DATE DUE

MA~~~~~~~~		
DE~~~~~~ 05		

SHUTTING
DOWN
THE
COLD WAR

SHUTTING DOWN THE COLD WAR

The Politics
of Military
Base Closure

David S. Sorenson

St. Martin's Press
New York

UA 26 .A2 S67 1998

Sorenson, David S., 1943-

Shutting down the Cold War

ta

Sorenson, David S., 1943-
    Shutting down the Cold War : the politics of military base
closures / David S. Sorenson.
        p. cm.
    Includes bibliographical references and index.
    ISBN 0-312-21090-6
    1. Military base closures—United States. 2. United States-
-Politics and government—1989-   I. Title.
    UA26.A2S67 1998
    355.7'0973—dc21   97-45915
                                                  CIP

Design by Orit Mardkha-Tenzer

First Edition: July 1998
10 9 8 7 6 5 4 3 2 1

Contents

Abbreviations

AAC	Air Combat Command
AFB	Air Force Base
AFBCA	Air Force Base Conversion Agency
AFCEE	Air Force Center for Environmental Excellence
AFMC	Air Force Materiel Command
AGMC	Aerospace Guidance and Metrology Center
AGS	Air Guard Station
ALC	Air Logistics Center
ARMS	Armament Retooling and Manufacturing Support
ARS	Air Reserve Station
BRAC	Base Realignment and Closure Commission
BUR	Bottom-Up Review
CBO	Congressional Budget Office
CDTF	Chemical Decontamination Training Facility
CENTCOM	Central Command
CERCLA	Comprehensive Environmental Response, Compensation, and Liability Act
CERFA	Community Environmental Response Facilitation Act
COBRA	Cost of Base Realignment Actions
DERP	Defense Environmental Restoration Program
DFAS	Defense Finance and Accounting Service
DOD	Department of Defense
DOE	Department of Energy
EPA	Environmental Protection Agency
FAA	Federal Aviation Administration
FISCO	Fleet and Industrial Supply Center Oakland
FMC	Federal Medical Center
FOD	Foreign Object Damage
FUDS	Formerly Used Defense Sites
GAO	General Accounting Office
GGNRA	Golden Gate National Recreation Area
HHS	Health and Human Services
HUD	Housing and Urban Development
IAP	International Airport
ICBM	Intercontinental Ballistic Missile
JCSG	Joint Cross-Service Groups
JPATS	Joint Primary Aircraft Training System
LRA	Local Redevelopment Agency

MCAS	Marine Corps Air Station
MV	Military Value
NAS	Naval Air Station
NASA	National Aeronautics and Space Administration
NAWC	Naval Air Warfare Center
NCP	National Contingency Plan
NEPA	National Environmental Policy Act
NESEC	Naval Electronic Systems Engineering Center
NOAA	National Oceanic and Atmospheric Administration
NPL	National Priorities List
NPS	National Park Service
NSC	Naval Supply Center
NSWC	Naval Surface Warfare Center
NSY	Naval Shipyard
OPM	Office of Personnel Management
OSD	Office of the Secretary of Defense
PCB	Polychlorinated Biphenals
PTR	Pilot Training Rate
QDR	Quadrennial Defense Review
RAB	Restoration Advisory Board
RCRA	Resource Conservation and Recovery Act
SAC	Strategic Air Command
SBA	Small Business Administration
SDIO	Strategic Defense Initiative Organization
SOCOM	Special Operations Command
SOS	Save Our Shipyard
SSA	Social Security Administration
SSBN	Strategic Ballistic Missile Submarine
START	Strategic Arms Reduction Talks
SWC	Strategic Warfare Center
TABS	Total Army Basing Study
TAC	Tactical Air Command
TCE	Trichloroethylene
UPT	Undergraduate Pilot Training
USAF	United States Air Force
USCM	United States Marine Corps
USN	United States Navy
VA	Veterans Administration

Preface

O ne of the advantages of being a faculty member at the Air War College at Maxwell AFB in Alabama, is having the chance to interact with the numerous visiting faculty members who spend at least a year with us. Recently, I was fortunate to work with one such individual who has many traits I admire, including a blunt sense of honesty and a zero-level tolerance for boredom. I was particularly interested in her reaction when I told her that I was starting to write a book on military-base closures. She looked at me as though I had lost my senses, logically assuming that the book would be about the base-closure process, a subject that can easily bring visions of spider-web charts littered with circles and arrows and names in microscopic print. So I quickly explained that the book would emphasize the politics of base closure instead of the closure process itself. When I gave her some hints about the sometimes bizarre directions that base-closure politics could take, she began to sound interested, much to my relief. I hope she will find the finished product interesting as well.

I selected a number of bases for study after they had appeared on a closure list. I had particular reasons for choosing those bases. First, I chose bases that were proximate to my location in Montgomery, Alabama (Meridian Naval Air Station [NAS] in Mississippi and Fort Mc-Clellan in central Alabama), because I work for the Air Force and spend the taxpayer's money on my research. There was no point in running up travel budgets to far-off places when base closings were happening in my backyard. When I did journey to more distant bases (such as Carswell and Kelly AFBs in Texas), I was able to perform a job for the Air Force (in that case, faculty escort for the international officer class at the Air War College) to justify my use of an Air Force plane for transportation. I was able to visit the Fleet and Industrial Supply Center Oakland (FISCO) for the first time in 30 years in conjunction with travel to the American Political Science Association Conference across the Bay in San Francisco. While there, I was driving back from Sausalito with my youngest daughter and noted a sign pointing to a turnoff to the Presidio of San Francisco. For the next four hours the two of us explored the closed base, wandering through empty bowling alleys and climbing up fire escapes to look into third-floor rooms to find out what was left (in one case, only a vacuum cleaner). The base was important because it had received a reprieve once after closure in 1988, but our first-hand survey made it much more interesting to include in this study.

I selected other bases because I had access to individuals who had been a part of their closure (Loring AFB in Maine, MacDill AFB in Florida, and Carswell). As an Air War College faculty member, I worked for former base commanders from Loring and Carswell who had joined the Air War College faculty after those bases closed. Third, I chose bases that I had once visited, simply because I was more familiar with them. I spent a week at Wurtsmith AFB in Michigan while doing research for a previous book, and, much earlier, I was stationed on two ships homeported at the Naval Supply Center in Oakland, California. When I was a faculty member at Denison University in Granville, Ohio, Newark AFB was six miles away, and I occasionally gave lectures there. The Long Beach Naval Shipyard sat near the dingy part of that city's port and petroleum area where I once raced at the Lions Associated Drag Strip in an earlier life.

The task of writing a book is made easier by the labor and cooperation of many others who rarely get the recognition that they deserve. Those who have assisted me in completing this work include Col. Gary Schneider, USAF, former commander of the 42nd Bombardment Wing at Loring AFB; Col. Richard Szafranski, USAF, former commander of the Seventh Bomb Wing at Carswell AFB; Col. Kenneth Boykin, USAF, former commander of the 379th Bomb Wing at Wurtsmith AFB; Col. Joseph M. Renaud, former commander of the Air Force Guidance and Metrology Center, Newark AFB; Ms. Jo Avalos and Lt. Shawn Bergen at the Fleet and Industrial Supply Center Oakland; and Mr. Joe Pesce at the Naval Air War Test Center at Point Mugu, California. I also thank Capt. Stephen Sudcamp, USN; Lt. Col. Tom Brehm, USMC; Lt. Col. Daniel Runyon, USAF; Ms. Mary Bridgewater; Lt. Col. Dan Steele, USAF; Lt. Col. Robert Bivens, USAF; Lt. Col. David Kovach, USAF; Lt. Col. Jeffrey Larsen, USAF; Lt. Col. Ronald See; and Maj. Clayton Church, USAF. The staff members of Air University's Fairchild Library were magnificent, particularly Sue Goodman and Terry Hawkins. Our departmental secretaries, Debbie Smith, Heather Brown, and Maria Robinson spent hours improving the draft of this book, as did Airman Richard Smith. There are other individuals who provided valuable information but were reluctant to have their names appear in print. I respect their wishes, but the reader must understand that the book contains some unattributed statements as a result. In all cases, I tried to substantiate information provided by individuals (named here or not) with a secondary source, but that was not possible in all cases. I am also very grateful to Grant T. Hammond, Donald M. Snow, and James Gosling, who helped me clarify a number of issues in the text. I have also benefited by discussions with Jeffrey Record, who served on Senator Sam Nunn's (D-GA) staff during some base-closure years. The faculty at the Air War College provided yet another invaluable resource for anyone working on a defense-related project—experience. When I encountered a question about bases, I often went to the office next door or down the hall. There I got a thorough education on some base or some problem at a base from someone once stationed there. The Air War College students were another invaluable source of information, and I am grateful to the Classes of 1996 and 1997 for sharing so many insights with me. Most important for me, no one in official position at the Air War College implied that this study could not be unfavorable to the Air Force or the Department of Defense should the facts so indicate. The Air War College is a great place to work as an academic. At St. Martin's Press I thank Michael Flamini, Elizabeth Paukstis, Wendy Kraus, Chris Cecot, and Mary Cooney for all their efforts in making this a better book.

As a final caveat, I should state that I am solely responsible for the opinions and conclusions contained in the book, which do not necessarily reflect the views of the Air War College, United States Air Force, or the Department of Defense.

Introduction

I wrote this book for several reasons. First, base closure became a significant issue in the wake of the Cold War, and the very controversy of the process indicated that it deserved a study. Between 1988 and 1995, the Base Realignment and Closure Commissions (BRACs) voted to close 330 military installations. Another 173 would end up on realignment lists, meaning that some functions on the base would close or be moved elsewhere. Base closure cost hundreds of thousands of jobs, and shuttered bases impacted hundreds of communities across the nation. The military wound up spending billions of dollars cleaning up and closing installations across the country. Bases kept open beyond their usefulness by congressional pressure quickly showed up on closure lists as military officers recognized the opportunity to save money for other, more favored programs.

Yet, the base-closure issue was but a microcosm of the larger impact of defense reductions after the Cold War. A defense budget that once consumed 25 cents of every federal dollar spent in the 1970s took only 13 cents of that same federal dollar by the mid-1990s. An entire institution, the Department of Defense, along with a multibillion-dollar defense industry had to regroup, restructure, and adjust to post–Cold War realities in the 1990s. And even this large sector of American society is a part of something even larger—the downsizing of government almost everywhere. The American experience of smaller, leaner, and more efficient government reflects worldwide trends. From Ulan Bator to Granite City, public enterprises close or pare back. Base closure, while more dramatic than many government-reduction processes, deserves an examination because it is a classic example of governmental reduction, to be studied for lessons about both the benefits and the hazards of government contraction.

The base-closure *process* is described elsewhere, mostly in government-produced manuals, with every regulation and every step in the years-long process spelled out in mind-numbing detail. So prospective readers who are searching for a thorough description of the base-closure process that has shuttered hundreds of military installations across the nation will need to look elsewhere. Here I detail process information only when it helps to understand what is the most important (and interesting) part of base closing—the political actors and processes that first dictated an effort to take the politics out of base closure, and then later turned around to make that effort almost impossible.

This study also attempts to fill the gap between two subdisciplines in political science—national security studies and American politics. The term "national security studies" has many definitions, but it generally focuses on military force as an instrument of statecraft. National security scholars, though, generally examine the links between military force and politics at the strategic level, and things like military bases are left hanging, often dismissed as "infrastructure." Students of American politics usually avoid discussions of things military, perhaps fearful of straying into someone else's academic turf. However, decisions about politics in the American political system can potentially explain things military as well as things civilian, and academic barriers should not stand in the way. Kenneth R. Mayer and Anne M. Khademian recognize this point, stating: "First, most studies of American politics assume that defense and civilian policies are so different that they belong in separate fields. Second, most defense analysts adopt the normative assumption that defense policy making should be above politics. As a result, scholars in both fields avoid thinking about the connections between political structures, political relationships, and defense policy outputs."[1] It is my hope that this study bridges these connections.

Theories remain the foundations of political science, and scholars have an obligation to subject them to repeated trials. In this case, theories purporting to explain both congressional behavior (constituency service) and military behavior (bureaucratic politics) are utilized as frameworks to examine whether military base policy fits these theories' central tenants. Base-closure policy additionally presents an opportunity to consider another theoretical notion on "lesson-drawing" over time. Richard Rose and others have formulated ideas about how policymakers learn and adjust from past policy experience.[2] The base-closure process as examined in this study covers three biennial iterations of the same process. It thus offers an opportunity to examine how the actors in the process learned across those three sequences. That is one major reason that I organized the study around the three BRAC years of 1991, 1993, and 1995. Did organizational learning occur over time, at the BRAC level, the congressional level, and the military level? Base-closure policy gives us one of the most ideal cases to study organizational learning because of these scheduled two-year intervals between closure years. We can closely examine exactly how these three organizations did or did not learn to further their objectives based on what happened in a prior base-closing year.

As I began to develop this project, other reasons for doing it emerged. I found few studies on the policy-commission process. The base-closure process is part of a larger trend in the United States to divorce politics from public-policy problems by turning them over to independent commissions. In recent years, the Social Security Commission, the Kerner Crime Commission, the Packard Commission on military reform, the Gates Commission on military conscription, and a host of others have wrestled with policy situations eschewed by elected officials. Often those problems are too politically hot to handle, and base closure is only one of them. No one wanted to cut Social Security payments to elderly recipients who rivet their political attention to this issue, yet bankruptcy threatened the system. During the 1996 presidential debates, President Bill Clinton suggested another crime commission to consider again solutions to the problem, and after his election he proposed another commission to resolve expected Medicare shortfalls.

Defense-policy issues are ripe for solutions recommended by commissions because the political stakes are almost always high, and feelings run deep on both sides of the issues involved. Weapons-procurement reform, military reorganization, roles and missions, and human affairs in the services are just some of the issues that commissions have either addressed in the past or are likely to address in the future. The roles-and missions debate plaguing the military since the end of World War II is illustrative. Several years ago, the military tried to resolve internal conflict between the services over roles and missions, but critics widely derided their effort as simply trimming around the edges of the problem. So Congress and the president created a roles-and-missions commission that proposed a more substantive reshaping of service responsibilities. In 1988, Congress and the president (George Bush) created the Base Realignment and Closure Commission for the same reason—despite requests from the Defense Department to do so, Congress had not closed a single base in the previous ten years.

This begs the question, though, about how successful the commission solution really has been. Can such contentious issues as crime, Social Security, and military-base closure really be depoliticized, given the high visibility and resource values attached to them? This study endeavors to find an answer to that question in the base-closure case.

The base closure commission process happened because Congress and the president made a serious effort to "rationalize" public decision making about resource allocation. Both Bush and Congress surrendered something that politicians rarely let go of—political power. In this case, political power was budget power. Budget power is about allocating resources, rewarding friends, coercing enemies, and increasing the chances for election or reelection. On its face, giving up such power seemed unthinkable; after all, military bases have long been seen as a case of "pork-barrel politics," representing direct pipelines into states and districts for federal money. Power is usually guarded jealously by those who have gained it, and to surrender it is highly unusual. Part of the research in this study was designed to investigate why it happened.

I was aware before I started this project that there were serious environmental pollution problems at many military bases. But I learned during the course of this research that environmental problems were sometimes used to close bases or keep them open, depending on circumstances. For instance, when Warner Robins AFB in Georgia suddenly appeared on the 1995 BRAC closure list, base officials revealed that several decades ago they had poured forty million gallons of highly toxic chemicals into a lagoon near the main runway. That revelation may have been a ploy to keep the base open, given the potentially staggering cost of just locating the waste, never mind cleaning it up. On the other hand, BRAC provided special funding to clean up toxins, thus saving the military the cost of cleaning them from their own funding. That fact alone may have tipped the scales in a close case to a decision to close a base. There were many other environmental cleanup issues that also factored into the politics of base closure, including the long delays that cleanup posed for base conversion.

Chapter One conceptualizes base-closure decision making. It introduces the varieties of military bases and examines their importance to the military and to the surrounding communities. It then proposes three models to explain the behavior of the different actors involved in the politics of base closure. Chapter Two discusses the politics of base-closure issues. What are the economic implications from base closure? How are environmental problems handled? What is the military impact of base closure? How can a base be converted once it is designated for closure? Then the specific BRAC years of 1991, 1993, and 1995 are covered in Chapters Three through Five, which examine some specific bases closed during those years. Part of the reason for covering those years separately is that the political climate spanning them changed from year to year. Another reason is that a sequential comparison offers a chance to explore learning behavior by all parties involved over time. Chapter Six summarizes the findings.

Each of the BRAC years added bases for closure or realignment. However, BRAC did more than recommend closure in each of its rounds. A considerable amount of BRAC time was also spent reconsidering previous closure or realignment decisions. In some cases, a base previously listed for closure might get a second decision based on information since the closure recommendation. Carswell AFB in Texas, voted closed by BRAC in 1991, was instead realigned in 1993. The Presidio of San Francisco, closed by the 1988 BRAC, was given a delay in closure and new closure plans by the 1993 BRAC. So while most of the bases selected for close examination in this study involved closure decisions, some such as Carswell AFB and MacDill AFB in Florida, were realignments, and others, such as the Presidio of San Francisco, experienced delayed closure and/or reexamination.

In the pages that follow, I detail what I consider a fascinating effort on the part of a myriad of political actors to fight the battles over base closure, with all of the heat and passion that normally accompanies a high-stakes political issue. The purpose is not to look under rocks for scandal, or to point fingers at alleged wrongdoing, but to analyze what happened, and to explain why.

CHAPTER ONE

Explaining Base Closure

In the State of Utah, we've got a little base called Fort Douglas. Fort Douglas is a historic base. Johnson Army [sic] went out there to put [sic] the Mormon uprising in 18 whatever it was, found out there wasn't such a thing; we kept POWs there during World War I, you've got all kinds of history there and a few little reserve units and that's about it. I think it should be closed. . . .
—*James V. Hansen, Representative of Utah*
Congressional testimony, 1990

Some of the more egregious examples of waste were Fort Douglas, an Army post established in 1862 to protect Pony Express mail routes and which now sits in the middle of the University of Utah campus. . . .[1]
—*Congressional Hearings, 1991*

The military is the dog that gets wagged by the tail when it comes to base closure . . . Operating base structure is expensive as hell. You don't win wars with base structure, but with weapons systems. We always want to close more bases than we can get away with. But we always get zinged by the political community.[2]
—*Gen. John Herres*

H ow to study military-base closure? To simply describe it in all of its forms and complexities over the many years of the process is difficult. The process is actually many processes, managed by myriad actors and conducted over many years. To be understood and analyzed, it must be separated into manageable parts, with a manageable conceptualization of the issue. This chapter lays out the frameworks used in this book to capture the process from different angles. It introduces three theoretical approaches to public decision making—*constituency service, bureaucratic politics,* and *learning over time*—as models to guide the study and analysis of the three years of base closure that follow. After identifying the topic, this chapter probes the commission process, the procedure used to guide the base-closure process since 1988.

WHAT EXACTLY IS A MILITARY BASE?

Military bases often started out as little more than collections of rough-hewn buildings surrounded by a wall of sharp-pointed logs— "fortifications" was gradually reduced to "fort," and even today Army bases are called "forts." They were located near cities to protect them or adjacent to trails to keep control of them. Forts were not the only military installations—the fledgling United States Navy constructed shipyards to build and maintain its small fleet of warships. These, too, were located in the growing cities of the East and the South, largely because they needed access to a large labor force and the small industries that produced canvas for sails and metal fittings to assemble the wooden vessels.

The military could not operate without bases.[3] Bases are where the military lives, trains, and operates outside of wartime or military exercises. They bring to one place all of the things that the military does to prepare for war. They are organized by function—training, combat, maintenance, finance, and so on. A training base has firing ranges, barracks for trainees, eating facilities, street sweepers, a fire department, and thousands of other things that allow it to function as a unit. Bases are self-contained in order to allow operation without dependence on the outside world. Military tradition holds that what the military does is so specialized that only the military can do it. So military vehicles are maintained on base, military births happen in military hospitals, military meals are served to military members, and military religious services are conducted in military chapels by military chaplains. Military police keep watch at base gates to keep out civilians who do not have a reason to be on base grounds.

Many of the functions carried out at military bases could be carried out anywhere, and it would be easier in some cases to perform them in nearby communities. That is happening in the decade of the 1990s. The military is closing military hospitals to save money. Service members could (and sometimes do) attend civilian religious institutions off base (some informal estimates put the number attending base chapels at 25-50 percent of the military stationed there). More and more military personnel live off base as cutbacks in military-construction budgets make it more difficult to replace deteriorating housing on base.

Since the end of the Cold War, there has been a growing trend to "civilianize" some traditional military functions, and it is not uncommon to see a majority of drivers passing thorough the main gate of a military base wearing civilian clothes instead of uniforms. Some in the military believe that this trend signals more delegation of things military to the outside world. The base, in other words, was once a kind of insulation between the military and civilian worlds, but, as bases close or reduce in size, the prospect of a takeover by the civilian sector of military functions erodes one fundamental purpose of having bases in the first place.

The size of bases ranges from a few buildings and a radar site to facilities that sprawl over many acres and resemble small cities. Some generate thousands of jobs in their communities, while others may barely be noticed even in the communities they are near. Some stretch over hundreds of thousands of acres of uninhabited land that the military uses for target practice or weapons testing. The land dedicated to military use in the state of Nevada (most of it target and test ranges) runs to more than four million acres, almost one-third of the state. The vast Air Force Range 473 stretches over several western states. It takes almost five hours for a B-52 bomber just to fly through it—down a centerline flight path with the military owning the four miles on either side of it. Flight maps of the range are dotted with circles and squares, indicating where lawsuits and noise complaints have originated. This is one of the problems of co-location, one of the reasons the military would like to have many of its bases far away from civilians.[4]

Military bases have a varied impact on civilian society. The most significant is economic, but it also carries over to the personal, the environmental, and the social. Service members sometimes meet prospective spouses in towns located near bases. Military fire departments and other emergency services often support or supplement emergency facilities in local communities. Intoxicated service members become a problem for both military and civilian police. Military waste intermingles with civilian waste and, when toxic, poses health problems for towns located close by. Bases, in other words, bring both benefits and costs beyond the economic impact to their civilian neighbors, and those costs and benefits are also issues given prominence when base closure becomes an issue.

Most military bases are not located near or in the county's largest cities anymore. Land costs and urbanization have forced bases close to cities to close, and most did long ago. New York City has no remaining bases left from the days when they ringed the city to keep the harbor safe from naval attack. San Francisco saw its last base, the

Army Presidio, close in 1993. The Dallas-Fort Worth area lost Carswell AFB in 1991 (though it never really closed); Detroit has no major bases; and both Boston and Philadelphia lost their naval shipyards. Several cities still have naval bases as neighbors, but, with the exceptions of San Diego, California, and Norfolk, Virginia, most seaport cities lost their naval yards some years ago. The Washington D.C. and Brooklyn naval yards shut down so long ago that now there is scarcely any trace of them left.

Many bases were located in rural America, in places like Rantoul, Illinois; Big Springs, Texas; Moses Lake, Washington; Olathe, Kansas; Willow Grove, Pennsylvania; and Barstow, California. There were a number of reasons for this. Rural America offered more room to maneuver, to fly, to make noise, to conduct secret operations—to do all of the things that need both space and privacy. There was another reason, though, that had more to do with a sense of military identity. For the professional military, there was something corrupt about the civilian world that soldiers and sailors were best kept away from. The civilian world was too undisciplined, too filled with temptations that ran counter to military professionalism and sacrifice. For young trainees, in particular, isolation from the civilian world was an essential part of their remaking as warriors. The military prides itself on its purposeful effort to set itself off from civilian life; witness the uniforms and the language with its colorful descriptors of even the most mundane things (particularly in the Navy, where almost everything has a different name). The Uniform Code of Military Justice is a set of laws with some sharp differences from civilian justice. So military bases protect their members from the world that most of them originally came from. They enshrine tradition and preserve the history that is so influential for the military. Samuel P. Huntington makes this point poignantly in the last pages of his classic *The Soldier and the State* when he compares West Point, with its strong military ideals, to the village of Highland Falls, just south of the academy, with its disordered materialism and lack of common purpose.[5] But if the military had to be near civilians, better that those civilians hold the small-town values of Manhattan, Kansas, or Moses Lake, Washington, rather than Kansas City or Seattle.

The other side of this argument is demonstrated by the problems that military bases impose on nearby communities. Towns and cities near military installations sometimes suffer from drunken brawls, rape, vandalism, and other such crimes committed by service members who do not hold the kinds of values Huntington places at West Point. Some of the seedier elements in society—tattoo artists, prostitutes, gamblers, and other con artists—congregate in military towns to peddle their wares to vulnerable service members. Towns like Phenix City, Alabama, Junction City, Kansas, or San Diego, California, are examples.

None of this suggests that members of the military have better or worse moral values than their civilian counterparts. Nor would most Americans (including the military) claim such. The separation should not be too great, because it is a part of American political tradition to fear the aloof professional military as a potential threat to civilian values. It is to suggest, though, that rural and middle-town America is more likely to feel the impact of base closure than the nation's largest cities are. And that fact is only one fact of the politics of base closure—one part of a larger process that the rest of this book works to unravel.

While the principal justification for military bases was to provide for the common defense, they also contributed economic prosperity to nearby communities. Soldiers from the bases shopped in these communities, and, as the fort grew, so often did the community. Navy shipyards also offered jobs with each ship contract, and members of Congress who controlled the naval budget realized that political success and shipbuilding money were related. It was not uncommon for members of Congress to work with the secretary of the Navy in ordering ships to be constructed in their states and districts. Finley Peter Dunne's Mr. Dooley once commented that the sole requirement for a secretary of the Navy was that the only salt he might have seen was in a barrel of pork.

The coming of the military airplane opened the way for expansion of the American military-base structure and the opportunity for more political benefits. Members of Congress could look with glee on the new possibilities of locating a base at home, but they found themselves at odds with the new Army Air Corps (AAC) in the 1930s. The AAC favored siting bases in strategic locations, such as along seaboards so that it could carry out coastal-defense missions. It favored states such as Texas and California so that its developing heavy bombers might reach South America should that continent be invaded by foreign forces. In the end, Congress gave in to the Air Corps and, in drafting the Wilcox Bill of 1933, left the final base-location decisions up to Air Corps.[6] That did not eliminate political haggling, though. In 1925; the Colorado congressional delegation opposed the Army's wish to establish a training school at Chanute Field in Illinois.[7] So the Air Corps wound up having to fund both Chanute and the new Lowry Field near Denver.[8] Later, when the Air Corps wanted to expand its basing structure even further

in response to possible war with the Axis powers, it had to keep the locations secret for fear that city politicians would interfere with AAC
base-location choices.[9]

World War II changed the American landscape in many ways, but
one of the most permanent changes was the mushrooming of military bases from coast to coast. By February 1944, Florida alone had 64
Army Air Corps bases. Some bases were little more than mud fields,
tents, and tar-paper shacks that rapidly disappeared after the war. But
other bases grew to the size of small (or, in some cases, large) cities,
which endured throughout much of the Cold War period. These
bases became more than simply supporting facilities for military missions. They generated millions of dollars in jobs and spending money
for the communities in which they were located. As such, they drew
understandable support from members of those communities, who
elected congressional representatives pledged to continue the flow of
federal dollars through those bases. In many cases, a military base was
the major—sometimes the only—major source of federal funds for a
congressional district. Sometimes they were the largest population
centers in rural areas. They provided jobs for many civilians who lived
adjacent to them, and often these jobs were plentiful since they
tended to be low skilled. Janitor, secretary, vehicle driver, dishwasher,
and painter were just some of the jobs offered to civilians, and the
number of such jobs increased during the 1960s and 1970s as the military increasingly turned traditional military positions over to civilians. Civilian secretaries, barbers, maintenance workers, cooks, and
the like were accepted because such jobs were considered "not mili-
tarily essential." Later more critical positions, such as aircraft maintenance and communications technician, were contracted out to
civilians. There were reasons for this: Civilians cost less in general
(they did not require military health care, commissaries, housing,
and other such benefits); moreover, the military discovered that military morale tended to improve when uniformed personnel did not
have to perform menial jobs. "Civilianization" was also good for the
economy, particularly in times when unemployment was a sensitive issue. So the presence of a military base in a region generated economic dependency that would be difficult to break. And that
dependency could be the dominant part of the local economy. For
example, in the traditionally naval city of Norfolk, Virginia (the
largest city in the state), the Navy operated nine large facilities that
generated more than 19,000 civilian jobs in 1988, making the Navy
the largest single employer in the city by far. In Long Beach, California, in the same year, the Naval Shipyard contributed 6,000 jobs

alone, while the 1988 total job base from military installations in Charleston, South Carolina, stood at near 14,400.

Bases generated economic benefits in other ways as well. Military personnel stationed at them spent money in the local communities, purchasing everything from tattoos to houses. While bases were once relatively self-enclosed from the local community, the past several decades have seen an expansion of military personnel establishing economic roots in localities. For one thing, the Defense Department realized that it was less expensive to subsidize their personnel to live off base than it was to build and maintain new housing for them. In 1995, approximately 70 percent of military families lived off base, receiving subsidies that were supposed to cover about 85 percent of their housing costs.[10] While military personnel could use their commissary privileges, sometimes a limited selection of goods drove them into the local community market. For both enlisted personnel and officers, the finite selection of meals in their respective clubs on base often made local community restaurants tempting. So total spending by military personnel could exceed the spending by community members in even a large town.[11]

Communities with bases also benefited from federal impact funds to offset the cost of a military base nearby. As more and more military members moved into the community, funds for schools, sewage and water expansion, road construction and repair, and a variety of other things came in from Washington. Such an infusion of money often allowed a town to expand projects and reap benefits for the local political leadership. It is hardly surprising that political figures who received such clear political benefits from having a base in their district would be reluctant to close it even if it could be clearly demonstrated that the base no longer had enough military usefulness to keep it open. As Representative David O'B. Martin (R-NY) noted in 1988 when the Base Realignment and Closure Commission legislation was introduced: "Each and every Member who has a base in his or her district is naturally going to try and protect it. That is understandable and in fact necessary for the individual Member. So we do have a parochial interest and it does manifest itself in the behavior of our colleagues."[12] When such parochialism manifests itself at the congressional level, though, it makes disposal of bases quite difficult.

Communities near bases attract not only workers and military families, but also military retirees. Those retiring from the military have certain, though limited, privileges, including the use of base facilities. Retirees have access to base hospitals (though that access is not guaranteed) the base golf course, and may also shop in base commissaries.

In 1996, the average savings between prices in supermarkets and commissaries was almost 30 percent.[13] When bases close, so usually does the commissary (the number dropped from 384 in 1993 to 312 in 1997),[14] and retirees can mobilize their political muscle to oppose base closure. In at least one case (Carswell AFB, noted in Chapter Three), the commissary remained open on a limited basis to serve retirees.

MILITARY BASES AND MILITARY POLITICS

Of course, politics did not drive all, or even most, basing decisions. Strategic reasons often dictated base location, though those reasons often disappeared long before the bases did. The Army, for example, located a number of its bases near the mouths of harbors to protect them against attack, though some of those bases, such as Fort MacArthur overlooking Los Angeles Harbor, did not close until decades after the threat against U.S. ports had disappeared. Another base, Fort McNair in Washington, D.C., was strategically located to keep the British out of that city (though they took it anyway in the War of 1812), and yet it remains open today. Other bases were located to protect trails against Indian attacks (Fort Riley in Kansas and Fort Sill in Oklahoma, both still open in 1997).

Strategic reasons weren't the only considerations, however. The Army Air Corps preferred bases in the South and West because of better flying weather in those regions. Florida, Texas, and California offered almost year-round flying weather, which was particularly important in a time before aircraft carried the kinds of instruments that allowed for night and bad-weather operations. Because of this, a number of fledgling aviation companies also located in Texas, California, and Washington State, and it made sense for Army and Naval aviation to co-locate with them in order to cooperate on experimental military aircraft.[15] The Army Air Corps, which sought independence from the Army during the 1930s, gained autonomy by relocating some of its forces in the West.[16] The farther away from Army Headquarters in Washington, D.C. the less likely Army leaders would try to interfere with the fledgling Army aviators. Naval aviation, too, drew opposition from traditional surface naval leaders, so it made sense to locate naval air stations in places such as North Island in San Diego, California, or Chase Field in Texas to keep some distance from the Navy Department in Washington.

Strategic reasons for base siting remained important, though. In the 1950s, the Strategic Air Command (SAC) responded to the "New

Look" doctrine of President Eisenhower by expanding its bomber bases, locating many of them in the northern part of the United States for shorter flying times to the USSR.[17] Missile bases needed abundant land, since the missile silos had to be dispersed over hundreds of square miles to limit the possibility of an attacking nuclear weapon damaging more than one silo. Francis E. Warren AFB, a missile base nominally located in Wyoming, actually stretched over the three states of Wyoming, Colorado, and Nebraska. Whiteman AFB in Missouri covered thousands of square miles of Missouri and Kansas.[18]

BASES, POLITICS, AND MILITARY REQUIREMENTS

Whatever the original reason for base locations, they ultimately tangled with politics. That was the heart of base-closure politics. The military needed bases for preparation for war and other military activities. But, in the face of the inevitable defense drawdowns that follow war, the military wanted to dispose of what had become surplus facilities. Congress had the authority to either keep bases open or close unnecessary ones, but the individual needs of its members made it impossible to shut down as many bases as the military sometimes desired. But Congress, as an institution, seemed to recognize that there are times when the surrender of power is necessary to prevent policy paralysis. So as they had done in 1921 when they gave the president the power to create the federal budget, members of Congress in 1988 gave the power decide the fate of bases to an independent commission—and, restricted the power of the president to interfere with base closures in the process.

This is not to suggest that base closure was impossible before then. There is nothing new about base closures—indeed, closures seemed to follow each military buildup. Thousands of hastily erected Army camps closed after the Civil War, the Spanish-American War, and World Wars I and II. The process was much simpler than it has become in recent years; in some cases bases were removed or abandoned in less than a day, with scarcely an impact on local communities. Base closures also followed each downturn of the defense budget after World War II. In March 1961, the Kennedy administration announced the reduction or closure of 954 military bases. While some of these were small facilities, the list included the Brooklyn and Portsmouth Naval Yards, four large Air Force maintenance depots, and a number of Strategic Air Command bases.[19] Another round of base closings followed in the wake of the Vietnam War. The defense budget for that period peaked in 1969 and was followed by almost ten years of decreases during the Nixon-Ford years and into the Carter administration, bringing bases down with it. But in these years, the Defense Department made the final decisions on what bases were surplus to their needs. While individual members of Congress expressed their reservations (and sometimes stopped closure), they usually worked to assist the targeted base with conversion to other functions.

As congressional oversight over the military increased, however, members found that it was possible to legislate restrictions that made base closure by the Defense Department almost impossible. The cost of surplus bases was becoming a drag on military readiness and other programs, and the base infrastructure was becoming more difficult to justify in the face of the massive reductions in the size and scope of the military following the end of the Cold War. Between 1989 and 1996, the defense budget declined by more than $100 billion in 1996 dollars, and the size of the force was slashed by more than 100,000 uniformed personnel and 45,000 civilians.[20] The Air Force budget shrank 40 percent from 1985 to 1996, and it lost 300,000 personnel, both civilian and military, over the same time period. Its inventory of fighters and intercontinental ballistic missiles declined by 50 percent; its long-range-bomber force by 75 percent. By the end of the decade, the Defense Department was planning for an active force of 1.5 million troops, down from 2.2 million, and a civilian work force cut from 1.1 million to 729,000.[21] The need for substantial base closure became obvious, and it was for this reason that the Base Realignment and Closure Commission (BRAC) came into being.

BASES AND THE DISTRIBUTION OF POLITICAL GOODS

The question that this book addresses is: how has the process actually worked, and how well has it worked? Did the independent BRAC actually take the politics out of the base-decision process? Were the decisions based on objective criteria like cost and requirements, as specified by the law that created BRAC? Or were the best-intended efforts of both the Congress and the president to substitute "rationality" for "politics" doomed to failure because of a combination of vague "requirements" and cost figures coupled with politics entering through the back door of the process? Would the efforts to "rationalize" the political distribution of base benefits that had existed since before World War II succeed in the face of a shrinking defense pie?

These questions get to the heart of a rarely solved political dilemma. On the one hand, politics can be viewed as a marketplace for the distribution of public goods, in which the stronger get more than the weaker because they have more capacity to influence the processes that allocate public resources. The result is a relatively amoral distribution that mimics a true "free market" economy. There may be a few rules (against violent redistribution, for example), but mostly what one member of society gets depends on relative power and the capacity to utilize that power in political bargainmaking. Self-interest is the driving motivation here, and non-violent political conflict is the mode that determines relative winners and losers. The only difference between politics as described here and the market place is that the goods are state provided—things that the private sector does not supply to society because there is no gain from doing so. States supply military goods for this reason, because there is no profit in private armies. But that is the only difference. State distributions do not have to be *equitable*, only *rational*. That is because politics can also be viewed as a *rational* process with resource allocation governed by regulations to maximize the efficient use of state resources. Such a process requires such things as a clear statement of purpose, a clear understanding of the available resource base, and a clear weighing of the different policies that might achieve the policy objective. Claimants for public goods compete for their share of distribution, and those who do the best by objective criteria get the largest share of the pie. Such is the stuff of "public-choice" theories, which attempt to place all of the above into formal statements of objective maximization. While no one who has studied public choice (or is at least familiar with it) pretends that decisions in public life are actually made this way, it can be assumed that public choice and its preference for rational decisions can be approximated, if only roughly.

Another view of state distribution does emphasize equity. While private markets may favor those better endowed with resources and ability, state markets should minimize unequal shares. The purpose of the state, in this view, is to make society's distribution of goods more equal, and that is particularly true of *government*-supplied goods. Such expectations generate the "fair-share" hypothesis that emphasizes even-handedness rather than performance. Since it might be argued that performance criteria are highly subjective, they cannot be useful as a basis for disbursement of resources. So all potential claimants should be treated the same, and no one should suffer disproportionate losses.

These notions form a basis of the expectations of those who operate a base or who benefit by its proximity. Their willingness to accept BRAC as an adjudicating mechanism for deciding on the fate of bases is partly predicated on their view of what the proper role of government distribution mechanisms is.

Congress and Defense Budgets:
The Theory of Constituency Service

There is no shortage of theories attempting to explain why Congress behaves as it does. That is hardly surprising; Congress "behaves" in different ways over different time spans under different leadership. Congress is hardly predictable, with sources of irregularity coming from the whole body, the committee system, the leadership, and the internal thermostats that are supposed to regulate it. But within the discordance on how and why Congress and its membership behave as they do, there are a few constants. One is that members of Congress work for the electorate, and they must reapply for their positions every two or six years. So there is a general set of theoretical approaches that can be lumped under the heading "constituency service" that focuses on how and why members of Congress direct political objectives toward their reelection.

Members of Congress are elected to serve their constituencies. That sounds simple enough, but what exactly does "serve" mean? What policy mechanisms can representatives use to service constituencies? And what do senators and representatives expect in return?

Service means many things, including "good public policy" and action taken on a variety of issues rarely salient to voters. However, representatives must be returned to their jobs, and that means that they must generate both voters to vote for them and political donations to get their message to those voters. One method to gain both is to bring federal money into the state or district and to raise political funds to advertise the fact. It also means protecting these established flows of resources, such as agricultural subsidies, rivers and harbors funding, construction of post offices, or other federal projects. Construction, in particular, is useful to representatives because it creates not only initial jobs, but also investments for future spending. A federal prison generates jobs for guards, custodians, secretaries, and other employment opportunities, for example.

Congressional Spending: Is It Pork Barrel Politics?

Military money may be the most effective way of channeling resources to districts and states, because of its widespread impact. Government subsidies for asparagus growers may benefit only a small percentage in any state or district, but defense spending tends to come in large packages and spreads easily once it arrives in the area.

It usually generates follow-on employment from defense contracts and at military bases.

Federal funding generated by elected representatives responds to real needs for the services and goods such money provides, yet it also funds things that are not needed by the nation but are approved because such funding enhances the electoral chances of its sponsors. Because in earlier times southern planters doled out barrels of salt pork to their slaves, the name "pork-barrel politics" has stuck.[22] The term sometimes describes "wasteful" projects in which the costs exceed the benefits;[23] John A. Hird defines it as "geographic legislative influence extending beyond commonly accepted notions of social welfare (for example, efficiency and equity)."[24]

It must be understood at the outset that it is difficult to distinguish between worthy projects and pork-barrel spending. It is rare that "pork" is blatant—funding projects built with absolutely no social worth beyond buying votes. Generally, pork projects have some limited worth, but often the cost far outweighs the benefits to society at large. During the Carter presidency, Congress funded a dam in Colorado whose primary benefits fell to nine families who farmed the area below where the dam was to be built, and who presumably would vote for the representative who proposed the project. Still, there were limited benefits to others in the region from recreation and flood control. Moreover, the pork-barrel hypothesis does not apply universally. While some scholarship points to pork motivations, other research finds the explanation lacking or mediated by other variables. John Ferejohn does find pork in the area of rivers and harbors policy,[25] as does Hird, though the latter tempers his own study of water projects by claiming that ". . . legislators are driven not only by a selfish desire for pork but also by a regard for project attributes commonly thought to reflect 'public interest. . . .'"[26] Morris B. Fiorina finds that pork is far more useful to members of Congress for maximizing reelection chances than is support of large nationally oriented initiatives like the Civil Rights Act.[27] Two former staff members of the Grace Commission of 1982 reported widespread pork-barrel spending on projects ranging from education to defense.[28] For others, though, it is closer to "it depends." Robert M. Stein and Kenneth N. Bickers looked at the changes in district awards from Congress over time and found that, in general, "tenure in the House is not significantly related to the change in the proportion of new to total grant awards."[29] That was in the aggregate, though. At the individual member of Congress level, they did find a relationship between "the increase in the proportion of new grant awards and electoral margins for incumbent House candidates."[30] To help bring information about those awards and other benefits to their constituents, they need to finance their election campaigns, and that, in turn, requires fund-raising. The cost of such campaigns, even for incumbents, has become so high that the old methods of passing the hat in church or calling constituents to send in their checks are simply inadequate. David B. Magleby and Candice J. Nelson note that the cost of House and Senate campaigns rose from $66 million in 1972 to $407 million by 1988.[31] By 1996, it had reached $2.65 billion, a threefold increase over campaign spending of twenty years before.[32]

Of course, members of Congress have other resources to enhance their chances of reelection beyond the tangible flow of money into their electoral bases. They can also act symbolically to appear as good representatives even when they either cannot or will not do something. Lawmakers have the power of the speech, the press release, the carefully timed visit to their district, and other communications tools to act as though they are doing something that they are not. For example, representatives powerless to stop legislation unpopular in their district may threaten a filibuster or other delaying tactics and then quietly use the threat in legislative chambers to get something else they want. They may generate howls of protest over a tobacco tax in their tobacco-growing regions and then quietly let it pass without opposition. Such symbolism is particularly effective in policy areas such as base closure when two clear needs—the interests of the nation and the interest of the district—are clearly in conflict.

CONSTITUENCY SERVICE AND CONGRESSIONAL DEFENSE POLICYMAKING

In describing congressional constituency service through the defense budget, Barry M. Blechman states: "There is nothing wrong with congressmen acting this way. Our system of government is built on this play of local interests in the Congress. . . . "[33] Indeed, members of Congress are elected to represent their districts and to channel federal dollars to those districts. Bruce M. Russett notes that, on defense issues, the alignment of members of Congress ". . . is related, in no insignificant way, to the economic importance of Department of Defense payrolls and employment to their constituencies."[34]

The problem lies, as Blechman states, in the clash between national interests and local interests. Should the national interest involve reducing the federal deficit or avoiding budgeted items that the military does not need, and the predominance of local interests stands in way of the national interest, problems will follow. For members of Congress, though, local interests can win elections and are, in the end, much more influential than national interests in that regard. While all members of Congress may symbolically be against the federal deficit, for example, such a position rarely stops them from supporting federal spending in their states or districts. Thus, members seek positions on the authorizing or appropriations committees that specialize in the kinds of programs that will benefit those back home. Members from farm states seek membership on the agriculture committees in their respective chambers; urban members work for membership on housing and urban affairs committees. members from defense-dependent states or districts seek armed services committees (which in the House of Representatives changed names in 1994 to the Committee on National Security). Congressional members can work on such committees to support projects that will bring federal dollars to their constituents—defense contracts, reserve facilities, federal impact funds, and the like. There is a belief that the more senior the member becomes on the committee, the more likely he or she is to get defense funds for the state or district.

Examples of constituency service on defense issues abound. Representative Thomas Downey (D-NY), normally a "dove" on defense issues, explained his support of the threatened A-6 Navy plane: "When the A-6 Intruder was going to be killed, I'm the Representative from that district and I'm on the Armed Services Committee. It's my job, whether I think the A-6 is good or not, to support it."[35] Senator Edward Kennedy (D-MA) set aside his customary criticism of the defense budget to defend the Navy and Marine Corps F/A-18 aircraft, whose engines are built in Massachusetts. Senator Alan Cranston (D-CA) tempered his criticism of the Reagan defense buildup with support for the B-1 bomber, built largely in California. Representative Richard Gephardt supported the Joint Strike Fighter (a follow-on aircraft for the twenty-first century) when McDonnell Douglas, in his St. Louis district, was a potential winner of the program. But when McDonnell Douglas lost in the first round of competition for the aircraft, Gephardt began to question the very worth of the program.[36]

Other legislators combine a voice of support for the military with support of defense spending benefiting their constituents. Senators Sam Nunn (D-GA) and Henry Jackson (D-WA) both bucked their party's relatively antidefense mood in the 1970s to support defense-budget increases. They also managed to get benefits for their states while doing so, largely because of their position in the Senate. Both chaired the powerful Senate Armed Services Committee, on which most senators with defense interests in their states would dearly like to serve. That committee, and its House counterpart, is a vehicle for legislators to influence defense issues that impact areas they represent. In the 105th Congress, which convened in January 1997, the Senate Armed Services Committee has only two members out of eighteen who do not represent states with either large military bases or large shares of the defense industry.[37] The influential Subcommittee on Seapower of the Senate Armed Services Committee has among its members Joseph Lieberman (D-CT), whose state has a large submarine-construction yard at Groton; John Warner (R-VA) and Charles Robb (D-VA), representing Virginia and the Newport News Shipbuilding Company; Robert Smith (R-NH), whose state is home to the Portsmouth Naval Shipyard; and Olympia Snowe (R-ME), who watches out for Bath Ironworks, a shipyard that is the largest employer in Maine.

Does such membership matter as a vehicle to direct contracts toward one's constituencies? Former Senator William Cohen (R-ME) used his position as chair of the Seapower Committee of the Senate committee on Armed Services to gain a contract for an Aegis-class cruiser at Bath Ironworks and a $28 million grenade contract for a Maine-based company.[38] Other members of the Maine congressional delegation worked in a similar way to land a contract for the Arleigh Burke-class destroyer, some to be built at the Bath Iron works.[39] A tug-of-war broke out over the contract between Cohen and Senator Trent Lott (R-MS), the Senate majority leader, who attempted to use his influence to shift the contract to the Ingalls Shipbuilding yard in Pascagoula, Mississippi.[40] Cohen became President Clinton's secretary of defense in 1996, and shortly after he assumed that post a study overturned Lott's earlier successful effort to get half of the destroyer order built in Pascagoula—a reversal that benefited the largest private employer in the state that Cohen represented for many years.[41]

After Cohen's resignation from the Senate, Senator Warner took his position on the Senate Seapower Subcommittee. In April 1997, Warner released a report from Chief of Naval Operations Adm. Jay Johnson praising an innovative shipyard plan to "smart buy" a new carrier by starting investment in 1997 for construction beginning in 2002. The shipyard gaining the contract was Newport News, located in Warner's home state of Virginia.[42] The support given by Senator Joseph Lieberman of Connecticut to the Seawolf submarine, a Cold War program saved by President Clinton, reportedly to preserve the submarine industrial base, is another example of pork-barrel spending. So, for that matter, was the opposition to Seawolf displayed by Senator Lott, who complained that it would take away naval spending for ships at Mississippi's Ingalls Shipbuilding.[43] Like the Bath Iron Works, Ingalls is Mississippi's largest employer, and the company as well as its labor unions have donated significant amounts to Lott's electoral campaigns.[44]

Ships are not the only examples. Senator Nunn helped Georgia's Lockheed plant in Marietta gain contracts for military aircraft, following on the heels of Senator Richard Russell (D-GA), who did the same thing. The House voted in September 1995 to include additional money in the defense budget for the B-2 Spirit bomber above what the Air Force (and the Joint Chiefs of Staff) had requested, with considerable support coming from representatives from southern California, Texas, and the Pacific Northwest, where most B-2 contracts are located.[45] Another notable example is Senator Daniel Inouye (D-HI), who used his chair position of the Senate Defense Appropriations Subcommittee to direct millions to his state each year, often for projects that the military did not want.[46] For example, he managed to insert funding for a "maritime technology program" into the 1998 defense appropriations bill. Senator John McCain (R-AZ) described the measure as a ". . . multi-million dollar bailout for a cruise ship line."[47]

Seniority outside the defense committees may also bring benefits. Speaker of the House Newt Gingrich (R-GA) has reportedly used his seniority to benefit Lockheed-Martin's C-130, built in its plant in Gingrich's Georgia district. Described as ". . . powerful patron for the plane," Gingrich supposedly pressured Defense Department Comptroller John Hamre to hasten contracts for the aircraft.[48] The reported quid pro quo for Lockheed-Martin was a contribution of thousands of dollars to Gingrich's campaign and contributions to tax-exempt foundations allied with the Speaker.[49]

The hope of campaign contributions also may fuel support for pork. One of the more blatant examples came from Representative Bill Chappell, Jr. (D-FL), who played a key role in keeping a lightweight Army weapon alive after the Army wanted to cancel it. Litton Industries which built the weapon, provided Chappell with contributions of $6,500.[50] Chappell also worked to preserve a Navy program built by Unisys, which contributed $20,0000 to his campaign coffers.[51] He also got other kinds of assistance from the defense industry—Avco and Martin Marietta representatives paid off his unpaid debts.[52] Sometimes congressional behavior crosses the line into illegality, as was the case of former Representative Robert Sikes (D-FL), who resigned under scandal, and former Representative Mario Biaggi (D-NY), who was convicted in a felony case for taking bribes from the Wedtech Company, a defense contractor.[53]

Pork extends beyond the water's edge. In 1996, the Senate authorized $4.6 billion for the Navy to buy 100 additional Norwegian-built Penguin air-to-surface missiles. The Navy, did not want them, so why were they ordered? Norway has indicated that it wants to upgrade its F-16 fighter aircraft fleet; if it does, the benefits would flow to the Lockheed-Martin Company, with numerous plants and subcontractors across the United States. The sale of Penguin missiles to the United States, with which Norway runs a negative balance of trade, might well be the ticket to future F-16 sales to Norway. That is particularly important to Lockheed-Martin, which since 1996 produces F-16s only for foreign military sales.[54]

Some critics of the defense-budget process argue that there is an "iron triangle," composed of defense contractors, the military, and congressional "defense hawks," who conspire over a common interest to keep the defense budget growing. That also means corporate support—to vote in favor of certain defense-budget items may bring in money from defense-corporation political action committees (PACs).[55] The military orders weapons not required by national-security needs, and contractors locate their production (and especially subproduction) in as many states as possible, thus forcing majority congressional support for them. Critics argued that the contract for the B-1 bomber distributed benefits over 48 states and concentrated in key states with considerable electoral votes just to sustain the program.[56] That often means spreading out contracts in unusual ways to get as much support as possible. Sometimes such benefit spreading can approach the absurd; for example, the list of B-2 bomber subcontractors included such unlikely names as Antelope Vacuum, Dale's Hitchin' Station, the Elite Car Wash, Frank's Radio Service, Kwik Key Service, and Clark's Pest Control.[57]

Constituency service is about more than simply getting benefits; it is also about keeping them. The base closure issue offers the best examples of such actions, but they extend beyond base closure. Legislators fight to keep defense industry and military units in their jurisdictions. Sometimes their struggles reach creative heights; Senator Wendell Ford (D-KY) became so angry at the Air Force for trying to move four C-130 aircraft out of a Kentucky Air Guard base that he held up the promotions of five senior Air Force generals.[58]

Is It Really Pork, Though?

The "pork barrel" hypothesis about congressional defense spending needs careful examination. There are clear cases in which members of Congress have rejected opportunities for constituency-based defense spending, such as when Representative William Minshall (R-OH) found himself opposing the MBT-70 tank, whose engine was to be made in his Ohio district. When Minshall got a demonstration of the prototype tank, he found that the driver's compartment was cramped and that the driver could barely see out from it. He labeled the tank a "turkey" and successfully led the opposition to it.[59] Representative Ronald Dellums, a California Democrat and later the chair of the House Committee on Armed Services, once opposed a contract for a naval vessel that might be built in his district—though he is reported to have said that if the ship were built, he would work to get it built in Oakland.[60] On a larger scale, Kenneth R. Mayer finds that at both the procurement contract and subcontract level, ". . . there is . . . little evidence that Congress as an institution routinely votes on defense issues solely because of pork barrel concerns. . . . "[61] This does not, of course, refute the connection between defense spending and congressional preferences for projects in their states or districts. It simply reminds us that there are other interests that guide congressional behavior, including the national interest. But Mayer also notes that senators and representatives do find ways to channel defense funds to their constituents, even if such behavior is not the norm.[62]

Supporters of legislation also use defense spending to gain support for it. As Paul Stockton notes: "One way a chair can gain support for his mark is to include the constituent-oriented programs favored by committee members. By dangling the funding carrot in front of project-hungry legislators, and cobbling together their various requests into the mark, a chairman can seek bipartisan support for his legislation."[63] Chairs of defense-related committees have a ready-made vehicle for this in spending for, and support of, military bases, found in almost every state in the Union.[64] During the hearings for the fiscal 1997 budget, the House National Security Committee made an unusual request to the services. The committee wanted each service to specify how many jobs an additional $15 billion of add-on defense projects could create, and the location of those jobs by congressional district.[65] Representative Duncan Hunter (R-CA), representing a defense-dependent district in San Diego, stated that he wanted to use the list to note how many jobs the Republican add-ons would create in key states.[66] Said Hunter: "Our president [Clinton] was going to places like California and standing before all the McDonnell-Douglas workers and saying, 'My defense bill means jobs.'. . . "The rest of the story is that while the President's bill might mean jobs, so did the bill that we were putting together in the Armed Services Committee."[67] While such statements do not in themselves prove "pork-barrel" motivations, they lend support to the importance of defense-related job creation, particularly during times when defense-budget cuts produce job reductions.

Congress and Military Bases

Military bases are one of the most common sources of defense dollars for a state or district. Even without new projects on a base, it generates millions of dollars annually, and congressional members benefit from that alone. Bases are also ripe for military construction contracts, often awarded to local contractors, increasing the take of defense dollars into nearby communities by additional millions. That fact has been obvious to members of Congress for decades, and certainly long before World War II with its vast base expansion. Efforts to close or consolidate unneeded defense posts in the 1930s were met with congressional outrage, and wartime expansion brought about protests from those members of Congress whose states or districts did not get what they felt was their fair share.[68]

Before congressional reforms in the 1970s, power and seniority flowed together. Because of the "one-party South," senior southern Democrats serving on the Armed Services Committees got the bulk of bases located below the Mason-Dixon Line. It was said of Representative L. Mendel Rivers of South Carolina that if he located one more base near Charleston, the whole district would sink into the sea. Rivers was hardly the only one—Senators John Stennis of Mississippi and Richard Russell of Georgia were also adroit at getting and keeping open bases in their respective states. For Russell, it did not hurt that one of the longest-serving chairs of the House Armed Services Committee, Carl Vinson, was also from Georgia.[69] Vinson got Warner Robins AFB located in his district rather than in Atlanta due to his ability to "call Macon" to the attention of War Department officials making the base decision, and further to pressure the railroads and realtors in the area to meet War Department demands.[70] Alabama's Senator Lister Hill was instrumental in making Maxwell AFB a permanent base after the Army threatened to close it after World War I.[71]

Southern Democrats were not the only successful representatives in the game of base politics. California Democratic Representative

Harry R. Sheppard rose to seniority on the Military Construction Committee in the 1930s and, when the Army Air Corps began to look for training bases and aircraft depots in the West, Sheppard worked with local officials to get both Norton and George Fields located in his district.[72] Around the same time, another California Democrat, William Kettner, was working to secure naval facilities in San Diego, aided by fellow Democrats in Congress who wanted to enhance his re-election chances in a normally Republican district.[73] When Army Air Corps officers looked for bases in the Northeast, Representative Charles R. Clason of Springfield, Massachusetts, persuaded them to locate near his city by pointing out that the variation in elevation of local tobacco fields was only one foot, making them ideal for runways. Thus, Westover Field (later Westover AFB) was located in Springfield.[74]

After World War II, representatives had more difficulty obtaining bases, since a considerable surplus existed. But they became adroit in protecting the bases they had in their jurisdictions. President Carter's secretary of defense, Harold Brown, estimated that he had to spend $1 billion per year on marginal military bases that Congress refused to close.[75] To help keep those bases open, the House Armed Services Subcommittee on Military Construction voted in 1982 to spend $300 million on bases the Pentagon wanted to close.[76]

Sometimes moving a mission to an existing base added jobs to the area. Democratic Representative Joseph Addabbo, representing Stewart Air National Guard Base in upstate New York, found a way to add a Marine C-130 unit to the base. The commandant of the Marine Corps turned down his original request, so Addabbo, reportedly with the assistance of Navy Secretary John Lehman, went back to the Marine Corps and argued that the East Coast needed a new air refueling unit. While the Corps suggested locating the unit at the Marine Base at Cherry Point, North Carolina, Lehman ordered it to put the unit at Stewart. Addabbo got $3 million-$5 million spent in his district as a result. Representative John Murtha (D-PA) managed a similar feat in his district. He worked to get a Marine Apache helicopter unit located at an Army National Guard base near Johnstown, again against the objections of the Marine Corps. According to Marine studies, the base location on a floodplain produced foggy weather in all but 110 days a year. Still, the construction went ahead. Senator Byron Dorgan, elected to the Senate from North Dakota as a Democrat in 1996, took his new seat on the Senate Armed Services Committee, announcing that he would use his position to push for funds to maintain and re-engine the B-52 bomber.[77] Since Minot AFB, one of a few bases left with B-52 bombers, was in Dorgan's home state, the position was clearly intended to save the base, which would likely close if the venerable old bombers were retired by the Air Force.

Secretary Lehman's name is associated with another, much larger, scheme to add military bases to the nation's inventory. As Navy secretary during the Reagan administration, Lehman sought support for increasing the size of the United States Navy to 600 ships. He recognized that congressional opposition to such a plan might be overcome if representatives saw self-benefit in it. So Lehman offered a proposal known as "Strategic Homeporting" that would add a number of naval bases for the purposes of homeporting the Navy's additional vessels. Lehman proposed ports in such electoral-rich places as California (at San Francisco or Long Beach), New York (Staten Island), and other states, including Louisiana, Rhode Island, Texas, Washington, and Alabama.[78] The Navy considered more than two-dozen cities, with a price tag of somewhere between $1.6 billion and $2.2 billion in military-construction costs alone.[79] The plan never came to fruition, and in the end, the BRAC process shuttered those bases.

According to some, this congressional dependency on bases was commonplace. R. Douglas Arnold argues that "Congressmen have little choice but to work to protect the military installations in their districts, because local beneficiaries see such installations as semi-permanent benefits."[80] Fitzgerald and Lipson report that efforts to close bases in 1963 generated an amendment to a military construction bill that would have given the House Armed Services Committee final authority over base closings.[81] President Ford vetoed a similar effort in 1976, and the override attempt failed by only 11 votes, showing the sentiment in Congress about claims of presidential base-closing authority.[82]

Not all agree about the degree of congressional power to stop base closings, though. Fred Thompson notes that, during the period of time Arnold covers, Robert McNamara and Melvin Laird, secretary of defense in the Nixon administration, closed literally hundreds of bases [83] Thompson also notes that, while Congress made base closure more difficult in 1977, the measure exempted the almost 4,000 bases that employed fewer than 300 civilian employees.[84] True enough, Congress did not pass an outright ban on base closures, but it did pass strict environmental provisions not mentioned by Thompson and, thus, made even these bases difficult to close. More to the point, though, in 1976 these bases were of less interest to many members of Congress simply because they did not generate the kinds of jobs that the larger facilities did. Many of these smaller installations mentioned by Thompson were nothing more than small radar sites that had minimum economic impact on their local communities. By excluding them from the closure limitations, Congress did not appear to be quite so driven by "pork" objectives. And there is one more piece of interesting information on the political impact of base closures on congressional reelection. According to Charles L. Wilson and James L. Weingartner, who examined the impact of both the 1989 and 1991 base closures on subsequent reelection success, there was no difference in the success of representatives who had a base on the closure list and those who did not.[85] That does not mean that representatives may not act as if base closure could hurt them politically, it is just that, in the aggregate, it does not seem to be the case. They still act as though harm may come if bases are closed or reduced. Senator John Glenn (D-OH), for example, opposed DOD decisions to reduce bases in Ohio because "the State of Ohio is being asked to bear a disproportionately large share of the Defense Department's cutbacks. . . . "[86]

Since some members of Congress may at least believe themselves to be politically dependent on military spending for their districts, the threat to close a base in representative's district can be an effective means for presidents to gain congressional compliance on issues. Representative Dick Armey (R-TX) claimed that, "To put it bluntly, there is a widespread fear in Congress that an Administration with unrestricted base-closure power may use that power as a political weapon to intimidate Congress."[87] There were stories about how presidents had in fact exercised their options to close bases. President Lyndon Johnson reportedly closed Amarillo AFB in Texas because the surrounding county had voted in favor of his opponent. Johnson also supposedly closed Walker AFB in New Mexico because the local community had voted for Republican presidential candidate Barry Goldwater in the 1964 election. One consequence of Walker's closing may have been the defeat of the Democratic representative of the district, E.S. Johnny Walker, who lost his seat in the 1968 election, in part due the fact that Walker's closure had meant the loss of 6,000 military personnel.[88] A similar fate befell Brookley AFB in Alabama, again for the same reason. Alabama voted Republican in the 1964 election, and newly elected Republican Jack Edwards found himself representing Mobile and the suddenly closed Brookley AFB. Edwards, though, survived base closure, and was re-elected throughout the 1960's and 1970s.

Weida and Gertchner argue that the Defense Department under Republican President Reagan punished Michigan Senators Carl Levin and Donald Riegle, Jr. (both Democrats) in 1983 by deactivating a fighter interceptor squadron at K.I. Sawyer AFB that would make the base vulnerable to closure, especially since the base was left with only a B-52 bomb wing.[89] The B-52 wing at K.I. Sawyer could have been replaced by a B-1 bomber wing, but Senator Levin in particular had been a bitter critic of the B-1 procurement program, and the Michigan press gave the message to the state's voters that K.I. Sawyer was vulnerable to closure because of Levin's B-1 opposition.[90] Reports hold that President Nixon closed a number of bases in Massachusetts in 1973, after that state became the only one to go against him in the 1972 election.[91]

Congress also reacted severely to the unilateral base-closure efforts initiated by Defense Secretary Robert McNamara in the early 1960s. Some 60 bases appeared on a list generated by McNamara's staff, placed there on the basis of the "cost-effectiveness" studies that made the secretary famous (or infamous, depending on the point of view). McNamara had become convinced that the Defense Department had depended for too long on requirement analysis done by the services or their "think tanks" and that this analysis had built-in service bias. He insisted that entire programs (including their bases) be scrutinized through "systems analysis," factoring together the system's requirements, performance, and cost.[92] Not only did McNamara not consult with the military (whom he expected to strongly oppose the move), but he announced the decision to close bases right after the 1964 elections when Congress was not even in session.

In response, Congress found ways to make presidential base closings more difficult. While Congress could not prohibit base closures directly, they could make the process more difficult. So during the 1965 congressional session, representatives tried to take control of base closures, but the measure did not have enough votes to survive President Johnson's expected veto.[93] In 1976 Congress passed the O'Neill-Cohen Act, which in Section 2687 specifies that the National Environmental Protection Act must apply to any base closing. The measure required the Environmental Protection Agency (EPA) to inspect the land at a candidate for closure and certify it to meet federal environmental standards. The O'Neill-Cohen act (co-sponsored by Senator William Cohen of Maine, who had already suffered one base closing at Dow AFB), anticipated the vast environmental problems at many bases; the consequence of disposal practices that pre-dated environmental laws. Tons and tons of almost every imaginable toxic substance accumulated for decades at most bases, and to certify compliance could have been so expensive as to virtually prohibit base closures.[94] During that same year Congress also passed and sent to President Carter for his signature a bill that would further complicate base closure through notification. The measure required the Defense Department to notify Congress whenever they selected a base for closure, to submit reports on the economic, strategic, and environmental impact of that perspective closure. It also required a 60-day grace period so that constituents could appeal to Congress. The law also required Congressional approval for any closure effecting 300 or more civilian employees.[95] Given that the largest and most politically sensitive bases (such as aircraft maintenance depots) had thousands of civilian employees, the provision made base closures almost impossible. These Air Force depots, in particular, are of considerable political importance, given the value of the work done in them. In fiscal year 1996, the Defense Department spent about $15 billion (about 6 percent of its total budget) on various forms of maintenance, with the Air Force accounting for almost $4 billion of that amount.

In 1982, Congress found another way to preserve Air Force and Navy air bases by requiring that they be considered for civil-aviation use. The Airport and Airway Improvement Act (Public Law 97-248) required the secretaries of defense and Transportation to submit a plan to Congress for making military airfields available for joint civil-military use.[96] Bases vulnerable to closure, including Chanute AFB in Illinois, NAS Memphis in Tennessee, Bergstrom AFB in Texas, March AFB in California, and Wheeler AFB in Hawaii, were included on the list of potential joint sites.[97] Ironically, all of these facilities were closed, most by one of the four BRACs, but not for lack of congressional effort to keep them open.

As noted above, representatives also have access to symbolic power. That would serve them well, in particular, when protecting a base from closure. They often recognized the national requirements for reducing excess military capacity yet wanted the appearance of putting up the good fight. L.R. Jones notes that "Some congressional opposition (to base closure) was clearly intended merely to show constituents that their representatives were working on their behalf despite little chance of overturning closure decisions."[98]

The result of all of this congressional action was that not a single base had closed for a decade when the hearings creating BRAC opened in 1988. During that intervening period, the Cold War was ending, yet that fact had almost no impact on base structure. Clearly, BRAC was an idea whose time had come, at least for the military, who wanted to reduce what at that point had become a bloated base structure.

THE MILITARY AND MILITARY BASE POLICY: DOES "BUREAUCRATIC POLITICS" APPLY?

Graham T. Allison popularized the term "bureaucratic politics" as a model to explain how organizations draw upon their own parochial goals to influence their stances on broad national decisions.[99] For Allison, and those who follow in his footsteps, organizational interests are key ingredients in the formulation of organizational policy. While organizations may serve some larger interest, that interest may be only abstractly connected to the needs of organizational members and leadership. The "national interest," in particular, is an amorphous concept difficult to link to concrete policy. [100] Organizational members may not see their own fate and future connected to such an abstraction. But organizational success in the policy marketplace, in which agencies compete for scarce resources by scoring success on critical measures, is something all members can keenly support. Thus, organizational policy priorities are shaped by the needs of organization membership and, thus, by organizational leadership. In Allison's terms the position taken by an organizational leader ". . . can be predicted with high reliability from information concerning his seat.[101] In the competitive world of politics, organizations vie for resources in the name of organizational survival and growth. How they do this depends in part on the observer. For some, the process turns pernicious—organizations concoct false objectives, manipulate information, limit outside oversight to satisfy their own internal needs, and form coalitions with other interest groups to support mutual objectives.[102] Others see the motives that drive the process as less deleterious and even argue that some good above the selfish organizational motives can come from bureaucratically driven outcomes.[103]

The bureaucratic-politics model has generated its share of skeptics. Stephen Krasner argues that the bureaucratic-politics approach devalues the power of central authorities to shape agendas.[104] David A. Welch agrees, noting that in the case of the Cuban Missile Crisis, which Allison used to demonstrate the theory, ". . . few players stood where they sat, where the decision-making processes contained no 'bargaining,' where pulling and hauling was limited to the realm of persuasion and debate, and where the president and Khrushchev held all the cards in their respective 'games.'[105] Edward Rhodes, in an examination of naval procurement patterns, finds that during the Cold War the chief of naval operations did not represent his particular subbranch in recommending naval-force structure, contrary to the expectations of bureaucratic politics.[106] Still, the concept has too much potential for explanation of military organizational behavior, in particular, to be neglected in a study of base closure.

THE MILITARY THROUGH THE BUREAUCRATIC POLITICS LENS

For the military, in particular, bureaucratic behavior is reflected when the services organize and plan to sustain their own share of the defense-resource pie. The U.S. military is divided into roles based on mission—sea, land, or air—and those operational areas sometimes subdivide into naval air, ground support air, strategic air, and such.[107] There is almost a natural competition between functional services for resources and, thus, roles and missions. In 1920, for example, as military aviation was growing in importance, Rear Adm. Bradley A. Fiske demanded that, "For the sake of the U.S.N. and the U.S. of America, let's get a Bureau of Aeronautics. . . . If we don't get that Bureau next session, Gen'l Mitchell and a whole horde of politicians will get an 'Air Ministry' established, and the U.S. Navy will find itself lying in the street. . . ."[108] Other cases of alleged military parochialism included the Army and the Air Force competing for the intermediate-range ballistic missile in the 1960s[109] and earlier Army and Air Force competition for the continental air-defense mission against enemy bomber attack.[110] The degree of military parochialism during the Eisenhower administration is reportedly why Secretary McNamara demanded independent analysis from that he was getting from the services.[111] The split between McNamara and his service chiefs may be typical in that military officers often hold different views on military policy from their civilian counterparts.[112] In some cases, a wide gap opened between the secretary of defense and senior military leaders. In other cases, compromise bridged the potential gap, as generally occurred during the Nixon administration with Secretary Laird reaching agreement with the Joint Chiefs on an exchange between autonomy and withdrawal from Vietnam[113] or during the Reagan administration between Air Force Secretary Verne Orr and the Air Force.[114]

How can military views and positions on military policy best be understood? One way is to consider the way that the military ranks policy issues in terms of importance. For Morton K. Halperin, the military services adopt a kind of "organizational essence" that ranks what organizations deem vital, and why.[115] According to Carl H. Builder, each service has its own personality, its own goals, and its own ways of doing things, even its own concept of war.[116] That means that each service wants autonomy to field and maintain the forces that best suit its concept of war. Air Force officers, for example, obviously value airplanes more than water trucks, but they also value combat aircraft more than cargo aircraft. Among combat aircraft, they value fighters and bombers more than ground attack aircraft, because fighters and bombers are closer to what the Air Force considers its "organizational essence." Why? In I.M. Destler's view, "They [bureaucrats] tend to press for their resolution [of issues] in the direction that will most strengthen their ability to do their jobs."[117] For the Air Force, "the ability to do its job" relates to its ability to put bombs and bullets on targets.

For some, the real focus of military bureaucratic politics is on defense budget shares, which constitute measures of relative success in the battle over defense resources.[118] There is also competition at the military service level for a more tangible level of resource. With the creation of the modern service structure in the late 1940s, competition splits three ways over which service can get the largest shares of the defense budget. Since resource shares are obviously related to the value of the mission, the services have also competed for significant missions.[119] It should not be surprising that services also compete for bases, given that bases are directly related to roles and missions. And to complicate matters, there may be *intra*-service rivalry as well as inter-service competition. Naval aviation, for example, competes for resources with the submarine forces, and Air Force bomber missions compete with tactical air. When the Strategic Air Command (SAC) received a majority of the Air Force budget in the 1960s, it came at the expense of the other Air Force commands. When the commander of the Tactical Air Command (TAC) designed the so-called TFX (later the F-111) aircraft in the late 1950s, it was in part to gain back resources TAC had lost to SAC.[120] That would mean, among other things, more bases under TAC control.

Service identity and goal preference also ties to professionalism and a sense of autonomy that resists decisions from "outsiders." The military generally defers to elected or appointed civilian officials on matters of national strategy, but prefers professional autonomy on matters it considers "military."[121]

B U R E A U C R A T I C   P O L I T I C S   A N D   B A S E   C L O S U R E

Theories of bureaucratic politics may also offer some light on service decisions on basing. While the services often wanted excess bases disposed of, the expectation was that it would be done *equitably*. No service wanted to take a disproportionate share of the closures; the services believed that if BRAC closed bases, each service should take an equal share of both the pain and the benefit. So it did not matter whether the service wanted to close its bases to reallocate its resources elsewhere, or whether the service needed bases targeted for shutdown. Whether each service should be reduced at the same rate, or whether the post-BRAC base percentage should be more evenly distributed was another issue. In 1986, the Air Force had more bases than did the other services, at 405. The Navy was second with 253, the Army next with 210, and the Marines had 25. As noted in subsequent chapters, the service share would emerge as a controversy in each of the three BRACs examined in this study. Bureaucratic-politics explanations predict that services will demand that each get a relatively equal share of base closures. That demand may not be not be visible in any single year, but the expectation is that closure equity will occur over multiple years.

The services will also expect that their professional need (or lack thereof) for bases will get careful consideration in base-closure decisions. Since their voice was muted in the past by congressional power, they must be expected to be unwilling to see BRAC simply become an exception of that power. In a similar sense, they will demand that BRAC be sympathetic to their needs and will attempt to shape both the BRAC-creation process and the BRAC-decision process accordingly. They may act in ways that frustrate civilian domination of the closure issue. As in the case of nuclear weapons, the military can complicate base-closure issues in ways not easily discernible by appointed staffers or civilian commissioners.[122] Data on base value, for example, are arcane and specific to the process generating them—the process is often impossible for the uninitiated to understand. Data may be either withheld or released selectively to influence outside decisions. And while the military cannot directly engage in political action to increase its impact on base-closure decision making, there are many ways to engage in informal actions that may have the same effect.

LEARNING OVER TIME

If policy making is to improve, it must be assumed that lessons from the past are somehow worked into policy making for the present and the future. Students of political learning note that both individuals and organizations struggle with the process. For Richard Rose, "Most policy makers draw lessons in an unreflective way; a lesson is no more than an assertion of 'what everyone knows.'"[123] At the organizational level, Jeffrey L. Pressman and Aaron Wildavsky note starkly that "Inability to learn is fatal."[124] James H. Lebovic states that "Military organizations appear unable to learn from observation and require direct experience. . . . [T]hey might respond only to failure or direct civilian intervention"[125]

The question is really *how* and *what* policy makers learn from the past. For many there are repeat processes that offer learning opportunities. First-term representatives have ample opportunity to learn the rules of the game in their legislature. Mistakes made in their first year become things to avoid in subsequent years. The first bill a brave member introduces often winds up in a legislative version of a dead letter office. The rookie member either learns from the shortcomings of the measure, or she or he may quickly become politically irrelevant. So it is with bureaucrats and just about anyone else who works in regularized political processes. Learning over time is about personal and organizational survival and growth.

BRAC was a regularized process in its last three interations. There was an initial opportunity in 1991 to learn from the difficulties of the 1988 process, even though 1991 brought new procedures. The years 1993 and 1995 gave all parties to base closure two more chances to sequentially learn how to better their own positions. BRAC members could learn from past errors and successes, as could the military, congressional members, and local officials. Often the same actors participated in all three BRACs. Several commission members had overlapping memberships and were in a position to pass information to the new members. A majority of the members of Congress faced all three BRAC years, as did most officials at the local level. There was, in other words, an opportunity for all to learn how to improve their positions. The question is: Did they? Did community base supporters learn about how to better respond to the challenge of base closure? Did the services learn how to protect bases they wanted or to increase the chances of base closure for the installations they did not want? Did members of Congress learn more about base closure and thus how to respond to base closures in their jurisdictions? A policy sequence divided into three parts, each separated by a two-year time span, provides an excellent opportunity to find out.

THE POLITICS OF COMMISSIONS

"When you cannot decide, create a commission." That axiom might characterize American politics in the second half of the twentieth century. Both presidents and Congress seem almost eager to avoid hard political choices by turning political problems over to the more "rational" process that seems to epitomize commissions. The president, after all, appoints commissions, often with congressional input, to take politics out of the decision-making process and reach policy solutions through a commission recommendation. Since such recommendations are rarely binding or enforceable, elected officials can ignore them if they do not agree with them (as President Nixon did with the findings of the Kerner Crime Commission). When commission outcomes are binding or difficult to overturn, elected officials are allowed the opportunity to do something politically unpalatable while blaming commission members for their actions.

The primary political expectation about commissions is that they be neutral. The expectation arises from the belief that so few things of importance get done politically because of political partisanship. Different ends of the political spectrum either cannot agree at all on critical answers to issues, or they compromise to the point that policy actions are so watered down as to be ineffective. If commissions are perceived as politically nonaligned, their chances of success are perceived as higher. One important prerequisite for commission membership is that candidates have no stake in the issues with which the commission deals. Or so the theory goes, though that may not always be the case. It is an assumption that is critical, though, to the success of commissions, because if, indeed, they are supposed to take the "politics" out of an issue, they can hardly be effective if the appointment process is, in itself, not independent from the very politics that logjammed the decision system in the first place.

Social Security is typical of issues delegated to commissions. Several years ago, when a deficit in the Social Security fund loomed, a Social Security commission was created to consider options that ultimately would give the system more years of solvency, and, more important, take the issue off the political front burner. Pornography was the subject of the Meese Commission on Pornography. Postal rates got scrutiny by a postal rate commission. Such issues are simply too hot to handle for elected officials, who eagerly turn them over to unelected temporary commissions. According to Thomas R. Wolanin, one of the more important reasons to create and sustain commissions is to provide both policy analysis and a means around issue avoidance.[126] Policy analysis is useful, states Wolanin, when objective information is required to override strong political preferences.[127] If the commission then carries out policy recommendations based on such objective analysis, politicians can claim that they were simply overwhelmed by it, though they can still protest the outcomes.

The Defense Department has increasingly turned to commissions. One of the best known was the Packard Commission, created in 1985 by President Reagan in response to growing criticism about military inefficiency. The Packard Commission delivered a number of recommendations that were adopted as legislation in the Goldwater-Nichols Defense Reorganization Bill, passed in 1986. These reforms included a new chain of command that included regional military commanders, a new position of vice chair of the Joint Chiefs of Staff, a restructuring of the defense acquisition system, and a variety of other features. Most observers regard the Packard Commission as successful, and many give the changes initiated by it considerable credit for the reshaped military that did so well in the war against Iraq in 1990-1991. So after the services failed to resolve the questions over service responsibility for roles and missions in 1992, the secretary of defense created a Roles and Missions Commission, headed by John White.[128] After the commission delivered its report in 1995, the DOD announced that it would accept more than 70 of the 100 recommendations of the commission, rejecting somewhere between eight to ten altogether and submitting the rest "for further study."[129]

The base-closure commission process, to an extent, became a model for the depolitization of defense issues. The BRAC decision-making procedure required the participants to:

- Generate a statement of purpose;
- Generate a statement about how base functions contribute to that purpose;
- Generate multiple criteria for achieving those functions;
- Rank the bases according to the strength of their relative contribution to the purpose;
- Make choices based on the highest scores.

This was supposed to take politics out of the process. Further assurance that politics stopped at BRAC's front door was provided by allowing all who wanted to, to witness all procedures. It was, in other words, a typical effort to rationalize the resource distribution process. This is what commission decision making is all about—a back-door approach to solving political dilemmas that have such high stakes attached to them that they have created political deadlock. The question addressed in this book is whether decision making by commission actually accomplished its goal of depoliticizing military base decisions so that rational decisions could be made on the nation's military-base infrastructure.

SUMMARY

From the theoretical perspectives outlined above, the following expectations emerge from a sequential look at base-closure cases:

First, members of Congress with a base in their electoral district will find ways to get around the BRAC "depoliticization" process to preserve their facility. They will try to influence the selection of BRAC members and to sway the outcome if it is unfavorable. They will adopt tactics that position them to be seen as striving mightily to save jobs at their base even if, in the end, they fail. Members of Congress will also learn tactics sequentially so that their measure of success should be greater in 1993 and 1995 than it might have been in 1991, since 1991 was a baseline learning year for future year base-closure lessons.

Second, members of the military will attempt to get "excess" bases closed, but under conditions that retain their control over the final selection. They will try to influence BRAC staff and members to accept their base preferences with little adulteration. At the service level, military officers will fight to close a rival service's base, and at the subservice level they will offer up another command's base over their own command's facilities. At the base level, base commanders will try to save their own base at the expense of other bases. "Not in my backyard" is the operative instruction. Military members will also learn from the past and glean information that will help them further their own organizational goals. Again, 1991 was a significant baseline year for lessons to take into 1993 and 1995.

Third, learning over time will also occur at the BRAC level. BRAC members (some with overlapping terms) can draw from previous failure to close a base to craft more successful policy in subsequent years. Their measure of success was on one level to accomplish at one level the congressional mandate expressed in the legislation that created BRAC—to close one-third of military bases by 1995. However, BRAC commissioners were not political neutrals. Their appointment to the commission was sometimes due to their particular capacity to protect a designated base. They would have the opportunity to learn the fine art of political horse-trading so as to protect their own bases by sacrificing others. After 1991, they could learn from the mistakes of their predecessors (do not wind up with your face on a T-shirt sold in communities where you recommended a base for closure, for example).

More important, they could learn that, while BRAC supposedly took the politics out of the base-closure process, there was plenty of politics left to play.

There are actually four levels of explanation in this quest, though they overlap somewhat (see Table 1.1).

Table 1.1: Base Closure Expectations

Approach	Expected Behavior	Use of Information
Constituency service	Act to keep bases open/ close rival bases	Manipulative
Bureaucratic politics	Act to close surplus bases/ seek equity	Manipulative
Learning over time	Reduce losses/ maximize gains	Objective
Commission politics	Stay above politics/ referee	Objective

Essentially, individual and organizational self-interest drives all forms of behavior: Legislators want to avoid punishment for perceived income losses from base closure; military organizations want to reduce overhead expenses while avoiding suffering an unfair loss; commission members want to maintain the objectivity that is the primary reason for their very existence; and all want to minimize loss by absorbing lessons from past experiences. Subsequent chapters examine how well these expectations are born out.

CHAPTER TWO

Bases and Politics

Early in 1941, the officer in charge of Luke Airfield, just east of Phoenix, was ordered by the War Department to locate a desert area for air combat training. A site was needed that was large, uninhabited, and consisted almost entirely of public land. The task of finding such an area was then assigned to a young officer named Barry Goldwater, an Arizona native familiar with the State's resources. Thus, the future Senator drew the original boundaries of Luke Air Force Base, which at that time contained nearly 1.1million acres.

—*Congressional Hearings, 1990*

*N*ot all U.S. senators have been so fortunate as Goldwater to have a chance to both carve out and then reap the benefits of a huge base in their states. But, as discussed in Chapter One, bases and politics still mix well. This chapter examines how the political requirements of elected officials exerted an impact on the base-closure process. It then considers the various mechanisms for base disposal and the politics involved in each. The economic impact of base closure and the complex problems of environmental cleanup are also addressed here.

As noted in Chapter One, military-base decisions result from a complex nexus of military and political needs. It should hardly be surprising that that same matrix impacts on base-closure decisions.

"REQUIREMENTS" VERSUS "POLITICS" IN BASING DECISIONS

Bases are the infrastructure of the military and are essential to military operations. While spending on base construction is a relatively small part of the defense budget (3-8 percent of the total), the value of bases themselves is far higher. They provide living spaces, runways, piers, hospitals, maintenance facilities, training grounds, laboratories, and myriad other capabilities for the military. When the military wants to construct a new base (something that has rarely happened in many years), it must submit a host of documentation to justify its requirements. When construction is required to modernize or repair an existing base, yet more paperwork must be submitted to the approving agencies within the military, as well as to Congress. Also, when bases are proposed for closure, the process starts by comparing how well each base meets military requirements. There is no question that military requirements drive much of the decision making on base construction, repair, and, ultimately, on closure. But how much? Given the economic value of base-generated military spending, politics also plays a role.

The Impact of Defense Budget Cuts and their Impact on Base Infrastructure

The harsh realities imposed by downturns in the defense budget affected bases in particular. The pattern of the American defense budget has demonstrated peaks and valleys since the end of World War II, with the peaks coming at the height of the Korean and Southeast Asian wars and at during the peacetime Reagan buildup. Sharp downturns in defense spending followed those peaks, sometimes lasting as long as ten years, as occurred after the peak of the Vietnam buildup.[1]

During the periodic defense budget declines since 1945, the military sought to reduce overhead expenses by cutting back on its base infrastructure. But those efforts were consistently resisted by political leaders who feared voter retribution. When, for example, Secretary of Defense Robert McNamara wanted to close the Boston Naval Shipyard in the 1960s, he was reminded by President Kennedy that the workers there would do two things in response: draw their first unemployment check and vote Republican in the next election. Since Democratic House Speaker John McCormick then represented the district, Kennedy withdrew the shipyard from consideration. Later, in the 1980s, when Senator John Tower (R-TX) suggested that all senators who wanted to reduce defense spending offer up a base in their state for closure, only Democratic Senator Robert Byrd from West Virginia offered to do so. West Virginia has no military installations of any consequence.

The military, on the other hand, realized that a bloated base structure could deny it money for important projects, so it periodically campaigned to reduce the number of bases. Ultimately, compromises were reached, and some bases did get the shutdown orders. Strategic Air Command (SAC), once the powerhouse of the Air Force, was the primary tenant at 55 bases during the peak of the 1950s manned bomber period. By 1994, only five Air Force bases hosted strategic bombers. While some of the bomber bases reverted to other uses, 31 closed, 16 alone during the tenure of Defense Secretary McNamara, who worked hard to get SAC to relinquish its bombers in favor of long-range ballistic missiles.

Bomber bases were not the only bases targeted during defense budget reduction years. The Navy lost yards (the Washington and Brooklyn Naval Yards), and the Army saw a number of its facilities drop from its base list. Some states were particularly hard-hit by closure prior to the creation of the Base Realignment and Closure Commission (BRAC). Alabama, for example, lost two of its three large Air Force bases (Craig AFB and Brookley AFB) in the 1960s and 1970s; Michigan lost two (Kinchelo and Selfridge AFBs), and Kansas also saw two close (Forbes and Schilling AFBs). Even in Texas with its large congressional delegation, large bases such as Amarillo, Biggs, Ellington, Webb, and James Connally AFBs got closure notices before the BRAC process started. In all, 94 large bases were closed between 1961 to 1981.

Congressional reaction to such executive actions was to make the closure process more difficult. The military tested these new restrictions by sending a base-closure list to the White House in May 1981, reportedly containing 50 bases to be closed.[2] They may have enlisted the assistance of budget director David Stockman, who believed that President Reagan needed a symbolic measure to demand cuts in military as well as civilian budgets.[3] But Defense Secretary Caspar Weinberger delayed consideration of base closure, knowing that Congress would make such an effort very difficult, particularly in the face of large defense budget increases requested by the Reagan administration. It would clearly have been difficult to ask Congress to increase, say, the weapons procurement budget while at the same time shutting down bases in congressional districts. So, again, politics thwarted the military in its efforts to reduce its base inventory.

However, the end of the Cold War meant that the "business as usual" efforts at base closure had to come to an end. The services' plans for dramatic force structure cuts demonstrated a clear need to formalize the base-closure process and try to remove it from politics. With a cut in the number of aircraft, ships, troops and other military force components, base structure quickly became excessive. The BRAC was the answer.

The 1990 legislation creating BRAC attempted to systematize the process by trying basing decisions to military requirements. In Section 2903, the measure specifically required the secretary of defense to prepare three estimates, for fiscal 1992, 1994 and 1996, the three years prior to the BRAC decision years. The estimates were to specify "probable threats to the national security" and a description of the anticipated force structure responding to such threats.[4] The bill also required the secretary of defense to specify the criteria used to make recommendations for base realignment and closure, so that such criteria might reflect "military value" with reference to the force structure and threat estimates noted above.[5] To help assure oversight on these estimates, the measure required the secretary of defense to turn over all information used in generating them to the comptroller general of the United States, thus making them available to the General Accounting Office (GAO) for independent analysis. The obvious hope of Congress in creating the authorizing legislation was to link the closure process to national security requirements rather than politics. The question remains as to how well these aspirations were realized.

THE CREATION OF BRAC

While the Reagan administration is best remembered for an increase in defense spending, it is also remembered for its antigovernment stance. The president railed against government inefficiency and cost, claiming that, in many cases, private efforts should replace government functions. The Defense Department is part of the government, though, and clearly Reagan did not want to submit the DOD to the same criticism that he was ladling out to the rest of government— he might well jeopardize his build-up. Not surprisingly, he created a commission, even though he did not call it one. The "President's Private Sector Survey on Cost Control," formed in 1982 and chaired by industrialist J. Peter Grace, recommended a number of things, including a reduction of about 10 percent in the military-base infrastructure. By accepting the so-called Grace Commission report, Reagan implicitly accepted its recommendation on closing bases. However, the road to reducing bases still ran through Congress, and Congress had little inclination to move on the subject. After all, the Reagan defense budget increases were flowing into their states and districts, and they were benefiting from the largess. So no action on base closure was taken during the Reagan presidency.

By 1988, though, it was clear to even the most jaded politician that something had to be done about the size of the military-base infrastructure. While the Bush Administration pushed ahead with plans for a substantial reduction of military force, the barriers to reducing the number of bases loomed ever larger.

Congress Resists, Then Relents on Base-Closure Power

Congressional reluctance to close bases remained strong. Fearful of another Lyndon Johnson axing bases to punish uncooperative members, Congress had passed legislation in 1977 requiring that the Defense Department notify Congress should any base become a candidate for closure. The 1977 stipulations also applied enforcement of the National Environmental Policy Act (NEPA) to base closures. The NEPA required, among other things, that environmental impact statements be formulated for any base facing closure. This act was largely the work of the Maine congressional delegation, which was startled to see an Air Force request for the closure of Loring AFB, which, had it succeeded, would have been the second bomber base closed in the state—Dow AFB near Bangor was the first.

Members of Congress also prevented base closings by refusing to authorize or appropriate money for the implementation of base-closure actions. They refused to allow the Army to build facilities to replace Fort Douglas in Utah, for example, and stopped funds that the Navy wanted to spend to transfer helicopter training from Naval Air Station (NAS) Whiting Field in Florida to Fort Rucker in Alabama. They refused the Air Force money to even study the closing of Mather AFB in California.[6] This is not to imply that no bases closed; as noted above, a large number shut down before 1977. According to R. Douglas Arnold, though, these were bases not fortunate enough to be located in the district of a member of Congress who belonged to one of the committees dealing with military affairs. In return, according again to Arnold, ". . . members of the military committees worked to keep off the congressional agenda proposals to allow greater congressional involvement in decisions about base closings."[7]

Things were changing, though. The Reagan increases in defense spending tapered off by the mid-1980s, and, as the Defense Department faced a dramatically reduced military force, it was clear that something had to be done. Momentum began in Congress that would lead to the formation of BRAC. Debate began in 1988 on how to create such a commission, which would effectively allow Congress to delegate its base protection powers. During that debate, representatives defeated a series of measures to block the process and also killed the provision to adhere to the NEPA that had so successfully stymied base closings in 1977.[8] So Defense Secretary Frank Carlucci chartered the Defense Secretary's Commission on Base Realignment and Closure in May 1988 and ordered it to conduct a study to recommend base closures and realignments.

There was initial congressional support for BRAC from both conservative Republicans and liberal Democrats. For liberals, BRAC represented an opportunity to cut defense spending and thus free federal funds for domestic programs. For conservatives, BRAC would allow the transfer of money spent on bases to other more important defense projects. For Republicans the base-closure process was appealing for several reasons. For one, they had campaigned hard for a balanced federal budget (a goal that would paradoxically hurt their presidential candidate in 1992), and closing bases would help to achieve budget balance without really cutting into military muscle. Some Republicans may also have been inspired by the analogy of private corporation restructuring. For the corporate world, restructuring was necessary to rid the firm of obsolete or unneeded capacity; so it should be with the military and its surplus bases.[9]

Initial Problems with BRAC

While BRAC process was intended to be non-partisan, it did not take Democrats in Congress long to notice the "non-partisan" results of the 1991 BRAC list. As Representative Patricia Schroeder (D-CO) opened Congressional hearings on the list, she noted that, of the 21 major bases slated to be closed, 19 were in districts represented by Democrats, and claimed that 99 percent of the civilian job losses from those closures were in Democratic districts.[10] For Schroeder, the implications were clear. In her view, Secretary of Defense Richard Cheney, working for Republican President Bush, and Cheney himself being a former Republican Member of Congress from Wyoming, had stacked the list in order to hurt Democratic incumbents in coming elections. Schroeder also mused: "We hope that we don't get into trading bases for B-2 votes, [but] that possibility is always there. This place is always a political bazaar, and people are always trading things for things. . . ."[11]

Part of the reason that politics continued to influence the process was the 1988 BRAC legislation making BRAC directly responsible to the secretary of defense. The 1988 Commission developed its own list of prospective base closures, and then presented them to the secretary of defense. But the secretary of defense was a political appointee, and reported directly to the president. The president could still pressure the secretary to load the base-closure process with preferences based on party rather than on need, and, once the secretary received the list of proposals, he could pick and choose based in part on partisan politics. It is impossible to demonstrate convincingly that such favoritism occurred, but, because of the suspicion by legislators that partisanship could occur, the 1988 process lacked congressional support.

Other flaws in the 1988 process included its secretive nature and the failure of commissioners to visit bases recommended for closure. The hearings were closed, and transcripts of those hearings became difficult to obtain. Thus, it was almost impossible to determine the extent to which partisanship influenced decisions. Members of Congress also might have realized that closed hearings would prevent them from appearing publicly before the commission and lobbying on behalf of their bases. The commissioners did not visit most of the sites targeted for closure, so members of Congress in particular complained about poorly informed decisions. They also expressed concern that the commissioners did not appreciate the impact on local communities that their recommendations would carry. Another concern was that the data the 1988 Commission used was faulty, and there was no oversight process to verify its accuracy. In short, the 1988 BRAC process clearly failed to take politics out of the base-closure process.

Changing BRAC Procedure for 1990

On November 5, 1990, Congress passed the Defense Base Closure and Realignment Act of 1990. In an effort to replace politics with rational means tests, the act provided specific criteria and a specific process for base decisions. Specifically, the act directed the Defense Department to consider the following criteria:

1. The military mission of the base and its impact on operational readiness;
2. The availability of land and other resources at both existing and alternative bases;
3. The ability to absorb contingency mobilizations;
4. The cost and manpower implications;

5. The extent and timing of potential costs and savings from closure or realignment;
6. The economic impact on communities;
7. The ability of communities' infrastructure to support forces and missions;
8. The environmental impact.

The law did give some leeway to the services to influence parts of the process. For example, in the 1993 BRAC, the Directorate of Operations, deputy chief of staff (plans and operations) gave the Air Force depots 35 supplemental questions along with the regular questions submitted to all Air Force bases.[12] The services also set their own standards as to how they valued bases.

The 1990 Defense Base Closure Act also tried to insure objectivity by involving the GAO in the process review. The act required that the Defense Department submit data on closures and realignments to the GAO. The GAO, in turn, passed its analysis of these data to both BRAC and Congress. The database alone was massive—for just the Air Force, the requirements of 8 main evaluation criteria and 212 subcriteria produced 500,000 data points on 105 Air Force bases located in the continental United States, Alaska, Hawaii, and Guam. It was almost impossible for the GAO to substantiate every entry in the data submitted by the services. According to some familiar with the data-collection process, that was exactly the point.

The GAO findings were then made a part of the BRAC final report to the President. All of this was intended to produce objective evaluations, and, indeed, some of the language used by the service evaluators sounded as though it would produce such outcomes; a system described as "A multi-layer, hierarchical filtering process is used to evaluate the relative impact of closing each base. . . . The system can perform both tabular and graphical access to base data, and utilizes customized stoplight screens to . . . compare bases . . . filter values . . . receive instant feedback on the sensitivity of the revised criteria."[13] However, to simply quantify vast amounts of data does not in itself guarantee "objectivity." Douglas P. Gorgoni performed a separate objectivity test, subjecting the "military value" criteria for the 1988 and 1991 BRACs to 12 Air Force experts. Gorgoni's panel concluded that "Military value is difficult to quantify . . ." and recommended no fewer than 27 improvements to the definition process.[14]

The Base Realignment and Closure Commission: Taking out the Politics?

Before BRAC, the decision process for base closure was informal, to say the least. Set out in the 1990 legislation creating BRAC were criteria to allow an assessment of bases in terms of their military, rather than their political, significance. That was the hallmark of BRAC— the built-in safeguards to assure objectivity in the politically charged atmosphere of base closings. That objectivity has been put forth time and time again by BRAC's defenders, who point out, as Assistant Secretary of Defense for Economic Security Joshua Gotbaum did in 1995: "The base realignment and closure process was designed to be as objective, as public, and auditable as any process in government. The law requires every realignment and closure recommendation in accordance with the force posture. It must be made in accordance with a specific set of published criteria."[15] The criteria are hardly clear, though. For example, when the Navy included the Long Beach Naval Shipyard in California on its list, Secretary of the Navy John Dalton indicated that it was chosen over a similar facility at Portsmouth, New Hampshire, because Long Beach could not serve the Navy's nuclear fleet.[16] On the other hand, the shipyard had the only dry dock in California large enough to handle aircraft carriers, most of which are nuclear powered.[17]

While the intention of the BRAC process was to take politics out of base closure, there is considerable evidence that this objective has not been fully met. For example, the state of Georgia, with a considerable population of military facilities, was not touched by any of the four BRACs.[18] While proof is impossible, it is difficult not to connect that outcome with the fact that Senator Sam Nunn (D-GA) was the Senate Armed Services Committee chair prior to the 1994 elections and ranking minority member prior to his 1996 retirement. Virginia saw the Norfolk Naval Station get through three rounds of BRAC without closing (with two senior senators, Republican John Warner and Democrat Charles Robb, on the Senate Armed Services Committee). Exceptions do exist—Senator John Glenn (D-OH) could not keep Ohio's Newark AFB open, and South Carolina's senior senators Strom Thurmond and Ernest Hollings lost both the Charleston Naval Shipyard and Naval Station in 1993.

Service priorities crept into BRAC as well, even though the process was intended to minimize them. The list of bases submitted by the Air Force in 1995 reveals how long-held priorities shaped its unwillingness to give up bases that the end of the Cold War made unnecessary.

The Air Force has two areas of base surplus, former strategic bomber bases and aircraft depots. The strategic bomber bases were a legacy of the Cold War, located in remote regions of the United States where both the aircraft noise and the danger of a nuclear strike from the USSR were minimized politically because of the small adjacent populations. While some of these bases closed under BRAC (Wurtsmith, Carswell, Loring, for example) a number of them remained even after the Air Force submitted its 1995 closure to BRAC. Minot AFB, and Grand Forks AFB in North Dakota, Ellsworth AFB in South Dakota, and Fairchild AFB in eastern Washington state. With a substantial drop in the strategic bomber force and no continuing need to threaten a mass bomber attack against Russia, most of these bases should have closed. Part of the reason they remained open may have been Air Force nostalgia for the strategic bomber mission.

Other survivors of the first three base-closure rounds included all five of the large aircraft maintenance depots: Ogden, Utah; San Antonio, Texas; Oklahoma City, Oklahoma; Sacramento, California; and Warner-Robins, Georgia. Rumors spread that at least two of these huge facilities would be placed on the 1995 closure list by the Air Force. President Clinton took one, Sacramento, off the 1993 list after heavy lobbying by California's two new Democratic senators, Dianne Feinstein and Barbara Boxer. Thus, its value to the Air Force would have been even less in 1995 than it had been in 1993 since the Air Force was even smaller two years later. But the Air Force did not include any of the depots included in BRAC 1993. Why? In part because they employ huge armies of civilians whose release from federal payrolls would spell economic disaster for the regions around most of these depots—consider the opportunities for alternate employment around Warner Robins or Ogden. The Air Force also wanted to maintain aircraft in its own depots. The depots had become more important to aircraft operators after the Air Force made changes to the maintenance system in the early 1990s that moved some functions (avionics and engine repair, for example) away from the aircraft bases to the depots. Having thus made the depots so much more important for aircraft operations, the Air Force was reluctant to give up any of them, despite surplus capacity.

When the commission reviewed the Air Force submissions for 1995, it surprised both the service and the depot's political supporters by placing four of the five (Sacramento, Warner Robins, San Antonio, and Oklahoma City) on its closure list. The 1995 final BRAC list included both Sacramento and San Antonio. Their stories appear more fully in Chapter Five.

Protecting Bases Under BRAC: The Game Changes

While the 1991 BRAC was closing bases around the country, some astute politicians were actually able to gain bases. One of the best at getting federal funds to his state was Senator Robert Byrd (D-WV), who had promised to bring a billion dollars to West Virginia in five years.[19] In 1992, Senator Byrd got $25 million in construction moneys for improvements to the Eastern West Virginia Regional Airport in Martinsburg, West Virginia, along with 4 Navy C-130s and 319 jobs.[20] That was significant for a state that has no coastline or even a major lake. Representative Norman Dicks (D-WA), a senior Democrat on the House Armed Services Committee, managed to gain force increases at almost all of Washington's bases. At McChord AFB, 24 A-10 attack aircraft and 8 more C-141 transports were secured from bases closing elsewhere. At Fort Lewis 6,000 new troops arrived in 1995. In 1992 space increased at the Bremerton Naval Shipyard, the Madigan Army Medical Center next to Fort Lewis, and the Everett Naval Station got enough new piers to base two major warships and an aircraft carrier.[21] Not only did these additions provide new jobs for the state, they also helped avoid base closures in Washington by the 1993 and 1995 BRACs.

Politicians with bases in their districts and states often find clever ways to keep those bases open. One tactic is to increase the monetary value of the base. Since base-closure decisions are usually made partly on the basis of the value of the installation, one logical response is to get new construction that increases the dollar value of the base. The connection between new construction and base saving was demonstrated aptly by Representative Robert Matsui (D-CA), who stated for the record in 1995 that "The gentleman from California [Mr. Fazio] and I have worked to get $400 million of construction programs for McClellan (AFB) in the last decade and a half. . . .The gentleman . . . did a tremendous job in doing whatever he could to save McClellan Air Force Base.[22] Another creative example of base preservation involved the efforts of Representative William Dickenson (R-AL) in saving Gunter AFB in Montgomery. Gunter was a relatively small base without a major mission after its runways closed in the 1960s and, thus, vulnerable to closure. Dickenson, though, used his position as ranking minority member of the House Armed Services Committee to get Gunter redesignated as an annex of Montgomery's larger Maxwell AFB, so both bases would have to be closed in order to close Gunter. Dickenson was also able to pepper Maxwell with new construction and gain new missions for the base, thus diminishing the probability that it would close.

Another avenue for avoiding base closure is to re-mission a base. Consider Whiteman AFB near Knob Noster, Missouri. During the Cold War it was a Minuteman intercontinental ballistic missile (ICBM) base; thus making it ripe for closure as the Minuteman force shrank. It was located near a small village of about 2,000 residents, so the impact of closure would be minimal with respect to the numbers of people. But with the advent of the B-2 "Spirit" bomber, the base, located in the district of Representative Ike Skelton, (D-MO)was designated as the B-2's only base, saving it from consideration for closure in the 1995 BRAC.[23] After the B-2s arrived at Whiteman, the Air Force did withdraw the ICBM missiles. A similar retasking may have saved the Oklahoma Air Logistics Center (ALC) at Tinker AFB from BRAC closure. As it became clear that at least one of the five Air Force aviation depots would be closed in 1995, B-2 bomber software maintenance work transferred from the Northrop-operated facility at Palmdale, California to Tinker, shifting 350 to 400 jobs to the Oklahoma facility in the process.[24] But once it reached Tinker, the base remained potentially vulnerable to closure since B-2 software maintenance was clearly capable of being moved elsewhere. So to give the base more protection, a high-ranking civilian employee at Tinker briefed members of the Oklahoma congressional delegation that the B-2 software program was moving again to another maintenance facility. Surprised and shocked, the representatives returned to Washington and got a promise from the Air Force that Tinker would keep the capacity. The briefer had, in fact, misled the delegation—the B-2 system was not moving. When the truth was learned, the civilian received a simulated "firing" by his commanding general, who was in on the ruse. It worked, though: The Air Force did not place Tinker on its 1995 list, and though BRAC added it, in the end, the base survived.[25] The tactic also worked for Senator Edward Kennedy (D-MA), who visited Hanscom AFB in Massachusetts in 1995 to "urge the expansion of Hanscom" by adding missions to the base that would presumably make it more difficult to close.[26] As noted below, he succeeded.

The Air Force has been particularly adroit at re-missioning its bases—so good that its efforts have drawn suspicion from Congress. In 1991, Representative Bill Alexander (D-AR) asked pointedly: "Can the Air Force give the Subcommittee good faith assurances that it has not prejudged—and reduced—the potential for winding up on the April 15 base-closure list by including these 'new missions' military construction projects in the fiscal year 1992 budget proposal?" His question was in response to finding requests for "new mission" construction at no fewer than 20 Air Force bases, some for new missions for the B-52 bomber.[27] The Air Force answered by saying that the money was not specifically designated to keep threatened bases open, or to make it easier to transfer B-52s from bases it considered excess. Alexander may have had reason to wonder, though, as B-52s from Eaker AFB in his state transferred to a number of other Air Force bases, whether the Air Force had singled out Eaker as a base it wanted to close in order to preserve more favored locations. The same question was asked in 1991 by Representative Robin Tallon (D-SC), who wondered why, after he requested a new mission for Myrtle Beach AFB, ". . . the Pentagon [told] me that it cannot give the Myrtle Beach Air Force Base another mission because they do not have another mission to give."[28] Myrtle Beach AFB, which served primarily as a wing of A-10 attack aircraft, was clearly vulnerable when the Air Force stopped buying the A-10 and began transferring existing planes to the Guard and Reserve forces. It appeared as though the Air Force did have new mission money for bases it wanted to keep open, but not for Myrtle Beach, which it wanted to close.

One of the more successful examples of re-missioning as a strategy of resistance against base closure is Goodfellow AFB near San Angelo, Texas. Goodfellow has enjoyed a phoenixlike stature—it was first re-missioned as a training base in 1947, then, after losing its flying mission in 1958, it got the Air Force Security Service training mission. In 1978, the secretary of the Air Force planned to phase out the Security Service, but, with some help from then-Chair of the Senate Armed Services Committee John Tower (R-TX), the intelligence-training consolidation moved to Goodfellow. So did a PAVE PAWS, a phased-array radar site that was a part of a national warning network against a ballistic missile attack from sea.[29] Re-missioning also affected Maxwell AFB in Alabama. The mission of training officer candidates moved there from Randolph AFB in Texas, and a modern and expensive classroom and dormitory building was built to house the Air Force Judge Advocate General School. Maxwell also gained a new building to house the Air Force Quality Institute. Even though a decision was made to move the Quality Institute to Randolph AFB before completion of the building at Maxwell, construction continued and the building itself was re-missioned. It became the new headquarters of the Air Force Doctrine Center, a nonexistent mission when the building was first planned.

Air Force cutbacks hit New Mexico in particular—Cannon AFB lost an entire wing of F-111s. The state might have been cut even more had not pressure from a New Mexico senator made the Air Force move the F-117 Nighthawk "fighter" from its super-secret base at Tonapah, Nevada, to Holloman AFB, in New Mexico.[30] The move cost millions of dollars in added security measures to protect the F-117. Holloman originated as a research base (it had been the site of the first atomic bomb test) and was operated in the years immediately following World War II by the Air Research and Development Command. It had been the site of many rocket and space experiments but had no history as an aircraft operational base.[31] So its conversion to an operational base with the F-117 represented a fairly unusual step.[32] Georgia was also the beneficiary of re-missioning, and the influence of Democratic Senator Sam Nunn, the ranking minority member of the Senate Committee on Armed Services, was hard to miss, when Warner Robins AFB, in the face of cuts elsewhere, got a new surveillance wing, bringing 2,214 military and 53 civilian jobs along with it.[33] BRAC placed the depot at Warner Robins on its closure list for 1995 (the Air Force had put no depots on the 1995 list), but it was removed in the final round.

Another avenue for political influence in the BRAC process is the right of senators to make appointments to BRAC. Senators interested in protecting bases in their states will try to nominate members for the commission who might work to avoid closing those bases. For example, Democratic Senator Tom Daschle (D-SD) nominated the former lobbyist for his state's Ellsworth AFB to the commission in 1995; in the same year, Senator Bob Dole (R-KS) nominated the former commander of the First Mechanized Division at Fort Riley, Kansas, to BRAC.[34]

The Politics of Resisting BRAC Closure

Clearly there are ways for political figures to make bases less vulnerable to closure in anticipation of future closure efforts. But for those who were less successful in doing so, facing BRAC closure with a vulnerable base meant adopting other types of tactics. Perhaps the most common response involved advertising the merits of the facility. For example, even as President Clinton was naming the final membership of the 1995 BRAC, legislators from Massachusetts were meeting with the Secretary of the Air Force to fence off Hanscom AFB, and the Maine and New Hampshire congressional delegations were selling the benefits of New Hampshire's Portsmouth, Naval Shipyard to the chief of naval operations.[35] Hanscom not only was spared, but it got additional benefits as well. In its list to the 1995 BRAC, the Air Force proposed closing its Rome Laboratory in upstate New York and transferring Rome's business to Hanscom, which already had 2,200 military, 2,000 civilian, and 6,400 contract workers.[36] So it was not surprising that both New York senators, Democrat Daniel Patrick Moynihan and Republican Alfonse D'Amato, delayed confirmation of the 1995 BRAC members because Hanscom would gain work that would be shifted from the Rome Laboratory in Plattsburgh.

A second type of defense tactic is to charge that the decision to close a base is "unfair"—that is, that "politics" is responsible, and the BRAC process is skewed by partisanship. In the case of Plattsburgh, both Senators Moynihan and D'Amato were still smarting after the 1993 BRAC closed Plattsburgh AFB (leaving the Rome laboratory untouched, though) instead of McGuire AFB in New Jersey. There was more than the usual New York/New Jersey rivalry, though. The 1993 BRAC chair was former New Jersey Republican Representative Jim Courter, and both New York senators believed that Courter had done his home state a favor at their expense. Courter denied the charge, pointing out that, as a *former* member of Congress, he no longer had to do favors to be reelected. Senator Arlen Specter (R-PA) used a similar tactic in 1992 when he echoed the suspicions of a union president at the New Cumberland Army Depot, saying: "If this is a deliberate way to make this facility come short so they could use that as an excuse to move it to Virginia. . . . I need to know." [37] Specter never indicated who the "they" were, and little came of the charge, but it at least gave the appearance of some wrongdoing, with the vigilant Specter ready to get to the bottom of it.

Representative Ronald Dellums (D-CA) was even more blunt about the unfairness of base closures when four bases located in his northern California district made the 1993 closure list. Dellums, noted for his persistent criticism of the Defense Department and defense spending, charged that he was being "punished for his political views."[38] Dellums' general counsel hinted that the chair of the House Armed Services Committee might retaliate by denying the Navy money for upgrades to its naval stations in San Diego and Washington State, which were rivals to Alameda.[39] A similar charge in defense of Fort Devins in Massachusetts came from Representative Joe Moakley (D-MA), who stated that the Army was punishing Massachusetts for its "liberal views" by closing the only large Army base in the region.[40]

Since the purpose of BRAC is to save Defense Department dollars, another means of resistance is to challenge the estimates of savings related to base closure or the impact of such savings in the near-term future. For example, in 1995, Representative Constance Morella (R-MD) stated that it would cost $143 million to replace a high-velocity wind tunnel at the Naval Surface Warfare Center (NSWC) at White Oak, Maryland (placed on the 1995 BRAC list), and $102 million to move the facility.[41] Sometimes cost challenges come from unexpected quarters, such as members of the commission itself. In the 1995 process, commission member Rebecca Cox challenged the "official" BRAC cost calculations on closing the Air Force's Rome Laboratory in upstate New York. Cox stated that the listed cost of $79.2 million was incorrect and that BRAC analysts had recalculated the new cost at $118.6 million, meaning that the time to recoup closure costs would be more than 100 years.[42] The Economic Development Advisory Board of Alameda County California, charged that "Neither the Navy nor the Department of Defense have offered to refute knowledgeable local experts who claim that it will cost $2 billion to relocate activities (at three naval facilities on the 1991 closure list) which must be retained."[43]

Another challenge involved the closure of Missouri's Richards-Gebaur Air Reserve Base (ARB) (mostly closed decades earlier save for a Reserve fighter wing). The Committee to Delay the Closure of Richards-Gebaur claimed that the Air Force was spending $16 million to renovate buildings at Whiteman AFB, also in Missouri, to receive the Reserve wing after Richards-Gebaur closed. The group argued, though, that the some buildings at Whiteman would not become available until 1996, thus calling for a delayed closure of Richards-Gebaur to save the $16 million.[44]

Senator Specter launched one of the more original efforts to save a BRAC-targeted base when the Philadelphia Naval Shipyard made the 1991 BRAC list—he sued. Joined by 18 other political and labor union officials, Specter argued that the base-closure process should be subject to judicial review—that federal courts should review wrongdoing in the BRAC process, even though the 1990 Base Closure and Realignment Act specifically exempted the laws resulting from that act from judicial review.[45] In the end, Specter lost his case, but not for a lack of trying.

Not all of the politics surrounding BRAC involved closure resistance—some of it was pro-closure. Of course some, pro-closure politicking is really about closing a base somewhere else so home bases can be spared, but sometimes there are other reasons. Other political figures genuinely want base closure because they calculate that base land is more valuable for alternate use than for military use. So Mayor Richard Daley, Jr. of Chicago wanted BRAC to close or move two Air National Guard units at O'Hare International Airport to expand the commercial part of the airport. Daley, who claimed that he was "the only mayor in the country who actually wanted a base closing in his city" (incorrectly, it turns out, as noted below) did not initially get his wish. The first BRAC decision in March 1995 left the units intact, and the only good news for Chicago was that the city would not have to pay up to $300 million to move them, as they had agreed to do in 1993.[46] But Daley's persistence led to BRAC's final decision to move the units from O'Hare because ". . . the community's desire to move the units undermines the typical community-base support relationship found at other bases and could be detrimental to future mission accomplishments."[47] The catch was that the City of Chicago had to pay for the costs of moving the units (to Scott AFB and several smaller regional airports) and redeveloping the facilities and remediating any environmental problems resulting from a faster close than DOD planned.[48] Also fortunate was Mayor Leonard Kiczek of Bayonne, New Jersey, who welcomed the news that the 1995 BRAC closed the Military Ocean Terminal in Bayonne. Kiczek believed that commercial development of the property across the river from New York City would generate more revenue than did the base.[49] In another case, the city of Sacramento reportedly wanted land used by the Sacramento Air Logistics Depot for airport expansion, but in the end the Air Force scratched the depot from the 1993 BRAC list and did not include it on its 1995 list. It was included, along with four other Air Force depots, on BRAC's 1995 list and ultimately became one of the most controversial facilities on that list.

DISPOSING OF BASES

One of the thorniest issues in the base-closure process is the ultimate disposal of former military facilities. The process would be much easier if the military could simply walk away from surplus bases, as it did after World War II. For example, the military abandoned numerous military airfields (which coincidentally helped to form the sport of drag racing as hot-rodders found the fields safer places to race than on public streets). Camps for training personnel often disappeared under bulldozers for urban housing. The larger bases that remained after World War II were too important economically to simply shut down, or their mission remained essential to the services. But even after military necessity waned and a service wanted to close a base, economic factors intervened to make the process easy. A variety of methods have been tried to find new tenants to operate base facilities or to build a new infrastructure at a former base. But finding new tenants was only one answer to successful base closure. Other barriers to base closure remained, such as the presence of toxic waste left by years of military dumping.

At many bases, environmental cleanup caused years of delay, as discussed further later in this and subsequent chapters. In yet other cases, infrastructure changes were needed before industry could move in to a closed base. Bases were not originally built with conversion in mind, so often closure requires wholesale replacement of facilities before a base can become a suitable commercial property. Even when facilities are appropriate for conversion, they often need repair and upgrading, since most bases slated for closure did not usually receive much military-construction money to maintain their buildings and other infrastructure.

Other factors that complicate base disposal include lawsuits tying up the closure process, and political efforts to continue some kind of military mission at the facility. Rarely have base closings and transitions to alternative functions been smooth or rapid. Often entangling regulations and priorities delay conversion efforts. Zoning issues, environmental requirements, and multiple layers of authority can add years to base land transfer and alternative utilization. In 1995, Representative Jerry Lewis (R-CA) complained that ". . . George AFB is a demonstration project of how not to handle base closure. Fifteen months after the lock was put on the gate at George, the Air Force is still playing around with who is going to do the planning and future development of the facility."[50] At that point, most of the early closure plans had fallen through, and the closure process was marred by 32 lawsuits, including one filed by the city of Adelanto over water well rights, an issue that dates back to 1942.[51] Representative Lewis was not the only one to complain; for all four rounds, base closure took longer on average than predicted at the time of the closure announcement.

Developing the Base-Closure Process

Base disposal may sound like a mechanistic process whereby the best alternatives are selected for the particular nature of the base and its surrounding environment. Experience suggests, though, that the process is much less structured, though amenable to learning over time. Some lessons from previous base-replacement policy got extensive study both inside and outside the Defense Department in order to extract lessons from it. Many of those lessons were political in nature.

Base disposal is also not divorced from the political priorities of those impacted by it. The stakes in replacement are high, since politicians may believe that they need to replace base economic contributions to their constituencies or face possible punishment in elections. Politicians may also regard base-replacement policy as a means of rewarding political contributors with favored treatment, such as obtaining low-cost or free base land for a firm as a result of a contribution from that firm or in the expectation of receiving such a contribution. Therein lies the possibility that favoritism plays a role in selecting replacement activity. At a December 1993 Defense Department news conference on base closure, the question was asked:

> Can you explain why this would't [sic] be open to rampant corruption? Or at least pork barreling? Let's say I'm Senator X from Georgia, a very powerful Senator. He calls up DOD and says, "I've got this base and I want it to go to Joe Schmo who wants to build a box factory there. Why don't we give it to him?" What stops that? I don't understand the process here that keeps it clean.[52]

The answer was not particularly reassuring:

> One of the things that stops it is that the particular entrepreneur isn't going to be able to get the land for nothing. . . . (H)e will have to pay for it.[53]

The questioner was apparently not satisfied, since the response was: "It keeps the corruption at a lower level."[54] However, there is little evidence of such "corruption" in the politics of base conversion. One case that has surfaced involves allegations that Staten Island Borough President Guy Molinari and his daughter, Representative Susan Molinari (R-NY) benefited from an arrangement over housing at the former naval base at Staten Island. According to reports, the Molinaris pressured the Navy into transferring the housing at the closed base to developers who had previously contributed some $40,000 in campaign contributions to the Molanaris.[55]

This is not to imply that most, or even some base, transfers are marked by shady political dealing or favoritism. Rather, base transfer is about political goods changing hands, and political outcomes get shaped by certain factors. One such factor is simply the necessity to do something with a base so that it does not represent lost opportunity. Base transfer is also a way to preserve some of the base's previous employment, or a chance to draw new employment to a political jurisdiction. It also may be portrayed as a vehicle to address social problems. In short, the politics of base transfer are driven by a combination of political needs along with the hope by the military for a rapid closure process. Given these needs, base disposal varies both in the means by which it is done and the potential for political opportunity.

1. Transferring the base to another government tenant. Sometimes city or state government takes over base property, as was the case at Alabama's Craig AFB, now the location for training and medical facilities for the Alabama State Patrol. Public housing and a community-college campus are also located at the former Craig site. The Charleston Naval Complex in South Carolina now houses the Charleston County Park and Recreation Commission. The county of Sacramento now operates the aviation facilities at Mather AFB. The San Francisco Police Department's field operations agency moved to the Hunter's Point Naval Annex in July 1996, [56] and the city of San Francisco obtained some of the newest housing stock in the city after taking over the naval base at Treasure Island and renting out hundreds of the houses there to add to city revenues.[57]

A federal-level takeover is also possible. In 1994, the Presidio of San Francisco transferred to the National Park Service. So did land at Mather AFB, Castle AFB, and Fort Ord, all in California. Twelve former Air Force bases were incorporated in the Military Airport Program sponsored by the Department of Transportation, the Federal Aviation Administration, and the Office of the Assistant Administrator for Airports in order to increase civil-aviation capacity. The former Naval Air Station at Lemoore, California, reverted to NASA (National Aeronautics and Space Administration).

Bases may also be transferred to another agency in the hope that their facilities might be used to address social problems. Representative Patricia Schroeder (D-CO) strongly supported the use of Lowry AFB in Denver to house homeless persons, perhaps administered by either a state or a federal agency. By 1996, 1,100 civilians lived at the former base site, with plans for another 3,000 new homes to be built over the next ten years. The state of Alabama looked to two closed bases, Fort McClellan and the naval station in Mobile, as possible sites to house juvenile offenders, to be run by the state's Department of Youth Services.[58] Homeless shelters also appeared at Hamilton AFB, Mather AFB, and the Sacramento Army Depot.

The federal Bureau of Prisons is a potential claimant for former bases—it runs several prisons located on or near military bases, including Vandenberg, Maxwell, and Eglin AFBs. Military bases offer ideal facilities for prisons: spartan barracks, remote locations, a hospital, and so forth. But bases also have neighbors, who are not likely to welcome a federal prison in their backyards. Prisons are depressing places where the danger of escape is always present. Prisons also offer fewer job opportunities than commercial industries, and the land and facilities are not taxable. So despite its legal advantage as a claimant of base property, the Bureau of Prisons has deferred to community desires and will not locate prisons on former bases unless the community wants such a facility.[59] Still, there is support generally for building more prisons, and the land on bases can be less expensive than commercial or farmland. Representative Ken Calvert (R-CA) introduced legislation in June 1996 to permit the federal government to allow the transfer of closed or realigned military bases to the Justice Department for final transfer to local officials to use for either prisons or other public-safety needs.[60] Local experience with such conversion was already in place by mid-1996, as the Navy brig at Treasure Island Naval Station in San Francisco Bay filled up with female prisoners from the Bay Area's overcrowded jails even before the base finally closed.[61] Given the cost of building new prisons at both local and federal levels, this replacement idea was sure to spread. During 1996 alone, the federal Bureau of Prisons leased 940 acres at George AFB, 660 acres at Castle AFB, and 685 acres at California's Sierra Army Depot.[62] Also, the state of Indiana constructed a medium-security 1,000-bed prison at Grissom AFB.[63]

A similar situation existed with the provisions of the McKinney Act, which require that surplus federal property be evaluated for the purpose of housing homeless persons. But, in some communities, housing homeless individuals is about as popular as providing prison facilities. So despite the requirement, there has been a willingness to defer to local preferences, and few bases have been converted to shelters for the homeless. Sometimes compromises occur, as in the case of the Sacramento Army Depot, where Foodlink, a McKinney conveyance applicant distributing food to the homeless, agreed to withdraw its application for base space when Packard Bell computers, the base's major relocation tenant, objected. To get Foodlink off the base, the city of Sacramento paid the organization an $840,000 relocation fee.[64]

Due to the controversy surrounding the McKinney Act, it was modified in 1994 by the Base Closure Community Redevelopment and Homeless Assistance Act. The legislation, passed unanimously by

Congress, exempts base-closure property from automatic inclusion for homeless shelters and instead establishes a new process requiring a balance between homeless-assistance needs and the needs of economic development.[65] The wording is: "The Secretary [of Defense] shall ensure that the needs of the homeless in the communities affected by the closure of such installations are taken into consideration in the redevelopment plan with respect to such installations."[66] The act also turns much of the decision making on development issues over to the local communities, which may still decide to use base facilities for homeless shelters. The Los Angeles City Planning Department recommended this alternative when it examined surplus housing left over from the closing of the Long Beach Naval Station.[67] Despite efforts at clarification, some confusion resulted from the vague phrase "take into consideration . . ." as was evidenced during debate in Alameda. The closure of Alameda NAS provided land that fell under the jurisdiction of the Alameda Redevelopment and Re-Use Authority, which set an objective to "urge (though not mandate) individual businesses to hire 15% of their respective workforce from a pool of homeless persons."[68] Alameda's mayor had to reiterate several times during debate over the issue that the quota was ". . . a goal, not a set-in-stone quota."[69]

Former base land also serves to provide facilities for troubled children. An agency known as Hope Meadows was established in 1994 at the former site of Chanute AFB in Illinois to house and care for children with behavioral problems. With support from President Clinton, a federal grant of $1 million was used to refurbish duplex housing at the base, and state funding of about $650,000 per year covers the operating expenses.[70]

Sometimes the military service that operates the base can make a transfer easier by lowering the price of both buildings and property, sometimes to zero. For example, when the Air Force left Kinchelo AFB in Michigan in 1977, it discovered that the original 1941 base leasing agreement required the service to restore the back to its original condition—farmland. But the Air Force successfully offered a compromise. It would turn the base over to alternative users completely equipped, including fire fighting equipment, furniture, and motor vehicles—everything except military equipment. The state of Michigan built a prison there for $3 million that otherwise would have cost ten times that much. Michigan also initiated an industrial park of 13 industrial companies on the foundations of what the Air Force left.[71] Fort Ord, on California's Monterey Peninsula, became the site for a similar scheme. Part of the installation, closed by the

1991 BRAC, became home to California State University at Monterey Bay, largely because the federal government transferred the land to the state of California without charge and sold family housing on the base for $1 per unit. That allowed Cal State Monterey Bay to own probably the cheapest dormitories in college history.[72] The Naval Air Station at Alameda donated parts to allow a machine shop to locate on base property.[73] And, as noted in Chapter Five, facilities at the Fleet and Industrial Supply Center Oakland (FISCO) were leased to the Port of Oakland for $1 a year. The Port then leased them to private firms for between $23,000 and $26,000 annually. Discounted electrical power is available at about half the cost at former bases because of a provision in the National Defense Authorization Act of 1994.[74] This same act also institutionalized the transfer of property to local reuse officials, apparently applying the lessons that the Air Force had pioneered at Kinchelo many years earlier.[75]

2. Turning the property over to private interests. The most common form of base transfer is to private tenancy. Base conversion to factories, transportation centers, warehouses, or maintenance facilities are very common. It is not the easiest form of conversion, for reasons noted below. However, private conversion efforts are often the first avenue of relief for communities around closed bases and their political supporters.

Sometimes finding a suitable tenant is difficult, though. For one thing, there are probably more available bases than commercial operations looking for more property. Moreover, base property had to compete with property that became available when defense industries also scaled down or closed due to the end of the Cold War. Many large factories that had once produced aircraft, tank parts, engines, and all the other things consumed by the Defense Department suddenly became available for commercial use. Unlike many bases, these facilities were designed specifically to manufacture things and were often more suitable than were base facilities. Still, conversion costs were steep, so Congress tried a number of measures to minimize the economic impact of defense-industry-plant conversion during the 1980s. Funds were appropriated for worker retraining, relocation, and management retooling, and, while some funding included military bases, not all of it did.[76] It is also true that both management and labor in the defense industry have more political clout than the military does in terms of gaining political funding for defense conversion.

There are other barriers to commercial conversion. Even when civilian enterprises want to establish operations at a former base, complications can arise. The neighbors of Rickenbacker AFB near

Columbus, Ohio, apparently tired of constant aircraft noise after years of B-52 flights over their houses, blocked an attempted transfer of base property to Flying Tiger Air Cargo, which wanted to operate a cargo hub there. Years went by before a scaled-down version of the operation was approved.[77] In 1996, voters in Orange County, California, also disapproved, by 60-40 percent, a reuse plan for the closing El Toro Marine Corps Station (MCAS) for similar reasons.[78] At San Jose's Moffett Field, a former naval air base, NASA received the airfield from the Navy but found itself in a sea of red ink to the tune of $3.5 million annually. Trying to stem the deficit, NASA proposed that commercial air cargo carriers be allowed to use the facility under an agreement that would exempt them from local noise restrictions. The nearby cities of Sunnyvale and Mountain View opposed the plan, which San Jose supported because its own airport had a noise curfew.[79]

Bases arc often difficult to convert to private use. For one thing, they were built for a particular function that rarely had any commercial or nondefense governmental counterpart. A large naval base, for example, is difficult to convert to a marina, and most naval bases were built before the containerization-vessel era and require extensive conversion to be used to service civilian container ships. The vast buildings found at an aircraft maintenance facility are rarely useful for manufacturing anything not resembling the aircraft and aircraft parts that once filled them. Many bases were not located near transportation hubs and instead were purposefully built in remote areas to keep their interface with the civilian world outside to a minimum. There the military took advantage of such things as lower property values and available land to practice maneuvers. There were also fewer citizens to complain about noise and fewer chances for young enlisted personnel to get into the kinds of trouble lurking in large cities, sometimes with bars, brothels, and strip joints just outside the main gate.

Rural locations, provide both opportunities and challenges for commercial base conversion.[80] The giant B-52 hangers at Walker AFB in rural New Mexico proved useful for a commercial aircraft maintenance operation after that base shut down in the late 1960s.[81] A British charter airline now lands at what once was Dow AFB in Bangor, Maine. In all of these cases, noise complaints were fewer simply because there were fewer people to complain, and more who were grateful for the economic advantage because there were few other economic opportunities in the area after the base closed. Information on locating at England AFB in rural Alexandria, Louisiana, notes specifically that ". . . the airside operations of this former military installation offer no noise restrictions. . . ."[82]

The other side of the rural-location situation involves the lack of infrastructure, an educated work force, and the kinds of cultural and social amenities needed to attract businesses and other enterprises. Compare, for example, the location of Rantoul, Illinois, or Olathe, Kansas, with the facilities at the former Mobile Naval Station, in Alabama. The latter base was in the middle of the Port of Mobile, at the terminus of the Tennessee-Tombigbee Waterway, the Mobile River, and the Gulf Intercoastal Waterway. Interstates 10 and 65 were close by, as were four national railroad carriers, along with other amenities located in Alabama's third-largest city. It is hard for rural bases to compete with such city-based advantages.

Despite these and other difficulties, there are hundreds of former bases that are now the location for a variety of industries and government activities. Sacramento Army Depot, closed by the 1991 BRAC, became the home of Packard Bell after the computer company lost its Northridge, California facilities to an earthquake. Packard Bell moved its entire manufacturing and distribution operations to Sacramento; as a result, almost all of the base's 3,000 former employees were reemployed.[83] At England AFB in Louisiana, also closed in 1991, a truck-driving school found the base's expansive runways ideal for its operations. The school, coupled with a civilian airport and an industrial park, has more than replaced the jobs lost when the base closed.[84] According to local officials at the England site, housing prices are rising and sales-tax revenues have increased over three years since closure.[85] A private contractor refurbishes military aircraft at Alabama's Craig AFB. Ohio's Banc One credit-card-labeling operation moved to vacant facilities at the former Gentile Air Force Station (AFS), and in New Hampshire, Cabletron Systems took over the first floor of the former hospital at Pease AFB to build a new training facility. In 1997, a billionaire Hong Kong investor announced plans to convert California's Treasure Island Naval Station into a lavish resort complete with a hotel and golf course.[86]

Former Air Force and naval air bases are especially useful because runways provide capability for air cargo flights to deliver parts and fly out finished goods. The Mather Airport at former Mather AFB has both Airborne Express and Emery Air Freight operating on its 11,300-foot runway. The Arkansas Aeroplex is located at the site of Eaker AFB, where commercial operators take advantage of existing facilities, including a 11,600-foot runway and a 1.8-million-gallon-capacity fuel farm serviced from a Mississippi River fuel terminal, saving the cost of moving fuel over land.

Bases already have networks of roads, lighting, sewer and water delivery systems, trees and lawns, and buildings—the basic ingredients of an industrial park. When Pease AFB closed in 1991 (the first base closed under BRAC to actually shut down), the property included an 11,300-foot runway (longer than at Kennedy International Airport in New York), and 1.2 million square feet of commercial office, light-industry, and warehouse facilities.[87] Best of all, it has already been paid for and thus was available for other compatible activities at a fraction of the cost of a new industrial park.

There are sometimes costs for such conversions. Often when former base property is purchased for industrial or other alternative use, the whole base comes in the package, so some unneeded things come along. Businesses locating on the base may have little use for barracks, military prisons, or tank obstacle courses, but such things can be demolished and still the entire base cost is still a small fraction of the cost of new facilities. And firms can use a portion of a base that may be best suited to their needs. Shipyards, for example, use sandblasting equipment to remove old paint from ships, so the Jeffco Painting and Abrasive Blasting and Coating Company signed a lease for 79,000 square feet of warehouse space at California's Mare Island Naval Shipyard. The firm was able to expand its operations from the cities of Richmond and Martinez without having to build completely new facilities; with the reduced cost, it was willing to take former shipyard employees to fill the 80-100 new positions at its new facilities.[88]

Congress established a program called Armament Retooling and Manufacturing Support (ARMS) for former ammunition plants in 1993. The program allows government-owned, contractor-operated contractors to "use and market idle capacity for other work, both government and commercial."[89] Congress authorized the Army, which administers ARMS, to offer a number of incentives to contractors, including land, buildings, loan guarantees, planning grants, and other inducements to get the contractors to locate their enterprises at old ammunition plants. The plan is designed to allow conversion "to thriving manufacturing centers while awaiting environmental remediation."[90] Contractors working under ARMS thus enjoy government benefits, but, at the same time, they must pay the potential penalty of operating under the hazardous conditions of highly toxic waste often found at old ammunition plants.

While such transfers may make the alternative use of bases cheaper, they apparently happened without much regulation or oversight. In some cases, property on the base was either sold or donated free by base authorities even though the property belonged to another federal agency. There were also cases in which military maintenance funds were spent improving property for the base's new tenant. To try to regulate property transfers, the Defense Department issued Regulation 32 CFH 91(h), which details the ways that base property can—and cannot—be transferred to the new user. A document produced in May 1993 (updated in August 1995) by the assistant secretary of defense for economic security, called *Closing Bases Right: A Commander's Handbook,* spells out these procedures.

More base-conversion innovation came from land swapping. Firms owning land in federal areas may swap that land for land on military bases. The actual purpose of land swapping involves adding to land under protection for environmental reasons, but creative trading may land a good deal for developers. The Barron Collier Corporation proposed a switch of land it owned in the Florida Everglades for land at either the Orlando or San Diego Naval Training Centers, the Treasure Island Naval Station, and several other closed bases.[91] The Farm Act of 1996 encouraged the idea by allowing developers to swap land parcels in the Everglades that then could be put under environmental protection. The Desert Protection Act does the same thing with desert lands.[92]

3. Allowing mixed development. Given the large size of many bases, some combination of government and private usage is often possible. Many former bases are now home to both state institutions—university campuses, for example, or prisons—and private enterprises. The plans for Vint Hill Farms Station in Virginia, a 7,000-acre Army intelligence post closed by the 1995 BRAC, reflected this type of conversion. Plans developed by the county called for mixed use, including high-technology industry, homes for the elderly and homeless, schools, and a golf course.[93] The Charleston Naval Shipyard and the Charleston Naval Station, both closed by the 1993 BRAC, also featured mixed-use plans. A plan to convert both bases into a civic and maritime center, to include an industrial park, a marina, and a 470-acre waterfront park, was proposed that included mixed funding, both private (but unspecified) funds and up to $50 million in federal funds.[94] California State University at Long Beach received 30 acres of former Cabrillo Naval Housing, which the university planned to develop in partnership with private industry for a research and training center.[95] The center was expected to generate 3,000 new jobs and $83 million in revenue annually.[96] The Economic Development Administration of the Department of Commerce was expected to contribute $4.5 million to the project, making it truly multiagency.[97]

One of the more successful cases of mixed use is at Lowry AFB in Denver, Colorado. Lowry, closed by the 1993 BRAC, will have 10,000 residents, 10,000-12,000 new jobs, and 10,000 students at several campuses located there by the year 2005, according to the Lowry Redevelopment Agency.[98]

An even more innovative use for bases was tried by the California and San Francisco film commissions, which used a number of California bases for movie locations: *Jack* was shot at the Mare Island Naval Shipyard, and *Copycat* and *James and the Giant Peach* were made at Treasure Island Naval Station and Hunter's Point Naval Annex.[99] Some estimates put the value of film shooting on former base locations at $50 million annually. The motion pictures were made before these bases closed, possibly setting a precedent for open bases.

4. Keeping limited military facilities at the base. One of the more common ways of doing this is to turn a base over to either Reserve or National Guard forces. Since Reserve and Guard forces generally require less by way of facilities than do regular forces, a base can be reduced in size and scope and still remain open. This is because both Reserve and Guard components serve only part-time, living in the communities and thus not requiring such things as barracks, hospitals, and the other facilities that full-time troops need.[100] Carswell AFB near Fort Worth, Texas, was closed in 1991, but subsequent BRAC decisions in 1993 converted the base to a joint Navy-Air Force Reserve Base, the first of its kind.

Rickenbacker AFB was a SAC base until the 1970s, when a part of it was turned over to the Ohio Air National Guard, which operated tankers out of the base until the mid-1990s. March AFB in California, one of the Air Force's oldest bases, also went through a similar transfer. Dow AFB in Maine, a former SAC base, now hosts a Maine Air National Guard Air Refueling Wing and elements of an air-defense squadron. Pease AFB in nearby New Hampshire is also home to an Air National Guard wing. Since the Air Force (like the other services) did not reduce its Guard and Reserve forces nearly as much as its active forces (partly for political reasons and partly because they are less costly to operate), a number of former active-duty bases were converted to Guard or Reserve forces. The Guard and Reserve units also do not have to use all of the land on the base in order to keep a portion of it open. For example, the Alabama National Guard asked for about 30,000 of Fort McClellan's 45,600 acres after the base-closure announcement was made in 1995.[101] This parcel of land would give the Guard a majority of the land, while permitting other parts of the base to be converted to other uses.

5. *"Privatizing" the functions performed at the base.* There are several meanings to "privatization." In Europe, it has meant selling government assets to the private sector. In the United States, privatization generally means turning over operations of public-sector activities to private operators while retaining public purpose and funding.[102] The assumptions behind the practice are that private vendors can perform public services more efficiently than public agencies can because they must make a profit and because they must compete for a public contract. Whether greater efficiency actually results is a matter of debate, but the concept was popular in the 1980s, in particular, during the Reagan presidency. The President's Private Sector Survey on Cost Control (the Grace Commission) issued a report on privatization in 1983 that stated that ". . . privatization is an implementation option in which Government sets a policy to provide a service, but opts to have the private sector produce it."[103] Examples of privatized public services include hospitals, day care, and military commissaries; report estimated annual savings of $597 million to be gained from privatization.[104] In this case, it could be argued that commissaries could compete successfully with commercial supermarkets under private management.

The President's Private Sector Survey on Cost Control's *Report on Privatization* did not consider anything as large as an aircraft depot. However, when the two depots at San Antonio and Sacramento finally wound up on the base-closure list, President Clinton made a quick decision to announce privatization of their functions. The 1995 BRAC authorized such a shift at Kelly AFB in Texas and for some of the work done at the Sacramento ALC at McClellan AFB in California.[105] The Clinton administration never clarified the details of privatization at the time of the 1995 BRAC announcement. It left the impression that private contractors would move onto the former bases and resume maintenance operations left by the Air Force, but it was never stated specifically that contractors would use the base facilities themselves. Indeed, the Air Force had entertained proposals from aircraft manufacturers that their production facilities be converted to aircraft maintenance capacity in order to preserve the defense-industrial base. Even though senior Air Force leadership rejected these proposals by the time 1995 BRAC announced its work, they still could be resurrected in the face of the announced closures at Kelly and McClellan. Thus, "privatization" could have meant the transfer of maintenance jobs from San Antonio or Sacramento to somewhere else, forcing those former depot workers lucky enough to get jobs in a private firm to relocate. It is hardly surprising that workers at Kelly viewed privatization with some skepticism. President Clinton, in an effort to reassure them and to shore up his political chances in Texas, spoke to those workers on October 17, 1995. The president announced to an audience of 8,000 Kelley employees that the Air Force, the Federal Aviation Administration (FAA), and the city of San Antonio had reached an agreement to allow joint use of Kelly's runway by both the public and the Air Force.[106] Said Clinton: ". . . even eight years from now, more that two-thirds of Kelly's jobs will still be here working for the Department of Defense. But at the same time, we'll create even more jobs."[107] It was difficult not to notice that the president did not provide any specifics.

Ohio's Newark AFB was the first privatization test. Newark, the smallest base in the Air Force, was home to the Aerospace Guidance and Metrology Center (AGMC). Its primary function was to calibrate the guidance systems used by both aircraft and ballistic missiles. With the end of the Cold War the bulk of the work on intercontinental-ballistic-missile guidance systems declined, until by 1995 it was only half the workload—the other being aircraft systems. Anticipating that drawdown of workload, BRAC approved Newark's closure in 1993. At the time, the most likely scenario for the aircraft-calibration work was to transfer it, possibly to Wright-Patterson AFB, about two hours away. But the Air Force was also considering privatization as a possible solution to keeping the base open without support from the federal budget. The 1993 BRAC endorsed the idea, with Newark AFB proposed as a trial site. The choice had some real advantages. The facilities had been designed for the specific task at hand (after first being built to stamp out aircraft wing spars), and there was little superfluous property to maintain.

According to the GAO, though, transferring the work at Newark from the Air Force to private contractors who would run the complex would cost $456 million more than if the base were kept in Air Force hands.[108] Still, Boeing and Rockwell International (which has a plant in the city of Newark) bid for the operation, though other contractors dropped out citing contract restrictions.[109] Finally, the contract was split between Rockwell International and Wyle Laboratories. Rockwell got the contract to repair guidance systems, and Wyle contracted to operate the measuring-sciences program. By October 1, 1996, the base, renamed Rockwell Guidance Repair Center, had become totally private.[110]

Whether money will be saved is another issue. By some estimates, up to 100 years might be necessary to generate the projected savings from closure and privatization.[111] Rockwell, though, was guaranteed a profit from the cost-plus contract it received to run the facility, and it began cost-cutting measures to enhance those profits, including pay and benefit cuts.[112] These decisions promoted a successful unionization drive by workers, with unforeseen consequences.[113]

The Clinton administration cited Newark as a model for bases like Kelly and McClellan, though Newark is much smaller and much more specialized than the two large depots, and the work force of 1,400 hardly compares with the 11,000-12,000 at the Texas and California depots.[114] Newark also lacks a flying mission, a runway, housing hangers, a base hospital, and all of the other things that normally dot an Air Force base. Newark occupies only 70 acres, compared with McClellan at 3,700 acres and Kelly at 4,600 acres. It is difficult to find many similarities between Newark and any other Air Force base.

According to the commander of the AGMC, though, there were commonalties between Newark and the larger depots, and he had consulted with McClellan on lessons learned.[115] Many of those lessons remained to be learned when the 1995 list rolled around, since Newark had yet to privatize. But, in the highly political climate of base closure, Newark became a potential example of a process that might help the president in the next election. That was important since the final closure for Newark was scheduled for October 1996, a month before the general election, so it was important to have a "privatization" success story to tell the voters. To help ensure that privatization would be successful, arrangements were made to reduce contractor costs. The land itself would be transferred to the Local Redevelopment Agency (LRA). Rent would be zero because the transfer would take place from the AFMC (the original major command), through the contractor, through the LRA, to the Air Force Base Closure Agency (AFBCA).

In reality, planning privatization for Newark led down an unknown policy direction in 1995. That fact was reflected in the terms of the operational contract (actually two, one for maintenance and one for metrology), which was for only nine months, with four possible one-year options to follow. It would appear that neither the contractor nor the AGMC was willing to risk a longer-term venture in the absence of hard knowledge about how well privatization would work. The command also made backup plans for failure, in which case the closure date would slip, and the base would wind up in long-term caretaker status under the direction of the AFBCA. The potential political fallout from failure was not discussed in the AFBCA plans for Newark's privatization failure. But, in the wake of the publicity accompanying the grandiose plans for the privatization of the huge depots in California and Texas, a failing at Newark could have huge consequences for the politicians who promised that it would save jobs and make closure of the two depots politically acceptable.

Some decisions to privatize did not wait for results from Newark, though. Under guidance from local community leaders, the Naval Surface Warfare Center (NSWC) in Louisville, Kentucky, transferred operations through contracts to Hughes Missiles Systems Company and United Defense on August 15, 1996, thus fully privatizing the facility.[116] Clearly, going down the privatization road was preferable to closing the base completely, despite the uncertainty involved. It was the most expedient thing to do politically.

THE ECONOMIC IMPACT OF BASE CLOSURES

Base closings may bring either boon or bane to adjacent communities. Sometimes they bring both. These effects, can be magnified by reports that tout the advantages of base closure for communities (as Defense Department analyses accompanying the 1995 BRAC round were wont to do) or by gloom-and-doom stories pushed by representatives trying to keep a base in their district open. Reality, as usual, lies somewhere in between. Issues involved include employment lost or gained, the loss or gain of tax revenues or other federal funds, and the spillover effect on the community from military spending there.

Jobs Gained and Lost

In 1988, BRAC opted to close Chanute AFB in Rantoul, Illinois. The small town located in the center of the state was expected to suffer economically from the closure —a study by two economists from the University of Illinois predicted a 29 percent drop in both retail and wholesale sales. But after the gates finally closed in September 1993, parts of the town's economy appeared to be growing instead.[117] Some private industry had moved into the vacated base buildings, and the end of competition from Chanute's commissary had benefited local business.[118]

Chanute may not be an isolated example of a successful base closure. Two years before the creation of the BRAC process, the Defense Department issued a study showing that the economic impact of a quarter-century of base closures in the United States had been largely positive. In the summary of 100 bases closed between 1961 and 1986, the study found that, while 93,424 jobs were lost as a consequence of base closure, new activities at those closed bases generated 138,138 new jobs.[119] The study also reported that 24 colleges and 33 vocational schools enrolling 53,744 students had replaced military activity on closed bases, along with 42 municipal or general aviation airports.[120] The study did not count the military positions lost when the base closed. While those were not jobs lost (military personnel are simply transferred elsewhere upon base closure), the departure of the people who held them did affect military spending in the local community. While most military personnel spend at least some of their income on the base (at the base commissary, gas station, bowling alley, and so forth), they also spend in the community, for such items as automobiles, furniture, appliances, and meals in restaurants. Moreover, some of the military spending on base benefits the community—the commissary may purchase, for example, its fresh dairy products and produce in local markets, and local utilities provide base electricity.

The 1986 study also revealed some real differences in job replacement after base closure. In some cases, there were dramatic gains in employment in the postclosure term—Walker AFB in New Mexico lost 379 civilian jobs when it closed in 1967, but replacement activities (including a Levi Strauss manufacturing plant, the Transportation Manufacturing Company, and a campus of Eastern New Mexico University) gained 2,770 new jobs and 1,400 students at ENMU. When the Brooklyn Army Terminal closed in 1981, 336 civilians lost their jobs, but the New York Rail Car Company and other smaller activities brought back 1,250 positions. In other cases, though, severe losses occurred. Brookley AFB in Mobile, Alabama, was a large aviation maintenance depot that employed 12,300 people. However, in the years after it closed in 1969, only 3,500 new jobs were created despite relocation of a number of businesses and activities, including Teledyne-Continental Motors, International Paper, International Systems, a municipal airport, and the campus of the University of South Alabama. Other locations more or less broke even. Fort MacArthur in the San Pedro hills above the Los Angeles harbor closed in 1975, taking with it 750 jobs, but some local-government operations (mostly related to schools) brought back around 720 positions.[121]

The closure of George AFB near Adelanto, California, by the 1988 BRAC, cost 600 jobs directly and 3,600 indirectly, plus a lost operating expenditure of $460 million per year.[122] By 1990, most hopes of recovery were based on converting George's runways to an international airport, linked to Anaheim by a "super train" designed to ride on a wave of magnetic energy and be in place by 1998.[123] By 1998, though, there was no super train and no "high-desert international airport," and neither appeared even on distant horizons.[124] Southern California's growth had slowed in the face of considerable defense-related cutbacks, and there was no real demand for yet another regional airport.[125] Yet, a Rand Corporation study of the communities surrounding George AFB revealed population growth and increases in the value of housing and retail sales after the base closed.[126] The study found similar results at Castle AFB and Fort Ord, both closed by the 1991 BRAC. Several possible reasons for the unexpected results were the departure of military spouses (opening up jobs for local citizens) and the shift by military retirees from the base exchange to stores in the community.[127]

A number of studies concentrated on the economic impact of bases closed before BRAC. John E. Lynch's study of 12 base closures during the 1960s is one of the more comprehensive.[128] The results suggest that the type of local response to base closure, and local coordination with both private and governmental actors, were factors that made a difference in the postclosure economic impact. At Presque Isle AFB in Maine, local leaders did not try to resist the closure decision but instead began immediately to plan for what turned out to be a successful transition to a civilian economy at the base.[129] Even in cases of closure resistance, such as Donaldson AFB in South Carolina, the local economy recovered with resilience.[130] The three Air Force depots examined by Lynch also demonstrated successful economic conversion that largely minimized the closure impact.[131] Another study of the time looked at the regional impact of nine closed bases and found that it varied in terms of county. The immediate county in which the base was located did better in economic-development terms after closure than did the surrounding counties, but only in the short run. Over a longer period of time, every base county save one declined below state average levels, while the surrounding counties did better economically.[132]

A more recent study was done on the impact of closing Fort Ord in California. Placed on the 1991 BRAC list, Fort Ord was one of Monterey County's largest employers. Lewis J. Coyle used an economic impact forecasting system (EIFS) to estimate the impact of replacing Fort Ord with an educational, science, and technology center. He found that, after a short-term loss in the area's economy, such a center would generate 13,000 new jobs in the community and draw up to 25,000 new students. Moreover, despite the loss of 16,000 military and civilian jobs on base, Coyle projected that local sales volume would increase by $235 million and in local personal income by $49 million.[133] After Coyle's study was published in 1992, the state did establish the new California State University at Monterey Bay on the former site of Fort Ord. Somewhat similar conclusions came from the Mare Island Naval Shipyard in northern California, closed by the 1993 BRAC. The unemployment level in neighboring Solano County remained almost unchanged from March 1993 (8.5 percent) July 1995 to (8.4 percent) despite base-employment numbers shrinking from 6,200 people to 2,350 over that same period. Of the almost 4,000 employees who did leave the base, more than one-third retired, and around 1,350 took advantage of the Defense Department's Priority Placement Program and relocated elsewhere. Another 1,150 took the Separation Incentive Program that offered them up to $25,000 to leave.[134] Recovery also seems underway in Charleston, South Carolina, hit hard in 1993 by the closure of the Charleston Naval Shipyard and Naval Station. By mid-1996, Charleston's unemployment rate had fallen, and new companies had moved into the area.[135]

Federal-Revenue Loss and Gain

There may be other benefits from base closure if new work is located on the former base. The flow of federal money to the community from base activities could be episodic. Cold War–period defense budgets (in real terms) rose and fell like a roller coaster, with sharp highs reached during the Korean and Vietnam wars and the Reagan buildup of the 1980s. Deep troughs followed each of the peaks, though, with defense spending often dropping to prebuildup levels. During the increases, the benefits to base communities increased as well (though not always proportionately), leading to new construction, new jobs, and new opportunities. During the drawdown, the jobs sometimes disappeared, and the buildings constructed during the upswing sometimes wound up with boards over the windows as business slumped off due to reduced spending from the nearby base. The result was a cyclical economy that could discourage investment in communities highly dependent on spending from bases. In some cases, local officials expressed a mix of reactions to base closures. They regretted the loss of income, they also noted, that alternative sources of income at former bases were, at least, more stable than income from base-generated expenditures.

Lessons Learned

Previous base shutdowns provide some useful lessons, but the time context needs to be considered. For one thing, the decade of the 1960s was a time of rapidly expanding higher education, and thus many closed bases became the new sites for a college or university campus.[136] The decade of the 1990s shown the opposite trend, as higher education contracted in response to overbuilding and the declining student-age population. So offering to locate a university campus on a closed base may no longer be an option.

Another difference is that base closures in the 1960s and 1970s targeted individual bases for the most part, and those cut from the payroll on one base could move to another. BRAC, though, cut waves of bases; with a much larger shutdown, interbase employment mobility may not be as great as it was in the past. A further distinction may lie in the value of the so-called "multiplier effect," the multiplied impact of money as it spreads through the economy. The multiplier effect from base spending varied from 2.06 in San Antonio to 1.0 around Fort Carson, Colorado, during the 1960s.[137] With that much variation, the economic impact of closings even in a single time period varied considerably, but, over 30 years, the comparison may be almost impossible to make.

What is the point of examining the actual economic impact of base closures? Despite the fact that a majority of studies find that, in the longer run, base closings actually help local economies, most elected officials choose to fight such closings when proposed for their constituencies. It is likely that the politician's fear of the short-run impact generates such opposition. Never mind that the local economy may, for example, improve from an immediate postclosure slump in two years; what matters most is that an election will come before the two years will come. There is evidence of such behavior on the part of elected officials. Edward R. Tufte notes that, in presidential elections, voters are motivated more by short-run prosperity than by long-run gains, and they pay particular attention to disposable income in the month preceding an election.[138]

THE ENVIRONMENTAL IMPACT OF BASE CLOSURES

The 1990 legislation chartering the last three BRAC rounds was quite specific about the responsibility for cleaning up environmental damage at closed bases. That legislation placed base-closing actions under the limited jurisdiction of the National Environmental Policy Act of 1969 with respect to property disposal and functional relocation as the result of a BRAC action.[139] The actual environmental response to base closure, though, would tax the language of the authorizing legislation in many ways.

The military performs many different operations at its bases, not all of which are environmentally benign. At maintenance bases, for example, the functions carried out often create considerable quantities of waste, some of which is highly toxic. At aircraft and vehicle repair facilities, solvents to clean parts and paint remover were often disposed in earthen pits and later filled and covered over with dirt. But because protective material rarely lined these pits, the waste later leaked into the groundwater below, creating a serious pollution problem. In naval shipyards, workers often dumped tons of chemical waste from paint removers, fuel-tank cleaner, and other deadly liquids into the waters around the yards. The cost of cleaning up Hunter's Point Naval Annex in south San Francisco is a case in point; it is estimated at more than $200 million[140] in one study and more than $356 million in another.[141] The Annex, once part of a larger shipyard closed in 1974, has 52 sites identified, some listed as "beyond remediation."[142]

Even more minor maintenance on motor-pool vehicles could accumulate; base dumps filled up with decades of automotive lead batteries, used motor oil, antifreeze, worn out tires, and other junk. When the dump site reached capacity, it sometimes was filled over and became the location of some other facility, such as the base golf course. In time, the waste, gradually leaching into the groundwater below, was conveniently forgotten. After building demolition, the remains, including leaded paint and asbestos, were buried in pits or sometimes conveniently pushed to the perimeter of the base, where the material lay for years, gradually disseminated by the elements. In times past, there was little attention paid to contaminants because little was known about their dangerous effects. Lagoons and rivers were especially convenient; at Warner Robins AFB in Georgia, 44 million gallons of industrial chemicals and solvents, including cyanide and trichloroethylene (TCE), were dumped into a lagoon south of the base runway between 1963 and 1978. The base was not trying to hide its waste dumping, because during those years it was entirely legal[143]—the lagoon was just more convenient because the waste would gradually float away or sink to the bottom.

The Nature of the Base-Contamination Problem

How bad is the base-pollution problem? According to one report in 1995 there were 27,700 contaminated areas in what the Environmental Protection Agency (EPA) labeled as formerly used defense sites (FUDS), with problems ranging from small to large. Another measure of the problem is the number of sites listed on the National Priorities List (NPL).[144] At the end of 1992, there were 107 base sites on the NPL, and the most common contaminants were petroleum, solvents, acids, heavy metals, and pesticides.[145]

Decades worth of poisons remain buried at many bases, and often the location of those wastes is unknown.[146] Sometimes a base-closure environmental study reveals such unknown contamination sites. It appears, for example, that, sometime between 1943 and 1945, the Army dumped mustard-gas agent, red fuming nitric acid, and potassium cyanide at the Raritan Army Arsenal in New Jersey. Periodic excavations at the site in 1961 and 1988 produced evidence of chemical drums, sprayers, and a substance that "smelled like mustard," but the substances were not cleaned up, and the Army found that it had to go back in 1992 and complete the job.[147] At Maxwell AFB in Alabama, a road-rebuilding project in the early 1990s was delayed for months when bulldozers accidentally uncovered buried aircraft fuel tanks apparently dating back to the 1920s and 1930s. At Arnold AFB, a large Air Force testing facility in Tennessee, a limestone leaching pit was discovered that had been used between 1953 and 1972 to dump such wastes as nitric, hydrochloric, phosphoric, and sulfamic acids, perchloroethylene, and trichloraethane, plus a variety of petroleum. Cleaning just this one pit required the treatment of 8,000 tons of soil—dug up, heated to 800 Fahrenheit and then further treated by an off-gas system and finally dumped back in the pit.[148] At the Seal Beach Naval Weapons Station TCE, hexavalent chromium, pentachlorophenol, antimony, arsenic, manganese, nickel, asbestos, vinyl chloride appeared in a site survey.[149] At giant Castle AFB in central California, 26 toxic waste sites were found on the base's 2,777 acres.[150] They involved both surface and subsurface contamination, including solvents, waste oil, pesticides, cyanide, cadmium., PCB, TCE, and other volatile organic compounds that made the base's drinking water unsafe to drink.[151] The Twin Cities Army Ammunition Plant ranked as Minnesota's worst Superfund site. Such problems were typical of most large military installations.

Changing Environmental Rules

In response to such findings and to the increased concern over environmental contamination, a number of federal environmental laws were enacted requiring disposal of base contamination in accordance with prescribed procedures.[152] These requirements are outlined in the Comprehensive Environmental Response, Compensation, and Liability Act (CERCLA), the Resource Conservation and Recovery Act (RCRA), the National Environmental Policy Act (NEPA), Executive Order 12580, the Superfund Implementation, the Community Environmental Response Facilitation Act (CERFA), the National Contingency Plan (NCP), and the Defense Environmental Restoration Program (DERP). Base waste policy also came under the jurisdiction of other legislation, including the Clean Water Act, the Clean Air Act, the Safe Drinking Water Act, the Toxic Substances Control Act, the Asbestos Hazard Emergency Response Act, the Lead-Based Paint Poisoning Prevention Act, the Residential Lead-Based Paint Hazard Reduction Act, and the Federal Insecticide, Fungicide, and Rodenticide Act. The combined weight of these acts had a significant impact on base cleanup in that they required monitoring and cleanup of almost every toxic element known. And bases had most of them. Thus, base commanders had to search for such hidden or forgotten waste dumps and clean them up in accordance with both state and federal requirements. That process added considerably to the final cost of base closure, and could also delay the time period for converting former base property for other uses, sometimes by years. All of this naturally raised substantial concerns in communities hoping to transfer the base to some other enterprise. For example, Pease AFB in New Hampshire (closed by the 1988 BRAC) had an initial list of 17 contaminated sites. Cleanup began in preparation for a Delta Airlines maintenance facility and a biotechnology plant, but, as it progressed, the number of contaminated areas grew to 35, and it became highly doubtful that Pease could be turned over to the new users on the original cleanup schedule.[153] The estimated cost of that cleanup was $11 million in 1988, but it rose to $114 million by 1992. At Mather AFB, in California, $40 million was spent between 1989 and 1996, though cleanup had begun on only three small waste projects and the majority of sites remained to be cleaned.[154]

Even in the earlier BRAC rounds, the environmental costs became prohibitive. But for opponents of a particular base closure, such costs might work in their favor. Representative Barbara Boxer tried that tactic to try to save the Presidio of San Francisco, in her district.[155]

Boxer claimed that the BRAC environmental cleanup estimate of only $2 million ignored the Army's much higher estimate of $82 million to dispose of the contents of dumping landfills holding asbestos, PCBs, and other toxins.[156] The dumping of chemicals into the lagoon at Warner Robins AFB in Georgia suddenly appeared in the press just as the base came under BRAC 1995 closure consideration.

The Defense Department was required to pay for cleanup of closing bases, but there was obvious reluctance to spend money to clean up past sins, no matter what the moral or legal obligation might be. In an era of constrained budgets, no organization likes to see its appropriated funds paying for the past instead of investing in the future. That presented a dilemma for the military: There was clear interest at the service level in closing excess base structure, yet reluctance to pay for cleanup at disposed bases. One way out was to ask for more environmental cleanup money and enhance the chances of getting it at a strategic time. So on March 29, 1991, with the service list of recommended base closings due in two weeks, the Defense Department suddenly added 3,000 new base sites to its pollution list, bringing the total to 17,482.[157] Whether or not the announcement was timed to influence the base-closure process or not, the Defense Department asked for an additional $1.3 billion for cleanup in fiscal 1992, a 22 percent increase over the levels for fiscal 1991.[158] Those amount hardly touches the problem when the cost of cleaning up just the most polluted bases is considered. As of 1995 there were 81 bases in which individual cleanup costs exceed $100 million, topped by Rocky Mountain Arsenal in Colorado at $2.1 billion. Aberdeen Proving Ground in Maryland followed at $1.8 billion, McClellan AFB in California at $887 million, Twin Cities Army Ammunition Plant in Minnesota at $773 million, Otis Air National Guard Base in Massachusetts at $586 million, and California's Edwards AFB at $565 million.[159]

Congress tried to address this problem in 1990 by including language in the Defense Base Closure and Realignment Act of 1990 stipulating that the Defense Department complete environmental cleanup within six years on bases expected to be transferred to nonfederal jurisdiction or to the private sector.[160] In addition, the Comprehensive Environmental Response, Compensation, and Liability Act (CERCLA) requires the Defense Department to certify that "all remedial action necessary to protect human health and the environment" has been taken before base property can be sold or transferred.[161] Of course, such a certification may be impossible to achieve, and the possibilities for compromise are clear here. Given the combination of a service eager to close a base (and terminate the costs of cleaning it up) and a community (backed by political representatives) eager to replace the military activity with other revenue-generating functions, compromise is almost inevitable. It is most likely in cases involving the most difficult aspects of cleanup such as groundwater treatment. A variety of things gradually contaminated groundwater deposits near bases, including leaking underground fuel bunkers and cleaning solvents, and the requirements for cleaning groundwater are staggering. It must be pumped to the surface and treated with scrubbing devices, then returned to the ground. That is after it has been located, a difficult task in itself, requiring the drilling of many search wells (each of which must be filled with concrete after being drilled) over many thousands of acres.

In 1995, the Defense Department had located 113 sites where groundwater required treatment, but no one knew how many more sites existed or what the cost to clean them would be when they were found. Moreover, the time required to research water-table pollution can stretch to years. One official testified in 1992 that, ". . . at Otis Air National Guard Base, since 1978, we have spent $21 million studying ground water contamination, but no cleanup."[162] It was not clear whether the cause of the delay was lack of information or money or lack of will. It did indicate how long delays can be even in critical situations where, again according to the testimony, "All the while, the contaminated ground water continues to migrate toward drinking water supplies."[163] In response to this type of problem, Representative Richard Ray (D-GA), chair of the Environmental Restoration Panel in the House, proposed a change in the existing laws. The change would allow a base transfer even if the cleanup effort was incomplete. Ray was looking at MacDill AFB in Florida, closed by the 1991 BRAC and targeted for complete shutdown in 1994 (though saved by subsequent BRACs). MacDill's cleanup schedule did not call for completion until 1998, which, under existing laws, would prevent the transfer of the base for four years. While the local community supported the cleanup measures, there were also fears that the consequences might leave local governments holding unsellable contaminated property.[164] As will become apparent later, Ray's measure was only the first attempt; Senator (later Defense Secretary) William Cohen (R-ME) attempted the same thing in his effort to make the transfer of Loring AFB possible. Even bases not on closure lists saw delays in cleanup that dismayed their political representatives. At the Navy's submarine base in Bangor, Washington, inspectors identified 42 contamination sites. However, some years later, the deputy assistant secretary of defense (environment) was unable to

answer Representative Norman Dick's (D-WA) question: ". . . why after $3.8 billion at a Trident submarine base, do we only have one site
cleaned up?"[165]

One school of thought on cleanup holds that, even if sites are located, they can never be fully cleaned.[166.] As this view became more
widespread following initial waste-removal efforts, it led to efforts to
relax strict compliance criteria. However, other problems occur once
the absolute conditions are compromised away, leaving less precise
guidelines. Then the temptation for those who want a rapid base
transfer is to push for less and less compliance, which usually generates a counteraction by those who insist on maximum cleanup standards. Whether or not local concerns about health problems
stemming from unresolved base-contamination problems will outweigh concerns about the local economy suffering from an empty
base because of pollution problems is difficult to say. Generally,
though, the economy takes precedence over the environment, particularly if environmental problems are seen as either relatively small
or relatively expensive to remedy. The economic consequences of
cleanup-imposed delays show up much more rapidly than do the consequences of toxic chemicals, which may take years to manifest themselves in health problems.

The Ammunition-Contamination Problem

Some of the most dangerous contaminants on military-base land are
the thousands of tons of unexploded ordnance that has accumulated
for decades at many bases—in 1995 estimated at 620 sites.[167] The
magnitude of the problem is indicated by the fact that 55,000 acres of
former base property is so contaminated with unexploded munitions
that it will have to remain the property of the federal government in
perpetuity.[168]

One of the more common military functions is weapons operation, which involves firing-range activity, in which live fire simulates
combat conditions to improve the skill of gunners, bombardiers, and
pilots. But shells from land artillery, tanks, and naval vessels, and
bombs dropped from aircraft do not always explode, and rarely does
anyone look for those that do not detonate. Over time, the live ordnance simply sinks deeper below the surface, to be discovered (if at
all) only years later. Other bases manufacture ammunition, and over
time faulty rounds and spilt chemicals get dumped into nearby rivers
or pits, sometimes forgotten until a site survey discovers them.

All too typical was the problem at Fort Devins in Massachusetts, listed for closure in the 1991 BRAC and scheduled for shutdown in 1996. The range south of the base had so much unexploded ordnance that, according to a study by the Business Executives for National Security, the land might never be used again for civilian purposes for safety reasons.[169] The state of Maryland received 75,000 acres of Fort Ritchie from the Army, under the stipulation that they could be used only as a wildlife habitat. This was because the land had formerly been a firing range, and there was simply too much unexploded ammunition requiring removal. As one colonel put it: "Better for Bambi to step on a round than a hunter. Bambi can't sue." Yet, these sites posed fewer problems than most ranges, which often were in remote locations (desert valleys, small islands—some shelled for more than 50 years), making cleanup obviously difficult and expensive. Naval vessels shelled islands off both the California and Hawaiian coasts for so long that it was rumored that the masses of steel buried in the island's sand distracted ship compasses from true north. Firing ranges at closed Fort Ord in California had accumulated so many spent lead bullets that much of the beach area (to become a state park) had taken on a gray color.[170] A far more serious problem existed at Fort Ord's 8,000-acre impact range, where the Bureau of Land Management proposed to limiting access to the 8,000 acres in order to minimize risks to the public."[171] The cost of cleaning up ammunition at Fort Ord may exceed $300 million and take more than 10 years.[172]

To locate unexploded ordnance, bulldozers fitted with special armor must scrape off many feet of surface soil. The process must be repeated because deeply buried shells tend to slowly migrate closer to the surface. The ordnance then must be carefully loaded and transported to locations for detonation or defusing.[173] The procedure is difficult enough on land, but it becomes more complicated still for ordnance located in water. Practice bombing against naval targets left many unexploded bombs under water, where they could remain dangerous for decades. The Army's cleanup efforts at Fort Sheridan in Illinois included searches for unexploded bombs in Lake Michigan, dropped there years before by aviators practicing their ability to sink ships.[174]

Sometimes the ammunition problems remain buried for many decades, discovered only by accident. During the Civil War, the Navy manufactured ammunition for its warships at the Mare Island Naval Shipyard in California. Faulty shells got dumped into the Napa River, which runs through the east side of the base. In subsequent years, the Navy had to dredge the river to keep the shipyard channel open; and in the process, it dredged up the old rounds, which had become so unstable that they exploded when exposed to air. When the base closed in 1995, no one really knew the extent of the contamination problem, but it had become so serious that firefighters refused to put out grass fires in the area filled in by dredge material because of frequent ammunition explosions.

Changes in Base Cleanup Policy for 1995

For the 1995 base-closure round, the Defense Department used its experience from previous BRACs to streamline base-cleanup problems. One proposed solution was the "fast-track cleanup." Much of this effort involved the creation of more committees to involve more actors in the cleanup effort. For example, base environmental and local officials and the Environmental Protection Agency (EPA) formed a BRAC cleanup team. "Fast-track cleanup" sped up the report deadlines and required the military to "attempt to complete its environmental impact analysis no later than 12 months after receiving the LRA's approved redevelopment plan."[175] The Environmental Baseline Survey must be completed no later than 18 months after the base-closure list becomes final.[176] The real purpose of fast-track cleanup is not necessarily to speed up the physical cleanup process itself, but rather to "cut thru red tape bureaucracy & speed up the entire process".[177] In other cases, a new form for cleanup promises to save considerable funds. The technique, known as "natural attenuation and degradation," is another term for "do nothing" and hope that natural dispersion and decay will ultimately render the contamination neutral. The state of California approved the first natural-attenuation measure for the groundwater under the former Sierra Army Depot. The decision, which saved the Army approximately $10 million, requires only that water not be tapped from suspected contaminant-migration sites and that those sites be monitored.[178]

While cutting through bureaucratic delays is commendable, it may fail to address the kinds of base-closure environmental problems noted above. A RAND study noted the potential discrepancy between the areas in which the pollution exists and the areas that may be the prime land for conversion. Toxic areas, defined as "operable units" under CERCLA, may be ". . . drawn to enhance the convenience and economy of a total base cleanup rather than to isolate the most risky hazardous waste sites."[179] The fast-track process may gain political points by giving the appearance of hastening cleanup at bases, thus making them more quickly available for alternative use. It also gives local community members more of a voice in cleanup efforts—an effort formalized in July 1993 with the creation of Restoration Advisory Boards (RABs). These bodies form when requested by the local government, or by petition from 50 local residents, or automatically if the base is placed on a closure list. RABs also involve the Federal EPA and state environmental agencies working with local community members, so they afford better interagency coordination, as well as citizen involvement. Of course, such involvement may also result in policy paralysis when substantial disagreements occur.

Other, more modest efforts to hasten cleanup involved shortcuts like field testing instead of laboratory testing, as was tried by the Navy at the closed Treasure Island Naval Station in the hope that such procedures might reduce the "site characterization" costs by 30 percent.[180] Using the present work force to clean up pollution was another innovative solution, as practiced at the Mare Island Naval Shipyard, where workers attend cleanup courses offered by the University of California while applying what they learn to actual cleanup of the base.[181]

Another environmental problem associated with base closures was future liability for base pollution by the new owners of the land. After some years of experience, recognition of undiscovered environmental problems at former bases grew, and with it grew fears that future operators would either be held liable for damages or would suffer business losses. Initial efforts by the Defense Department to create an indemnification policy were rejected by Congress in 1993 as "confusing,"[182] and several years passed before DOD crafted a replacement that Congress accepted.

One way to avoid the cleanup problems of base closure is to avoid closing the most toxic of bases. Level of contamination, though, is not one of the factors by which bases are judged for closure. In 1993, BRAC Chair James Courter tried to make that explicit by warning Defense Department officials not to exclude bases from their BRAC lists just because of contamination levels. The deputy secretary of the army assured him during hearings that decisions on base closure were "not based on environmental factors."[183] However, the principal environmental director for the deputy assistant secretary of defense revealed that the decision to exclude the Tooele Army Depot in Utah was based on the "level of contamination and the length of time needed to complete restoration" of the environment.[184] Tooele had been the site for storage of nuclear and chemical materials, among other things.

The Military Impact of Base Closures

If there was a clear proponent for base closure, it was the military. Saddled with what it considered a bloated and costly infrastructure, the military openly lobbied to close bases long before the Cold War had ended. But the military has paid a price for base closure, and in ways it probably did not expect.

One consequence of base closure has been an increase of anxiety and stress levels on the part of military personnel stationed on targeted bases. As Air Force chaplain Thomas P. Azar stated, military personnel "have invested more than time in their workplace. They have an emotional investment that carries no measurable price tag. They have established relationships . . . that enhance one's patriotic and family commitments."[185] Bases become, in other words, home to the people who live on them, however briefly. Bases link personnel to squadrons, battalions, divisions, companies, and other military organizations that become identified with the base. Fort Bragg in North Carolina will long be known as the home of the 82nd Airborne Division, California's Camp Pendleton as home of the Marine Corps on the West Coast, and Carswell AFB in Texas as home for the Seventh Bomb Wing for decades. To shut down a base often means closing down the attached military units. The 379th Bomb Wing at Wurtsmith AFB in Michigan, for example, was deactivated after the base closed its gates for good in 1993.[186] In the early 1990s, Gen. Merrill McPeak, the Air Force chief of staff, brought back some of the so-called "legacy wings," the famous fighter and bomber wings of World War II, to reinforce the Air Force's connection with its past. But base closures were dismantling wings faster than they could be brought back from the history books. And bases were often reminders of that history—many named for historic figures. The Air Force named most of its bases for Army or Air Force flyers killed in action, and the Army often named its bases for famous Army generals. Some officers privately expressed concern that these memorials to their late heroes would be lost forever after their closure.

For the military, other disruptions also stem from base closure. Personnel transfer, often without replacement, even though they may still be important to base functions. That means that maintenance is not done completely, that fuel may not be delivered, that leaking toilets are not fixed, and that there may be a shortage of gate guards, forcing those remaining into double duty. The hospital may begin to reduce its staff and facilities, forcing those remaining on the base to wait for hours for medical care or to have to go to civilian hospitals.

The forms required for military decorations may not get processed, and those who have earned such decorations may leave the base without receiving them.[187] Military golf courses close, including some famous courses at such places as Fort Benjamin Harrison in Indiana, or at Fort Ord and the Presidio of San Francisco in California.[188]

At the other end of base-closure for the military is relocation, or "permanent change of station" in military parlance. While relocation is a regular part of service life, base closure means just one more relocation for the military family who may have moved onto the base six months previously. It also means that entire military units move to an unfamiliar base next to an unfamiliar town, where they set up again in unfamiliar buildings and have to look up unfamiliar phone numbers when something goes wrong.

When personnel and units move to a new base from one closing, problems also occur. Units presently at the base must get used to sharing base facilities with a new unit. Base operations are suddenly faced with a new overload when a closed base's functions transfer to another base. The firing range is suddenly more crowded, and the motor pool has inadequate vehicle maintenance facilities for the newly arrived vehicles from a closed base. A specific example: The chemical-weapons-disposal facilities at Fort Leonard Wood, Missouri, are suddenly overtaxed when chemical weapons once destroyed at Anniston Army Depot in Alabama are transported to Missouri for destruction. Base laundries cannot handle the influx of new troops from a closed facility. And so on.

These costs are difficult to measure. But they are real costs, and the military pays them for each round of base closure.

THE LESS TANGIBLE IMPACTS OF BASE CLOSURE

There are less tangible cost factors in the base-closure process. Communities that lost bases suffered more than just reduced revenue. In many ways, the military members do much more for the local area than just spend money there. They often join in community activities. Military personnel coach soccer and little league teams, participate in church and civic activities, donate blood in local hospitals, and provide backup emergency services and disaster relief. Of course, there is also the seamier side of the military impact on communities, such as the strips of bars adjacent to the base where civilian and military police sometimes to work overtime subduing young service people hampered with too much alcohol and not enough sense. But that problem was worse in the 1960s and 1970s, when most young enlisted members were single, and fun consisted of going out to a bar instead of going to a movie with the children. There were few military efforts to curb alcohol abuse and its related consequences, with 25-cent-per-drink "happy hours" sending the wrong signal about the consequences of drinking too much. In the 1990s, the military has made a concerted (if not wholly successful) effort to curb drinking, and a majority of military personnel are married. Even incoming recruits are more likely than ever to have spouses.[189] While that has meant more problems for the military (such as divorce and spousal abuse), those problems are more likely to occur on base, or at least to fall under the jurisdiction of the military. Since more military personnel are married, there are fewer singles out on the town. The average age of soldiers during the Vietnam era was 19 years; by 1996, it had risen to 27.5 years.[190] In many cases, the military person was more likely involved in the church choir than in a barroom brawl. Thus, while base closures 20 years ago might have brought the side benefit of less trouble from military people, that was less true during the BRAC process. Closures are now more likely to deprive communities of the positive values of having the military around.

HISTORICAL AND NATURAL PRESERVATION AT MILITARY BASES

While U.S. military history is relatively brief compared to other nations, the military has been around long enough to have left historically significant things. Moreover, bases often comprise thousands or sometimes hundreds of thousands of acres—often shared with wildlife of many types. Base land itself might not appear as a significant issue, but both its historical importance and the wildlife often sharing it with the military emerged in the 1990s, in particular, as yet another base-closure issue involving political differences.

PRESERVING MILITARY HISTORY

Base land sometimes holds historic treasures. Army historic preservation efforts include protecting prehistoric human remains at Fort Bliss, maintaining the United States Military Academy at West Point, the oldest continuously used military installation in the country, and eighteenth-century houses of "extreme national significance" at Fort Eustis. The oldest Navy chapel in the country is located at Mare Island

Naval Shipyard, featuring carvings depicting naval history and signed Tiffany stained glass windows. But Mare Island is closing, and the future of the chapel, along with a number of other historical buildings is unclear.[191] At the Presidio of San Francisco, 520 of the total 870 buildings fall into the National Historic Preservation category requiring protection.[192] The Air Force preserves the building at Maxwell AFB where the Air Corps Tactical School developed theories of strategic bombing in the 1930s. The Wright brothers opened a flying school at that base in 1910, and the site where they perfected their heavier-than-air machine remains preserved at Wright-Patterson AFB. Some less attractive history is also preserved at Air Force bases, like the now dilapidated buildings set aside at a remote part of Maxwell AFB for Black soldiers during the racial segregation years of World War II.

The historic significance of some bases may mean more than just the loss through deterioration of old and valuable properties, though. The National Historic Preservation Act of 1966 mandates that every federal agency take into account how its undertakings may affect historic properties it manages. The act also requires each military service with a base to afford the Advisory Council on Historic Preservation a reasonable opportunity to comment on its proposed action, thus taking up even more time in the already lengthy base-closure process.[193] No transfer may happen until any structure more than 50 years old is assessed and classified for historic-preservation value.[194] The National Historic Preservation Act is but one of many such laws at the federal level. Others include the American Indian Religious Freedom Act (which, among other things, grants Native Americans access to religious sites), the Archaeological and Historic Preservation Act, the Bald and Golden Eagle Preservation Act, the Coastal Zone Management Act, the Endangered Species Act, the Fish and Wildlife Coordination Act, the Migratory Bird Treaty Act, the Native American Graves Protection and Repatriation Act, the Watershed Protection and Flood Protection Act, and the Wild and Scenic Rivers Act. In addition to this plethora of federal legislation, states may have their own preservation requirements. The Defense Department also promulgates a variety of directives and instructions on preservation at military bases. All have an impact on base closure, since bases are often the location of historic buildings, Indian grave sites, wildlife preserves, and other such things covered by the above acts.

There are different methods to preserve facilities at military bases. One is direct custody transfer to another agency. As noted above, the Presidio transferred to the National Park Service. To preserve the battle site at Midway Island, the Fish and Wildlife Service took custody of the Naval Air Station there after its closure by BRAC in 1993.[195] Another means is to provide incentives to maintain and enhance buildings or other property through tax credits. There are several such incentives, including a rehabilitation tax credit of 20 percent for reconstructing "certified historic structures" and a 10 percent tax credit for rehabilitating any structure built before 1936.[196] The purpose of such incentives is to reduce the temptation to tear down dilapidated base buildings and instead restore them.

Other things of historical value lie in military museums, often located on military bases. Some of those displays might move elsewhere after base closure, such as the Chemical Warfare Museum and the Women's Army Corps (WAC) Museum at Fort McClellan in Alabama. Other displays are not so mobile, including the historical aircraft often collected at base museums at Air Force bases. Castle AFB in California had 44 aircraft on display, including a B-24, a B-36, and an SR-71. The B-36, the largest bomber ever built, is not in flying condition and not easily moveable. March AFB, with its 50 aircraft, received $250,000 from the Air Force, but March, like Castle, saw its Air Force contribution stop when the base closed.[197] McClellan AFB likewise will lose its $185,000 in annual operating funds from the Air Force should the base close, leaving in doubt the fate of the 32 restored aircraft in its museum. While the foundations operating these museums may try to take over the displays, fund-raising becomes difficult since the original agreements with the Air Force to establish base museums stipulate that any collection items may be pulled on 60 days' notice.[198]

Should some of these bases become shopping malls or university campuses, no assurance exists that such preservation efforts will continue. Clearly, at one of the Army's most historical places, the Presidio of San Francisco, preservation efforts halted for at least six years after the first closure decision in 1988. The property once occupied by the Long Beach Naval Station became attractive to a Chinese shipping firm that wanted to construct a cargo terminal there. But Long Beach Heritage, a group dedicated to preserving historic buildings there, opposed the plan. Said a spokesperson: "President Roosevelt built this as the headquarters of the Pacific Fleet in 1940. That's the part Long Beach Heritage would like to save."[199] As of 1997, the fight continued.

In one somewhat unusual incident, preservationists and environmentalists split in a fight that delayed environmental certification at the Mare Island Naval Shipyard. Since the yard worked on nuclear-powered submarines, sometimes radioactive materials leaked into the yard's dry docks. At the bottom of the dry docks were huge blocks of granite to support the weight of a ship. The only way to demonstrate that radioactive materials had not leaked into cracks in the granite was to drill into the stone. Preservationists halted the effort, though, noting that the granite had supported the dry-dock frames for a considerable period of time and, thus, had historical significance.

Wildlife Preservation at Military Bases

Another base-closure issue involves a base role in preservation of endangered species. In 1996 the Army devoted significant resources, approximately $4.5 million annually, to the protection of approximately 280 federally listed threatened or endangered species on sixty-three installations. In that same year the Navy managed some 3.5 million acres of environmentally sensitive land. Aberdeen Proving Ground in Maryland, boasts one of the largest bald eagle populations in the Department of Defense."[200] The Seal Beach Naval Weapons Station shares its area with a national wildlife refuge that provides a home for at least five endangered species in an adjoining salt marsh.[201] Over 1000 of the 5,000 acres of the base are so designated. Fort Bragg in North Carolina, is home to one of the nation's largest populations of the endangered red-cockaded woodpeckers.[202] Marine Corps Base Camp Pendleton in California is the only preserved habitat for the least Bell's vireo, an endangered species. The Marines have identified its habitat as "mine fields," to be avoided during exercises, and thus assisted a 200 percent increase in the bird's population.[203] The Palos Verdes blue butterfly, once thought to exist only at the end of the runway at Los Angeles International Airport, was discovered in 1993 at the Defense Fuel Supply Point in San Pedro, California. This base (managed by the Defense Logistics Agency), is the only site where this species lives, and base officials work with the Navy and the Fish and Wildlife Service to preserve it. The Mare Island Naval Shipyard is home to the salt-marsh harvest mouse, the only known mammal to drink pure saltwater. Arnold AFB in Tennessee hosts populations of gray bats, Cumberland pigtoe mussels, and Eggert's sunflower. Eglin AFB in Florida contains more than 90 endangered species, including the Okaloosa darter, Florida black bear, the naked-stemmed panic grass, the white-topped pitcher plant, and a salamander so new to science that it remains unnamed.[204]

It is unclear what happens when bases with endangered-species protection close. If base lands set aside for breeding or nesting are bulldozed for shopping malls in an effort to replace lost base jobs, a fight could develop over habitat preservation. Such a fight broke out in the city of Alameda, California in 1995 when efforts to use the runways of the former Naval Air Station for a least tern bird preserve met with some resistance from those who wanted the land for development.[205] However, the Fish and Wildlife Service received considerable acreage from bases for wildlife preservation purposes, and established a 900-acre bird refuge at Alameda, along with other land at former naval facilities at Skaggs Island and the Mare Island Naval Shipyard.[206] Other Fish and Wildlife Service areas include land at Fort Devins in Massachusetts, the Joliet Army Arsenal in Illinois, and Midway Island.[207] Efforts were underway in 1997 to find a way to preserve Mare Island's saltwater-drinking mouse as that base closed. [208]

Some base closures actually generate habitats for endangered species. One of the more surprising examples is Rocky Mountain Arsenal, a former chemical weapons depot. Once thought to be so contaminated with chemical weapon residue that it could never be cleaned up, the former base is scheduled to become the Rocky Mountain Arsenal National Wildlife Refuge. After a 20-year cleanup effort costing almost $2 billion, the land will be the home to over 300 wildlife species, including bald eagles, prairie dogs, and white-tailed deer.[209] If such a habitat could be established at Rocky Mountain Arsenal, certainly others could be established at less toxic sites.

SUMMARY

Military bases are the focus of significant political priorities. They are classic cases of many of the dilemmas facing the divided American political structure, including local versus national interests and organizational interests versus elected leadership interests. This means that clear decisions on base-closure situations are almost impossible, since the only way that the American political system can adjudicate such politically charged outcomes is though compromise. It means that, in the absence of any clear rule to make such choices as are involved in base closure, the participants will try to make their own rules, and the existing rules (such as those defining the BRAC procedures) will be bent and even broken by a variety of participants.

Prior to the establishment of BRAC, base closure was almost impossible for a decade after 1977. But, at a general level, the establishment of BRAC forced those with a stake in preventing base closure to be more innovative and to invest more effort at either resisting the closure altogether or working to soften its economic and political impact. Re-missioning, funding pork-barrel construction projects, and the generation of questionable cost data were just some of the tactics used to save bases, while privatization, low-cost land transfer, and shifting from a military mission to a nonmilitary mission at a base were some of the means used to ease the impact post closure.

This chapter examined the politics of base closure along topical lines. Since base closure occurred over four iterations, a comparison of the last three of these sequenced processes lends additional explanation to the politics of base closure. The following chapters analyze the base-closing years of 1991, 1993, and 1995. The study excludes 1988, the first official BRAC year, since the BRAC process changed for 1991. Each chapter looks at the BRAC process for that year and examines some select bases targeted for closure. Not all bases so chosen were actually closed—some survived the scrutiny of the process, and some did not. Others closed in a particular year, only to have a later BRAC open them up again or at least find something to keep a marginal capacity there. So, the year that the base is picked does not necessarily signify the end of the base. Some are examined twice (Fort McClellan in Alabama, for example), and some appear in only one year (like MacDill AFB in Florida in 1993) even though Fort McClellan was examined first in 1991 and a final decision not reached until 1995. The process is complex, and many bases do not fit neatly into an organization structured after BRAC years. Still, the process is always interesting and often unpredictable. What follows are classic demonstrations of high-stakes politics.

CHAPTER THREE

1991

Mr. Browder [referring to two chemical weapons sites at Fort McClellan, AL]: I see the nightmare of us being dominated as America's two-seat toxic toilet.
Mrs. Schroeder: Two-seat toxic toilet. That is amazing.
—*Congressional Hearings, 1991*

There are not too many things in this world that are cigar shaped and run on nuclear power.
—*Unemployed submarine worker, Mare Island Naval Shipyard, 1991.*

*I*t took considerable political struggle to finally complete a base-closure round in 1988. In the face of a decade of no base closures, though, it was apparent that politics still dominated the process, a situation that became even more obvious when Congress rejected a preliminary base-closure list in 1990. Embarrassed by the initial failure of the process, Congress searched for remedies. As noted in Chapter Two, Congress proposed substantial revisions for the BRAC process, with a changed role for the Defense Department, an open decision process, and oversight by the General Accounting Office (GAO). In a way, it was a reflection of the so-called "sunshine on government" process that had had an impact on so many political bodies in the 1970s, when public faith in the overall governing process waned considerably.

Major reductions in both the military force structure and the defense budget by 1991 helped mandate substantial base closure. In April 1989, the Bush administration submitted a defense budget with a cumulative five-year value to $1,665.9 billion, then revised it downward in January 1990 by $167 billion.[1] Moreover, there were some real cuts in force structure that could have been used as reasons to reduce the supporting base structure. Projections through 1994 called for the reduction of 2 Army divisions (out of 18 original), the retirement of 2 battleships, 2 nuclear cruisers, 8 nuclear-powered submarines, 14 B-52 bombers, the Minuteman II ballistic missile, and an assortment of smaller items for a total reduction of $5.7 billion.[2] These reductions were not unnoticed by the political actors involved in shaping the changes for the 1991 and subsequent base-closure rounds.

1988: THE FIRST BRAC EFFORT

Congress wrestled with base closure seriously for the first time in ten years when it reluctantly passed a limited base-closure bill. The chief sponsor of the measure, Representative Richard Armey (R-TX), wanted to remove Congress from the process completely, but in the end a compromise came from the House and Senate Armed Services Committees that gave Congress numerous loopholes to impact the process.[3] Then House Armed Services Committee Chair Representative Les Aspin (D-WI) and Government Operations Committee Chair Jack Brooks (D-TX) modified the measure, with Aspin's version keeping Congress less involved than Brooks's, though both more so than Armey desired.[4] Armey fought back, and the final bill created an independent commission that would provide a list of proposed base closures to the secretary of defense. The secretary then forwarded the recommendations to the president, who in turn would have 15 days to decide to close all or none of the selected bases. Congress could only vote to approve or disapprove the secretary's actions.[5] In the end, the 1988 commission targeted 16 bases for closure.

Fortunately for President Bush, the 1988 BRAC base-closure list appeared in December 1988, a month after he defeated Democratic challenger Michael Dukakis. While the election was not all that close, the president did need to carry large states like California, with numerous electoral votes and military bases. The bad news for California in December was the BRAC shutdown of six bases, which hit the state hard. Victims included the historic Presidio of San Francisco, Mather AFB near Sacramento, and George AFB and Norton AFB, both located in Riverside County inland of Los Angeles. Altogether the state stood to lose 17,000 jobs. Some installations gained jobs, such as March AFB (closed by the 1991 BRAC), which would get 3,400 new positions from transferred functions, and the San Diego Naval Shipyard, which picked up about 1,500 new jobs.[6] San Diego would benefit by a decision not to build additional facilities at the Hunter's Point Naval Annex, which itself closed two years later. It was, in part, a small battle in the larger resource war between northern and southern California.

The estimated 1988 BRAC savings were more than $700 million yearly. That may seem like a considerable amount of money, but another way to look at it is to figure it at less than 1/280th of the overall defense budget. The Presidio of San Francisco got a reprieve until 1993. Many California bases shuttered, though, leading to charges that politics might have intruded in the first supposedly "objective" base-closure process. Senator Pete Wilson (R-CA) noted that bases in his home state plus the Northeast were closing, while southern states escaped with fewer base closures.[7] It was hard not to notice, for example, that the 1988 BRAC did not touch Georgia, a state with a large number of bases. Some tied that to the fact that Senator Sam Nunn (D-GA) was chair of the Senate Armed Services Committee. Others noted that the same was true for Wisconsin (with few bases, though), the home state for Representative Aspin, chair of the House Armed Services Committee.

1991: THE PROCESS REVISED

The base closure process for 1991 added new checkpoints from previous iterations to further distance politics.[8] To allow local officials a chance to defend bases and argue BRAC from economic positions, BRAC Chair James Courter expanded the on-site part of the process. The commission scheduled five hearings in Washington, and another eight held in particular regions of the country. President Bush got the final base-closure list on July 1, 1991, with modest changes. BRAC dropped four bases from the 31 bases initially submitted by the secretary of defense and recommended closure of an additional two bases. Efforts to repeat the 1990 experience in Congress failed in July when a resolution to reject the BRAC list failed in both the House Armed Services Committee and the full House. Given that both houses of Congress had to agree to either accept or reject the BRAC findings, Senate efforts to kill the BRAC list ended after July 30. The list received quick approval since the president had only 15 days to approve or kill the list entirely, and Congress had only 45 days to accept or reject the closure list.

At the Defense Department, Undersecretary of Defense Donald J. Atwood assumed oversight of the base-closure process. Atwood, considered one of the most powerful civilians in the DOD, distributed a memorandum on December 10, 1990, initialing the process and appointing Colin McMillan, the assistant secretary of defense for production and logistics, to be directly in charge of it. McMillan formed a steering committee to coordinate the effort across the services, placing OSD (Office of the Secretary of Defense) officials in charge of each service's base-closure effort.[9] He also specified the closing criteria to each service secretary in a February 13, 1991, memo that, among other things, emphasized the exploration of multiservice bases. One consequence of these developments was a transfer of power away from the uniformed services to the civilian officials in the OSD. The latter never made clear their assumptions behind this move. However, the OSD had less attachment to the current base structure than did the uniformed senior military, who had spent most of their careers as a part of that very structure. OSD civilians, therefore, might be less parochial in determining bases to be closed. This generated the potential for service resentment against these same civilians, who had not spent their careers in the military yet prepared to offer up bases without necessarily a thorough understanding of the military consequences of closing them.

Service Base Evaluation

Part of the reason for a smoother process at the top lies in the improved service base-evaluation process. While each service accomplished the task differently, all three tried to develop objective criteria to outweigh partisan efforts to save bases recommended for closure. The Army first categorized its bases by "mission category," which allowed a ranking of them by military importance. Those categories included (1) fighting installations; (2) training bases; (3) industrial bases; and (4) major training areas.[10] The Total Army Basing Study (TABS) rated each facility using a software program developed for that purpose. The final ranking, though, suggested that, for all of the rules that were to direct the outcomes, there were also exceptions. For example, Fort Richardson in Alaska and Schofield Barracks in Hawaii were ranked eleventh and twelfth among the fighting installations, yet the Army retained them because of the "geographical importance of their location."[11] However, the Army did recommend Fort Ord in California for closure, although it ranked tenth out of thirteen Army bases. Fort Devins in Massachusetts ranked higher than Forts Totten and Hamilton, both located in New York state, but the latter were spared "because their missions are exclusively area-oriented," according to the Army.[12] When the GAO reviewed the Army's process (another step in the revised BRAC to ensure objectivity), it concluded that the process was "well documented" although it could not be sure that the Army had always followed its own procedures. The GAO also commented that the Army's ". . . future plans are not precise and include some uncertainties" and it could not, therefore, judge whether Army consolidation plans matched future assessments.[13]

The GAO found more to criticize when it examined the Navy's base-closure process. According to the GAO, the Navy rarely seemed to document its decisions adequately, nor did the naval oversight process assure that data were accurate.[14] The Air Force, according to GAO, did a better job of providing documentation for its decisions, made largely by a board consisting of five general officers and five Senior Executive Service civilians. The Air Force created an ordinal ranking process for its bases, used by a working group to initially rank all Air Force bases for review by the executive group.

In 1991, the Air Force dominated the base-closure list, with no fewer than 11 major bases proposed. Five of these bases were home to Strategic Air Command (SAC) bomb wings, and their closure could not have come as much of a surprise, since the end of the Cold War had reduced the importance of SAC's nuclear mission (though not its conventional one). What was perhaps more surprising was that only two of the five (Loring AFB in Maine and Wurtsmith AFB in Michigan) were "northern tier" bases, while the others (Carswell AFB in Texas, Castle AFB in California, and Eaker AFB in Arkansas) were sunbelt bases. Five of the other bases were homes to fighter wings, still an essential part of the Air Force. Fighter numbers, though, were shrinking as the Air Force began to retire its older F-4s and the earlier versions of its F-15s and F-16s (which often went either to Air National Guard units or to other nations). As each fighter wing got smaller, consolidation became possible, allowing one base to shut down and its fighter wing to transfer to another fighter base.

The Army and the Navy had fewer bases on the 1991 list (that would change dramatically for the Navy in 1993), but one, in particular, that did appear on the 1991 list raised alarm bells in north-central Alabama. Fort McClellan had already made the first closure list in 1989, and its second appearance, in 1991, would not bode well for the largest employer in the county. In the end, McClellan would appear two more times in successive BRACs before its fate was finally sealed, which in itself makes it a fascinating political study.

Politics may have been involved at the service level, and within services. Critics charged, for example, that Secretary of Defense Dick Cheney picked Whidbey Island Naval Air Stations (NAS) in Washington

State for closure. According to Representative Al Swift (D-WA), in whose district Whidbey Island is located, the "light attack" aviators who fly the F/A-18 and A-7E naval aircraft out of Lemoore had gotten into a political turf battle with the "medium attack" aviators at Whidbey over who would get the new A-12 stealth attack plane. The A-12 was first slated to go to Whidbey, but for unexplained reasons the Navy shifted it to Lemoore. It never arrived, canceled instead by Secretary Cheney after allegations of cost overruns on the project. The fight between the two groups may have spilled over into the base-closure process when Whidbey Island made the closure list and Lemoore did not.[15] According to the Navy, however, cost and a planned reduction in the A-6E fleet at Whidbey drove the decision.[16]

POLITICS AND JOBS

The 1991 closure list produced some clear winners and losers on the job front. California lost the most jobs, a total near 27,000 from both closures and realignments. The closing of Fort Ord on California's northern coast would cost 16,000 jobs alone.[17] Florida would lose 19,000 jobs, but when Orlando's naval training facility relocated to Illinois, the latter state gained 14,000 jobs. While Orlando did pick up some jobs as the result of the closing of Williams AFB in Arizona, they would not match those lost by the training center's move.[18]

It would not take long for political figures to conclude that politics rather than rational choice drove the selections. House Armed Services Committee Chair Aspin, who would himself later have to close bases as secretary of defense, stated initially that the list "appears fair." A subsequent study by Aspin, though, found that 59 percent of the bases closed were in Democratic districts, and Democrats represented almost 82 percent of the jobs lost.[19] Secretary Cheney described that notion as "goofy,"[20] noting that the world situation had changed after the Cold War, and the United States was reducing its forces by more than 25 percent. In reality, Republicans suffered some painful base closings as well. Senator Arlen Specter (R-PA), who saw both the Philadelphia Naval Station and the Philadelphia Naval Shipyard appear on the 1991 list (with a total of 13,000 jobs lost), complained that "it looks like the Department of Defense has declared war on Pennsylvania."[21] The death of Senator John Heintz in a plane crash compounded the problem for Pennsylvania Republicans. They suddenly needed to fill a formerly safe seat in the 1992 election. Republicans also noted that such installations as Fort Dix in New Jersey, represented by James Saxon (R-NJ), were to be scaled back to just a few reserve units. When the BRAC list revised the service submissions to exclude Fort Dix, the possible connection between former New Jersey Representative James Courter, the BRAC chair, and the reversal of the Army's Fort Dix decision would fuel charges of unfairness and partisanship by BRAC.

The Bush administration apparently decided to respond both carefully and vaguely to congressional fears about base closures. When Senator Specter pointedly raised the closure of the Philadelphia Naval Shipyard with Undersecretary Atwood, the latter responded that no decision had been finalized by Secretary Cheney, stating further: "There are a number of studies that are going on, and will be going on, before a final recommendation is made."[22] Later in the same testimony, he tried to assure Senator Daniel Inouye (D-HI) that ". . . there are many bases that are listed on here that are not being closed but that there would be some consolidation of activities and realignments of people and realignment of functions."[23] Atwood also stated that factors such as economic and environmental impact studies and the dependency of retirees upon base hospitals might also change some decisions on base-closing recommendations from the Defense Department.[24] There appeared to be little inclination from Atwood or others in DOD to do little more at this stage than to try to soft-pedal the potential impact of base closings—an understandable, if timid, approach given the fact that Congress had flatly rejected the base-closing list of the year before. While the modifications to the legislation for 1991 would have prevented a repeat of this performance, the hostility in Congress to base closings was enough to warrant caution from DOD officials in this the first of three rounds.

The 1991 BRAC Commissioners

Congress approved the 1991 BRAC membership in April 1991. The members were:

- James A. Courter, the chair. Courter had been a Republican member of Congress from New Jersey and was an unsuccessful candidate for that state's governorship; he was in private law practice when selected for the 1991 BRAC.
- William L. Ball, a former secretary of the Navy and president of the National Soft Drink Association.
- Gen. Duane H. Cassidy, who had commanded the Military Airlift Command and the United States Transportation Command (a

merged command combining the Navy and Air Force transportation commands). He was vice president for logistics technology
for the CSX Corporation.

- James Charles Smith II, a former aide to Senator John Tower (R-
  TX) and vice president of Brown and Root, a Houston-based construction firm that had a number of major contracts with the
  Defense Department.
- Howard H. Callaway, the chair of GOPAC, a conservative politi-
  cal-action committee, a former secretary of the Army, and chair
  of the Colorado Republican Party.
- Robert D. Stuart, Jr., former U.S. Ambassador to Norway from
  1984 to 1989, and retired president and chief executive officer
  for the Quaker Oats Company.
- Alexander B. Trowbridge, secretary of commerce in the Johnson
  administration and former president of the National Association
  of Manufacturers.
- Arthur Levitt, Jr., former president and chief executive officer of
  the American Stock Exchange and chair of the Levitt Media
  Company.[25]

Three of the commissioners had clear ties to the Republican Party
(Courter, Smith, and Callaway) and one to the Democratic Party (Trowbridge). Trowbridge, though, resigned over a potential conflict of interest and was not replaced. Two other commissioners, Ball and Smith,
were former members of the Senate Armed Services Committee staff.

The commission gained a significant increase in political power
over past years because of the ways that Congress changed the process
after the rancorous 1988 round. In that year, Congress rejected the list
of 55 bases proposed by Secretary of Defense Cheney, charging that
the large majority of them were in Democratic districts. So in 1991, the
revised Base Closure and Realignment Act changed the procedure, removing the secretary of defense as an approving official. Instead, the
secretary nominated bases submitted by each service to the commission, which had to complete its own deliberations and submit its own
list to the president by July 1. The hearings had be open. The president, in turn, had 15 days to either accept or reject the list and submit
it to Congress, which had 45 days to reject or accept. Should the president reject the list, the commission had an additional four weeks to
make revisions, should it decide to do so. In reality, though, the rules
did not require BRAC to change its submission list—it could submit
the same list back to the president, or something close to it, and the
president could reject it again. Such a logjam has not happened, but

the prospect undoubtedly gave some incentive to both sides for early communication and cooperation. It was fairly clear in 1993, for example, that President Clinton worried about the impact of defense-related unemployment in California, and thus would be more willing to sign off on the closure list if McClellan AFB and the Presidio of San Francisco were removed from the original list. They were, and he did.

The 1991 BRAC members initially challenged the Defense Department's closure and realignment list, which contained 43 recommendations for closure and 29 for realignment initially, by adding 35 more bases. In the end, however, the commission voted to close only those bases originally submitted by the Pentagon. Whether or not the additional BRAC list of bases for consideration was only for a show of independence is difficult to tell. It is interesting that the BRAC additions contained 20 Navy, 6 Air Force, and 9 Army facilities, implying that the commissioners thought that the original DOD list was too light on its Navy offerings.[26]

Despite the mixed political backgrounds of the 1991 commission, the votes were almost always one-sided. The commission voted 76 times, and, of those 76 votes, 57 were unanimous. In only eight cases did two commissioners vote against the majority. In no case did more than two members vote in opposition.[27] In only six cases did the commission overturn the Defense Department's recommendation, and in all of those cases the decision was to strike the base from either closure or realignment.

The BRAC process is supposed to prevent situations in which either the president or the Congress picks and chooses bases to add to or exclude from the BRAC list. In reality, though, it was very difficult to remove such a valuable issue as base selection from politics. There was intense lobbying by political figures and interest groups to both keep bases open and close them. There was intense fighting over which bases made the initial service lists. Base supporters often mobilized impressive amounts of data to refute whatever claims the service may have made in justification of closure. Their aim was to make base closure more painful politically—by portraying it as irrational, partisan, or heartless. In the cases below, the political players used all of these tactics, sometimes successfully, sometimes not. But it was always interesting.

FORT MCCLELLAN, ALABAMA

Located near the town of Anniston, Alabama, Fort McClellan's very name seems a paradox—a federal Army fort in the self-proclaimed "heart of Dixie" named for one of the North's most reluctant Civil War generals. It would suffer the fate of appearing on the 1988, 1991, 1993, and 1995 BRAC lists, surviving the first three, only to fall in the end in 1995.

Fort McClellan started out as Camp Shipp during the Spanish-American War and was a combat training area in World War I. During World War II, the base served as an internment camp for German and Italian prisoners of war as well as a training base. The Chemical Corps Training Center was activated in 1951, the Women's Corps School moved there from Fort Lee in 1954, and the U.S. Army Military Police School was officially dedicated at Fort McClellan in 1975. In 1979, the Army Chemical School relocated to Fort McClellan from Aberdeen, Maryland. It was these small and somewhat unglamorous missions that gave Fort McClellan its reason for existence, but also much of its vulnerability to closure.

While most Army forts are home to infantry or artillery or armor, Fort McClellan had the dubious distinction of being home to a chemical warfare unit. Chemical weapons, according to many professional soldiers, are not a proper mission for a professional army, but rather simply weapons of mass destruction. It requires no courage to spray them or shoot them from afar or drop them from a high-flying airplane. They can easily cause civilian casualties, or casualties in one's own forces, should the wind shift. So particularly in times of budget scarcity, the Army may find chemical weapons and their associated facilities relatively easy to dispose. As discussed further in Chapter Five, when Fort McClellan again made the BRAC list in 1995, members of the Anniston Chamber of Commerce raised these suspicions.

Representative Glenn Browder (D-AL), whose district included the Anniston area, pointed to the danger himself in an effort to forestall Fort McClellan's closure. He noted that one of the storage areas for chemical weapons in the United States was at nearby Anniston Army Depot, co-located with Fort McClellan's chemical school (giving rise to the "two-seat toxic toilet" remark noted at the beginning of this chapter). ". . . The toxic chemicals stored at Anniston Army Depot could be the basis for a catastrophic chemical accident or incident,"[28] Browder warned, noting further that, should such a chilling incident occur, Fort McClellan had a memorandum of understanding that it was to provide assistance to the Anniston Army Depot. His warning was scarcely veiled; if Fort McClellan closed and thus was incapable of rendering chemical-accident assistance to Anniston, then ". . . it is obvious that the congressional mandate of maximum public protection has been ignored in many instances. . . ."[29]

The Army's recommendation for Fort McClellan was to close the base completely and to realign the chemical school to Fort Leonard Wood in Missouri. McClellan's military police school would also go to Leonard Wood, and the combined schools were to become the Maneuver Support Warfighting Center. This imposing but nondescriptive title would then allow other things that the Army regarded as "cats-and-dogs" to be sent to Fort Leonard Wood, which just happened to b? in the Missouri district of Representative Ike Skelton, a senior member of the House Armed Services Committee. One of Fort McClellan's other missions, the Defense Polygraph School, would be relocated to Fort Huachuca in Arizona.

The most dramatic action recommended by the Army was the shifting to caretaker status of the Chemical Decontamination Training Facility (CDTF). It was that action that gave community activists fighting for McClellan their primary ammunition. They were able to argue successfully that budget considerations rather than military value drove the decision. Thus, it appeared that the Army had violated one of the decision rules for BRAC by choosing cost savings over military priority. Moreover, the CDTF would not be able to be reactivated quickly in case of emergency, and, if it ever reopened, the Army would have to recertify it environmentally. Finally, start-up costs could have ranged from $4 million to $7 million, depending on the environmental or regulatory standards required, and the start-up time might have consumed three to five years.[30]

The testimony of chemical-weapons experts before the commission was important, since it could challenge the relative unimportance of chemical warfare in traditional Army thinking. The experts managed to convince the commissioners that chemical decontamination training was important and that either a new CDTF should be built at another base or the facility at McClellan preserved. Since there were no plans to build a new CDTF, the commissioners voted against the Army recommendation. That may have been, in part, a consequence of a chance event that otherwise might have left the base more vulnerable to closure. The recently concluded Gulf War dramatically demonstrated that chemical weapons could, indeed, be used in warfare, no matter how much some in the Army might have held them in disdain. The live television pictures of panic-stricken news reporters struggling with gas masks under Scud missile attacks in Saudi Arabia were convincing reminders of this terrible weapon.

So for a variety of reasons, Fort McClellan got a reprieve from its Army sentence. (It would be a temporary one, though). So, perhaps, did memories of the Gulf War and the warning sirens of pending chemical-missile attacks. Indeed, it is possible that the renewed efforts to ban chemical weapons on a global basis might have countered the reaction from Iraqi efforts to develop chemical munitions. Like many bases that survived a closure recommendation from the Defense Department, Fort McClellan would soon reappear almost like clockwork on both subsequent base-closure lists, and, ultimately the skill of its defenders would run out. In the meantime, though, Fort McClellan would get a few more years of life.

WURTSMITH AIR FORCE BASE, MICHIGAN

When the Army Air Corps expanded its operations at Selfridge Field on the Upper Michigan Peninsula in the mid-1920s, it also began to experience a rise in the aircraft accident rate. Aircraft suffering mechanical problems after takeoff had to try either to make a forced landing in an open space or to return to Selfridge. So in 1923, then-Maj. Carl Spatz (later a legendary Air Corps leader) visited the small town of Oscoda, Michigan, and arranged for the purchase of enough land to construct an auxiliary airstrip.[31] That strip, initially named Oscoda Army Air Field, later became Wurtsmith Air Force Base. During the latter part of the Cold War, Wurtsmith was home to the 379th Bombardment Wing, consisting of B-52Gs and KC-135 tankers. It was one of many "northern tier" Air Force bases originally located because they offered slightly shorter flight times to the USSR. At the height of its operations, Wurtsmith hosted 3,700 military personnel and their families.

The end of the Cold War spelled doom for these bases, as well as for the small towns located around them. By the summer of 1990, signs proclaiming "Say Yes to Wurtsmith" began to sprout up in the little town of Oscoda—the citizens there knew that the BRAC commissioners were going to take a hard look at their only source of income apart from summer tourism along Lake Huron. They had good reason to worry. For one thing, Wurtsmith's B-52Gs were the older version of the two B-52 models flying then; the last one had come off the assembly line in 1959. Their advanced age lead to higher repair costs and more lost time in Wurtsmith's repair facilities. The maintenance crews could not keep up with the problems, and sometimes the aircraft had to fly limited missions until the crews could schedule them into the shops.[32] The B-52G also used old J-57 engines, which required water injection to give the engines enough thrust to get the bomber airborne and had not been manufactured in years. The cost of making or reconditioning parts for the J-57 was high, and the plane could not land at takeoff weight in an emergency because the J-57 lacked thrust reversers. These and other aging problems doomed the B-52G, and Wurtsmith along with it. Wurtsmith had its own problems, though.

When SAC built practice low-altitude bombing ranges for its aircraft, it located them in remote areas—Wyoming, Montana, North Dakota, and Utah—to reduce noise complaints and safety hazards—B-52s based elsewhere had to fly to those locations for practice, a long and increasingly costly procedure. In fact, the 1991 BRAC report directly noted Wurtsmith's distance from low-altitude ranges as one of the best reasons to close it.[33] The flight on a fuel-guzzling B-52 to Ellsworth AFB in South Dakota, located proximate to the bomber ranges to its north, took about three hours. In August 1991, SAC selected Ellsworth as the site for the Strategic Warfare Center (SWC), where bomber crews could fly practice missions over the ranges and be evaluated afterward. The purpose of the SWC was to replicate the fighter training at Nellis AFB in Nevada using the same kind of training and technology. But Ellsworth posed another problem for the B-52s that came to practice at the SWC. It was home to the 28th Bomb Wing, fully equipped with B-1Bs but no B-52s. Therefore, Ellsworth's maintenance facilities had limited capacity and only a few spare parts to repair a visiting B-52. That could become a serious problem since the B-52s were aging rapidly and stressed considerably by long flights at low altitude through bombing ranges. Given that the wings on the giant bomber could flex up and down as much as 15 feet at the tips, parts of the wing surfaces could easily crack or break off. It became almost common for a B-52 to return to Ellsworth after six hours of practice with missing flap tracks or spoilers or other wing damage, meaning that the crews would have to wait at Ellsworth until the parts arrived from a B-52 base. So the problem for Wurtsmith was not only its location far away from the practice bombing ranges, but also the fact that its bombers were simply too old to get there and back in one piece.

On April 13, 1991, as crowds of townspeople joined with families to welcome back the crews from the 379th Bomb Wing who had fought in Operation Desert Storm (dropping 20 percent of all allied bombs over the Kuwaiti theater), the news broke that Wurtsmith would close and the 379th would be disbanded. The impact on the local community would be swift and painful. Wurtsmith was one of the larger employers in the northeast part of Michigan, with a work force of 700 civilians and a value of $145 million per year to the local economy. Given that the area's unemployment rate in 1991 was more than 11 percent, Wurtsmith's loss would be severe.[34]

The Air Force calculations for Wurtsmith's closure were highly favorable. Initial figures gave a closing cost of $29.1 million and the estimated annual savings of $63.3 million.[35] The service noted that Wurtsmith was the third cheapest to close in the Air Force and gave back the highest closure savings of any Air Force base on the 1991 list. That was, in part, because, like many SAC bases, the facility had only one mission—supporting the strategic bombers. There were no minor missions there, as was often the case for Air Force bases belonging to other commands.

Wurtsmith's local defenders argued the case against the Air Force. They pleaded that closing Wurtsmith would have a severe impact on the economy of northern Michigan. They probably weakened their case when they urged that K.I. Sawyer AFB on Michigan's Lake Superior coast be closed instead. They kind of had a point—K.I. Sawyer, also a B-52 base, while distant from training ranges, was closer to them than was Wurtsmith. But closing K.I. Sawyer would also hurt northern Michigan's economy, even if the primary pain would occur farther north. Ironically, K.I. Sawyer was not on the 1991 list, but it would not escape 1993, when, after an equally impassioned effort by its own defenders, BRAC closed it. The main gates shut permanently in September 1995.

If representation on an Armed Services Committee is an advantage for bases, then Wurtsmith should have been relatively safe from closure. One of Michigan's two senators (Democrat Carl Levin) and the two House members closest to Wurtsmith all had seats on their respective Armed Services Committee. But reaction to the news about Wurtsmith from members of Michigan's congressional delegation was mixed. Representative Bob Davis (R-MI), whose district contained Wurtsmith, said: "It's not over yet. Don't give up. We still have a shot at keeping it."[36] Davis was less specific about what chance Wurtsmith really had, but he could be gratified to learn at the same time that B-52s from Loring AFB in Maine and March AFB in California were scheduled for transfer to K.I. Sawyer AFB, also in Davis's district. Democrat Levin stated that he would investigate the reason given by the Air Force for closing the base—its distance from training ranges—and also he pleaded with BRAC commissioners to allow each impacted state to be heard ". . . if only for an hour." There was not much optimism in this first reaction to the announcement, and Levin probably knew that Wurtsmith had little to offer in its defense. Most likely relieved by the news that BRAC had spared the Army Tank-Automotive Command in Warren, Michigan, with 5,000 jobs, from closure after the Army put it on its submission list, Levin probably realized that he had been fortunate to only lose Wurtsmith and its 700 civilian jobs.[37]

Environmental Problems at Wurtsmith

Like most SAC bases, Wurtsmith had a pollution problem. Over the years, fuel spills (some of them from dumping and igniting fuel for fire drills, some from a 1986 tanker crash) had caused the accumulation of toxic material in nearby groundwater. Workers had poured degreasing agents to clean jet engines down waste drains. These chemicals contained trichloroethylene (TCE), a suspected cancer-causing agent, and, over time, they reached groundwater levels. As a result, two plumes of contaminated underground water had moved away from the base into a nearby lake and the wells of at least four homes close to Wurtsmith.[38] The Michigan Department of Natural Resources estimated that the cost of cleaning up the waste would be close to $10 million, and it wanted the Air Force to accomplish it before Wurtsmith closed.[39] What was curious about the announcement of Wurtsmith's pollution problems it that is was made by the state attorney general just weeks before the announcement of the 1991 BRAC list. Whether or not the announcement of Wurtsmith's toxic problems was intended to influence the final decision on the Air Force's choice to recommend the base for closure is impossible to prove. But the timing was at least interesting. The pollution situation at Wurtsmith had been public for some time, and the Air Force had initiated efforts to remedy the situation. Following unsubstantiated reports of an increase in birth deformities at the base hospital and of TCE in local meat and fish, workers attempted to extract the TCE from the soil. The task would end up costing $44,000 for each ounce of TCE and, in the end, was not successful. Once workers cleaned a parcel of land, the chemical simply migrated back to it from adjacent contaminated areas. So Wurtsmith's pollution problems would delay closure of the base and its ultimate potential for transfer to an alternative use. That delay became significant when the township of Oscoda wanted to receive a parcel of base housing with 96 of the most highly valued houses. The problem was that a plume of TCE ran under the property. In response, the Air Force more carefully defined the boundaries of the plume, and the state of Michigan raised its maximum contaminant level from 2.2 parts per billion to 5, allowing the transfer to take place.[40]

Wurtsmith After Closure

Michigan's two senators were unsuccessful in challenging the decision to close Wurtsmith, but there were still political ramifications that they apparently felt the need to address. In September 1993, two years after the closure decision, Senator Donald Riegle, Jr., (D-MI) introduced an amendment to the Senate requiring the Defense Department to justify selection for closure of any base it had previously listed for closure if that base was rejected by BRAC. While such an action could not save Wurtsmith, it did place Riegle in a position to be seen as a protector of bases (and especially Michigan bases) for the next round.[41] Senator Levin appeared to be more responsive to Wurtsmith itself by introducing legislation to make surplus military equipment available to communities suffering economic hardship because of a base closure.[42] The hope was that this equipment would be useful in assisting community redevelopment, but there was also the prospect of getting surplus equipment from Wurtsmith (such as fire engines, office equipment, and so on) distributed free to Oscoda and the other small towns in the area that clearly would suffer when Wurtsmith closed for good.

Michigan's governor, John Engler, created a base-conversion authority in 1991 to assist in economic development of Wurtsmith. Three years later, he dissolved the group, claiming some limited success: a new public airport, 250 jobs created, and "the largest-ever defense conversion grant in order to develop a regional water supply system to support future expansion of reuse of the base. . . ."[43] According to other calculations, 425 new jobs came from aviation, educational, and industrial activities located on former base property.[44] The new tenants included Alpena Community College, American International Airways, Oscoda Plastics, Classic Container, Earth Tech, and a number of local agencies, including the Huron Shores Educational Consortium, the Office for Economic Development, and the U.S. Forest Service. The town of Oscoda took possession of the base properties, and the Air Force agreed to provide water and sewer service payments until September 30, 1998.[45] The community also gained the base theater for the Shoreline Community Players under the agreement.

Indicative of Wurtsmith's state of redevelopment was the fact that, of the 4,626 base acres, 2,801 remained available by 1996, five years after the closure announcement. In response, the Iosco Country Board of Commissioners voted to apply for designation as a "renaissance zone" under Michigan law, which would allow businesses locating at Wurtsmith to gain tax exemptions for up to 15 years.[46]

The rolling roar of B-52s straining for altitude over Lake Huron stopped for good on June 1, 1993, when Wurtsmith padlocked its gates. Not only did the base close, but its bombers went to the desert storage facility at Davis-Monthan AFB in Tucson, Arizona, ultimately to be chopped into small pieces as a part of the START (Strategic Arms Reduction Talks) agreement that scrapped a large quantity of nuclear weapons and their delivery systems. The tanker aircraft were transferred to the Air Force Reserves, and the historic 379th Bombardment Wing that dated back to World War II's Kimbolton Field in Great Britain was deactivated. But by then the Cold War was over, and few seemed to notice—except for those living in the small towns outside the main gates whose lives would be changed for a long time to come.

CARSWELL AIR FORCE BASE, TEXAS

Posters printed to celebrate Carswell Air Force Base showed giant B-52 bombers flying out of the base and over the city of Fort Worth, its proximate neighbor. These illustrations may have inadvertently displayed one of Carswell's problems—the flight paths of the base's bombers and tankers reportedly took them too close to the civilian airliners using the Dallas-Forth Worth Airport. But the possibility of midair accidents was just one problem that put Carswell on the 1991 list of base closures.

Carswell had been a fixture outside of Fort Worth for years. First named Tarant Field in March 1942, Carswell (named after a World War II Medal of Honor winner) became Fort Worth Army Airfield a few months later and took its final name in 1948.[47] In the early 1950s, it was home to a wing of B-36 Peacemakers, the world's largest bomber (one of which remains in the lake off the end of Carswell's runway). It had long been the home of the Seventh Bombardment Wing, and the Fort Worth community had long since become used to the sound of bombers on takeoff and landing.

Carswell provided thousands of jobs for the Dallas-Fort Worth community, a military hospital for its military retirees, and military personnel who spent their money in the community. Carswell's military personnel were also attracted to the area by the kind of nightlife provided by places such as Billy Bob's Texas, a legendary watering hole favored by B-52 crews. Billed as the world's largest honky-tonk, Billy Bob's was packed on Friday and Saturday nights, an indicator of the contribution made to the Fort Worth community by Carswell.

Carswell was vulnerable to closure, though. Its location in the southern part of the United States meant that its B-52s would have farther to fly in the event of a war with the USSR. In 1991, even that possibility was growing increasingly remote, though, as the Soviet

Union and its European empire disintegrated. The primary reason for Carswell's existence was the strategic bombing mission aimed against the Soviet Union, but by 1991 the end of the Cold War made that mission increasingly unnecessary. That was perhaps best symbolized when B-52s (from Barksdale AFB in Louisiana) flew a goodwill mission to a former Soviet bomber base that was once on their nuclear target list, while a counterpart Soviet Bear bomber visited Barksdale. The number of bomber bases was clearly excessive. The BRAC final report for 1991 cited the high density of air traffic in the Dallas-Fort Worth area, claiming that it was the worst in the country.[48] The poor quality of Carswell's base housing was also a factor in the decision to close. The housing had been under renovation, but the contractor had defaulted, and the Air Force had little hope that the project would restart anytime soon.[49]

Carswell's liability to closure may have come from another quarter, though—politics. For decades, Representative Jim Wright, the powerful Democratic Speaker of the House, represented the district containing the base. Wright protected the base during his tenure in office, but when the Speaker was ousted in a political scandal, Democrat Peter Geren won Wright's seat. There was speculation around Fort Worth that Wright's resignation would hurt Carswell and that bases represented by senior members of Congress would fare better than Carswell would with its freshman legislator. One unnamed commentator stated that Fairchild AFB in Washington state—"a mirror image of Carswell"—would not be closed because of the influence of House Speaker Thomas Foley (D-WA).[50] While such a claim is impossible to prove, it probably contributed to the sense in the community that politics dominated the base-closure process and was, therefore, unfair to Carswell.

Closing Carswell: The Politics Start

Whatever the reasons for closing Carswell, the decision brought with it a number of associated problems. One was the loss of Carswell's hospital, which served not only the approximately 7,200 active-duty personnel at the base but also the large (numbering more than 100,000) community of military retirees in the Fort Worth area. In fact, 21 percent of Texas's 147,000 retired military families chose to live in Fort Worth, partly to be close to Carswell.[51] Military retirees are represented by such powerful lobby groups as the American Legion, the Veterans of Foreign Wars, and the Retired Officer Association, giving them considerable political clout. So it did not take long for a political challenge to BRAC's decision on Carswell. It came initially from Representative Geren in a letter to the GAO complaining that the Air Force had been unresponsive to his counterarguments about the value of Carswell, including the economic impact on Tarant County, "Carswell's role in regional air space coordination efforts," and a memorandum "outlining DOD and Air Force willful NON ADHERENCE [sic] to the intent and spirit of the law when conducting their internal base closure and realignment review."[52]

Shortly after the 1991 BRAC list became public, Geren met privately with Air Force officials connected with the Carswell decision, including Gen. James Boatright, who had served as deputy assistant Air Force secretary for installations. From that meeting, Geren concluded that the Air Force had placed little importance on four of the eight evaluation categories. Among those criteria, according to Geren, was the base's potential for new military use, which Geren had argued was "excellent," citing "new-wave fighter jets, AWACS (Airborne Warning and Control System), KC-135s, and C-17 transport planes."[53]

Geren's argument had its flaws, though. There were ample bases already existing for the aircraft he named, and it was unlikely that any of the planes would have been transferred to Carswell, given the air-congestion problems around it. That might have precluded expansion of the Dallas-Fort Worth International Airport and raised safety questions in the flying public's mind.

Representative Geren faced other obstacles as well. Normally, a member of Congress can count on fellow representatives from the state to assist in fighting base closures. But one neighboring member had to duck the fight to save Carswell. Representative Dick Armey (R-TX) was a sponsor of the original BRAC legislation that had closed 86 bases since its passage. Armey realized that there were probably some members who were waiting for a chance to get back at Armey by closing a base in his own state. As him put it, "I'm the one guy who is capable of hanging a bull's eye on Carswell. . . . There are times when discretion is the better part of valor."[54]

The Economic Impact of Closing Carswell

Initial reports implied that Carswell's closing would cost 880 civilian jobs, coupled with the loss of 4,600 military personnel and their paychecks.[55] The indirect impact estimates were the loss of 12,000 jobs in the community, costing $212 million annually.[56] The president of the Fort Worth Chamber of Commerce, Terry Ryan, questioned the accuracy of the figures, calling them "exaggerated."[57] Still, the economic impact on the Dallas-Fort Worth area was serious, particularly when coupled with the decline in defense-industry employment at such military stalwarts as General Dynamics and Bell-Textron. The political consequences of such unemployment gave emphasis to alternative plans for Carswell. However, initial conversion efforts mapped out by the James Toal Company indicated that the options were limited at best. Aviation development was the best option to avoid competition with other area industrial parks, but reuse related to aviation would compete with expansion plans for the Dallas-Fort Worth International Airport.[58] Other options involved aircraft maintenance, pilot training, or aircraft manufacturing,[59] but the air-traffic-congestion problems that helped close Carswell in the first place would surely rise to challenge any new aviation-related base-conversion efforts. So the political incentive grew to keep a portion of Carswell open and operated by the military. That would make correction of the base's severe environmental problems easier since there would not be private interests waiting to receive clean base property.

Environmental Problems

Environmental problems cropped up at Carswell as they did at almost all bases scheduled for closure. One problem in particular was an underground aquifer contaminated with a plume of polychlorinated biphenals (PCBs). PCBs are difficult to remove in any circumstances, but these were located under the main runway, which posed an even more intractable problem. The Air Force had promised to keep the main runway open for the General Dynamics plant on the other side of the base. General Dynamics was building F-16 fighters there and needed an open runway to test the new fighters and ultimately to deliver them to their customers. To remove the PCBs, the runway would have to be dug up to get access to the soil and water aquifer below, a process that could have consumed years of time. There was also the question of who should pay to treat the plume, since it appeared to flow from the General Dynamics plant. The Air Force and General Dynamics blamed each other, and, in the end, the plume remained.

There were other environmental problems at Carswell. Landfills, underground storage tanks, TCE, and petroleum deposits littered the base. A strange reference to "low-level radioactive material from buried munitions" also appeared in a report.[60] Progress on all of the problems was slow. Despite the base-closure decision in 1991, by 1995 only surveys of some of the damage had been completed, and of Carswell's 3,196 acres, none had been certified as clean.[61] The U.S. Geological Survey initiated a project to determine pollution-migration patterns, to include wells at Lake Worth.

Carswell After "Closure"

Air Force estimates for Carswell's closure costs came to $45.6 million, with the payback at one year, after which the estimated annual savings of $45.5 million would begin to accrue. The total savings of $156 million were not close to Wurtsmith's, but they were still appealing.[62] The 1991 BRAC would review the Air Force's recommendation for Carswell with favor and voted it closed. That was not the end of Carswell, though—and it would not be the last time that Carswell would show up on a BRAC list, either.

The 1993 BRAC revisited the base, but this time the actions resembled Santa more than Scrooge. Commissioners voted to close the Dallas NAS and to send its aircraft to Carswell. The same fate befell the Navy and Marine Corps Reserve centers in Dallas. The Reserve aircraft relocated to Carswell under the somewhat strange argument that ". . . it would alleviate current air . . . encroachment restrictions."[63] But what had been one of the main arguments in support of closing Carswell? Air encroachment on the heavily traveled takeoff and landing patterns at Dallas-Fort Worth Airport—an argument dismissed by one knowledgeable observer as a "flagrant lie."[64] The 1993 BRAC report went on to note that ". . . the Federal Aviation Administration [FAA] supported the proposed relocation to Carswell AFB because it was compatible with the existing and future Dallas-Fort Worth Metropolitan Air Traffic System Plan."[65] But the most curious outcome of these transfers was that, by 1995, the allegedly crowded skies in and out of Carswell AFB would have more military airplanes flying through them than existed at the base when it was "closed" in 1991. At the height of its operation as a SAC base, Carswell had 27 B-52s, 27 KC-135 tankers, 24 F-4 fighters, and a handful of T-37 trainers—around 70 aircraft in all. By the late 1990s, there will be more than 100 aircraft at the base, including F-16 Air Force Reserve fighters and F/A-18 Navy combat aircraft in the Naval Reserve wing. Carswell also got some support groups as a consequence of other base closures. When Bergstrom AFB in Texas closed its gates in September 1996, the 610th Regional Support Group, the 610th Service Flight, the 810th Civil Engineer Flight, and the 610th Security Police Squadron all moved to Carswell, which at that date bore the official title of Naval Air Station Fort Worth Joint Reserve Base, Texas.[66]

When the Seventh Bomb Wing was the major base tenant, there were 6,000 active-duty military personnel stationed there. Plans call for 4,000 full-time Reservists and an additional 7,650 part-time Reservists to be stationed at the base, giving it a whopping 11,650 military personnel in all. Then there is the prison staff. After its closure, the base hospital was designated as a federal medical center (FMC), which houses 1,100 women from federal prisons who are sent to the FMC for medical treatment. The hospital's conversion caused considerable consternation among Fort Worth's military retirees, but retirees do not have a direct entitlement to military medical facilities and can use them only on a space available basis. They were appeased, though, by the fact that the base exchange, the commissary, and the golf course remained open and accessible to them. They owed that privilege to Representative Geren, who successfully drafted legislation to keep these facilities available to retirees. They might have rewarded him with reelection in November 1996, except that in late 1995 Geren announced that a desire to spend more time with his family had lead him not to seek another term. It was an interesting outcome, since Geren had probably done more than any other representative to keep his base going long after it had been "closed."

The economic impact of Carswell's "closure" was temporary—there was some unemployment and local business closures immediately after the Seventh Bomb Wing departed. In 1997, there were a few shuttered businesses near the base, but there also were signs of economic growth as well. The crowds at Billy Bob's Texas may not have been quite as large as before, but business was still good. However, the economic impact of drawdowns at Fort Worth defense plants was substantially higher than the temporary drop in Carswell employment. Employment at the General Dynamics F-16 plant declined from 27,000 to 13,000 in five years and, in early 1996, was running at around 30 percent capacity. Only 4-6 F-16s came out the front door, compared to 25-30 in the Reagan defense buildup of the 1980s. The Bell-Textron helicopter plant was just beginning low-rate production of the Marine Corps "Osprey" aircraft in that same year, with full production at least three years away.

Despite the obvious success at relocating groups to preserve Carswell, there is still much unused property. Thousands of base housing units sit empty and deteriorating. The vast concrete facility where bombers once sat on 15-minute alert armed with nuclear weapons is now vacant, and the alert shed where crews waited for the emergency klaxon to sound also sits abandoned. Even the concertina wire around the facility remains, but it guards only the earth mounds that cover the now empty nuclear-weapons-storage area. In the late 1990s, these facilities were only reminders of why Carswell's bomb mission disappeared, probably forever.[67] But the activity surrounding them was a testament to the political skills of those who, in the end, "saved" Carswell.

LORING AIR FORCE BASE, MAINE

When the news broke around Limestone, Maine, that Loring AFB was scheduled for closure by the 1991 BRAC, there was shock and anger in the local community, especially since Loring's B-52 bombers and KC-135 tankers had just finished participating in the Gulf War. In rural northern Maine, where Loring was one of the largest employers in the region, the announcement seemed particularly unjust after the flush of victory in which Loring's crews had been a part. In fact, members of Maine's congressional delegation quickly announced that they would use the 42nd Bomb Wing's participation in Desert Storm as a reason for keeping the base open. But, while that war was over, Loring's had just begun. In the end, the Desert Storm argument did not help Loring anymore than it did Wurtsmith; Loring could not overcome problems that were largely a function of its mission and its location.

Many SAC bases were located in the cold northern parts of the United States, but none was as remote and as cold as Loring. Located near Limestone, Maine, in the upper eastern corner of the state, Loring was a true Cold War base. It first opened in August 1953 as home to a B-36 wing, and the unique droning noise of the ten-engined monster planes became familiar over the northern Maine countryside. In 1956, the then-obsolete and expensive B-36s were replaced with B-52s and KC-97s; while KC-135s later succeeded the KC-97 tankers, the B-52 remained the mainstay bomber at Loring until it closed.

Loring AFB may have been 300 miles closer to the USSR than any other U.S. base, but with B-52s that advantage was becoming irrelevant. The B-52 could fly to the USSR and back from Louisiana or Arkansas with its long range, and the cost of keeping Loring open began to exceed its value to the Air Force. Loring was frigid in winter, and its runways required constant sweeping due to the average yearly accumulation of 105 inches of snow. Winter weather made aircraft operations hazardous and aircraft security improbable. In the event of an imminent nuclear attack on the base, bombers would have had to take off in the space of 15 minutes. If such an attack had occurred during a blinding blizzard or right after a snowstorm had deposited wingtip-level snow, a rapid takeoff and escape would have been practically impossible.

More ordinary problems came from Loring's weather, though. Heating bills were high, as were associated maintenance costs. So were morale costs—for Air Force personnel not used to long cold winters, Loring was simply "boring Loring." Snow buried buildings, and personnel required great effort getting from one place to another trudging through waist-deep snow. The only relief was Maine's short summer, remembered mostly by Loring veterans for the clouds of biting black flies and mud from the thawing snow.

Air Force efforts to close Loring actually began in 1977. Pilots with orders to Loring were told with certainty that their stay would be a short one, because Loring would close in the next year. Community members started a Save Loring Committee, and preparations for the fight began. But a fortuitous event would save Loring that year. President Jimmy Carter found himself in trouble seeking votes in the Senate to ratify his Panama Canal Treaty. Many Democrats, including Maine's Edmund Muskie, were wavering on the treaty, and Carter knew he needed Muskie's vote. So in a political swap, Carter rescinded the decision to close Loring, and Muskie voted in favor of the treaty. But, in truth, Loring's struggle had just begun. The Air Force again considered closing Loring in 1988, but again it ran into a significant political obstacle. Senator William Cohen (R-ME) Muskie, and Representative Thomas J. "Tip" O'Neill, Jr. (D-MA) combined to keep Loring open. When a base appears on previous closure lists, though, it is almost sure to appear on subsequent ones, and the "living dangerously" rule for threatened bases applied again in 1991. Having been spared from closure in 1988, Loring was sure to be examined closely by the new BRAC. The Cold War had faded considerably since 1988, and the need for Loring's B-52s was even more questionable. The base had ended its primary Cold War mission of nuclear response in 1985, and the B-52s there carried only conventional weapons. There were too many B-52 bases, and Loring was vulnerable. Still, the installation most vulnerable to closure was the Naval Station at Brunswick, Maine, in part because it had appeared on Defense Secretary Cheney's original list of closures. It was also felt that the economic impact of Brunswick's closing would be less painful in populous southern

Maine than Loring's closing would be in its rural north location.[68] Brunswick, though, never made the final closure list submitted to BRAC since the Navy made a strong argument to keep it because of the value of the anti-submarine patrols flown from the base over the North Atlantic.

The decision to keep Brunswick open was troubling for the future of Loring, since at least one base in Maine was expected to make the 1991 closure list due simply to the high cost of maintaining military facilities in Maine's extreme winters. But the citizens of the local towns around Loring had even more to worry about when they discovered that retired Air Force Gen. Duane H. Cassidy, the former SAC chief, was on the 1991 BRAC.

Given his former position at SAC, Gen. Cassidy was quite familiar with what he regarded initially as a strength at Loring: rapid-refueling capacity. Loring began to construct such a system, which should have given it an advantage over Plattsburgh AFB in New York, which did not. But Gen. Cassidy changed the priority from rapid-refueling capacity to "quality of life." He argued that upstate New York had a better living situation for Air Force personnel than did Loring.[69] Cassidy worried that the long winters and lack of cultural amenities might impact morale so much as to reduce re-enlistment rates. Why Cassidy changed his priority was never made clear. But his position was apparently persuasive—the Commission voted 5-2 to close Loring.

The Political Reaction to Closure

The political fallout from the announcement of Loring's closure was both quick and turgid. Some citizens chose to believe that the decision was politically motivated by the failure of Maine's congressional delegation to support the B-2, or as a way to get rid of the B-52 to make room in the Air Force inventory for the B-2.[70] Senators George Mitchell (D-ME) and Cohen sent a letter dated July 22, 1991, to Senator Sam Nunn (D-GA), Chairman of the Senate Armed Services Committee, detailing their objections to the methodologies used by both the Air Force and BRAC to select Loring. The letter bluntly stated that the Air Force had treated the Maine congressional delegation unfairly, offering the following as examples:

• The lack of cooperation from the Air Force in providing timely response to the Maine Congressional Delegation's requests for information and documents;

- The imposition of a "gag rule" preventing delegation members from obtaining unclassified information directly from Loring officials;
- Significant inconsistencies and inaccuracies in the Air Force data which consistently worked against Loring AFB while favoring other bases;
- The introduction of highly subjective considerations as "tie breakers" that the Air Force claimed were excluded from its review; and
- Reliance on active duty Air Force officers to act impartially as members of the commission staff.[71]

The letter elaborated on these charges, noting, for example, that Senator Cohen had requested information from the secretary of the Air Force communicated between SAC headquarters and Loring about the cost of upgrading Loring's conditions to SAC Code 1. Cohen wanted to know why Loring's estimate came in at $26 million while SAC costed out the same improvements at more than $111 million. According to Cohen, the Air Force responded to the request by providing only the SAC estimate, causing the Senator to charge "stonewalling." He then sought the same information through the Federal District Court using the Freedom of Information Act, but was still unsuccessful in gaining the Loring estimates. Members of the Maine congressional delegation then asked Commissioner William L. Ball to request a copy of the Loring upgrade estimates when they traveled to the base. The base commander did give Ball the cost information, and Ball passed it on to Senator Cohen's office. However, following that, according to Cohen, the Air Force ordered Loring AFB officials not to provide any more information, instructing them to advise anyone wanting such information to get it directly from Air Force headquarters. Cohen charged that accurate information about Loring was difficult to obtain without on-site visits, causing heavy reliance on what he said was misleading Air Force-provided data about the base that the commission staff had used to prepare its reports. For example, Cohen noted that, when three BRAC commissioners visited Loring in June 1991, the base engineer told them that figures supplied by Air Force headquarters of $34 million to upgrade Loring's roads were "absurd" and that his estimated cost was only $1 million. The Air Force, again according to Cohen, stated that, while Loring's roads were in disrepair, roads at other SAC bases (including Minot, Grand Forks, and K.I. Sawyer) needed no upgrading. Other cost discrepancies included hospital upgrades—Cohen charged that the costs to upgrade hospitals at six other SAC bases were dramatically understated (at Barksdale AFB, for example, from $14.7 million to $15 million) in order to preserve these bases while making Loring more vulnerable to closure.

Cohen seemed most disturbed, though, by the issue that had so aroused the ire of the local townspeople; the "quality of life" problem. Cohen charged in his co-signed letter that Commissioner Cassidy had stated ". . . I looked at everything . . . and I couldn't find anything but quality of life . . . as a discriminator (between Loring AFB and Plattsburgh AFB). This was patently unfair, wrote Cohen, since Air Force Gen. Eugene Habinger (co-chair of the Air Force Base Closure Executive Group) had stated in a letter of June 17, 1991, that "The quality of life issue was discussed with GAO. However, it was made clear that it was neither part of the Air Force criteria or process nor of any influence in the original process." [72]

The governor of Maine, John McKernan, Jr., echoed Senator Cohen's concerns, noting in a presentation at Loring: "We do not feel frankly . . . that we received a fair shake. We don't think that the criteria were followed as envisioned."[73] There was no evidence provided at this appearance to bolster the governor's statement.

The entire Maine delegation raised additional issues in a letter to the Comptroller General of the United States. In it, they charged that ". . . the Air Force did not actually weigh the economic impact of closing Loring in reaching its decision" and that, while the Air Force stated that Loring's facilities were "well below average" compared to other Air Force bases, the service discounted the value of more than $300 million in new military construction over the decade."[74] They noted, in particular, that Loring had a new hospital and "significant upgrades" to other facilities.[75]

The commission's final report did not even mention the "quality of life" issue. Instead, it focused on the usual estimates of closure cost and savings. The estimated cost was $46.6 million, and the payback period would start one year after closure. The annual savings of $61.8 million would quickly balance out the closure costs, at least according to the estimates.

After the final decision to close Loring, the economic impact on nearby communities was quick; according to the local newspaper: "Home values have plummeted. Business has declined at some stores because residents, worried about the future, are buying only essentials. Families are beginning to leave for new jobs."[76] In 1991 the base spent $71 million on payroll, equipment, construction and other activities that employed local workers. That flow stopped immediately after the base's gates closed. The community lost more jobs than just those at the base, though. The so-called multiplier effect (secondary jobs supported by Loring's workers) was $132.9 million, with some 761 of these secondary jobs created in all the places where Loring's civilian workers and military personnel spent their salaries.

Searching for Employment Alternatives

While the scramble to keep Loring open continued, alternative scenarios began to develop as it began to appear that Loring's fate was sealed. It became clear that if nothing was found to replace the Air Force at the Loring site, the local communities faced economic disaster. However, it was not easy to plan for a replacement. Caribou and Limestone were rural communities and offered little support to an industrial operation of any size. Northern Maine was primarily agricultural country, sparsely populated, and with little by way of infrastructure. There were not enough people living in the Loring area to staff anything but a small factory, and the chances of importing additional workers by a larger facility were usually dashed by the time the first signs of winter arrived, sometimes in August. The very problems that General Cassidy had noted at Loring could at least be overcome by the Air Force to a degree—personnel were simply ordered there. But alternate enterprises could hardly do the same for additional workers. So some other activity had to be considered if Loring were to have any chance of offering an alternative to the Air Force.

Senators Cohen and Mitchell began to consider a research facility instead. By October, they had inserted language into a Veterans Affairs appropriations bill directing the National Aeronautics and Space Administration (NASA) to prepare a study of the feasibility of a permanent research base at the Loring facility. Why NASA? In part because NASA had conducted research into ozone depletion from Loring in 1991, and these activities gave both Maine senators hope that such research could become permanent.[77] It was unclear how such research activity could replace even a fraction of the Air Force jobs at Loring, but at least it was a start. Mitchell and Cohen did not stop at NASA, though. They also proposed that the Department of Agriculture establish a national laboratory for the study of cold-climate growth and biotechnology at the Loring site, inserting a provision in an Agriculture Department supplemental appropriation directing the Agriculture Department to study such a possibility.[78] Senator Mitchell did address the research possibility earlier in September of that year when he complained that Maine was one of only four states that did not have a federal research and development laboratory. Noting that Maine used more firewood for energy than any other state, the senator said that this fact made Maine an ideal spot to study research on this alternate energy source.[79] Senator Mitchell also expressed the hope that northern Maine could be the location of research on the cleanup of hazardous waste—there would presumably be plenty at the Loring site. He suggested that the Environmental Protection Agency might "explore the possibility for developing cleanup training and research as part of a Federal facility in Maine."[80] Senator Cohen did not have to hope that the EPA "might explore"; he had directed it to do so, by inserting such instructions into another supplemental appropriations bill (this one for the Veterans Administration and the Department of Housing and Urban Development).[81] Leaving no stone unturned, the same two Senators had also directed the secretary of energy to investigate the possibility of establishing research on alternative energy sources (presumably including firewood) at Loring.[82]

Senator Mitchell, for his part, turned to the Department of Defense with a somewhat unusual request; might Loring become the site of a ballistic missile defense system? His inquiry, directed to the Strategic Defense Initiative Organization (SDIO) generated a relatively noncommittal answer from Henry Cooper, then director of SDIO. Cooper noted that, while the Missile Defense Act of 1991 did not specifically designate a site for ballistic-missile-defense experiments, SDIO was considering only one site, at Grand Forks AFB in North Dakota (site of a previous missile-defense system), for such research.[83] Cooper's letter noted also that the site, when built, would generate only 250-300 jobs.[84] Of course, a few jobs would be better than none, and Senator Mitchell could take credit for trying, even though he turned to an organization whose programs he had soundly criticized when President Reagan launched them in 1983.

In the meantime, others were considering private-sector alternatives. The Air Force Base Disposal Agency (AFBDA) was receiving (presumably) unsolicited letters from industrial interests inquiring about the availability of surplus Air Force property where they might locate their facilities. One such inquiry came from Hamid Butt, president of A & P Aviation, which sought hanger space to accommodate 747-type aircraft for A & P's maintenance operations (which, the letter specified, would be "preferably in an economically depressed area").[85] Colonel David Cannan of the AFBDA replied in a letter to Butt that, if the Air Force did have such facilities available, it would have to "advertise in the open market under rules of full and open competition."[86] However, Colonel Cannan noted, ". . . it is Air Force policy to assist local communities impacted by the current and pending base closures by considering applications for interim use of facilities as a means of creating replacement jobs prior to the transfer and disposal of closing base property."[87] He suggested that Butt contact the Loring Readjustment Committee (LRC) in Caribou, Maine, which, he wrote, "was interested in pursuing such an arrangement at Loring Air Force Base."[88] The Loring Readjustment Committee was, in fact, created for such a purpose and did pursue the opportunity offered by A & P. Unfortunately for the LRC, talks hit an impasse over financing, insurance, and a variety of other factors, including some scarcely veiled charges of bad faith on both sides.[89]

Environmental Problems at Loring

The environmental problems noted in earlier chapters also surfaced at Loring. There were 27 sites at Loring proper that required cleanup, with additional problems at some of the satellite facilities supporting Loring, such as the Dow Pines recreational site near the town of Great Pond. Some of the problems were easy to locate because there were records of storage or dumping sites. For example, some of Loring's hazardous waste had been stored in tanks, including 25,000-gallon tanks filled with a pickling solution containing hexavalent chromium (a suspected carcinogen), and these tanks were marked on maps. But other waste sites, such as dumping sites for jet fuel, were more difficult to discover. When a KC-135 tanker aircraft was overweight before takeoff, the pilot would swing the plane over to the side of the runway and dump fuel from the refueling boom under the tail. However, the procedure violated Air Force safety rules, so it was never acknowledged publicly.[90] Over the years, the highly flammable and toxic jet fuel drained through the topsoil and ended up in local water tables. In other cases, sewage lines leaked underground for years before the problem was discovered, and sometimes it was not discovered until after the closure decision was made.

The impact of Loring's environmental situation jumped from local to national with the discovery of radiation emitting from a building sealed for decades. Twelve workers received doses of radiation when peering into the building, and suspicions immediately turned to stored nuclear weapons. EPA inspectors discovered alpha particles when they stuck Geiger counters through a small hole in the building. When the issue made National Public Radio, the building was finally opened, and nothing but an old shirt was found. The emissions turned out to be radon gas. But the wider importance of the incident was that it called even more national political attention to the variety of potential environmental hazards at bases.[91]

The environmental situation represented both an asset and a problem for those involved in Loring's closure. On the one hand, there was a considerable amount of waste to be cleaned up before Loring could be offered for alternative use, which threatened to both delay the closure and hike its cost.[92] On the other hand, there was $239 million worth of business for environmental contractors. The Maine congressional delegation made sure that Maine-based waste disposers would have a chance for a share in the cleanup funds by asking that at least half of the funds be spent only on small local firms.

Unfortunately for the Maine delegation (and Maine-based environmental firms) the efforts of Maine's political leaders differed from the policy of the Air Force Center for Environmental Excellence (AFCEE), which had taken over all environmental cleanup policy for bases on the BRAC list. That policy was to be enforced directly by the Small Business Administration (SBA), whose representative stressed in a letter to Sawyer Environmental that SBA wanted firms "that have the capability to do environmental work on a national level; being able to address clean-up work at *any* Air Force facility in U.S. territories."[93] Sawyer, a small firm located in Hermon, Maine, may have found little solace in the final line of that letter, which noted that, ". . . some firms may have come away from the conference disillusioned at the sincerity of SBA's efforts to actively promote your involvement in these contracts."[94]

The Air Force was working at cross-purposes with the Maine congressional delegation, which was understandably trying to eke out what little benefits might be associated with a base closure in their constituents' home. Members of the delegation tried both sides of the environmental issue when they realized that the environmental problems at Loring threatened to delay transfer of Loring assets. In October 1992, Senators Cohen and Mitchell were able to announce that Congress had passed a bill (that they had introduced) allowing uncontaminated portions of bases to be transferred before all base cleanup work had been completed.[95]

By 1996, $130 million in BRAC funds had been spent to clean up Loring, and 50 percent of the contaminated soil had been removed. The bad news was that, five years after the closure announcement, only half of Loring was certifiably clean.

Loring After Closure

Loring AFB became the Loring Commerce Centre after the Air Force moved out. With some assistance from Maine's congressional delegation, $300 million was invested in new construction to make the site attractive to commercial ventures. The Centre actively marketed Loring's buildings, noting that many of them were of recent construction (many built in 1986 during the Reagan defense buildup) and in excellent condition.[96]

Loring also benefited from a Defense Department decision to consolidate the Defense Finance and Accounting Service (DFAS), creating five regional offices and twenty branch offices. Loring won a DFAS center, opened July 28, 1995, in a ceremony attended by Defense Secretary William Perry. The DFAS center was opened on the site of Loring's former hospital, which itself had been constructed in 1988 at a cost of $25 million, was expected to employ 500 staff members when fully operational. But DFAS was not Loring's only government tenant. The Department of Labor chose Loring as the site of a new Job Corps Center to house 380 students and employ a staff of 130. A Maine-based firm got the contract to operate the center, for an initial award of $10 million.[97] In addition, the Department of Interior chose Loring to locate a new 4,900-acre National Wildlife Refugee that opened in early 1997.

Some commercial enterprises started up at Loring, including the Limestone Country Club (because Loring, like almost all Air Force bases, had a large golf course), the Evergreen Bowling Center (because Loring had a bowling alley for service personnel), the Malabeam Lake Recreation Area (because Loring, like many other bases, had a recreation area). Even the former ammunition bunkers were utilized, by Ward Farms, Incorporated, which used them to store flax, and plans existed to build a scutching mill to extract fibers from the flax to make linen. Another business, the Weecare Day Care Center opened in June 1996 (because Loring, like most other bases, had a day care center), as did McDonald Enterprises wood and specialty products company, which employed 10 workers.

While these alternatives were clearly better than nothing, they added up to only 505 total, more than 200 short of Loring's total when the base was open. What was more discouraging was that the DFAS, a government agency put there specifically to provide employment, accounted for 294 of those jobs. Loring's future after closure had much to do with a transfer of government functions, mostly at the federal level. There was very little success in attracting commercial ventures to Loring, which was hardly unexpected given the base's extreme location and harsh winter climate.

Judging the Politics of Closure

While politics could not save Loring AFB despite heroic efforts, members of the Maine congressional delegation did manage to ease somewhat the pain of closure. At one level, their actions appear to have been based on parochial politics. But, from another perspective, they were simply doing what they had been elected to do. They were trying to protect the substantial economic contribution that Loring AFB made to the economy of northern Maine, which, according to Senator Mitchell, constituted around 20 percent of the total economy of the region.[98] For Aroostook Country, again according to Senator Mitchell, that meant 8,500 jobs (presumably both direct and indirect employment), $152 million in annual income, and $4.6 million in local revenue.[99] Unlike Carswell, northern Maine had no other economic alternative such as industry or raw materials production, that could help replace the losses from Loring's closure. The Maine delegation did try what seemed to be desperate tactics, but, from their perspective, the situation itself was desperate. In the end, they did what their constituents elected them to do—protect local interests from Washington politics and from the "rational" base closure process that BRAC represented. For the politicians and citizens of northern Maine, BRAC did *not* serve their interests; it harmed them seriously. In that sense, the politics of commission interfered with the politics of locality. And in large measure, local politics lost to federal priorities. At the federal level, the BRAC report noted, in an unusual addition to a base closure decision, "The economic impact on the Loring AFB community will be severe."[100] Indeed it was.

SUMMARY

1991 was the first year of the revised base closure process, modified by Congress in 1990 to try to remove what politics remained after the 1988 and 1990 efforts. It appears that the modifications were only partly successful, though the evidence is mixed. Bases that ranked lower in military value were selected for closure over those ranked higher. For the Air Force, the largest number of bases were SAC bomber facilities (Eaker, Castle, Loring, Wurtsmith, and Carswell);

an acknowledgment that the Cold War was ending in 1991. The heavy bombers would no longer dominate the Air Force as they had for so many years. Training facilities were also cut, an indication of the smaller numbers of personnel the military would be needing to fill the ranks. The Air Force closed Williams, Lowry, and England AFBs—training bases all—while the Navy put its training center at Orlando, one of three in the country, on the 1991 list[101] Another, Myrtle Beach AFB in South Carolina, was the home to an A-10 aircraft wing—an aircraft type that transferred to the reserves and Air National Guard. Some might argue that the closure list reflected a shift in power from SAC to Tactical Air Command (TAC) that occurred between the 1950s-1970s and the 1980s-1990s. There were no fighter bases on the 1991 BRAC list. The Army put Fort Dix, Fort Benjamin Harrison, and Fort Chaffee on its closure list for the same reasons. They all had as their primary mission some kind of training.

Politics marked the 1991 BRAC process despite the efforts to "rationalize" base closure. There were clear winners and losers, and their battles complicated the 1995 process—particularly the case of New York versus New Jersey.[102] But there were other inequities. While California suffered the closure of seven installations, Texas had only one "closure" of Carswell AFB—which, in the end, would not happen. The state of Washington lost only one base (perhaps surprising since Washington had Fairchild AFB, the home of a B-52 wing, and the Naval Submarine Base in Bangor, the site of a Trident SSBN base). By 1991, both the B-52 and Trident were playing a less significant role because they had been dedicated to the Cold War mission of strategic nuclear deterrence. Georgia also did not suffer a single base closure, even though the King's Bay Naval Base was also a Trident base. Critics of BRAC did not miss the point that Representative Norm Dicks (D-WA), a senior member of the House Committee on Armed Services, and Senator Sam Nunn (D-GA), a senior member of the Senate Committee on Armed Services, represented Washington and Georgia's respective interests in Congress. Another inequity was the closing of a number of Navy aircraft repair depots, including those in Norfolk, Virginia, Pensacola, Florida, and Alameda, California, while leaving the five large Air Force depots intact.

The Air Force had the largest number of base closures in 1991, with 14. By contrast, the Army had the fewest closures, with eight bases making the final list. Among those included were Fort Benjamin Harrison in Indiana, Fort Devins in Massachusetts, and Fort Ord in California. Fort Benjamin Harrison was an initial-training entry base, but, with fewer soldiers entering the smaller Army of the

1990s, there was less need for such bases. Fort Devins was the home of the Tenth Special Forces Group—and Special Forces have never been at the heart of an Army that honors most the infantry and armor tasks. Fort Ord was the home of an infantry division, but it was a so-called "light division," the Seventh Infantry Division. Such divisions were created late in the Cold War period, and some in the Army saw them as products of the "defense reformers" who rose to prominence in the Carter Administration. The Seventh Division was, in the end, transferred to Fort Lewis in Washington, and Fort Ord closed. For the Army, it is noteworthy that none of the large infantry or armor bases were closed in 1991.

The Navy had a relatively balanced list of closures—one large ship-yard (Philadelphia), two Naval Air Stations (Moffett Field in Califor-nia and Chase Field in Texas), two Naval Stations (Long Beach and Philadelphia), and several smaller facilities. The Navy seemed best at generating a relatively equal list encompassing most of the service's primary functions, including sea and surface air. The submariners, though, did not suffer a single closure.

No one saved from a base closure in 1991 could breathe a sigh of relief. BRAC 1993 was already being planned as the 1991 list was published.

CHAPTER FOUR

1993

The mother of all base closure lists clobbers Charleston.
—*Senator Ernest Hollings (D-SC)*

S enator Hollings's horror upon discovering that South Carolina's
worst base closure nightmare had come true is indicative of how
most politicians respond to such news. He realized that both the city's
Naval Shipyard and Naval Station were on the 1993 BRAC closure
list.[1] He had a point; the combined naval facilities in Charleston accounted for 19,000 direct military and civilian jobs.[2] And while the
governor of Guam complained that the list did *not* include the Naval
Station there (he wanted the land for development), most political
figures whose bases were on the hit list complained vehemently and
pledged to fight back.[3] In other words, the 1993 BRAC final list
brought the usual response. *The Washington Post* speculated that parts
of Crystal City would become "a high-rise ghost town," noting that
the 1993 BRAC might eliminate more than 11,500 jobs in northern
Virginia.[4] Some politicians, such as Republican Senator Strom Thurmond (R-SC), charged that the new Clinton administration was playing partisan politics; "unreasonable, unjustified, and outrageous" was
his reaction to the list. However, Democrats also lost bases; Representative Ronald Dellums (D-CA), lost four bases in his district.[5] Said Democrat Representative Robert A. Borski (D-PA) about the cuts in
Philadelphia, "This is another devastating blow to our local economy
that will have a terrible impact on the lives of thousands of people."[6]
The impulse, particularly among Republican representatives with
bases picked for closure was to blame the Democratic Clinton administration. The initial Clinton submission to BRAC by Secretary of Defense Les Aspin included 31 bases for closure and another 134

proposed for realignment. In the end, though, BRAC added more bases and in its final report recommended to the president that 130 bases close and another 45 be realigned.

The expressions of outrage by politicians following the final announcement were by now a predictable part of the base closure political drama. Wounded representatives and local officials blamed the president. Republicans blamed Democrats, and Democrats blamed Republicans. Everyone political blamed the BRAC members. It was clearly BRAC season again.

THE POLITICS BEGIN

The 1993 BRAC process almost guaranteed controversy. For one thing, it would be the first BRAC held under a Democratic president, Bill Clinton. The previous BRAC rounds fell under Republican president Bush (technically Ronald Reagan was still president in the first BRAC round in 1988, but Bush would inherit the political pain it caused). Republicans recognized that a large number of military bases were built and preserved in districts represented by senior Democratic members of the House and Senate Armed Services Committees. While most of the Democratic old guard in Congress had died or retired by 1993, newer Democrats still represented many of their districts. Thus, Clinton would face the problem of signing off on the shutdown of military facilities located in the backyards of senators and representatives whose support he would come to dearly need.

Another source of controversy returned as the Chair for 1993 was former Republican representative James A. Courter. Courter's tenure on the 1993 BRAC would prove to be even more interesting than his 1991 stint, especially when it came to the age-old political rivalry between New York and New Jersey, and even after that fight was over, its reverberations continued two years later.

With the exception of Courter and one other member, the rest of the BRAC membership was new for 1993. Including Courter, the commissioners were:

1. Peter B. Bowman, vice president for quality assurance for the Gould Corporation, a diversified corporation located in Newburypoint, Massachusetts. Bowman was a retired Navy captain who had a background in submarines, and the retired commander of the Portsmouth, New Hampshire Naval Shipyard.

2. Beverly B. Bryon, a former Democratic member of the House of Representatives from the Sixth District of Maryland. She had served as chair of the Military Personnel and Compensation Subcommittee of the House Armed Services Committee and also had been a member of the House Special Panel on Arms Control and Disarmament.

3. Rebecca G. Cox, vice president for governmental affairs at Continental Airlines. Cox had also served as assistant to the president and director of the Office of Public Liaison for President Reagan. She had also been assistant secretary for governmental affairs in the Department of the Treasury.

4. Hansford T. Johnson, a retired four-star Air Force general who had served as Commander in Chief of the U.S. Transportation Command and of the Air Mobility Command.[7] At the time of his selection, General Johnson was chief of staff of the United Services Automobile Association.

5. Harry C. McPherson, Jr., a partner in the Washington, D.C. law firm of Verner, Liipfert, Berhard, McPherson, and Hand. He had previously been a deputy under secretary of the Army for international development and assistant secretary of state for educational and cultural affairs.

6. Robert D. Stuart, Jr., former U.S. Ambassador to Norway from 1984 to 1989, and retired president and chief executive officer for the Quaker Oats Company. When he was appointed to 1993 BRAC, Stuart was president of Conway Farms, a real-estate development firm. Stuart, along with Chairman Courter, had served on the 1991 BRAC.

The commission appeared to be nonpartisan and balanced in favor of expertise and representation. The two retired military officers lent the committee some expertise, though the Army was not represented. Some of the other commissioners had ties to either the Republican or Democratic parties. McPherson had been special counsel to President Lyndon B. Johnson, and Cox was married to Representative Christopher Cox (R-CA). In addition to her work on the Reagan staff, she had served on the staff of Senator Ted Stevens (R-AK). Bryon had served as a Democrat in Congress. Republican President Reagan had appointed Stuart ambassador to Norway.

Some commissioners came from states with bases vulnerable to closure. Courter was from New Jersey, which had several Army bases and McGuire AFB. Bowman was from Massachusetts, with Fort Devins, the only large Army installation in the Northeast. Byron came from Maryland, also a state rich in bases. Cox resided in southern California, particularly rich in Navy and Marine Corps bases.

Congress produced a few changes in the BRAC process that were attached to the Defense Department authorization bill for Fiscal Years 1992-1993. Those changes included a sort of back-door provision for the president to subvert the base closure process altogether by refusing to submit commissioner nominees by the specified date (January 25, 1993, and January 3, 1995, for the two remaining BRACs), although in 1995 it was Congress who was slow in submitting its own nominees to President Clinton. Congress tried to reduce the influence of the Defense Department by limiting the number of analysts that could join the commission staff from one-third to one-fifth. Congress also attempted to increase the independence of Defense Department staff assigned to the Commission by mandating that no member of the Department of Defense could write the evaluation reports for such personnel. That way, staff members who might submit negative information about a base belonging to their service could not be punished by a negative evaluation after they returned to their service duties. That was one step designed to increase the accuracy of service information to BRAC; another effort was new language mandating that senior Defense Department officials certify as true the information that they passed on to the commission. That requirement originated from the 1991 BRAC experience in which there were numerous accusations of bad or misleading information submitted by the armed forces. Finally, Congress demanded that environmental costs for closed bases be submitted for each fiscal year as a part of the annual defense budget request.

The new Clinton administration made a few changes to the BRAC process as well. Noting criticism about the slowness of previous base closures, Deputy Defense Secretary William Perry assured Congress that he intended to change the process. Perry noted that, in the past, base closure had been accomplished in three phases, starting with the military moving off the base. Then cleanup began, and only after cleanup was finished could the General Services Administration begin to dispose of the property. To speed the process, Perry announced that the new administration would integrate these activities under the undersecretary of defense for acquisition.[8] That position, created under the Bush administration, was the locus for defense acquisition reform. It was unclear, though, how coordinating base closure activities under one office might hasten the closure process.

Another political controversy for 1993 was the McKinney Act which mandated that base facilities be considered for homeless shelters. The

Clinton administration struggled with the provisions of the act, which seemed to remain in place partly out of respect for the late Representative Stuart McKinney (R-CT), who had died after passage of the bill named after him. The Defense Department, however, found itself in the unpopular position of having to defend the bills provisions against charges that it favored the homeless over job creation at base closure sites. The following exchange at a 1993 news conference held by DOD officials indicated the nature of the problem:

Q: But ultimately, the homeless, all things being equal, have priority over jobs.
A: They do have the legal priority.
Q: Over jobs?
A: Yes, they do. But we believe that given the size of these installations and the scale these sorts of requests usually are, that there's plenty of room for negotiation with local officials.
Q: Once we get the word out here, a lot of people are going to want to call and talk to somebody. Is there an 800 number available now, or someone people can talk to?
A: No, we don't have an 800 number yet. . . .[9]

The respondent then referred the questioner to the Commerce Department for further information, indicating that, bureaucratically, the Defense Department wanted to get as far away from the McKinney Act as possible. To have to defend the rights of the homeless (not exactly a popular constituency) against the availability of replacement jobs at closed bases was something no agency wanted to do.

BASES FOR 1993

With the publication of the final BRAC list for 1993, the service share of the pain clearly fell on the Navy. While the Army had only one major facility placed on the list (Fort McClellan, in Alabama, later removed and added to the 1995 list), Fort Monmouth, New Jersey, and Vint Hill Farms Station, Virginia, two smaller Army facilities, also made the 1993 list, and four Army depots were also realigned or closed.[10]

The Air Force had only four large facilities slated for closure, but the Navy placed twenty-three of its bases on the initial closure list. The Navy lost two major shipyards (Mare Island in California and Charleston in South Carolina) and four major air stations (Tustin Marine Corps Air Station [MCAS] in California and Naval Air Stations at Barbers Point in Hawaii, Cecil Field in Florida, Agana in Guam, and Alameda in California). Naval Stations in Charleston, South Carolina, and Treasure Island, California, also made the closure list. The famous old submarine base at New London, Connecticut, also was closed by the 1993 BRAC.

Two other Naval Stations making the 1993 list were Mobile, Alabama, and Staten Island, New York. Both were part of the "homeporting" schemes of the Reagan Administration. Then-Secretary of the Navy John Lehman assiduously courted local and national political figures in his effort to build support for a 600-ship navy. Neither facility had been completed when the closure decision was completed, making them easier to close, but there was considerable disappointment in both Mobile and on Staten Island. It also could hardly be missed that four of the Navy installations (eight total) slated for closure by the Navy were in or near the district of Representative Ronald Dellums.

A careful examination of the Air Force list of bases revealed that the Air Force placed only two large active bases on the list, K. I. Sawyer in Michigan and Griffiss AFB in New York, both SAC bases. Homestead AFB in Florida was on the list, but had been devastated by Hurricane Andrew the year before. The Air Force announced that the damage at the time was so severe that they wanted to shut down Homestead and move the fighter wing based there to Moody AFB in Georgia. Ironically, Homestead was later removed from the list, allegedly to reconstruct it for a jobs program. The other two facilities on the Air Force list were Newark AFB in Ohio, the site of the Aerospace Guidance and Metrology Center (AGMC), and a Reserve facility at O'Hare International Airport in Chicago. Newark AFB was particularly vulnerable to closure since its main function was to calibrate the guidance systems on ballistic missiles, and the U.S. ballistic missile force was being reduced because of the end of the Cold War. Newark AFB was a smaller facility, as Air Force bases go, although it was the largest employer in its county, with 1,679 jobs. In short, compared to its 11 bases listed on the 1991 BRAC report, the Air Force was clearly going to do better in 1993. However, as BRAC added bases to the service lists, Gentile Air Force Station in Ohio also got a closure notice even though the Air Force had not recommended its closure.

The Air Force's 1993 submission included New Jersey's McGuire AFB. A historic installation named after the second-ranking American fighter ace of World War II, McGuire had become an airlift base hosting a wing of C-141s. It was located in a remote part of New Jersey, and the nearest town, Wrightstown, was nothing more than a strip of bars and tattoo parlors. Air Force personnel stationed there ranked the quality of life low. The base facilities were deteriorating, and many stationed there preferred to commute rather than live on base. So the base was recommended for realignment, which would have brought about the same impact as outright closure. All of McGuire's active force would be transferred, leaving only a small Air National Guard and Reserve force behind. The cost of such realignment would have been 8,000 military and civilian jobs.[11]

Plattsburgh AFB, located in upstate New York near the Vermont border, was considered a good quality-of-life base. It also had ample runway for the B-52Gs and KC-135s stationed there as a part of SAC's nuclear deterrent force. The base had only one handicap for the Air Force—aircraft fuel had to be shipped in by truck or by barge up a nearby river. During the winter months, the river froze, and fuel was unavailable in wartime quantities.

When it came to choosing between McGuire and Plattsburgh, the Air Force chose McGuire. One plan was to move Plattsburgh's bombers and tankers to another SAC base and relocate McGuire's C-141 mission to Plattsburgh. But the Air Force had not counted on the stiff political rivalry between the New York and New Jersey congressional delegations. Representative James H. Saxon (R-NJ), who represented McGuire's district, fought hard to keep the base open and to close Plattsburgh instead. In the end, Saxon won, but there would be a bitter residue of the fight that would last into the 1995 BRAC, when New York's two senators delayed confirmation of BRAC nominees in retaliation for the 1993 loss of Plattsburgh. The impression remained that McGuire stayed open due, in part, to the influence of Chairman Courter.

The inevitable rivalry between bases intensified in 1993 over the shipyard issue. Next to perhaps Air Force depots, naval shipyards offer more civilian jobs than any other type of military installation, and when the Charleston Naval Shipyard made the 1993 list, the impact showed. Charleston Naval Shipyard provided 35,656 jobs to military, civilian, and contract workers, dwarfing the Medical University of South Carolina (the region's second-largest employer) at 7,700 workers and Charleston AFB (number three) at 6,000 employees. The vast majority of shipyard workers were civilians. Charleston's defenders realized that the Navy's surplus capacity in shipyards would have to be reduced substantially before 1995, or, even if Charleston survived 1993, it would surely make the 1995 list. So to get close to reducing the surplus 3.8 million "man-days," of workers, Charleston supporters argued that the Norfolk Naval Shipyard in Virginia should close instead.[12] They could have targeted the Portsmouth Naval Shipyard in New Hampshire, but they recognized that even if both Mare Island Naval Shipyard in California and Portsmouth closed, there would still be a surplus 900,000 man-days of work—and, of course, one of the 1993 BRAC members, Peter Bowman, had been the former commander of the Portsmouth shipyard. If Norfolk closed, then all but 126,000 excess man-days would be eliminated.[13] Their choice pitted Charleston against the second-highest-rated shipyard in the Navy, and Charleston's defenders against the powerful Virginia delegation of Republican Senator John Warner and Democrat Charles Robb. In the end, Norfolk was not even dented by the attempt, but it showed that service ties are quickly forgotten in the rough-and-tumble battles over base closure. That would become most evident in the case of perennial survivor of the base closing wars, Meridian NAS in Mississippi.

MERIDIAN NAVAL AIR STATION, MISSISSIPPI

Located in the gently rolling countryside in east-central Mississippi, Meridian NAS hosts a training facility for Navy and Marine Corps aviators. With 9,000 acres of land, Meridian is one of the larger Navy bases in the country, at least in terms of area. But the size had more to do with Meridian's use as a training range for gunnery and ordnance than it did with Meridian's importance to the Navy. Naval philosophy on bases is fairly simple; they are needed for all the reasons that services need bases, but they are less important than ships. When the Navy has to choose between bases and ships, the choice is inevitable. When it has to choose between different types of bases, they choose bases directly related to ships (shipyards, and naval stations) over bases that are only indirectly related to ships (training bases). So Meridian was clearly vulnerable, along with other training facilities, to closure. The only question was: how vulnerable? The base was first put on the 1991 closure list by the Navy as an alternate to another base, but the 1993 list saw Meridian as a prime closure candidate. Its position as a training base was especially vulnerable, not just because the Navy valued training bases less, but also because of the changing political climate. The end of the Cold War clearly meant fewer aircraft and, thus, fewer pilots. Second, undergraduate pilot training (UPT) is fairly common across the two flying services, and the Air Force was facing the same dilemma. So, consolidation of Navy and Air Force UPT bases was a likely prospect in the 1990's era of jointness.

Second, both the Air Force and the Navy were working on a new basic-training aircraft, the JPATS, which, when delivered at the end of the decade, would make consolidation of training bases even more likely. While this would not have a direct impact on Meridian NAS (no primary training was conducted there), the smaller number of Navy pilots would ripple up through the service, and soon there would be less need for the intermediate-strike training at Meridian. So the Navy command at Meridian and the leaders in the community had few assets to fight the closure decision when it was first announced, and when the official word from the Navy became "toe the line," there was an inclination to do so—at least until some of the local leaders in the town of Meridian became suspicious that the Navy's official justification for the closure of the Naval Air Station was misleading at best, and fraudulent at worst.[14] Moreover, they began to suspect that other Naval Air Stations had conspired against them in a fight to see which one might survive closure.

The Meridian Community Involvement

While such traditional port cities like San Diego, California, or Norfolk, Virginia, are usually considered "Navy towns," Meridian, Mississippi, could also qualify. Town-base relations had been quite good over the years (an exception occurred when base personnel were detailed to search for the bodies of three civil rights workers killed in nearby Philadelphia, Mississippi in 1964). Many of the Meridian NAS personnel lived in the city, and used its facilities on a regular basis. Meridian NAS made its fire-fighting equipment available to the city, and Meridian, in turn, supported the Military Spouse Employment Program, which made it easier for military family members to gain jobs in the community. The local Navy League, with more than 1,000 members ranked fifth in the United States in terms of both membership and support of Meridian (and became heavily involved in efforts to save the base). Meridian offered hospital space for service members and dependents, and military personnel provided natural-disaster assistance to Meridian when required. But the most important connection was the $87 million per year that the base and its payroll pumped into the local economy—about 12-13 percent of the total. So when the base made the BRAC, the community mobilized. The local Navy League (without support of the national Navy League) joined with other organizations to fight closure. Those groups included labor unions whose members worked at the base, the head of the local utility company that sold Meridian NAS its power, and merchants from Meridian. They raised money (the city, county and private interests had raised over $50,000 in 1991 to try to influence the decision) and organized a political response to the closure decision. Workers were encouraged to write letters (and given samples of what the letters should say) to Representative G.V. "Sonny" Montgomery (D-MS), the district's representative, and to Mississippi Senators Thad Cochran and Trent Lott. They were also encouraged to demonstrate their support for Meridian NAS at the BRAC regional hearings in Birmingham, Alabama, on May 4, 1993, and at the BRAC's subsequent visit to the base four days later. Meridian NAS had given the members of the public permission to drive onto the base, park their cars, and line up to greet the BRAC commissioners as they entered the facility. Leaflets called upon them to "show your southern hospitality" and to wave signs and flags. The planners had heard that the BRAC visitors had received unfriendly treatment at other bases and so made sure that the commissioners were taken to the base in a parade of cars, with citizens greeting them on the way.

Two committees actually formed—one to find ways to save the base, and the other to find alternatives for the base should it close. The overall philosophy of both committees was that if it was in the best interest of the Navy and the United States that Meridian NAS closed, then only the second committee would be activated. But as committee members scrutinized the data used to justify closure of Meridian, concern grew that the numbers were simply wrong.

Questions About Closure Data

According to a Navy report published in February 1993, the six naval airs training bases gave excess capacity for projected Navy needs to 1999. The requirements implied that two of these facilities could be closed, and some of their functions transferred to other bases. So the military value (MV) was used to evaluate each of the six bases. (See Table 4.1.)

According to this ranking, Whiting Field got a slightly lower MV score than did Meridian, yet Meridian and Memphis made the closure list. One reason stated in the commission report was that Whiting Field in Florida was closer to Pensacola, Florida, than was Meridian; an apparently important factor required that aircraft from both locations had to fly to Pensacola carrier-deck training.

Table 4.1: Military-Base Evaluations, 1993

BASE	*MILITARY VALUE (MV)*
Kingsville	83.2
Pensacola	78.2
Corpus Christi	74.5
Meridian	76.7
Whiting Field	73.2
Memphis	46.1

SOURCE: "Attachment S Recommendation for Closure: Training Air Stations," internal memo, Meridian NAS, n.d.

The Navy leadership joined with the local Save Meridian committee to challenge the closure decision. They looked at the bases that would be receiving Meridian's aircraft if the base closed and realized that there would be a cascading effect that would ripple across several naval training facilities. For example, Kingsvillle NAS in Texas would get all 66 of Meridian's TA-4s in addition to operating its own 44 T-2 aircraft. That would cause an overflow such that Corpus Christi NAS, also in Texas, would have to take half of Kingsville's T-34s and T-2s from Pensacola, apparently to consolidate all T-2 operations at Corpus Christi. Thus, NAS Whiting would have to take half of Corpus Christi's T-34s. An internal memorandum suggested that one opposition strategy for Meridian would be to ". . . Mention all limitations that you can think of at Corpus—FOD (foreign object damage), noise, only one dual runway, only one runway with arresting gear at Pensacola—would need to move NFO jets, etc."[15] The Navy Meridian Team (formed by the Navy at Meridian to respond to the BRAC decision) noted a number of additional problems potentially posed by Meridian's closing. For example, the team claimed that it would not be feasible to locate all T-34 aircraft at Kingsville, since the total 384 aircraft would exceed Kingsville's primary training requirements (PTR) of 200. Additionally, Kingsville's T-45 military construction program was incomplete, whereas Meridian's military construction program would be completed by 1994. The Meridian team also noted that the real excess in training capacity was not in strike training, but rather in primary, maritime, and helicopter training. Moreover, the Meridian team stated that Pensacola would not be adequate as a T-45 relocation site because that action would only increase Pensacola's air-traffic density (already the highest in the country) and thus increase the chances of mid-air collisions (Meridian carefully noted the 304 near-misses there from 1986 to 1991). Pensacola also suffered from noise-abatement problems, limited access to training ranges, no T-45 environmental impact study, and, noted in bold letters by the Meridian team, a significant hurricane risk.[16] Meridian had its own target range, ample overland airspace, no aircraft-density problems, and the chief of naval air training had designated the base as a hurricane evacuation center.[17] The Meridian team also raised the question of future aviation training. It pointed out the potential for helicopter training with the Army at Fort Rucker, Alabama, and noted that primary pilot training could shift to the Air Force for all services (no matter that the Navy had vigorously opposed such consolidation in the past). Better to wait, warned the Meridian team, until resolution of these joint issues. Meridian also looked to the state of Mississippi for its justification to remain open, arguing that Mississippi had adopted legislation providing up to $10 million for capital improvements on the base "as incentive to remain open or to expand schools/military operations."[18] Finally, the Meridian team pointed out that the savings from closing Corpus Christi NAS would be $297.9 million versus only $157 for Meridian. It also noted the "noise, FOD, and air traffic/airspace issues" at Corpus Christi (apparently following the suggestions noted above) went on to observe "HURRICANE risks: six hurricanes hit Texas Coast since 1980."[19] If that was not bad enough, the Meridian team's study noted that there were "significant environmental clean-up costs to expand facilities; substandard landing pads, parking aprons, 31 percent of hangar space less than adequate (for what was not reported); corrosion control inadequate; housing deficiencies" at Corpus Christi.[20]

The Competition to Survive Closure

Meridian had another problem to cope with. Representatives for Chase NAS in Texas began to plot a similar strategy to that of Meridian once they found their base on the closure list. Their counter, though, involved targeting not only the surviving NASs, but also those slated to close, presumably believing that at least one would be spared in the final BRAC decision-making process. They noted that, like Meridian, Chase was located close to a target range, but that, unlike Meridian, Chase could be potentially closer to a home port, and thus to the carriers from which the pilots might ultimately operate from.[21] Representative Greg Laughton (D-TX), representing Chase's district, noted that, "Meridian, Mississippi is home base for 30 percent of the aircraft carriers and 10 percent are based in Pensacola, Florida," adding: ". . . An aircraft carrier always should have been in south Texas, except that we didn't have a place to house it. Now we have a new base that Texans donated one-third of the cost to construct."[22] He was referring to the promised new naval station for Corpus Christi, part of Secretary of the Navy John Lehman's "home porting" scheme for his projected 600-ship navy. Laughton's conclusion was obvious: ". . . it would appear to make sense to consider consolidating all advanced jet training requiring aircraft carrier operations in the Corpus Christi Bay area. . . ."[23] His argument depended on funding for the completion of the Corpus Christi NS, which remained unfinished despite the generosity of Texas. Even if it been finished, though, his argument would likely not have won the day, since it was unlikely that Corpus Christi itself would have homeported more than 10 percent of the aircraft carriers in the fleet. Still, Meridian had to ward off one more attack from another naval air station in the bidding stakes to survive closure.

All of these arguments could have been undercut by the reduction in Navy pilot demand. There would simply be fewer training bases, eliminating the requirement for consolidation. Navy projections at the time assumed that the number of carrier battle groups in that the post–Cold War era would drop from 12 to 10. However, a recalculation of post–Cold War defense requirements called the Bottom-Up Review (BUR), initiated by Secretary of Defense Les Aspin in 1993 surprised the Navy. While the other services suffered cuts under BUR, it preserved the number of carrier battle groups at 12. Had the number fallen to 10, the Navy could have conducted its strike training from 1.5 training facilities, which would have meant that Meridian could close and a part of its operations could be transferred elsewhere. As it would turn out, though, the BUR findings would greatly assist Meridian NAS in staying open—at least in 1993.

Representative Montgomery and Meridian NAS

Meridian's member of Congress was well placed to help save the base. Representative Montgomery, a veteran of many years on the House Committee on Armed Services, had staunchly opposed the original 1988 base closure legislation, stating then: "I don't really need any more people on welfare in my state. . . . The military bases are a good economic treasure for my people."[24]

With the release of the 1993 list, Montgomery muted his response more than did some of his colleagues. He stated simply, ". . . It's a big mistake. I'm sad."[25] While Montgomery could not challenge the decision directly, he had his staff assist the local committees at Meridian by providing them with data to challenge the Navy's numbers. In the end Montgomery's staff work would provide a critical edge that would ultimately allow the local committee to show a different case for Meridian than that made for it by the Navy.

The final BRAC report vindicated Meridian, noting that there was, indeed, excess capacity in naval pilot training but not in Naval strike pilot training. The commission also accepted Meridian's argument that support of both current and future PTR justified a second full-strike training base like Meridian.[26]

In the end, Meridian NAS survived—removed from the 1993 BRAC list in part because the efforts to close it had been so underhanded. Those who had worked so hard to save the base were less than relieved, though. They knew that, despite the tactics used against it, Meridian was vulnerable to the scheduled closure process in two years. The Cold War had ended, the Navy was downsizing, and Meridian's status as a base would be questioned again. They were right; the base would reappear on the 1995 closure list, but once again, the arguments that won the day for Meridian in 1993, coupled with additional assistance from Representative Montgomery's office, would help Meridian to survive the 1995 round as well.

THE PRESIDIO OF SAN FRANCISCO

The Presidio of San Francisco, California, was first ordered closed by the 1988 BRAC. But the base was one of several to enjoy a temporary respite from closure—the 1993 BRAC looked at the Presidio decision again and made fundamental changes to it. As a consequence, the Presidio got a new lease on life, and a new set of problems. It would again be considered in 1995, when it became apparent that even the 1993 solution was inadequate. So while the 1993 chapter of this book tells the story of the Presidio, it started much earlier and ended later.

Preserving Presidio History and Setting

Few other military bases hold as much history as does the Presidio. Originally built by the Spanish, the Presidio opened in 1776, transferring to United States ownership after the Mexican War. The only part remaining from the Spanish period is a small piece of adobe wall (now preserved in the Officer's Club). The fort grew with the arrival of gold seekers landing in San Francisco and expanded again in 1854 as the Army developed coastal-defense bases in the nation's harbors. The city of San Francisco grew around it, but the base protected 2.5 percent of the city from development. Real estate speculators had coveted the area since the 1870s, and, after fears that the Army might abandon the post surfaced in the 1960s, then-Representative Philip Burton (D-CA) managed to get the entire base included in the Golden Gate National Recreation Area (GGNRA) in 1972. Thus, it followed that when the 1988 BRAC voted to close the base, they decided to turn custody over to the National Park Service, the managing agency for the GGNRA.

The decision to include the base in the GGNRA is not surprising, given its history and its value. The facility covered more than 1,400 acres and featured more than 800 structures, including many of historical significance. In addition to the Sixth Army Headquarters, the base held 54 other tenant organizations and 18 separate military commands. The old part of the base at the site of the original Spanish garrison was base headquarters, marked by graceful old buildings and a parade ground. The Letterman Army Hospital complex included part of the original infirmary (built in 1899) and a modern multistory hospital and living quarters. The residential areas, 14 in all, included everything from old Victorian homes to modern apartment-style barracks. The base land also included beaches and dunes on San Francisco Bay and an old forest with towering Monterey pines, cypress, and eucalyptus with miles of hiking trails running through it. Base land also enclosed a national military cemetery and Crissy Field, site of some very early military aviation feats.

The Presidio's landscape alone made prospects for conversion difficult. The base was described as a "barren place" in the Nineteenth Century because animal over-grazing destroyed most of the ground cover. So in 1883, a Major Jones developed a landscape plan giving the base its abundant forests and landscapes. Much of the vegetation was on the endangered species list at base closure time— some 11 types in all. Around one-quarter of the 160 species of birds visiting the base bred there, and a candidate for the endangered species list, the San Francisco Tree Lupine Moth, lived near Baker Beach on the base. Base property also included the only free-flowing creek in San Francisco.

Efforts to Close the Presidio—Again and Again

In November 1989, Congress approved the 1988 base closure list but recommended some changes for the Presidio. Those recommendations included retaining the Sixth Army Headquarters at the Presidio, maintaining Letterman Army Hospital, and giving the Army access to the commissary, the Child Development Center, and to base housing. From those recommendations, it was difficult to understand that the base was actually to close.

The 1991 BRAC reviewed the 1988 Commission's somewhat unusual transfer of the Sixth Army Headquarters from the Presidio to the National Aeronautics and Space Administration (NASA) facility at Ames, California. The Army initially identified the Ames facility (formerly the Naval Air Station at Moffett Field) as a candidate for the Sixth Army Headquarters because of the following:

1. 75 percent of reserve units attached to the Sixth Army were in California.
2. The principal ports of debarkation were in California.
3. The West Coast has a high need for military assistance to civil authorities.

It turned out, though, that the savings of moving the Sixth Army Headquarters to NASA Ames were quite small.[27] So a compromise was reached to retain the Sixth Army Headquarters at the Presidio while turning over the remainder to the National Park Service. But that solution was complicated as well. The National Park Service, for example, wound up owning base housing, which it then leased back to the Army, its original owner. Again, there was no cost savings.

The National Park Service Takes Over

The Presidio of San Francisco was transferred from the Army to the National Park Service in the hope of preserving and developing the historic fort.[28] While operation by the National Park Service precluded major commercial development at the Presidio, it did allow the Park Service in 1991 to solicit some rather interesting proposals for non-commercial activity at the base. The general superintendent of the GGNRA, Brian O'Neill invited the people from around the Bay Area to help plan that future. And help they did. Soon proposals poured in, many from the citizens of San Francisco, and included such things as:

- Artist Colony and Homeless Housing (to provide living/working space for artists in exchange for the artists' help in running a homeless shelter);
- Arts and Education Demonstration Project: Creative Use of Recycled Materials (sponsored by the Scrounger's Center for Reusable Arts Parts, or SCRAP);
- San Francisco Mercado Project (to retail value-added products such as textiles and sculptures made from second-hand materials recovered from San Francisco's waste stream);
- The Pickle Family Circus Center;
- Theatre Pomegranate (to provide theater performance to underprivileged children);
- Envision (to provide custom legal visual/communications material for litigants involved in morally and environmentally beneficial lawsuits);
- California Institute of Integral Studies (a graduate school emphasizing research in the integration of Western worldviews, philosophies, spiritual practices and cultural traditions);
- Multicultural Training Resource Center;
- University for the Earth (would relate human rights to global concerns);
- Sunship Earth Study Center;
- Greenpeace Western Complex;
- AIDS Day Health Center;
- Goodnews Tenderloin Center;
- Institute for Public Golf (to encourage more diverse participation in the game and lessen the environmental impacts of golf courses);
- The Peace Pole Project ("The Society promises a message that Peace Prevails on Earth, through World Peace Prayer Ceremonies, Peace Pole obelisks, . . . and the dedication of a large Pole at the Presidio").[29]

Along with these somewhat offbeat proposals came proposals from the Navy (to operate the hospital along with the Veterans Administration), the Red Cross, and the Defense Investigative Service. The Park Service did not anticipate, though, that BRAC 1993 would reconsider the 1988 closure decision, so all interest was put on hold. Later, one somewhat unorthodox institute, the Thoreau Center for

Sustainability, opened in part of the Letterman Army Hospital complex to house some twenty nonprofit organizations.

Politics to the Rescue

The National Park Service found itself with inadequate resources to adequately restore and operate the Presidio. To the potential rescue came Representative Nancy Pelosi (D-CA), who represented California's Eighth District. Pelosi attempted to get legislation through Congress that would create an independent agency to run the Presidio as early as 1994. The bill passed the House, but failed to come to a vote in the Senate.[30] In March 1996, Pelosi reintroduced the bill.[31] Circumstances, though, had changed since 1994, with a Republican-controlled Congress interested in paring government spending. Pelosi recognized the changes, and prudently co-introduced her bill with Representatives Stephen Horn (R-CA) and Ben Gilman (R-NY). Their 1996 bill proposed creating a Presidio Trust to administer control over about 80 percent of the Presidio, leaving the National Park Service with just the beaches, Fort Point, and Crissy Field.[32] The Presidio Trust itself would be an independent government corporation whose mission was to increase revenues to the federal government through the use of Presidio facilities. If, at the end of 15 years, the Presidio was not self-sufficient, the General Services Administration (GSA) would take possession of the property and dispose of it by sale.

The bill quickly got a dose of 1996 electoral politics when Senator Bob Dole (R-KS), the then-front-runner for the 1996 Republican presidential nomination, cosponsored the bill. Even retiring senators got into the act as Senator Bill Bradley (D-NJ) put a hold on all bills coming from the Natural Resources Committee (where Pelosi's bill was referred) until New Jersey's Stirling Forest, the state's last major woodland, got Congressional protection.[33] Politics entered again when Interior Secretary Bruce Babbitt urged President Clinton to veto the entire measure if it included funding for a controversial Utah wilderness designation.[34] Pelosi, as well as a number of environmental groups, opposed that issue, which was sponsored by Utah's two senators. Pelosi remained optimistic that both Clinton and Dole would somehow resurrect protection for the Presidio since, presumably, both needed the pro-environmental vote in politically important California.[35] Yet if the bill was not complicated enough, Senate Minority Leader Tom Daschle (D-SD) attempted to attach an amendment to it increasing the minimum wage.[36] Senator Bradley, meanwhile, threatened a filibuster over the Utah wilderness measure, and California's two Democratic Senators, Dianne Feinstein and Barbara Boxer stated that they would join him, thus, potentially killing the Presidio Trust part of the legislation.[37] At that point, the bill had mushroomed to include some 50 different measures concerning land transfer and land funding. Dole reentered the fray in late March and attempted to break the Democratic filibuster but failed on a 51-to-49 vote.[38] He then pulled the entire bill from the floor. Bad feelings ran high, and it appeared that there were no winners. Senator Orrin Hatch (R-UT) said, "As far as I'm concerned, there ain't going to be any Presidio," noting that, while he supported the Presidio, he got no support for his Utah amendment from Senators Boxer and Feinstein.[39] California's two senators found themselves in a difficult position of not wanting to alienate environmental activists who opposed the Utah bill because it did not, in their judgment, set off enough land for protection. But 1996 was an election year, and political failure might have had an impact, in particular, on Senator Dole's chances to win the White House. So, on May 1, Dole got an agreement from Senate leaders to drop both the Stirling Forest and Utah wilderness provisions.[40] Senator Hatch was a close Dole ally and undoubtedly realized that protecting the Presidio might help Dole's presidential chances in California, while Bradley, a lame duck, did not have the political clout to protect his amendment. Both Pelosi and Boxer then touted the self-financing part of the Trust legislation to make it more appealing to majority Republicans: "It is fair to say the bill does incorporate (Republican) ideas," said Boxer.[41] Those tactics seemed in doubt, though, as other senators rushed to get their land-protection measures attached to the now-stripped-down bill. Senator Patty Murray (D-WA) wanted a Vancouver park in the bill, Senator Edward Kennedy (D-MA) sought to include a whale park in New Bedford, and Senator Max Baucus (D-MT) objected to a land-provision transfer in his state.[42] Dole, ever the political compromiser, assured his Democratic Senate colleagues that their issues either were or would be taken care of, and the bill passed the Senate unanimously. It wound up in conference committee after easy House passage, and the president himself took political advantage of the situation to take a shot at Dole. Campaigning in San Francisco with Feinstein, Boxer, and Pelosi, Clinton strolled Crissy Field (to be returned to its natural habitat as a marsh) and said: "We need the Presidio bill; we need it now . . . we need it clean; we need it unhampered," and Boxer added: "I say to Senator Dole, in your last two days in the U.S. Senate after a very distinguished career, why don't you join with our president and join with all of us, get this bill out of the conference committee so we can send it to the president's desk."[43] (Dole had decided to resign from the Senate to run for president full-time.)

Yet, for Presidio supporters in San Francisco, the bloom was coming off the bill as it progressed through the political system. House passage was assured only after Representative James Hansen (R-UT) inserted a provision giving the Presidio Trust just 12 years to reach financial self-sufficiency and requiring 80 percent self-sufficiency in five years.[44] Opposition grew, some voiced by Amy Meyer, chair of People for a Golden Gate National Recreation Area. Noting the strict self-sufficiency requirements, Meyer charged: "What they are aiming for is failure."[45] San Francisco Supervisor Angela Alioto also expressed dismay at the bill, asking, "Why are we giving in to corporate interests?"[46] That issue galvanized criticism among early Presidio conversion supporters, who wanted to avoid commercial development of the base.

In a political year, no one should have been sanguine about the fate of the bill. Once thought secure after Dole's efforts in the Senate and Pelosi's in the House, the legislation emerged from conference committee with another new load of additions, making it more than 700 pages in length.[47] Given California's political importance to both parties, it was hardly surprising that the new bill contained numerous provisions for funding California projects. They included a $440 million habitat-restoration project for San Francisco Bay, federal designation of the AIDS Memorial Grove in San Francisco's Golden Gate Park, and the designation of Japanese-American World War II internment camps in California's Inyo County.[48] Most controversial, though, was a measure easing Alaskan logging restrictions, opposed by environmental groups, and thus provoking a veto threat by President Clinton. That put Clinton at odds with Senators Feinstein and Boxer, who urged him to sign the bill[49] Senator Frank Murkowski (R-AK) derided the President as "standing tall, perhaps, but standing in the mush."[50] The fight intensified as time was running out on the bill as a governmental shutdown loomed. Back in went the Stirling Forest protection, along with the Tall Grass Prairie Preserve in Kansas. Democrats insisted that they would block the parks bill unless Republican initiatives disliked by environmentalists were dropped from the package.[51] Said Representative David Obey of Wisconsin, "We are no closer than we were at the beginning of the day."[52] The president again threatened a veto, pleasing some Republicans who wanted him to take the blame for the death of the Presidio bill.[53] Senator Boxer was, in the end, able to clear a final hurdle erected when she reached a bargain with Alaska Senator Murkowski, who wanted to ease logging in the Tongass National Forest. Boxer got White House Chief of Staff Leon Panetta (a former California Democratic representative) to agree to provide a three-year supply of logs to the sawmills in Tongass.[54] But with the intense political fighting that accompanied the measure, the controversy did not die, as House Democrats charged that Republicans stalled in turning over the legislation to the White House for signing, thus denying President Clinton a visible bill-signing ceremony close to the election.[55]

The particular nature of San Francisco politics almost guaranteed opposition to the measure. A loose coalition calling itself United for the Presidio issued a critique of the legislation, complaining that it could turn the land over to commercial interests without much oversight from the community.[56] In an article on the Internet, the group also complained that no public hearings were held in San Francisco and encouraged readers to contact Clinton and urge him to veto the bill.[57] The group's membership was diverse (including the National Trust for Historic Preservation and the Cow Hollow Neighbors in Action), and it was impossible to predict its impact. But, given the intense nature of San Francisco politics, continued political turmoil over the future of the Presidio could never be ruled out.

In its final form, the bill created a seven-member board appointed by the president to oversee the leasing of historic buildings to generate funds. The seventh board member would be the secretary of the interior. The Trust got the best part of the old base, and could hire outside the civil-service system. It was also exempted from many of the government procurement regulations to streamline the acquisition of necessary goods and services.[58]

The legislation continued the $25 million annual funding initially but phased it out gradually, to be replaced by revenues generated by the activities monitored by the board. Their task was to find tenants to bring revenue-generating activities to the old post, which by the end of 1996 had Arnold Palmer Golf Management, Incorporated to run the base golf course and a Burger King.[59] There was clearly a ways to go.

The National Park Service saw its own clout threatened by the new measure. While the Presidio was the Park Service's most expensive park, at $25 million per year (compared to Yosemite at $18 million annually), the agency still wanted to appear innovative in transferring Presidio facilities. In April 1966, it got private funding to convert the Presidio's commissary to an exhibit hall[60] and, in June, it generated a plan to turn Crissy Field into what Brian O'Neill hoped would be "one of the world's finest waterfront sites."[61]

Environmental Problems at the Presidio

Given its long history, it was almost inevitable that the Presidio would have contamination problems. Those problems got public attention when a resident swan at the Presidio's Mountain Lake (once San Francisco's water supply) died of lead poisoning, and high levels of lead were subsequently found in the lake's water. They apparently came from soil dredged up from the base's target range and dumped into the lake.[62]

The main problems, though, were fuel dumps at Crissy Field and buildings filled with asbestos and leaded paint. Building 979, once a mine-storage facility, was found to be contaminated with chlorinated solvents. Sites once used in an air-defense missile system had soil containing polycyclic aromatic hydrocarbon, expected to be cleaned out by the spring of 1998. A total of 41 buildings contained asbestos and leaded paint. Some 27,000 linear feet of a fuel distribution system snaked through the fort, some of it running under historic buildings. All of it had to be either dug up or capped off under buildings, and the soil around it decontaminated from the leaks that had accumulated over the years.

These problems were hardly insurmountable, particularly compared to the large shipyards and bomber bases. The real problem came in the delay of funding to remedy the problem and to complete site surveys to certify that the land met specifications. The long battle over both closure and the operation by the National Park Service only delayed that funding, and, as of 1996, much of the old fort's land remained unsurveyed and uncleaned.

Summary

The Presidio is hardly a success story despite the value and beauty of its land. The prolonged fight to keep the base in operation, followed by the necessity to turn it over to the National Park Service only delayed what may still be successful conversion. Some time must pass before the conversion of the Presidio to a self-sustaining enterprise is deemed successful or not. Should it fail, the old post land may be sold to commercial interests, and the oldest fort in the country may finally disappear despite the often heroic (and unusual) efforts to preserve it.

MacDill AFB, Florida

The "sunbelt states" have long been attractive to aviators because of their good flying weather. So Florida became the home to more Navy and Air Force bases per capita than any other state except Texas. Most Air Force bases dated back to the time of the Army Air Corps prior to World War II and quickly expanded to fill wartime needs after Pearl Harbor. One of these was MacDill Field, later renamed MacDill Air Force Base after the war. Located in central Florida outside Tampa, MacDill became a training base for wartime flyers. Pilots trying to master the tricky takeoff conditions of the Martin B-26 medium bomber were perhaps fortunate that MacDill's main runway pointed toward water because, if the takeoff speed was inadequate, a wet landing was a certainty. "One a day in Tampa Bay" was a local slogan that described the problem pretty well.

After the war, MacDill grew, gaining a fighter wing and the beginnings of its problems. Local newspapers printed noise complaints as the open areas over which fighters flew filled up with houses. Local air-traffic problems also grew as two civil airports near MacDill expanded, often filling the skies with inexperienced private pilots. Space restrictions grew and, as they did, so did tensions over what had once been open skies.

MacDill's Closure Problems Begin

In the 1980s and 1990s, MacDill became the location for not one but two major joint military headquarters. Special Operations Command (SOCOM) and Central Command (CENTCOM) both located at MacDill. In 1988 SOCOM got its special advocate in Washington in the name of Charles S. Whitehouse, who filled the newly formed position of assistant secretary of defense for special operations and low-intensity conflict. As an article in the local paper pointed out, "That makes him the Washington advocate for U.S. Special Operations Command, the headquarters at MacDill Air Force Base that oversees military commando units."[63] It was never clear whether Whitehouse actively lobbied on behalf of keeping MacDill open, but the position clearly gave him the authority to do so, particularly when it became known that the Air Force wanted to close the base.

Both commands brought with them a four-star commander in chief (CinC) and a host of flag-rank officers on their staffs. A one-star Air Force general commanded MacDill. He had to host commands in which at least four or five flag-rank officers out-ranked him. It was in part for this reason that Air Force Secretary Donald Rice decided to realign MacDill by relocating its fighter wing and closing the runway and its associated flying operations. That way Rice could hope that some other service might take over the operations at MacDill, thus sparing the Air Force the cost of maintaining two large commands and the difficult tensions between the CinC staffs and the Air Force base commander. Thus, MacDill appeared on the Air Force's submission to BRAC in 1991. When the Commission reviewed the submission list, though, it initially recommended closing the entire base. But BRAC staff had apparently underestimated the huge cost of moving two command headquarters. Both commands had established a large communications network to link up with their far-flung areas of operations, and the cost of moving this equipment alone became prohibitive. During the BRAC visit to MacDill on June 10, 1991, commissioners received a 30-minute briefing on the highly classified nature of these operations and the cost to move them, and that briefing was followed by another in Washington a week later.[64] After the hearings on the 1991 closure list, the recommendation from the commission changed to essentially reflect the Air Force's initial position. The fighter wing moved to Luke AFB, and the runway closed.

The Air Force now faced the problem of disposing of the property. The initial hope was that the high value of Florida waterfront land would make disposal easy. Water surrounded MacDill on three sides; thus, the base held the potential for a resort or amusement park. But there was only one access road onto the base, and MacDill was near a declining neighborhood. The Air Force offered to sell the runway and the land around it to the city of Tampa, but the city did not want the runway itself, and interest in the surrounding land waned quickly when the extent of toxic contamination was revealed.

Environmental Problems at MacDill

Like most Air Force bases, MacDill had been less than careful when disposing waste from aircraft operations. Years of fuel spills had accumulated in the sandy soil and shallow water tables around the runway, and the staggering cost of cleanup would make property disposal difficult. The usual contaminants appeared; petroleum hydrocarbons, toxic metals, pesticides, underground storage tanks, solvents, and pesticides lay at various sites on the base. In 1991, 38 sites were located, but by 1995 a site investigation remained incomplete. Over a period of three years, the United States Geological Survey completed investigations of only half of the suspected pollution sites. On the basis of this incomplete evidence, total remediation was forecast for the year 2004, making it difficult to find a commercial tenant before then. So consideration turned to a possible government tenant. It would have to be an agency with airplanes—enough airplanes to justify keeping runway operations at MacDill open.

1993 BRAC Reviews MacDill

The 1993 BRAC would provide an answer to the future of MacDill, but not the one the Air Force wanted. Instead, BRAC reversed the 1991 runway-closure decision and instead offered the site to the National Oceanic and Atmospheric Administrative (NOAA), which relocated its aircraft operations from Miami to MacDill. Management of the runway shifted from the Air Force to the Department of Commerce, the parent organization for NOAA. The Commerce Department found itself in charge of a runway and a hanger for a small handful of planes, relieved of its rent payments to Miami International Airport. NOAA only operated about 15 aircraft worldwide, though, and the few sent to MacDill were hardly enough to justify keeping the facility open.

Natural and Political Pressure

An act of nature impacted on MacDill's future, though. In 1992, Hurricane Andrew ripped through Homestead AFB in Florida, leaving almost nothing undamaged. Homestead, which had escaped BRAC previously, suddenly emerged as a strong candidate for closure. Members of Congress from central Florida saw an opportunity to save MacDill's aircraft operations, thus making the base more difficult to close in the future. Homestead based the 31st Fighter Wing and the Air Force Reserve 482nd Fighter Wing. Given the devastation there, it appeared logical to relocate the fighter wing at MacDill. Moody AFB in Georgia was also on the closure list, but because it was also a fighter base, it became an alternative home for several squadrons in Homestead's fighter wing. The fact that Moody was in the home state of Senate Armed Services Committee Chair Sam Nunn (D-GA) did not hurt its chances to get the 31st.

Central Florida's congressional delegation developed an alternative plan that would take the Reserve 482nd Fighter Wing and locate it at MacDill. Some members of the 482nd (which was really just one squadron and a headquarters) began plans to relocate to the Tampa area by purchasing houses there. They were shocked to learn that the move was temporary, and the wing would relocate back to Homestead after its rebuilding.

Homestead was not without its own strong congressional representation, though. There were direct appeals to President Clinton to rebuild the base instead of closing it, and Clinton, facing a midterm congressional election in the next year, agreed. So money flowed into Homestead to keep a mangled installation while, at the same time, perfectly good ones were closed. While the 31st Fighter Wing was disbanded, the 482nd Reserve Wing would return to Homestead after temporary relocation at MacDill. The BRAC determined that the cost of moving the wing was excessive, though, and thus stayed there through 1995, when once again BRAC would find the Air Force wanting to close the installation.

BRAC Revisits MacDill in 1995

The Air Force tried again to close MacDill in 1995, but failed once more. The outcome was the same as in 1993, but in 1995 the Air Force apparently failed to anticipate the reaction of central Florida's congressional delegation.

The chief proponent of that delegation was Representative C.W. (Bill) Young, who represented a district adjacent to MacDill. Young was in a strong position to assist MacDill even though it was not in his own district. He rose in the congressional ranks to ultimately become the ranking minority member of the Defense Subcomittee on the House Committee on Appropriations. Young realized that he could use his position to influence the BRAC decision if he could convince members that closing the base would be prohibitively expensive. So he personally guided two BRAC members through the communications operations of the two commands at MacDill, convincing them that moving such equipment would cost ". . . hundreds of millions of dollars."[65] Young pointed out that ". . . this year we were in close contact with the members of the commission," and he was certainly correct.[66] There was a point to his efforts; while Young did not directly represent the district, MacDill employed more than 5,500 employees, and some of them lived in his district. With the coming of the tanker wing from Malmstrom, the job count returned to the 5,500 jobs that the base had had with now-departed fighter wing. So did the revenue that the base spread throughout several counties; according to a University of South Florida study, that value exceeded $2.2 billion annually, with the direct and indirect creation of about 70,000 jobs.[67]

Despite the role he played, it would be a mistake to give Representative Young all or even most of the credit for saving MacDill. The two Commanders-in-Chief with commands there wanted to preserve the runway, and they enlisted the support of the Chairman of the Joint Chiefs, Gen. John Shalikashvili, who pressed Air Force Secretary Sheila Widnall to keep the runways open. Air Force Chief of Staff Ronald Fogelman changed the earlier decision of his predecessor, Gen. Merrill McPeak, who favored closing the base. Other factors also weighed in to help keep MacDill from closing.

Given the difficulty that the Department of Commerce was likely to have in operating the runway at MacDill, BRAC 1995 gave back that operation to the Air Force, and a tanker squadron was moved there to justify keeping the base open. The 43rd Air Refueling Group brought 12 KC-135 tankers to MacDill from Malmstrom AFB, where the runway closed in 1996. The move brought with it $23 million in construction money, which might protect MacDill against any further closures. The base's aircraft inventory increased even more in mid-1997 with the addition of two EC-135 aircraft transferred from Warner Robins AFB in Georgia. Ironically, the two major command users that the Air Force had once used to justify its efforts to close MacDill were used to justify the tanker move. Said the 43rd Wing Commander, Colonel Mike Chester: "This offers us a unique opportunity to right there with our two biggest customers—U.S. Central Command and the U.S. Special Operations Command."[68] The EC-135s came with the same justification, since their primary purpose was support of CENTCOM.

Homestead AFB, meanwhile, was rebuilt, pouring millions of construction dollars to south Florida. It was removed from the inventory of active Air Force bases, though, and in 1998 was home to the 482d Fighter Wing, equipped with F-16 aircraft. To ensure that the wing would remain operational, an Act of Congress specified that it could not revert to a tanker wing, as had all the other reserve fighter wings. So because of that act, the 482d Fighter Wing is the only reserve fighter wing remaining attached to the Air Force.

SUMMARY

The 1993 BRAC procedure made changes from 1991, particularly in terms of "openness." The commissioners did realize that the 1991 closure process had left the taint of politics in the process, and one way to try to purge this taint was to open public access to the process. So beginning in April 1993, the commission held 17 regional hearings across the country. While not all commissioners attended these regional hearings, they did represent an opportunity for local leaders and citizens to press questions and concerns to those commissioners present. That process did not prevent the inevitable turmoil that normally accompanied base closings, but it at least offered more information for participants to fight about. Controversy remained just as high as it did in 1991. Nothing illustrated that more than the fight over the Presidio, which, among other things shows that base closure politics during an election year is particularly contentious given the stakes at hand. In the Presidio case, the original closure decision in 1988 carried over again and again, and produced just as much heat in 1996 as it had in 1988.

The events of 1993 also illustrated the point that base closings are sometimes never final, as the MacDill case showed. Even the interference of nature with the destruction of Homestead AFB derailed temporarily the efforts to achieve a solution to MacDill. And, again, the operating service, this time the Air Force, was thwarted in its efforts to get out from under the base and its two major command staffs. The Navy (particularly the Naval Training Command) likewise was stymied in its efforts to close Meridian NAS. Apparently, it underestimated the power of local politics coupled with the powerful but silent efforts of Representative Montgomery to save the base. Not having learned that lesson, the Navy would again be blocked from closing the base in 1995.

The Navy took the brunt of base closings in 1993. The Air Force saw two bomber bases targeted for closure—Plattsburgh AFB in New York, and K.I. Sawyer AFB in Michigan—but the five major aircraft repair depots survived yet another round of base closure. The Army had only one large base targeted for closure, but Alabama's Fort McClellan appeared on the 1993 list, only to once again disappear from the list after BRAC hearings. The citizens of central Alabama might have felt that, after its third appearance, Fort McClellan might be finally safe. So might the citizens living around the large Air Force depots in Texas, California, Utah, Oklahoma, and Georgia. Well protected politically, and with huge civilian workforces employed there, the depots seemed almost impervious to closure. But the 1995 BRAC would venture where previous BRACs apparently had feared to tread, and would move to usher in the real "mother of all base closures."

CHAPTER FIVE

1995

But I would say that it looks to me like the 1995 base closure list is going to be the biggest one of all. I do not know whether it is going to be out of two or what, but it is going to be bigger than the 1993, Ted, I think.[1]

—*Secretary of Defense Les Aspin*

What is so important about the Portsmouth Naval Shipyard? The importance of the Portsmouth Naval Shipyard is that the vast majority of its personnel live in New Hampshire, the state that has the first 1996 presidential primary. . . . The fact . . . has not been lost on Governor Wilson or Senator Dole.[2]

—*Representative Stephen Horn (R-CA)*

*T*he bad news for bases that had survived the 1991 and 1993 rounds of base closure was that 1995 would be worse. The original legislation creating BRAC specified closure of 30 percent of the existing base structure as of 1988 after the final round had been completed. The combined effects of BRAC 1991 and 1993, though, had closed only 15 percent of those bases, leaving another 15 percent for 1995. The problem was that the overall constant value of the defense budget had declined 34 percent between 1988 and 1995, and while 70 U.S. bases closed in the first three rounds, 495 remained untouched by the BRAC process.[3] Contrary to the quotation from Senator Hollings (D-SC) at the head of the last chapter, 1995, not 1993, really promised to be the "mother of all base closures." That it was not was symptomatic of the fact that politics was still alive and well in the base closure process.

BRAC 1995 promised to be not only the most severe BRAC, but also the most controversial. Bases targeted for closure in earlier rounds were now shutting down, and the pain of defense cutbacks in

general was spreading across the country. Another round of base closures on top of prior base shutdowns and defense plant layoffs would
surely generate even more political controversy than the last rounds
had. With that likelihood in mind, members of Congress from vulnerable states hoped to defer the 1995 round for two years. In September 1993, the Senate defeated 79-18 a proposal by Senator Dianne
Feinstein to delay BRAC until 1997.[4] The concerns expressed by Feinstein and others began to filter into the BRAC process even before
it began. For Republicans, in particular, the process seemed to be driven at least in part by political objectives, and even though Republicans captured the Senate and House in the 1994 midterm election,
the presidency remained in Democratic hands. Thus, Republicans
were concerned that he would pressure the services and the Secretary of Defense to protect certain bases in key states where Democrats
retained offices in the Senate and House. After all the president was
now on the defensive after the 1994 midterm elections, to protect
both his own re-election chances and those of his fellow Democrats in
Congress. It was also noteworthy that the president's choice for BRAC
Chair for 1995 was a former Democratic Senator from Illinois.

THE POLITICS OF SELECTING COMMISSIONERS

For 1995, the BRAC process was examined in light of previous experience to try to minimize political turmoil. BRAC was an open process
compared to other commission operations, with commissioners making themselves available to the public at various base visits and regional public hearings. For the last BRAC, though, the process was
opened even more, with televised live hearings on the final decision
process. Citizens previously unfamiliar with C-SPAN found themselves watching eagerly for hours on end as the commissioners
slogged their way through mounds of information on each base on
the list. At the end of discussion of each listed base, the members
would vote. While the process may have appeared impassive within
the hearing room, the emotion in living rooms and neighborhood
bars can only be imagined as bases lived or died on majority vote. The
names and faces of the commissioners became well known, even if
only for a few days. They were:

- Alan J. Dixon, former Democratic United States Senator from
  Illinois from 1981 to 1993 and a partner in a St. Louis law firm at
  the time of his BRAC appointment.

- Alton W. Cornella, president of Cornella Refrigeration.
- Rebecca C. Cox, vice president of Continental Airlines.
- James B. Davis, retired Air Force general.
- S. Lee Kling, chair of the board of Kling Rechter & Company, a merchant banking firm in St. Louis, Missouri.
- Benjamin F. Montoya, president and chief executive officer of the Public Service Company of New Mexico and retired U.S. Navy rear admiral.
- Joshue Robles, Jr., senior vice president, corporate controller, chief financial officer of USAA Financial Services, and retired U.S. Army general.
- Wendi L. Steele, professional writer.

The list was not confirmed without some political fighting. Senator Bob Dole, the senior Republican from Kansas, nominated Robles, who had previously commanded the First Mechanized Infantry Division at Fort Riley, Kansas. Prior to Robles nomination, Dole sent forth former Army Secretary Michael P.W. Stone as his nominee, but Stone's candidacy was withdrawn by Dole after undisclosed problems cropped up in a White House background check.[5] The White House also moved slowly on Robles's appointment, apparently concerned that his membership on the Commission was designed specifically to save Fort Riley and thus improve Senator Dole's political chances, both in Kansas and for the presidency in 1996. Dole, in a counter-move, postponed a full Senate vote on the first six BRAC nominees. He was joined in this move by Senators Daniel Patrick Moynihan (D-NY) and Alfonse D'Amato (R-NY) of New York, both of whom were still angry over the 1993 swap of New York's Plattsburgh AFB for New Jersey's McGuire AFB. The result was that when the commission first met with its new Chair, Senator Allan Dixon, it was a commission of one—Dixon.

It turned out that Robles was not the only member who had ties to military bases. Davis, nominated by House Speaker Newt Gingrich (R-GA), was a retired Air Force general who had worked for the Spectrum Group, a firm that assisted local communities in saving bases. Furthermore, he represented the city of Glendale, Arizona, which was trying to protect nearby Luke AFB. During congressional confirmation hearings, Davis told the House Armed Services Committee that he would cut his ties to Spectrum and recuse himself from decisions on Ellsworth AFB in South Dakota (which did not make the closure list). At that time Luke and Ellsworth AFBs were in competition to stay open, and Davis's support for Luke would have come at

Ellsworth's expense. Ellsworth, though, had its own advocate in Al Cornella. Cornella's company was located in Rapid City, South Dakota, Ellsworth's nearest community. Cornella, nominated by Senate Minority Leader Tom Daschle (D-SD), had lobbied on behalf of Ellsworth in 1993 when he headed the chamber of commerce effort to save the base. The base was probably vulnerable in both years because its primary tenant, the 28th Bomb Wing, faced disestablishment. The 28th consisted of B-1Bs, which in 1995 were under consideration for partial transfer to reserve and Air National Guard units. Ellsworth was also a "northern-tier" base with a questionable rationale for existence in the post–Cold War period. Cornella stated during confirmation that he would refrain from decisions on Ellsworth. His disclaimer did not appease Representative Richard Armey (R-TX), who had been the prime mover for the BRAC process. Armey called Cornella's nomination "a joke" and claimed that Cornella should be testifying before the commission, not as a member of it.[6]

Other commissioners with Republican ties also had connections to bases, even if they were somewhat less obvious. Rebecca Cox, vice president of Continental Airlines, was married to Republican Representative Christopher Cox (R-CA), who represented the district containing both El Toro and Tustin Marine Corps Air Stations (MCAS). She too said that she would recuse herself from decisions involving the two bases, as she had previously done when she was a member of the 1993 Commission that voted to close Tustin (and then delayed the closure date until 1999). But Commissioner Cox had another interesting connection that was not geographical, but rather related to her position at Continental Airlines. Senator Rick Santorum (R-PA) sat on the Senate committee that regulated airlines, including Continental Airlines. Santorum had a strong interest in saving Letterkenney Army Depot, located in Pennsylvania, which the Army recommended for realignment. One way to accomplish this was to close a competing arsenal. So Cox strongly defended Letterkenney by arguing in favor of closing the Red River Army Depot, defended by fellow Commissioner Robles. In the end, both facilities were "realigned," an action that saved jobs at both bases.

Wendi Steele, the professional writer, also brought political ties to the BRAC process. She had formerly served as an aide to Senator Don Nickles (R-OK), where Tinker AFB, a base containing the Oklahoma City Air Logistics Center (ALC), was located. The Air Force did not place the Oklahoma City ALC on its list of recommended closures, but BRAC included it for consideration. Unlike the other BRAC nominees, with ties to bases, Steele said that she would not recuse herself on decisions about Tinker AFB, arguing: "I'm committed to being fair. I don't think it could be an issue."[7] In the end, the Oklahoma City ALC was one of three air logistics bases surviving closure, though Steele's role in that decision is unclear. The depot issue was clearly complicated, as noted below.

Commissioner S. Lee Kling had ties to the Democratic Party, having served as finance chair of the Democratic National Committee. He had also served as national treasurer for the Carter-Mondale Election Committee, and as national treasurer for the Gephardt for President Committee in 1987-1988. His ties to Representative Richard Gephardt (D-MO), the former Speaker of the House, were fairly obvious, though it is impossible to prove that no significant installation in the state of Missouri was closed in the 1995 round due to Kling's membership on the commission.

The Senate Armed Services Committee members did realize that it would be very difficult to find commissioners who were not connected with military bases. Senator Sam Nunn said: "I think that everybody ought to understand that if we picked a Commission that had no connection with any base in the United States, we would be going to Europe or Japan for that Commission."[8] Perhaps, but at the same time, there are a number of states (Iowa, Wisconsin, Minnesota, Vermont, Oregon, and West Virginia, for example), that have no major military installations inside their borders, and it is difficult to believe that there were not suitable members for the 1995 BRAC with less visible ties to vulnerable bases than those ultimately selected. Their promises to recuse themselves from deliberations concerning bases with which they had connections were only partly reassuring for purposes of impartiality. Bases, it should be remembered, are closed competitively, and efforts to close one base may save another base. So any of the above commissioners could strongly support the inclusion of a base on the closure list without directly acting on their own base, yet their action could work in their base's favor.

CHANGING THE CLOSURE DECISION PROCESS FOR 1995

After three rounds of base closure, the 1995 round became a repository for experience on the process. The 1995 process saw a number of modifications, particularly in areas that had been marked by controversy in previous rounds. There was probably no more controversial element in past BRAC efforts than the quality and accuracy of the data submitted to support base closure decisions.

Because there had been numerous problems with the accuracy of submitted data on base value and use (recall Meridian NAS or Loring AFB, for example), the 1995 BRAC developed new rules to try to minimize the exactitude problem. All data submitted through the BRAC process had to be certified as accurate by an expert in the field. Moreover BRAC 1995 held 13 investigative hearings in Washington, D.C., in addition to its regional hearings so that experts from both other government agencies and the private sector might testify independently about base facts. The General Accounting Office (GAO) also played a major role in evaluating the Defense Department data.

Change occurred in another area as well. Previous base closure rounds had seen power concentrated and expanded at the federal level as each agency involved tried to expand both its expertise and its policy jurisdiction. By the mid-1990s, though, the long-standing refrain of "too much power in Washington" had its influence on BRAC politics as well. Two congressional acts of the previous year both gave power back to base localities and softened one of the more onerous provisions of federal control over base transfer, the McKinney Act. The Pryor Amendment to the National Defense Authorization Act for Fiscal Year 1994, sponsored by Senator David Pryor (D-AR), placed the resolution of a number of base-closure issues with local communities and weakened federal jurisdiction, and the Base Closure Community Redevelopment and Homeless Assistance Act of 1994 changed the demands of the original McKinney legislation that homeless housing had priority over economic development, requiring instead that the needs of the homeless only be "considered" in base redevelopment. The Environmental Response, Compensation, and Liability Act made "fast-track" cleanup easier and allowed base transfer prior to complete remediation of environmental problems at closed bases. Economic development took center stage as a clear priority of the Clinton administration, which, facing another round of base closures prior to the presidential election of 1996, already had crafted its base-policy response in the best of political terms.

In January 1994, the Defense Department issued guidance to the services for the selection of bases for closure and realignment. Each service then initiated its own review of base valuation, but this time with a new procedure recommended by the 1993 BRAC members. Since service jointness was gradually becoming important to the Defense Department (after being mandated by the 1986 Goldwater-Nichols Act), the department created the Joint Cross-Service Groups (JCSG) for the 1995 round. The JCSG represented five functional groupings (depot maintenance, military medical treatment facilities, test and evaluation, undergraduate pilot training, and laboratories—areas in which the potential existed for the services to combine what had previously been separate and often duplicative functions. What is somewhat telling about service attitudes toward jointness is that it took seven years for the services to institutionalize efforts to combine functions across base, and to judge bases on their capacity to handle joint operations.

THE AIR FORCE DEPOT PROBLEM

Bases barely surviving earlier BRAC rounds were especially vulnerable to closure in 1995, and rumors began to spread even before the selection of the 1995 BRAC commissioners. Since none of the Air Force's five large maintenance depots (technically called air logistics centers, or ALCs) had made earlier closure lists, they were particularly susceptible to inclusion in 1995. The depots, according to a GAO report, held considerable excess capacity, averaging 45 percent. The average was skewed somewhat by extreme scores; Warner Robins in Georgia had 26 percent excess capacity, while San Antonio in Texas had 58 percent.[9] The wing commander at Ogden ALC at Hill AFB in Utah used the base newsletter to try to calm nerves when rumors about Ogden's imminent closure became so frequent.[10] There were some cases of overconfidence as well. A colonel in the electronic-maintenance shop at Warner Robins ALC, considered safe from closure, said that he wished the depot would be placed on the BRAC list so the workers there would work harder.

When the Air Force first announced its 1995 BRAC candidates in February, no depots appeared on its list. But within the Air Force itself, there was considerable debate over this decision. Commanders of the operational Air Force commands began to lobby Air Force leadership to change the decision and add depots to the Air Force's 1995 closure recommendations.[11] They had suffered previous cuts in operational bases and believed that they could better preserve what they had left from cuts in 1995 only if some of the depots were offered up for shutdown. Prior to the 1995 round the Air Force Materiel Command[12] (AFMC) had cut only its small base operations, such as laboratories located at larger bases. In 1993, when the operating commands lost a number of large bases, the AFMC suffered only the loss of Newark AFB in Ohio. According to one report, a majority of senior Air Force officers believed that it was necessary to close at least two of the five Air Force depots.[13]

The initial 1995 Air Force closure list, though, was sent to BRAC without any depot closure recommendations. Air Force officials had initially placed two of the five depots on their draft closure list, but the same officials suddenly pulled them from it the night before the list went to BRAC. That may have been a response to political pressure from the White House, since earlier in 1995 the Air Force BRAC team had concluded that the service had an excess capacity of 1.5 depots (rounded up to two) and had ranked each depot in terms of its value.[14] Then, perhaps as a way to get the Air Force's attention, the BRAC commissioners astonished the service in May by placing four of the five (McClellan AFB in California with Sacramento ALC; Warner Robins AFB in Georgia with Warner Robins ALC; Tinker AFB in Oklahoma with Oklahoma City ALC; and Kelly AFB in Texas with San Antonio ALC) on its lists, leaving only Hill AFB with Ogden ALC. To add insult to injury, the commission also listed for closure the Defense Distribution Depots belonging to the Defense Logistics Agency at McClellan, Robins, Tinker, and Kelly AFBs. The BRAC members forced the Air Force to reconsider its closure recommendations, and, in a flurry of activity, that service found itself under considerable political pressure by supporters of the now-threatened depots. All the depots except Ogden and Oklahoma City were in vote-rich states, and the presidential election was slightly more than a year away. The Air Force recalculated its rankings of the depots and resubmitted them to BRAC, which ultimately voted to close McClellan AFB, including Sacramento ALC, and to realign Kelly AFB, with an option to privatize San Antonio ALC.

The action took many by surprise. The common belief that the large Air Force depots were too politically important to close was shattered. Those with a longer memory remembered that the Middletown Air Material Area at Olmstead AFB in Pennsylvania and the Mobile Air Material Area at Brookley AFB in Alabama were both closed in the 1960s.[15] In other cases, though, perceptions of depot vulnerability set in, particularly at Ogden and Oklahoma City. Community activism mobilized a human chain of support around the Oklahoma City depot, with a reported 30,000 citizens forming the chain. At a more political level, Senator Nickles was able to obtain military-construction funds to get a new runway for the base, since Air Force requirements had changed to mandate at least two runways for depots. That action, which cost millions of dollars, may have been helpful in saving Oklahoma City, as the base was ultimately taken off the 1995 BRAC closure list. The new runway was only in the planning stages in 1995, though, and, while it was later completed in terms of concrete, it had no navigation aids for landing, and thus was unusable.

Depots are highly desirable bases to have in one's district because they employ large numbers of civilian maintenance workers to repair military equipment. They contribute so many jobs to local economies that certain members of Congress formed what became known as the "depot caucus" to legislate their workload. The caucus was responsible for what is called the "60-40 rule," which mandates that no more than 40 percent of Defense Department maintenance can go to private companies. The members of the depot caucus would make themselves heard during the 1995 BRAC round.

One of the most controversial closings of the year was the aircraft depot at McClellan AFB in California, at least in terms of press coverage, though McClellan's loss of 11,000 jobs paled alongside the more than 20,000 jobs at the San Antonio Depot at Kelly AFB.[16] Still, Mc-Clellan seemed to be a magnet for criticism of the process, which focused heavily on the economic and political impact of closure. The nature of the military requirements tended to become clouded in the heat of the debate. For example, Senator Barbara Boxer (D-CA), in an opinion article in *USA Today*, noted with alarm the overall impact of McClellan, in particular on the Sacramento area, which, if closed, would add its 13,000 jobs (others claimed 11,000) to an estimated 13,000 other jobs already lost at other previously closed bases in Northern California.[17] While her piece was titled "Base Essential to Security," her only arguments about McClellan's contribution to security were that ". . . defense officials say that to close it would 'disrupt military readiness'" and that ". . . Air Force officials say that closing it would 'preclude the Air Force from carrying through with vital readiness and modernization programs.'"[18] However, the Air Force had already noted a 30-40 percent surplus in Air Force depot capacity, since the number of aircraft in its inventory had shrunk by more than 25 percent from the 1980s while depot capacity had remained unchanged since then. Moreover, aircraft depot work was being consolidated across the four services, providing even more depot capacity. So to argue that some unspecified "readiness and modernization" programs were threatened by the closure of McClellan rang somewhat hollow.

In its own evaluation of depots on "military value," the Air Force ranked them in the following order from high to low:

1. Warner Robins
2. Oklahoma City
3. Ogden
4. Sacramento
5. San Antonio

Representative Frank Tejeda (D-TX) of San Antonio challenged this ranking, claiming that "Kelly (San Antonio) has the best quality record with the lowest defect rate and fewest customer complaints of all ALCs. Kelly has the best educated work force and nowhere else in the Nation will you find employees who are as involved in their community than in San Antonio."[19]

Other political figures representing Texas were equally ready to do battle. Representative Henry Gonzales (D-TX) fired off a letter to President Clinton charging that the decision was "unsound on military and economic terms."[20] Republican Governor George W. Bush stated that "I know the commissioners took a long, hard look, but I think they made the wrong decision."[21] Representative Frank Tejeda went somewhat further, alleging that two BRAC commissioners with California ties had switched votes to close San Antonio after their bid to save Sacramento was defeated."[22] "Some of those votes were retaliatory votes," he said.[23] Other charges of dirty deeds were leveled by retired Air Force Brig. Gen. Paul Robertson, who led the effort to save San Antonio. He alleged that "the staff is out to get us," claiming that the BRAC staff had changed Air Force figures to show that the closure costs for San Antonio were $421 million rather than the $525 million figure generated by the Air Force.[24]

Sacramento's closing also generated stiff responses. Senator Boxer's main emphasis indicated where her real concerns were: Should Sacramento be added to the 22 California bases already closed or realigned, California's unemployment rate would surely rise. Representative Robert Matsui (D-CA) found conspiracylike behavior on the part of the commissioners. While he did not name names, he stated that ". . . this was the most outrageous around. Those commissioners, not all of them, but many of them had their own agenda. One who was a high-ranking Army official, for example, not only during discussions showed significant bias, but he was actually outwardly favoring Army depots saying all his experience with the Army led him to believe that we should save these bases. That is not the way this process is supposed to work."[25] Matsui was obviously referring to Joshue Robles, whose defense of the Red River Army Depot was noted above.

As President Clinton considered the impact of closing McClellan, he began to consider an alternative to his 1993 actions of asking BRAC to remove the base from the final list. He realized that the political impact of closing the base might be eased if he could assure the workers—and California voters—that the jobs could be "privatized" instead of lost. One question was: How many of the total jobs could be privatized? According to White House Chief of Staff Leon Panetta, the base would remain open for five years following the closure announcement and privatization could save 700 to 1,000 jobs for the following years.[26] Less than 10 percent of the total jobs, in other words, would be saved for a limited period of time. For the military, the second question was: Why? In the face of surplus depot capacity, why invest in privatizing the jobs, whose salaries would still be paid out of Defense Department funds? The program struck many in the Air Force as pure politics for a very marginal gain. Indeed, as one analyst indicated, the savings from closing McClellan would first be deferred for five years, then eroded by privatization.[27] Moreover, what would be the point of privatizing the jobs at McClellan (or Kelly, for that matter) when the Air Force had indicated that retaining these depots simply retained surplus capacity whether private or Air Force owned? Even the workers at McClellan—presumably the core of those Clinton needed to win—seemed skeptical about the privatizing plan. As one worker pointed out: "You lose all those benefits and start over at the bottom. . . . Besides, they say the jobs will stay in California, but will they stay at McClellan?"[28]

Privatization plans for San Antonio began to form by November 1995, and the job picture became somewhat clearer. According to Air Force projections, of the 19,000 civilian jobs at San Antonio, approximately 3,000 would leave between 1995 and 2001, with a goal of maintaining the remaining 16,000 until 2001.[29] Since 11,000 jobs would remain at the base due to the transfer of other functions at Kelly AFB, the total projected job loss was 5,000.[30] There were no good predictions about how many jobs would remain at the depot after 2001, when the Air Force was scheduled to sell the property to the city of San Antonio. So other plans were proposed to help economic adjustment, including designating Kelly AFB and areas surrounding it as an Enterprise Zone, thus making it eligible for tax incentives and other governmental allowances; expediting environmental cleanup, and supporting changes to the 60-40 rule.[31] Some of these proposals, particularly changing the 60-40 rule, sounded somewhat like wishful thinking, given the power of the depot caucus and the desire of its members to protect the remaining depots. But other proposals might allow for low-cost transfers to other activities, though at what could be considerable government expense.

The privatization plan generated opposition from several quarters. Some argued that to place traditionally military functions in private hands would be tantamount to disaster. "The services have a real requirement for a ready, controlled source of maintenance, because when it comes time for war they can't afford to start renegotiating contracts." So said Bill Johnson, legislative assistant for Representative Jim Hansen (R-UT), who was co-chair of the depot caucus in Congress."[32] Hansen and other members of that caucus had lobbied for years to keep the depots open because they were such an important source of employment. They understood the implications of privatization for that employment base. Said Hansen: "I'm an avid believer in privatization, but there have to be some things done by the military."[33] In the end, the depot-caucus members feared total privatization and lobbied hard to close Sacramento and San Antonio so that their workloads might be shifted to the remaining three depots, which, by 1996, were operating at less than 50 percent capacity.[34] Hansen himself saw the heavy hand of politics in the McClellan privatization decision, charging that "the administration has continued to play fast and lose [*sic*] with the law. On a recent visit to Sacramento, White House Chief of Staff Leon Panetta issued the following threat, 'If there is any action in Congress or by any other depots to try and inhibit the privatization effort, the President has made it clear that we will consider that a breach of process and he will order the McClellan [*sic*] to remain open.' I find that kind of blatant disregard for the law offensive and contemptuous of the law and of Congress."[35]

Another source of opposition came from defense-industry officials, who had hoped to transfer some aircraft maintenance work to their facilities to preserve them in the face of declining military orders. Don Fuqua, president of the Aerospace Industries Association, said: "We support privatization, but we have concerns about privatization in place, which could exacerbate the over-capacity problem."[36] His concerns reflected a dilemma facing the military aviation industry as the defense budget declined and orders for new aircraft dropped. In order to preserve defense industrial capacity and save jobs in the aviation business, proposals surfaced to shift maintenance work from military depots to commercial aviation plants. Fuqua expressed concern that allowing the depots to remain open under privatization would deprive aircraft manufacturers of a golden opportunity to expand their business—maintaining and building aircraft.

Still, plans for privatization continued. At San Antonio, the center commander announced that the C-5 maintenance facility would be the first to privatize, and by August 1996, managers had developed a time line for the process. There were so many assumptions in the time line and the associated employment levels that firm planning would be difficult. As the commander explained: "Based on a July '97 contract, we would set a reduction in force . . . effective data of March '98.

That assumes the transition to the contractor takes place over a nine-month period. . . . We believe we'll get the approval."[37] The commanders words were candid, but the caution with which he spoke indicated that there was still much uncertainty associated with the entire privatization enterprise even after it was adopted as the official depot conversion policy. But, of course, 1996 was an election year, and the choice was the most acceptable to President Clinton.

In late 1996, the GAO released a study critical of the depot privatization plans. It bluntly stated: "Because substantial excess capacity exists in both the public and private sectors, privatizing Sacramento and San Antonio workloads in place will result in missed opportunities to reduce the overall cost of Air Force depot maintenance operations."[38] The GAO report also noted that the "60-40 rule severely limited the amount of privatization. Air Force planners projected that, without the rule, around $600 million in depot workload would privatize, and that, should the law remain on the books, the remaining $1.05 billion workload would simply transfer to other depots.[39] The Air Force tried to delay that transfer in 1996 by halting consideration of transfer of ground-communications-electronics workload to the Army's Tobyhanna Depot in Pennsylvania to preserve jobs in Sacramento.[40]

The Clinton Choice—Protest and Accept

In the end, Clinton found himself with two unpalatable choices; send the base closure list back to the BRAC commissions for reconsideration (which would, in the view of some of his advisers, smack too much of pure politics) or accept the list. Since sending the closure list back to BRAC would appear "political," and since there was also no assurance that BRAC would make changes to it, particularly the changes that the president wanted, Clinton chose to accept the list while acting angry, perhaps to deflect some of the inevitable blame for the accompanying job losses. In what was described as a "lectern-pounding, finger-pointing outburst," Clinton tried to blame BRAC for the consequences of base closings, and even hinted that the 1995 list favored Republicans at the expense of Democrats.[41] Clinton also understood the politics of personal appearance. He dispatched Deputy Secretary of Defense John White to San Antonio with a check for $500,000. White claimed that the check was "just a symbol" and the first installment of funds to assist in base transition.[42] During his visit, White noted that while "it was not Clinton's idea to close the base," the administration would try to preserve at least two-thirds of the 16,000 jobs there.[43]

The depots presented an additional set of problems with their pollution levels. At Oklahoma City, for example, a 220-acre plume of toxins lay in the upper water aquifer. Additional pollution problems included underground storage tanks, waste pits, fire training areas, and low-level radiation areas. At San Antonio an initial survey in 1982 1988 located some 26 potential contamination sites, but further site investigation expanded the list to 52.[44] Problems included waste pits, oil-evaporation pits, contaminated groundwater, and several sites marked "radioactive disposal area."

There is no question that the 1995 BRAC actions were the most politicized of all. In response, Deputy Secretary of Defense John White (who had headed up the Defense Department's sensitive Commission on Roles and Missions before taking his Deputy position, felt obliged to explain that there was in fact no "playing politics" in the BRAC process. In an opinion piece in *The Washington Post* titled "Playing Politics? The Charge is Baseless," White actually conveyed the opposite impression; politics had indeed played a role, but not at the Defense Department's end of things.[45] Nor, for that matter, was the Clinton Administration playing politics. The politics playing was apparently done at the BRAC level, which, White claimed, was ". . . pressured by mayors, governors, senators, representatives, and many well-heeled lobbyists."[46] While White did not directly assert that the 1995 BRAC recommendations were based on political considerations, he did note: "The Commission protected 23 bases that the Defense Department said we couldn't afford. [47] So why did the president ultimately accept the list without sending it back to the Commission? According to White, "Since we believed that it was more important to preserve the process than to correct every Commission misjudgment, we recommended that the president accept the list."[48]

BRAC Chairman Dixon clearly resented the charge of politicization. In a letter to *The Washington Post* in response to White's editorial, Dixon claimed that the Defense Department was largely responsible for the pain inflicted by the 1995 list. He noted that BRAC had accepted 84 percent of the Defense Department's recommendations for 1995, the same percentage as in 1993 and one percent higher than for 1991.[49] Dixon claimed that changes in the Pentagon's list were necessary only when "errors occurred"—for example, when the Defense Department did not place any of the Air Force depots on the list despite "significant excess capacity at all five of the depots" reported by both the Air Force and the Defense Department Depot

Maintenance Joint Cross-Service Group.[50] Dixon also noted that the GAO had questioned the Air Force's cost estimates because they were based on incomplete studies, and had concluded that the Air Force had overestimated the cost of closing the depots and underestimated the saving that would accrue from such actions.[51] Dixon finally reminded his critics that "The decision to close any military base is a painful one. The Commission was created because Congress could not endure that pain."[52]

In the end, Congress voted in September 1995 to accept the entire list of 79 closures and 26 realignments. The vote did not come without a final struggle to reject the BRAC list; Representative Tejeda submitted a proposal to turn down the recommendations, but in the end his measure was soundly defeated by a 343-75 vote in the House. It was largely symbolic anyway; said Tejeda: "I have no illusions about the final outcome of this matter."[53]

Service Shares of BRAC 1995

In the 1993 BRAC round, the Air Force saw only three of its bases closed, while the Navy had the largest share of closures. If previous BRAC patterns were to be repeated, the 1995 round should have compensated the Navy (and, for that matter, the Army) by giving the Air Force the biggest cut. But when the Defense Department list was released by Defense Secretary William Perry, the Air Force again had the fewest bases. As noted earlier, the biggest surprise was the exclusion of the Air Force depots from the list. It had been reported that the joint service commission that had reviewed the initial service selections recommended that both McClellan and Kelly AFBs be closed.[54] But because of the potential political damage that could result from their closure, they were not on the initial list, prompting Oklahoma Republican Representative Nickles to query: "Where's California? Ten percent of the electoral votes. It makes one wonder."[55] The burden of closing aircraft depots thus fell on the Army and Navy, which prompted Representative Tillie Fowler (R-FL) to complain that it was unfair to expect those services to close their depots while the Air Force shut down none; "That was not an option given to the Navy and Army," said Fowler.[56]

That sense of bitterness from the Navy and the Army may have helped BRAC to re-insert both the Sacramento and San Antonio Air Force Depots on the closure list. But in fairness to all of the services involved in BRAC 1995, some of the difficulty lay in making comparisons across service bases. Each service was required to rank its bases on a value scale, but there was no common database to do this. For example, costing out the value of a base is difficult since most bases had been built decades before the closure process began, and there were no common models to use. Instead, each service developed its own costing models, and, in fact, those models produced disagreement even within the services. In the Air Force there was considerable disagreement between the major Air Force command headquarters and the Air Staff in Washington about the conclusions that cost models produced. So when the models proved to be less than useful in deciding closure issues at the service level, the conflict was resolved more through political pressures than through decisions based on objective data. And even though the GAO had to validate the results of service cost models, it is very difficult for even the most careful accountant to validate the products of inadequate models.

Winners and Losers

In 1995, there were some clear winners and losers from the military submission round. According to the calculations of the *Dayton Daily News*, Ohio would be a new winner, with a new gain of 1,825 jobs from closed bases. While some small facilities would be closed or reduced, Dayton's Wright-Patterson AFB would gain 3,730 full- and part-time jobs, while Texas lost 6,981, New Mexico 5,138, Alabama 4,946, Pennsylvania 3,600, and California 3,386 jobs.[57] It was difficult to see the hand of politics intervening here, at least not at the presidential level. While Ohio is an important state, Texas, California, and Pennsylvania are even more important in the electoral vote contest. While President Clinton bitterly complained about the job losses in those states, he either did not try to alter or was not capable of altering the final BRAC calculations.

FORT MCCLELLAN, ALABAMA

By 1995, the citizens of Anniston, Alabama, could not have been surprised that Fort McClellan appeared again on the BRAC list. It had appeared on every previous BRAC list, a record shared by no other base. The reasons given by the Army were the same as they had been in prior years—that the Army's chemical mission and its elements at McClellan could be transferred elsewhere. That mission was not important enough to justify retaining an Army fort. For the public around the base, though, the lack of justification meant the end of a $150 million annual payroll.

Base Vulnerabilities

Previous efforts to close Fort McClellan had revealed other vulnerabilities. The base lacked a single large school, but instead hosted a number of smaller schools that could be consolidated with other schools at other bases. There was no more land there for expansion, unlike at Fort Jackson in South Carolina, where there was room for both expansion and consolidation.[58] One way to get around these vulnerabilities was to bring in missions from other services as a way to get these services to support Fort McClellan. The Navy moved its Chemical, Biological, and Radiological and Defense Disaster Preparedness School to Fort McClellan, sending 550 Navy personnel to the school annually. The Air Force followed suit, moving its Disaster Preparedness School to Fort McClellan in 1994, training 1,000 airmen each year. The Marines sent 1,100 military police personnel along with 250 nuclear-, biological-, and chemical- warfare-specialists to Fort McClellan annually. If one of the goals of such multiservice usage was to help keep Fort McClellan open, it clearly failed. For the other services, the facilities required for such training could be moved to another Army base or maybe to one of their own.

According to Representative Glen Browder (D-AL), the Army initially testified to BRAC that the one-time cost estimates for closing Fort McClellan were $231 million, but one month later, the cost had increased to $391 million.[59] Browder also argued that the Army's net cost figures jumped from $110 million in June 1995 to $377 million in August 1995, a 243 percent increase.[60] Browder also gave dark forecasts about how much Fort McClellan's closure would hurt the country in military terms, noting that: ". . . in the future something is going to happen with chemical weapons, an incident akin to the Beirut barracks bombing of the past. . . ."[61]

Members of the Anniston Chamber of Commerce echoed the same complaints against the Army as they had in previous years—that the Army leadership was comprised of "traditional" soldiers from artillery, armor, and infantry and that such soldiers had little taste for chemical weapons. They would be, therefore, quite willing to shut down a base with chemical weapons as its primary mission in order to save a base in which the Army performs "traditional" missions. Since both Fort Riley in Kansas and Fort Carson in Colorado were rumored to be candidates for closure, the suspicions of the Anniston Chamber of Commerce members deepened when McClellan was the only major Army base to appear on the Army's submission to BRAC. Neither the Chamber of Commerce supporters nor other defenders of Fort McClellan would find much encouragement from at least one BRAC member, retired General Robles, who had formerly commanded a unit at Fort Riley, and had been nominated for the commission by Kansas Senator Bob Dole to ensure that one of his state's larger bases would not be touched in the 1995 base closure round.

Efforts to Save Fort McClellan

One strategy Fort McClellan's defenders had used previously was to try to add value to the base by requesting a $108.9 million chemical-disposal facility at the nearby Anniston Army Depot in 1993, with construction scheduled to start in May 1994.[62] Given that the United States had at that time 30,000 tons of chemical agent slated for destruction,[63] the facility at Anniston could have possibly helped keep Fort McClellan open, in part because it might have been easier to transfer and ultimately destroy Fort McClellan's chemical stockpile at Anniston than to transport it across state lines to another facility. Fort McClellan had a written agreement with the Alabama Department of Environmental Management to provide resources in case of a chemical-weapons emergency at Anniston. Thus Fort McClellan and a new chemical-disposal facility could work in tandem to dispose of chemical weapons, possibly delaying or preventing closure. On the other hand, there had been a considerable transfer of chemical weapons to other sites, including remote Johnston Atoll in the Pacific Ocean. Since there had been no major accidents in these transfers, the argument about the comparative safety of local chemical disposal may not have carried too far. When that facility was not funded, Representative Browder acted to kill a Senate-sponsored measure directing the Army to study how chemical weapons might be transported to other locations safely.[64] In a 1995 press release, Browder said he worked to kill the study out of concern that the Army might transport chemical weapons into Alabama for destruction at Anniston.[65] Said Browder: ". . . although we in Alabama are willing to destroy our own stockpile, we are absolutely opposed to other people sending their chemical weapons into our state."[66] He did not say that pressure to build a disposal facility at McClellan might increase if the Army could not even study how to transport McClellan's chemical weapons out of the state for disposal.[67]

The Politics of Chemical Weapons

Browder emphasized, in particular, the toxic nature of the weapons, noting that: ". . . Fort McClellan has poisons such as sarin and VX. A small drop of sarin on a man's skin can be fatal. VX is several times more lethal than sarin, and a small drop of the liquid evenly distributed can kill many people. Among the weapons stored at the Anniston Army Depot, each M-23 land mind contains 10 1/2 pounds of VX. Each of the 78,000 MSS 115-millimeter rockets . . . contains either 10 pounds of VX or 10.7 pounds of sarin. That is a pretty dangerous mixture."[68] Browder even took advantage of a 1995 chemical weapons attack in Tokyo, Japan by a terrorist organization to drive home his point about the value of chemical-weapons training: ". . . it is only a matter of time before terrorists, extortionists, or deranged individuals and groups targeted Americans. That is why I am asking American defense intelligence and emergency preparedness officials to tell me and the American people just what our Government is doing to prepare for chemical and biological terrorism here in the United States."[69] The presumed answer that Browder wanted was "not enough without Fort McClellan." He would subsequently ask ". . . all Alabamians and all Americans concerned about chemical weapons and terrorism to write or call President Bill Clinton and urge him to save the world's only live-agent chemical weapons training base."[70]

As though the chemical-weapons issue was not enough ammunition in itself to save Fort McClellan, Browder went doggedly after another issue, a $17 million Army request to buy land for a museum in Washington, D.C. Browder spoke several times on the issue, calling the proposal the "Potomac Pork Palace" and arguing that the Army already had 48 museums around the nation.[71] Browder would have known; he had three at Fort McClellan: the Chemical Weapons Museum, the Military Police Museum, and the Woman's Army Corps Museum. So why should he care about the Army's desire for a new Washington, D.C., museum? Because such a facility could incorporate Fort McClellan's three Army museums, thus removing one more reason to keep Fort McClellan open.

BRAC's closure decision moved Fort McClellan's Chemical School and Military Police School to Fort Leonard Wood in Missouri. Such decisions to move facilities are normally made on the basis of available facilities to absorb the transfer. But in Fort Leonard Wood's case, such facilities were unavailable for either school. So while base closure is intended to save money, the supporters of Fort McClellan may have been dismayed to learn that the cost of facilities for the Chemical School came to $32 million, and for the Police School, close to $27 million.[72] One of the beneficiaries of this construction was Representative Ike Skelton (D-MO), a senior member of the House Committee on National Security who represented the district in which Fort Leonard Wood was located.

After Closure: What Next?

After the news of Fort McClellan's closure, local officials formed a Reuse Authority to combat the expected 16 percent increase in unemployment. But there was a sense of pessimism in the group: "At Cameron Station, VA, where land sells for $1 million an acre, they're standing in line for redevelopment. The same may be true for Fort Devins, Mass. Here it's harder to sell the idea of redevelopment," said Robert Richardson, head of the group.[73] Richardson did not specify why he thought conversion would be more difficult at Fort McClellan, but he did indicate that, despite the fact that Fort McClellan appeared three previous times on closure lists, "We never had a back-up plan because we never expected the post to close."[74] Possibly part of the problem was that despite Richardson's expressed surprise at McClellan's closure, the Army anticipated it and did not fund much new construction on the base. Perhaps another dimension to the problem of re-use was the nature of the surrounding area. With a population of 116,000, there was not the available labor force that surrounded some other bases (though Cameron Station, Virginia, and Fort Devins, Massachusetts are also located in rural areas). The median income was also lower, at $20,700, for Calhoun County, compared to $28,000 for the United States in 1996.

One potential solution lay in expanding higher education by utilizing base facilities to locate college and university classrooms. In December 1996, the State Board of Education gave permission for a group of three Alabama colleges to apply to use some of Fort McClellan's land for their expansion programs. Ayers State Technical College, Jacksonville State University, and Gadsden State Community College formed a group called the Higher Education Center Consortium to combine some assets from each institution to educate local workers in industrial training.[75] The hope was to attract industry to the area by offering a trained work force by pooling higher-education resources. But earlier in the month Alabama Governor Fob James had expressed a desire to reduce the size and scope of Alabama's higher education system, which had already suffered the largest cuts in the nation in 1996. The only attractive offer from Fort McClellan that gave the Higher Education Center Consortium any chance of success was the requirement that the base must give away free property, facilities, furniture, and equipment when it abandoned the post in 1999.[76]

Fort McClellan was hardly the Army's largest base, but it still had 2,300 active-duty military with 3,600 dependents in 1996. It also employed more than 2,000 civilians. There were few prospects that most of the jobs lost to base closure could be replaced with civilian industry. So Fort McClellan remained one of the more pessimistic base closures of 1995. In contrast, the closure of the Fleet Industrial Supply Center in Oakland, California, would be one of its success stories.

FLEET AND INDUSTRIAL SUPPLY CENTER, OAKLAND, CALIFORNIA

The Fleet and Industrial Supply Center (FISCO) was a large complex of industrial warehouses, railroad tracks, and piers stretching along the Oakland waterfront just south of the Oakland Bay Bridge terminus. For most of its history, it was the Oakland Naval Supply Center (NSC), renamed only in 1993. From World War II to Vietnam, thousands of ships loaded there with military supplies and troops for the far reaches of the Pacific. Trains packed with soldiers arrived at the adjacent Oakland Army Base, and the soldiers were bused to the docks of the Oakland NSC, where they marched aboard large gray transport ships and then sailed under the Bay Bridge and on to distant theaters of war. Cargo stored in huge warehouses filled the holds of supply ships to support combat, as well as peacetime operations, thousands of miles away. It was unglamorous work, mostly done by civilians who moved to Oakland to take advantage of wartime jobs.

By 1967, though, the Navy declared the aged troop ships too costly for further service, and they joined the fleet reserve of mothballed vessels in Suisan Bay. The workload diminished for the Oakland NSC, but it continued to berth and load civilian cargo vessels and ships operated by the Military Sealift Command and the Maritime Administration. The center also continued to provide employment for the citizens of Oakland; despite the work reduction, the facility maintained

Vietnam-era employment levels through 1995, when 21 workers lost their jobs due to work reduction.[77]

The original site for the Naval Supply Center was selected in 1940 after a two-year rivalry among San Francisco, San Mateo County, and Oakland. By 1941 $20 million had been spent to develop the facility.[78] In the early 1960s, the Army base at Fort Mason, across the San Francisco Bay, closed, and the headquarters building for the Military Sea Transportation Service moved to Oakland NSC, adding to the importance and the employment levels of the complex.[79] It became one of the largest West Coast military shipping ports, supporting hundreds of military activities throughout the Pacific region.

The NSC Declines in Military Importance

The end of the Vietnam War was the beginning of the end for the Oakland NSC, though the end was long in coming. That was perhaps fortunate for the NSC, though, because while its workload declined, the influence and scope of the Port of Oakland grew. The Port of Oakland is an arm of the Oakland city government, which centralized most of the city's commercial transportation facilities under a commission first established in 1927. The Port manages 16,645 acres of property stretching from Emeryville to San Leandro, including marine terminals, the Oakland International Airport, Jack London Square, and 569 acres of commercial property under lease. A board of directors runs the Port and includes members with prior affiliations to the state Supreme Court, the Kaiser industries, organized labor, real estate, and education. The Port and its commission represent a powerful political force given that they manage activities that directly and indirectly create 24,400 jobs and a combined payroll of $1.23 billion.[80]

The Port of Oakland anticipated growth as trade with Pacific Rim nations increased in the 1980s, and the NSC infrastructure allowed for such expansion. Port facilities grew on unused land around Oakland NSC, and, by the early 1990s, the base was almost surrounded by Port operations, including the towering gantries used to offload cargo from container ships and acres of land used to store the containers themselves.

Oakland NSC, now the Fleet and Industrial Supply Center Oakland (FISCO), first appeared on the 1993 BRAC base-closure list, which included almost all large naval installations in the San Francisco/Oakland area, including the Treasure Island Naval Station,

Oak Knoll Naval Hospital, and Alameda NAS. Representative Ronald Dellums (D-CA) had most of these bases in his congressional district. Dellums, then chair of the House Armed Services Committee, bitterly protested a pattern that he claimed was the result of retribution for his refusal to support national-defense policy. Dellums often criticized the services, including the Navy for its alleged racial policies, and led a sometimes-lonely crusade for reduced military spending.

Representative Dellums and the Politics of Closure

Dellums himself once stated: "I did not join the Armed Services Committee to learn about missiles, planes, and ships; I joined because I knew I would need to become an expert in this field in order to argue successfully for military spending reductions that would free up resources for the desperate human needs that I see every day in my community."[81] Dellums was at least honest in his belief that the defense budget represented lost opportunity for other programs, rather than pork-based employment. But if the Navy wanted to send a message to representatives in Congress who failed to support its policies, this was a way to do it. Additionally, Dellums was an early advocate of "defense conversion," the process of converting military factories and bases to civilian use. He had encouraged local work in this area through connections to the East Bay Defense Conversion and Reinvestment Project, which had been authorized under a defense appropriations act and was headquartered in Oakland. In a sense, the base closures might provide Dellums a chance to put his beliefs into practice—or so the Navy might argue. Yet, there is no direct evidence that the Navy did punish Dellums by listing so many naval bases in his district for closure. On the other hand, there was no other congressional district in 1993 or 1995 that suffered as many base closures as did California's Ninth, Dellum's own. Dellums had found the process unusual as far back as 1991, when he coauthored a letter to the comptroller general of the United States over the closing of Alameda NAS, located just south of FISCO. The letter stated, in part, that: "This afternoon, we received — anonymously — the enclosed document. If this is a valid document, it clearly shows that the DOD study (on closing Alameda) is rigged, and that the taxpayer's money is being wasted in a sham study."[82] That study recommended Alameda's closing on economic grounds.

The Bay Area still reeled from previous closures, including Hunter's Point Naval Shipyard (mostly closed in 1974) and Fort

Mason. The other political reality was that President Clinton needed California to win the 1996 election, and the state was already suffering high defense-related unemployment. Clinton did not want to lose the base and possibly see Dellums, a fellow Democrat, defeated because of the resulting unemployment. On the other hand, the U.S. Navy, concerned about the closure of bases it wanted open, saw FISCO's closure as a way to save them. After all, the Fleet and Industrial Supply Center performed one of the least glamorous of military tasks, the storage and shipment of military materiel. While any Naval officer will concede that no operation can proceed without supplies, they are usually quick to add that, in a downsized Navy, no one wanted to pay the costs that it took to maintain the aging complex. The Army was drawing down from its Pacific commitments, and no troops had been moved by sea since the mid-1960s.[83] Moreover, the Oakland base was aging, and its older buildings needed repair. The southernmost pier had rotted away to the point that it was simply fenced off and abandoned.

The Economic Cost of Closing FISCO

Obstacles to closure remained, however. FISCO employed a work force of more than 2,000, almost all of them civilians. The nearby cities of Oakland and Richmond had historically high levels of unemployment, and several federal development projects had failed to stem the trend. In 1966, for example, Oakland's unemployment rate was 8.4 percent, compared to a 4.1 rate at the national level.[84] In 1969, the Economic Development Agency (EDA) reportedly invested $1,085,000 in business loans to Oakland that resulted in the creation of only 43 jobs.[85] High unemployment in California had already become a political issue in the 1992 election (probably helping Bill Clinton defeat President Bush), and its importance in 1996 was obvious.

The San Francisco–Oakland Bay area had already suffered from earlier base closures, including the Naval Air Station and Naval Station at Alameda (just south of Oakland NSC), the Hunter's Point Naval Annex in south San Francisco, and the Naval Station at Treasure Island. The closure of the Oak Knoll Naval Hospital also had an impact on military employment in the East Bay Area, and, to the south of San Francisco, the Army's Fort Ord had been shuttered. The issue rose when FISCO made the 1993 BRAC list, submitted by the Navy with an argument that FISCO supplied mostly local military facilities also recommended for closure. BRAC, though, disagreed with the Navy position, noting that FISCO's customers were spread across the Pacific region. More significantly, though, the commission noted that ". . . the quality, and often minority, jobs retained at FISC Oakland helped to mitigate the cumulative economic impacts of other Bay Area commands recommended for closure."[86] The commission noted additionally that FISCO had legal authority to lease land to the Port of Oakland for construction of a new container facility on FISCO property.[87] That authority had been given to Representative Dellums in 1993 to mitigate some of the negative impact of other closures in his district. While the report did not speculate, the clause could be seen as a hint that, if commercial port facilities were built on FISCO land, then the unemployment situation could improve. In other words, BRAC 1993 probably gave FISCO a two-year breathing space to negotiate with the Port of Oakland before it would appear on the 1995 BRAC base-closure list. So even after the base escaped the 1993 closure, proceedings began to lease land to the Port of Oakland, as some 195 acres of land changed hands.[88] President Clinton took credit for the plan that would lease land in some cases for $1 a year and also publicly asked federal regulators to speed up a plan to dredge a channel through the bay allowing larger ocean-going ships to get to berths at FISCO.[89] Another transfer developed into a made-for-politics event, as Representative Dellums and Oakland Mayor Elihu Harris appeared at a ceremony marking the conversion of six acres of FISCO land to the Port of Oakland.[90] The six acres went to the Union Pacific Railroad, which ran tracks to FICSO to move shipping containers to its vessels. This would later become part of the intermodal transportation hub planned by the Port of Oakland, which assumed an active role in creating alternatives for FISCO. Without such activism, other options for FISCO were problematic. The San Francisco Bay Area had already been developed by commercial ocean-going shipping concerns, and a considerable portion of those operations were already underutilized by 1995 as seaports from Seattle to San Diego competed fiercely to offer berthing space and offloading facilities for ships plying the Pacific trade routes. With the closure of the Alameda Naval Station just two years previously, the closure of FISCO threatened to render much of the East Bay waterfront a desolate empty row of unused piers and rotting warehouses. Worse, FISCO's adjacent facility, the Oakland Army Base, also made the BRAC list several hours after FISCO itself. Since the two facilities sometimes operated in tandem (since the Army used FISCO operations to support its overseas forces), the closure of the Army base made FISCO's closure even more likely. But the Port of Oakland developed grand plans for FISCO, including an "intermodal terminal" linking railroad, highway, and pier and involving the Southern Pacific, Union Pacific, and Santa

Fe Railroads. The entire facility "could generate $500 million in revenues and $15 million in state and local taxes by the year 2000, as well as hundreds of construction jobs."[91] Port officials went even further, claiming that six new planned cargo berths and a new railroad terminal might generate 4,100 new jobs and $187 million in wages by the turn of the century.[92] Since the base itself would not close until 1998, it was not clear how such a project might be completed in two years. Still, FISCO employed 2,000 civilians in 1996, and the Port's extensive plans offered not only to protect some of their jobs, but to add thousands of additional jobs as well. Whether or not these jobs would materialize by the promised date, their promise took much of the political sting from the FISCO closure.

The Adjacent Oakland Army Base

When BRAC got the Army's initial 1995 closure list, the Oakland Army Base was not on it. Deputy Secretary of Defense John Deutch called Senator Dianne Feinstein to let her know that, while the Defense Department would recommend closing Long Beach Naval Shipyard, it would spare Oakland Army Base.[93] The news was not universally welcomed in Oakland. "It's the only bloody site in the Bay Area that works as far as conversion goes," said Saul Bloom, executive director of the Arms Control Research Center in San Francisco.[94] The facility's 422 acres, with 30 miles of railroad, marine terminals, and freeway connectors, were well connected to shipment points, and speculation arose that the Port of Oakland might be interested in expanding onto the Army base land. Conversion to a produce market was another alternative, as was locating an alternative-energy site there.[95] In May, BRAC added the Oakland Army Base to the closure list, outraging Senator Feinstein, who pointed out that the deputy secretary of defense had specifically excluded the base from the initial closure list.[96]

Despite the obvious reduction in use since Vietnam, Army officials defended the port, arguing that it was necessary to support large Pacific military operations on short notice. They noted that Oakland Army Base was the Army's only West Coast port, and that the base's 2,200 civilian workers would be needed during a national emergency to handle the specific requirements of military cargo.[97]

BRAC analysts disagreed with the Army, though. The commission held that ". . . the normal workload of Oakland Army Base does not justify its continued operation as a military terminal."[98] It noted that the Army had not conducted an operational analysis of the facility with a ten-division requirement, which was the size mandated for the Army after the Cold War. Specifically, BRAC charged that "Oakland's role in a west region contingency is based on transportation feasibility analysis that models an obsolete force structure and stationing plan."[99] In fact, during the most recent large military operation, Desert Storm, two other military ports on the West Coast handled military cargo in support of that operation. So BRAC found that the Army had, in its often-repeated words, "deviated substantially" from the military-value criteria, and the commissioners decided to close Oakland Army Base.

The Navy had reached a similar decision on the Fleet and Industrial Supply Center, and the secretary of the Navy removed the base from the closure list. But BRAC analysts determined, as in the case of the Oakland Army Base, that the Navy had "deviated substantially" from criteria 5 and 6 and thus added FISCO to its 1995 closure list.[100] The issue was complicated by the fact that FISCO was actually three sites—the large facility in Oakland and two smaller facilities, the Point Molate Naval Refueling Station in Richmond and the Navy Supply Annex in Alameda. Both Richmond and Alameda wanted the land on which these two smaller stations were located, so that left the main facility in Oakland. The commission noted that, if the two smaller units were closed, the primary function of FISCO became that of providing office space for the Military Sealift Command (MSC) and the Defense Finance and Accounting Service (DFAS).[101] The MSC had moved its headquarters to Oakland in the 1960s from its old location across the Bay in San Francisco's Fort Mason; the building constructed for the move was more than 30 years old by 1995, and its value had diminished considerably. Besides, the MSC had become a part of the United States Transportation Command, which combined the MSC and the Military Airlift Command, with a headquarters at Scott AFB in Illinois. Since the MSC was a worldwide command, no particular reason existed to make sure its headquarters were near a body of water. Thus, it became easier to relocate the MSC, which would move to San Diego.

That decision raised a number of problems, not the least of which was what to do with the large work force in an already economically depressed area. But in the end there was no easy answer to the situation—after all the East Bay Area had historically suffered from high levels of unemployment, and neither Oakland NSC/FISCO nor a host of other federal projects had made much of a dent in it.[102]

Another problem involved the growing reluctance of commercial sea cargo operators to have their operations disrupted in order to handle military cargo. That was a significant issue because, since Oakland was the only large military terminal on the West Coast, movement of military goods would have to be done at commercial facilities. While such a program might be in line with the growing trend of privatization, it also disrupted normal commercial operations, and owners were increasingly reluctant to turn over scarce facilities for that purpose. The closure of the Bayonne Military Ocean Terminal in New Jersey by the 1995 BRAC compounded the problem, since the only military seaport left would be the one at Sunny Point, North Carolina, quite smaller than either Bayonne or Oakland. Representative Robert Menendez (D-NJ), who represented Bayonne, charged that deregulation by the Ocean Shipping Reform Act would create "megaports," thus reducing the number of commercial ports available for military shipping in times of emergency.[103]

Of course, the military could force a takeover of commercial facilities under something known as the National Shipping Authority Service Priority Orders, but those orders needed a significant national emergency to justify them. BRAC commissioners noted that the Defense Department and the Maritime Administration were engaged in initiatives to address the issue, though they did not spell out what those initiatives were.[104]

FISCO and The Port of Oakland

The Port of Oakland moved rapidly to assimilate FISCO's property once closure was announced. Port authorities offered to pay for a major part of the conversion and mapped out long-range plans to include the leasing of FISCO warehouses to private firms. With a serious shortage in warehouse space in the East Bay Area, the Port moved quickly to clean up the huge buildings, so that everything from cotton to timber to manufactured goods could be stored there once the Navy moved out. The negotiated fee of $1.00 a year for 50 years clearly made profits from warehousing automatic. But what to do with the aging FISCO facilities? The Port of Oakland announced that almost all buildings and piers would be demolished to make way for new containerized loading facilities and a recreational area where the piers stood. The Port also attracted commercial subtenants, who were already moving on to FISCO land even before final closure in September 1998. Indeed, things were moving so fast through the Port's efforts that the closure date for FISCO was moved up a year, saving the Navy money for the maintenance and operation otherwise required. A DFAS office was initially scheduled to locate at FISCO, but BRAC decided that it would move to downtown Oakland (another small plum for Dellums), and the MSC Pacific headquarters would move to San Diego. There were even plans for the Point Molate Naval Fuel Depot, which contained the historic 1909 Winehaven Vinter's Castle, part of what was thought to be the world's largest winery at the turn of the century. The castle, with 29 Spanish-style homes, was taken over by the Navy, but, at base-closure time, the city of Richmond, which got the property, was trying to market it as a conference center despite the fact that it could only be reached by a narrow winding road.[105] Contra Costa Community College also expressed interest in the facility, along with a group called Rescue Mission, for 29 housing units; the Homeless Collaborative, for a warehouse and office building; and Orchid Net, for a laboratory and office space.[106] The Alameda Annex, consisting of 169 acres on the inner harbor across from Jack London Square, was bid for by developers with plans for a residential development. Since the Port of Oakland managed Jack London Square, the package negotiations were relatively effortless.

Environmental Problems at FISCO

The environmental conditions at FISCO were not nearly as serious as those at many naval shipyards or Air Force bases. The most serious sites involved PCB spills from railroad cars and diesel-oil deposits from utility engines. A dry-cleaning operation and an auto hobby shop also made the environmental list. An initial survey revealed 13 sites, but that was reduced to six, with a cleanup cost of about $700,000. While, in most cases, the service operating the base must pay for the cleanup, the Port of Oakland chipped in to assist. The Port demolished the dry-cleaning plant and the hobby shop and cleaned the facility, and since 1996 the area has been used for storing shipping containers. This was all accomplished two years before FISCO was to close—without all of the delay and red tape common with such projects when they are done by the service responsible for the base. At the Point Molate facility, 24 underground fuel tanks required cleaning, but that was the extent of the environmental problems there.[107] The cost estimate was $20 million.

A potential environmental issue arose from the Save San Francisco Bay Association, an environmental group. The association noted that other military bases in the area fronting on the bay were built partly from landfill, "displacing some aquatic and wetland habitat."[108] While the association did not mention FISCO specifically, its Military Base Closure Project did note that "Base reuse authorities are under tremendous pressure to maximize the economic potential of these surplus military lands (noting specifically Mare Island and Alameda) by allowing housing and other economic development projects and are reluctant to support . . . environmental benefits. . . ."[109] A lawsuit by such an organization might tie up projected Port of Oakland plans for years. The Base Realignment and Closure Act did limit compliance to the National Environmental Protection Act and also limited court challenges to the act. A court of law might, though, have to determine what "limited" means, and that alone could mean considerable delay of development plans.

Rumors about the possible closure of Oakland NSC had begun in 1991.[110] It made the closure list in 1993, so local residents were not too surprised to learn that the base would finally close in 1998. The Oakland Army Base and FISCO initiated closure proceedings, and the local community could take solace that the Port of Oakland took interest in both developing the base and paying for that development. So it turned out that 1995 brought both closure of the Fleet and Industrial Supply Center and the Oakland Army Base and the return of the Raiders football team to Oakland from Los Angeles. By 1997, though, the Raiders were losing money, while prospects were considerably better for the old FISCO property. It is one of the more successful examples of base closure.

LONG BEACH NAVAL SHIPYARD, CALIFORNIA

The city of Long Beach had long languished in the shadow of its large neighbor to the north, Los Angeles. In the 1930s, it was a quaint seaside city, but during World War II it mushroomed into a city built largely on a military economy. The Douglas Corporation expanded its military aircraft operations there, and the Army Air Corps opened Long Beach Army Air Field. From the late 1930s onward, the Navy built up facilities with a Naval Shipyard, a Naval Station, and numerous other smaller facilities, covering 645 acres in all. The shipyard opened in February 1943. The Air Corps base closed after the war, but the Navy facilities remained open until the start of the Korean War, when the Navy closed the shipyard. However, the yard reopened in 1951 after an intensive campaign by Representative Clyde Doyle who represented the city.[111] Doyle argued that it could employ 3,500 workers when the state's unemployment numbers ranged between 7,000 and

8,000 as they had in 1951.[112] It would not be the first time that the yard's employment potential would be used to justify its existence.

Initial Efforts to Close the Shipyard

Initial pressure to close the Long Beach Naval Shipyard probably came shortly before the 1988 BRAC was to meet. Long Beach, as a government yard, competed with private shipyards, a fact noted in a letter to 1988 BRAC Chair Abraham A. Ribicoff from John J. Stocker, president of the Shipbuilders Council of America. In the letter, Stocker stated: "The Navy commanded in 1946 a fleet of 1,115 naval ships supported by 11 naval shipyards employing 93,600 civilian employees. At the end of fiscal 1987, the Navy had an active fleet of 568 ships supported by eight shipyards employing 72,400 workers."[113] The private yards had seen orders for commercial ships drop sharply, leaving the Navy as their primary customer. But the Navy had begun to modernize its own yards and became able to underbid its commercial rivals since there was no need for a government operation to make a profit.[114] Since the 1988 BRAC deliberations are closed, there is no record of whether the Shipbuilders Council of America had any influence on BRAC decisions. But anxious defenders of Long Beach Naval Shipyard realized that their yard was vulnerable to closure and responded with a spirited campaign immediately after Stocker's letter became public knowledge. A Save our Shipyard (SOS) Committee was formed and quickly generated figures on the value of the installation to the community. Save Our Shipyard noted that Long Beach was one of only two yards qualified to work on nuclear-powered carriers and was also qualified to work on the battleships that were being resurrected by the Reagan administration.[115] To counter a GAO report stating that private yards could perform similar maintenance for 10 percent less than public yards, the Save our Shipyard Committee claimed that Long Beach Naval Shipyard reduced its overhead by $20 million in one year, and, in a response to Stocker's organization, the head of SOS charged that "it would appear that the effort to close public shipyards is not directed at saving taxpayer's dollars but is an effort to enhance the private sector's profit motive."[116] The argument appeared to carry into 1991, as BRAC members visited Long Beach Naval Shipyard, but after the Navy excluded it from its 1991 list, BRAC did not include it. In 1993, Long Beach survived as well, with BRAC targeting shipyards at Charleston, South Carolina, and Mare Island, California, instead. But the shipyard's good fortune and political protection would not last.

1995: The Final Closure

The Navy included the Long Beach Naval Shipyard on its 1995 submission list to BRAC, claiming surplus shipyard capacity. By Navy calculations, the one-time cost to shut the yard would be $74.5 million, with annual savings of $130 million from the action.[117] Chief of Naval Operations Adm. Jeremy Boorda said that the Long Beach yard's functions would be handled by either the private sector or other naval shipyards.[118] BRAC agreed and voted to close the facility.

The decision created the expected immediate outrage from both national elected officials and local leaders. Representative Juanita McDonald (D-CA) spoke to a public rally at which she threatened the president: "If you want to keep your job in Washington, we better keep our jobs in Long Beach."[119] The city's mayor stated: "We're committed to fight, and we're going to win it."[120] Senator Boxer stated that she was "continuing to urge President Clinton to reject the unacceptable recommendations . . . to close Long Beach Naval Shipyard," charging that the decision ". . . was not fair to the hard working employees of the shipyard, the City of Long Beach, the Los Angeles region, and the State of California."[121] California Governor Pete Wilson, shortly before announcing his candidacy for president of the United States, called the closure decision "shortsighted" and "a great mistake."[122] The mayor of Long Beach also stated that an independent study showed that it would be cheaper to homeport carriers from the closed Alameda Naval Station at the Long Beach Naval Shipyard than at San Diego—$25 million for Long Beach versus more than $750 million at San Diego.[123]

By 1995, the Port of Long Beach had become the nation's busiest container-ship port, and potentially the 100-acre naval facility could have expanded that growth even further. But the Port's director indicated that "we've given money to the Save Our Shipyard Committee" to try to reverse the closure decision instead of planning to include the shipyard in future Port expansion plans.[124] To Representative Stephen Horn (R-CA), there was another explanation for the Long Beach Naval Shipyard decision. It was the result of Navy internal politics—"it is a matter of the air wing versus the surface fleet versus the underseas fleet. What happened in the case of the closure of the Long Beach Naval Shipyard, the only shipyard that has ever returned consistently money to the Treasury. . . ."[125] While Horn did not finish his thought on internal Navy politics, he implied that the surface Navy (largely conventionally powered) had been outflanked by the aviation and submarine branches, both of which use nuclear power.

They apparently put pressure on BRAC and the Navy to keep the Portsmouth Naval Shipyard in New Hampshire open because it was nuclear capable, while closing the conventional-capable Long Beach yard.[126] Horn offered no proof of his allegation, though.

The cost of maintaining the shipyard loomed large over the closure decision. Compared to a closure cost of $74.5 million, the savings between 1996 and 2001 were estimated at $725.6 million.[127] But the community task force countered with a "surplus-capacity" argument, claiming that Title 10, Section 2464, of the United States Code required the Navy to maintain surplus dry-dock facilities in case of war or other national emergency.[128] While the BRAC commissioners noted that there was a risk, they said that it was "manageable" and, that, in such an emergency, the Navy could use the large dry docks at Puget Sound, Washington, and Pearl Harbor, Hawaii. The BRAC report noted that West Coast shipyards would benefit from the closing of Long Beach Naval Shipyard (a considerable number of American private shipyards had closed during the 1980s) and that the community's additional efforts to get a carrier or two homeported in Long Beach were "operational," not "base-closure," issues. The final recommendation was to close the facility, except for a sonar dome shipyard and some housing needed to support the Seal Beach Naval Weapons Station. Along with it, a small contracting office, the Supervisor of Shipbuilding, Conversion, and Repair, was disestablished in Long Beach, and its function transferred to San Diego.

Environmental Problems

Since 1943, the shipyard had serviced thousands of ships, blasting paint off them, cleaning out their fuel compartments, [129] stripping their electric cables, lubricating their machinery, and piling up the waste that resulted. Shipyard workers stored the chemicals required for such jobs, along with gasoline, diesel fuel, solvents, battery acid, and other contaminants, in tanks that sometimes leaked or overflowed.

Preliminary inspections of the site revealed the usual pollution—petroleum hydrocarbons, paints, solvents, battery acid, trichloroethylene (TCE), and asbestos throughout the facility. Shipyard pollution is complicated by the fact that much waste winds up initially on the bottom of the waterways under the dry docks and piers. There it mixes with the bottom sediment and is swept around by the currents, which often disperse it widely. An initial study indicated that runoff from contaminants at the shipyard could deplete the oxygen content in seawater and be toxic to aquatic life and spawning grounds.[130] It also could blend contamination from other installations, as was likely with the Long Beach Naval Station, closed by the 1991 BRAC. At that base, preliminary surveys were turning up a variety of toxins, including arsenic in disposal pits.[131] Those problems were monitored in 28 test wells over a two-year period to try to determine the extent of the environmental problems. That would have to be determined before either cleanup or reuse could start. It was particularly important since some redevelopment plans called for dredging Long Beach harbor, and no one knew exactly what buried waste might be stirred up by the dredging.

Environmental problems were also complicated by the fact that the Long Beach military complex was not a Superfund site and, thus, was ineligible for Superfund cleanup money. That meant that, unless a Port of Oakland-like solution for cleanup arrived, the Navy would have to fund remediation; until the damage could be estimated, the Navy had no benchmarks for determining how much to budget for cleaning the Long Beach Naval Shipyard of decades of waste.

The Economic Impact on the Community

Long Beach found itself reeling economically from a variety of problems. In 1991, the Naval Station and the Naval Hospital closed, reportedly costing the city 17,000 jobs and $1 billion annually in lost income.[132] The next year, riots inspired by the Rodney King incident in nearby Los Angeles spilled over into Long Beach, costing $40 million in losses. The McDonnell-Douglas Corporation, the city's biggest employer, laid off 30,000 workers in the early 1990s in response to sluggish aircraft sales, reportedly costing the community another $2.4 billion yearly.[133] The shipyard's closing was just another blow, with its estimated losses at 10,000 jobs and $40 million in annual wages.[134] The total contribution of the shipyard to the regional economy had been estimated at more than $757 million annually.[135] Many of those jobs would head south, to San Diego. "San Diego will absolutely gain from Long Beach. All major repair work on the West Coast will be done in San Diego, helping the city's status as a megaport," a spokesperson for Representative Duncan Hunter (R-CA) noted.[136] There was serious concern, though, about what to do with the lost shipyard jobs. Port officials, noting that shipyard workers may have job skills not easily translated into other activities, estimated that no more than 450 of the more than 3,000 shipyard workers losing their jobs would find reemployment in replacement positions at the Port facility.[137]

The city of Long Beach has worked hard to transform itself from a fading seaport. The decaying old buildings that housed bars, tattoo parlors, and pornographic movie theaters were bulldozed to make way for a rebuilt waterfront complex. In place of the old Long Beach Pike amusement park, the city now features the ocean liner Queen Mary (moored to a dock as an entertainment feature), and once a year championship racing cars roar through streets once largely inhabited by sailors. In the wake of the 1991 and 1995 closures, new development offered hope, including a retail center, the Alameda Corridor Complex (a rail and truck route linking the Port of Long Beach to areas north), and the Queensway Bay Waterfront Complex (housing and retail) — all expected to bring 86,000 jobs and $3.1 billion in both public and private investment.[138] So in a sense, despite the loss of two major facilities, the city was already transforming itself from dependence on the United States Navy to economic growth from tourism and entertainment. Still, problems remained, with vacant lots along Long Beach Boulevard, gang-related violence, and a city budget that could not keep up with demands for increased services.

POINT MUGU NAVAL AIR WEAPONS CENTER, CALIFORNIA

Weapons are the instruments of war and require testing to prove their worthiness. Some military bases are dedicated to this purpose, and the Naval Air Weapons Center at Point Mugu on California's coast is one of the more important of these facilities. The base covers 4,490 acres of land, and also includes 36,000 square miles of sea test range and several offshore islands. First opened in 1944 as a carrier-based aircraft repair facility, the base became a missile-test facility, the Pilotless Aircraft Unit, in 1946. That mission grew to ultimately become the Naval Air Warfare Center Weapons Division (NAWCWPNS), Point Mugu's primary mission. NAWCWPNS tested aircraft-delivered weapons on a variety of ranges, including facilities at Point Mugu itself, China Lake in California, and Albuquerque White Sands in New Mexico. One of its features is a $100 million weapons-test building the size of three football fields. The purpose of the building is to allow live-fire tests of weapons under security conditions. A sizable base work force of 10,000 included numerous civilian technicians and support personnel.

Point Mugu first made the BRAC list in 1993 but survived closure because its defenders successfully argued that the Navy's data supporting its closure were erroneous. But the handwriting was on the wall, and, in anticipation of its appearance on the 1995 list, the Navy began moving facilities from Point Mugu to the Naval Test Center at China Lake, California. The consolidation between the two bases cost Point Mugu 2,000 jobs, but the worst threat was yet to come.

As the 1995 BRAC decisions neared, the Navy ranked Point Mugu second as a technical base, right behind China Lake and ahead of eight others. But Point Mugu appeared again on the BRAC 1995 closure list, and that fact sent community home values plunging. The initial plan would allow Point Mugu to keep its radar and missile-test-range monitoring facilities, but most everything else would move to the Naval Weapons Laboratory at China Lake. The runway would close.

While the Navy's facilities might move to other bases (China Lake and Eglin AFB in Florida, which coveted Point Mugu's missions), the Air National Guard facilities remained in doubt. Once the Hollywood Air National Guard, the unit moved to Point Mugu in the mid-1980s and spent $75 million constructing new buildings for its operations. The facilities cost the Guard $3.5 million annually to operate. Its mission at Point Mugu was unique in that it was the only C-130 unit west of the Rocky Mountains. The problem was that, if Point Mugu closed, the Guard might wind up as the sole tenant operating the airfield. For the Guard, the cost to operate both its runway and related facilities was simply too high, forcing it to seek another location should the main Navy installation close.

The Navy, which wanted to close other California facilities (particularly the Long Beach Naval Shipyard), rallied to save Point Mugu. Its cost estimates were straightforward. The Navy reasoned that the cost of relocation of more than 3,000 people and their equipment (mostly to China Lake) would be $805 million.[139] Factoring in inflation, it would take 63 years to recover the $805 million, which naval officials said was a conservative estimate.[140]

More practical problems surfaced when Point Mugu officials explored the alternatives. They derived four scenarios:

- Move all but the hardware in loop facilities, radar-cross-section-analysis chambers, ristatic chambers, F-14 A/D and EA-6B weapons-support activity, and electronic combat systems encounter laboratory;
- Analyze the workload and duplication of environmental facilities that exist between Point Mugu and China Lake. Move environmental facilities to China Lake;

- Retain Sea Range, but move Sea Range operations, control, and engineering facilities to China Lake;
- Close or mothball all remaining facilities, runways, and hangars.[141]

One called for moving the long-distance remote control over the Sea Range from Point Mugu, right on the coast, to China Lake, located in the California high desert several hundred miles and a mountain range away from the Sea Range. There were two ways to link China Lake with the Sea Range—microwave transmission towers (at an initial cost of $25 million) or fiber-optic cable, which was available but carried an annual leasing cost of $6 million to $7.5 million.[142] The main problem, though, was closure of the Point Mugu runway. Without it, aircraft using the Sea Range would have to fly with a live-weapons load over populated territory—something sure to gain the opposition of people living in the densely populated southern California area.[143] Another potential safety hazard emerged in landing the QF-4 drone aircraft (a remotely piloted version of the F-4 Phantom) on San Nicholas Island with instruments. If the range-operating functions transferred to China Lake, the remote-landing system, with its range of about 100 miles, would be insufficient to perform the drone-landing mission.[144] Potential coordination problems emerged from splitting the F-14 Weapons Systems Support Laboratory functions from flight-test operations. If the airfield closed, part of the testing facilities would remain at Point Mugu while the aircraft and crew would have to remain at China Lake. Then the upgraded aircraft would have to fly from China Lake to the Sea Range, using more fuel in the process.[145] Some aviators believed that a long training or test mission for either an F-14 or an F/A-18 would require aerial refueling, adding more to the overall cost.

The problems, in other words, involved both cost and coordination. While, in theory, most of the facilities at Point Mugu could move to China Lake, the Sea Range could not, and so, in the end, the costs began to outweigh the benefits of either reducing Point Mugu or closing it entirely. But other barriers remained.

Base closure is made easier if conversion to alternative uses is feasible. Any base with a runway represents the potential for conversion to a civil airport. Point Mugu is located in Ventura County, and that entity became interested in converting Point Mugu to a commercial cargo hub. That interest might have made Point Mugu's closure easier, but, unfortunately, Ventura County officials did not ask commercial air companies if they might be interested in the facility, so all they could offer was potential rather than actual conversion. Moreover, both Santa Barbara and Oxnard had airports, and the latter was the site of the former Oxnard AFB. Both airports had room for expansion without the often costly cleanup and other activities associated with base closure. So conversion options rapidly became limited.

When BRAC Commissioners Rebecca Cox (married to a Southern California Republican member of the House of Representatives) and Benjamin Montoya (a retired Navy rear admiral) visited the base, the Navy arranged to have them accompanied by high-ranking naval officers, including Adm. Ronald J. Zlatoper, commander in chief of the Pacific Fleet, and Adm. John A. Lockard, head of naval aviation. The chief of naval operations himself, Admiral Boorda, issued a letter to accompany the BRAC visit, stating that Point Mugu was "not only a critical asset for the Navy, but . . . a national asset as well."[146] The effort apparently paid off; in July 1995, BRAC commissioners voted 8-0 to exclude Point Mugu from their list of closures.

Political reaction was prompt. Senator Boxer noted that she "was proud to have been a part of the team that included Representatives Gallegly and Beilenson, Senator Feinstein and myself" that worked to exclude Point Mugu, noting her testimony on the value of Point Mugu before the BRAC hearings.[147] However, a major reason that Point Mugu remained off the final 1995 BRAC closure list was more likely the testimony of the commanding officer of the naval installation at Point Mugu, who told BRAC members that the projected savings from closure and merger with China Lake would not begin for 63 years.

Environmental Problems

The decision to keep Point Mugu open was largely a function of the cost to move facilities and the awkwardness of operating from two facilities. But the environmental cost of closure loomed in the wings. While a base spokesperson noted that the environmental problems associated with the base were "never an issue" because the decision to keep the base open was made before much of the contamination on or near the base was publicized, the problems existed nevertheless.

Among them were buried waste and contaminated water, including the entire lagoon at Site 4 (itself contaminated by two creeks). Chromium lay under the area where shops once stood, along with PCB and the usual petroleum contamination from underground storage tanks.[148] Point Mugu incorporates or borders one of the largest coastal ecosystems in California, including large tracts of salt marsh. The land is home to six listed and fifteen proposed candidates for the endangered- and threatened-species lists, and in May 1994 a pair of California light-footed clapper rail birds were spotted nesting near heavy-metal concentrations from former plating operations. The federally protected birds had not been seen in the area since the 1980s, so their plight was significant.

Rumors spread of worse contamination in the Sea Range area, including the dumping of a small nuclear reactor in the area. Substantial debris littered the range, including hundreds of thousands of rounds of ammunition and the remains of target aircraft downed over the years. That is hardly surprising since, on average, a missile is fired into the range every 15-20 minutes around the clock.

No one was quite sure if the range area would be included in the cleanup of Point Mugu should the entire base close, but just that possibility might have helped save the facility had the cost arguments failed. Should the base be placed on a future closure list, environmental problems may well surface again.

The Future for Point Mugu

Point Mugu escaped closure twice, partly because of the Navy's strong interest in keeping it open and partly because the cost and problems associated with closure were too high for BRAC to accept. However the post-1995 situation at Point Mugu was tilting against preserving the base in any future closure process. For one thing, Point Mugu was more than a test base; it also hosted a number of other smaller activities, as is typical of most bases. Two Reserve wings used base facilities, a P-3 patrol wing and an F/A-18 wing. The base also supported an unusual function, a squadron dedicated to supporting missions in Antarctica. But in a cost-cutting measure, that unit, consisting of special ski-equipped C-130 transports and helicopters, disbanded in the mid-1990s, leaving the base with one less organization and one less reason to remain open. Reserve units are relatively easy to move, because they can locate at civilian airports if necessary.

Point Mugu's primary justification for remaining open involved the cost of closure. The vast test building was calculated into that cost as a loss. But Point Mugu had other potential costs, and other bases spent large sums of money on modernizing facilities. The housing at Point Mugu dates back to World War II and was in fairly poor shape in the late 1990s. The cost of repair and replacement is obviously high. The other comparative cost factor involved the money expended by the Navy at its test center at Pataxent River, where large quantities of money bought much new construction between 1993 and 1997.

SUMMARY

On and around the bases left open after the 1995 round there were both sighs of relief and a sense of anticipation about the future. For the immediate future, those bases appeared safe from closure since there was no future BRAC scheduled. But, at the same time, the reductions mandated by Congress in 1988 had not been carried out over the last three BRACs, so the possibility of future closures was very real. Bases that barely escaped could not be assured that another effort to close them might not ultimately succeed. For one thing, the services still had excessive base capacity in some areas, and, in the face of still more defense-budget reductions, there were service-driven incentives to try to keep the pressure on for base closure. The services also knew that BRAC was not the only way to close a base. Between 1952 and 1983, 166 military airfields were deactivated and turned over to civilian use.[149] Moreover, the long-term pattern from base closures revealed that recovery from the initial economic downturn was not only possible but increasingly common. With a well-thought-out use plan, a closure-and-conversion project might get the kind of political support that had been lacking before BRAC. Additionally, there were rumors that consolidation would force still other bases to close. The remaining Air Force depots were particularly vulnerable, with reports that the Defense Department had decided that by 2000 there would be only two Air Force depots, with a third to be converted to joint use.

By the end of 1995, though, the verdict was still out on that year's hottest answer to conversion—privatization. For the two large Air Force depots at Sacramento and San Antonio, there were some prospects for success. In Sacramento, the Air Force depot had pioneered some high-technology processes that could be attractive to private investors once the depot had shrunk in size. Sacramento had been the Air Force's center, for example, in high-speed integrated circuits, fiber-optic communications, and advanced composites.[150] The depot had also cooperated with the automobile industry in producing electric vehicles, and with the medical profession in nuclear medicine, using the Air Force's only experimental nuclear reactor. It was also hoped that Sacramento could duplicate the experience of the

Army depot nearby that had closed several years previously and had experienced a pattern of job growth after closure. The mayor of Sacramento noted that the Army depot had employed approximately 4,000 people during its existence but that conversion had created an additional 1,000 jobs, with an expectation of 7,000 total by the next year.[151] San Antonio could not boast such facilities, but the fact remained that it, like Sacramento, could offer a well-trained work force for civilian contractors interested in either privatization of defense functions or locating industry on the base site.

The Clinton administration appeared to have learned from previous BRACs about the need to be up front on assistance and conversion efforts for communities impacted by base closure. In early August 1995, when the final BRAC vote was in, the Defense Department published a press release on ways communities might gain assistance in their conversion efforts. The publication listed information on planning grants, DOD technical assistance, other federal programs, and a "Community Guide to Base Closure."[152] One of the messages was that there would be much more federal assistance than ever before, which may have been good news to communities affected by a base closure, even as it raised questions about how much of the expected savings generated by base closure would be eaten up by assistance costs to offset closure.

CHAPTER SIX

Conclusions

Mr. Speaker, I am amazed, especially at my California colleagues. When they vote for a $177 million cut in defense, and California is the leader in the defense industry, and most of our bases are in California, what did they expect? What did they expect?[1]
—*Representative Randy "Duke" Cunningham (R-CA)*

Most observers consider the BRAC process an unparalleled success. It has already resulted in hundreds of closures and realignments within the United States, 70 of which are identified as "major closures." By comparison, in the 10 years prior to BRAC 88, the Department was able to close only 4 major facilities.[2]
—*Joshua Gotbaum, Assistant Secretary of Defense, 1995*

The end of the Cold War is generally dated to around 1989; by the end of 1995, the United States finally had the outline of a post–Cold War military-base structure. The closures of 1995 would complete a process that, over four interations, had changed the military landscape of the United States. Some of the country's oldest and most historic bases disappeared from the map. The Charleston, Boston, and Philadelphia Naval Shipyards that had served the nation since the Revolutionary War were shuttered.[3] Michigan, once home to three major Air Force bases dating back to the beginnings of military aviation, would not have a single Air Force base after September 1995. Nor would New York or Pennsylvania. Virginia and Ohio would have only one apiece. States such as Texas and California, once peppered with Air Force bases, had only nine and eight remaining, respectively. Historic March, Chanute, and Selfridge AFBs, opened during the biplane days, were gone forever. The Army's Fort McClellan, Fort Ord, Fort Devins, and Fort Benjamin Harrison also shut down and, with them, the memories of hundreds of thousands of soldiers who had served there.

Sentimental memories cannot keep unneeded bases open, though. With the end of the 1995 BRAC round, the military had waged yet another battle in its continuing war to close excess installations. It was a partial victory, though. Bases did close after Congress surrendered power to the BRAC. Presidents did sign the commission's decision, even after some considerable complaining about how unfair the process was. In the face of the defense cuts from the end of the Cold War defense posture, however, base cuts were inevitable. The United States Army had dropped from its Cold War structure of 18 divisions to 12 by 1995. A further reduction to 10 by the late 1990s became a part of the Clinton defense plan. The Air Force had fallen from 26 active fighter wings to 13 by 1995, and from 268 strategic bombers to 141. Naval combat ships declined from 546 to 373, and further declines were in store as the Navy was retiring more ships than it was building.[4] Under such cuts, the 1995 base structure, in particular, was highly vulnerable to a significant trim. And trimmed it was— by mid-1995 10 percent of the Cold War base infrastructure was either closed or realigned, with an additional 10 percent slated for closure over the following several years.

DID THE THEORIES EXPLAIN BRAC-RELATED DECISION MAKING?

The three approaches chosen here for analyzing the politics of BRAC are constituency service, bureaucratic politics, and learning over time. Theories are useful for organizing explanations of particular phenomena and, as they stand the effort of scholars to refute them, serve as increasingly robust predictors. The theories used here are not "tested" with the rigor normally found in a true scientific experiment, and their application differs from previous usage in several ways. Behavior, for example, normally attributed to Congress as a body is attributed to individual members of Congress, operating largely outside the institution. Their behavior is measured largely from statements they made about their bases or from letters they wrote on base-related matters. In some cases, behavior is simply attributed from an appearance (Representative Ronald Dellums's [D-CA] appearance at a land-transfer ceremony at the Fleet and Industrial Supply Center Oakland, for example). But scholars must deal with the evidence at hand and, while recognizing the limits of its usefulness, still attempt to draw conclusions.

CONSTITUENCY SERVICE AS AN EXPLANATION

The Constituency Service Model predicts that representatives act to protect investments in their districts because constituents vote on how well elected officials provide benefits flowing from those investments. Constituency-service actions may take the form of concrete efforts to delay or prevent closure, such as re-missioning a base, appealing for reconsideration, or finding fault with data used for closure, or it may be limited to symbolic actions taken in the face of a hopeless political battle to save a base targeted for closure.

Representative Peter Geren (D-TX) led one of the more successful base-saving efforts. Geren was a junior Democrat, replacing the legendary Jim Wright. While Wright's influence allegedly protected Carswell AFB during his tenure, the base was believed vulnerable due to Wright's departure. Geren, though, managed to bring enough other missions to Carswell that, in the end, he saved much of the base's employment. Deciding not to run in 1996 because of family commitments, Representative Geren never benefited from his success.

Other representatives worked in similar ways to preserve bases. Senator Don Nickles (R-OK) managed to insert construction money into the 1995 defense budget to construct a new runway at the Oklahoma City Air Logistics Center (ALC), contributing to a BRAC decision to strike the base from its closure list. Representative G.V. "Sonny" Montgomery (D-MS) worked twice to help get the Meridian Naval Air Station (NAS) from the BRAC list. Representative William Dickenson (R-AL) attached Gunter AFB to Maxwell AFB so that Gunter could not be closed separately.

Success in preventing base closure does not appear to be based on either party or seniority. Representative Montgomery was both a Democrat and relatively senior, having been first elected in 1966. Dickenson was the ranking Republican on the House Armed Services Committee. Nickles, though was a Republican in a Senate then controlled by Democrats. Yet while the Senate was in the hands of the Democrats, two senior Democratic Senators from Michigan, Carl Levin and Donald Reigle, lost Wurtsmith AFB. Maine Senators George Mitchell, then one of the senior Democrats in the Senate, and William Cohen, a moderate Republican who later became President Clinton's defense secretary, were both frustrated in their efforts to keep Loring open in 1991, though how much of that effort was symbolic is difficult to tell. But they did fight to preserve jobs in northern Maine, and by getting a Job Corps Center and a Defense Finance and Accounting Service (DFAS) center located there, they did mitigate somewhat the jobs losses after the Air Force left the base. Even if the number of jobs did not match previous levels, the dedication of a new federal facility is an activity that gets political attention, particularly in a rural area. In the end, both Mitchell and Cohen decided against running for re-election, and Mitchell's seat was won by former Representative Olympia Snowe, a Republican who had Loring in her district as a House member. It is impossible to tell how much her activism on Loring's behalf helped her win Mitchell's Senate seat, but it probably did not hurt her chances. It would appear, though, that both Senators Mitchell and Cohen did what they could for Loring as much for "the good of the people" as they did for their own careers, since each ended their political careers voluntarily three years after the fight for Loring.

Actions by lawmakers to preserve bases in their electoral districts tend to work best before the closure decision is announced. Success is not having your base listed for closure. Once the closure decision is made, the process of challenging it becomes much more difficult. Thus, symbolic gestures often replace policy change efforts after the closure announcement is made. Such actions appear particularly important for junior representatives and in those cases in which the stakes for base closure are particularly high. Such was the case in 1995 for California's two senators, Barbara Boxer and Dianne Feinstein. Boxer, in particular, tried to appear very active after some particularly large California bases appeared on the 1995 BRAC list, traveling frequently to the state to denounce closures, take credit for bases not appearing on the list, or work to help with conversion when all else appeared to fail. Typical of Boxer's actions was her performance at a U.S. Senate Committee on Environmental and Public Works hearing at Alameda, California, at which she stated that environmental technology developed for base cleanup also had a global market ("up to $200 billion per year . . . ") and that some was under development in California.[5] Boxer also showed up to announce that the naval facilities at Point Mugu, California had been stricken from the 1995 BRAC after initially having been included, though Boxer herself played only a marginal role at best in saving the facility from closure.

Learning the political system enhances constituency service, as does learning how to compromise within it. An excellent example was set by Representative Nancy Pelosi (D-CA), who persevered in a difficult battle to establish a private trust to manage the Presidio of San Francisco. Pelosi, a liberal Democrat, worked carefully with Republicans in 1996 (along with her Senate counterpart, Barbara Boxer) to fashion a compromise that angered some of her liberal allies in San Francisco but, in the end, probably saved the Presidio from complete deterioration. Pelosi had also managed to get the closure of the Presidio delayed when it originally appeared on the 1988 BRAC list, buying some precious time for a better solution to develop after the National Park Service, found that it had inadequate funds to transform the base after a 1993 Congressional decision to grant the NPS operation of the Presidio after the Army was to leave.

Members of Congress often fought hard to preserve military installations in their area, though the penalties for failing to do so seem minimal at best. The evidence suggests that representatives can survive, and have survived, politically after a local base closing. Even one of the most severe base closings of the 1960s, Brookley AFB in Mobile, Alabama, did not cause Representative Jack Edwards (R-AL) his seat. He was a newly elected Republican in a traditionally Democratic state, swept into office on the coattails of Republican presidential candidate Barry Goldwater in 1964. He should have been defeated if the loss of 12,000 base-related jobs mattered politically. However, he continued to be reelected, and even in 1998, the district remained in Republican hands. Both Senators Riegle and Levin of Michigan were reelected after Wurtsmith AFB closed. Representative Dellums received a large majority in each election year after 1993 and 1995 decimated his base-laden district. Paradoxically, Representative Geren worked hard to retain Carswell AFB, and then voluntarily retired from office, so one of the more successful base-saving cases did not produce a victor.

On the other hand, representatives have little to lose by either fighting or appearing to fight base closure—after all, risk minimization is one common characteristic of most representatives, and better to fight in the end, if just to make sure. Recall the old adage of "what have you done for me lately?" The most effective tactic for challenging base closures was to blame the BRAC members, which was one of the main reasons Congress created BRAC in the first place.

BUREAUCRATIC POLITICS AS AN EXPLANATION

The services welcomed the BRAC process on the one hand, and opposed it on the other. Why? Because the services desperately wanted to close surplus bases that drew money from operations they considered more critical—but they also wanted to exercise their own independence in choosing what bases would close. The Navy, for example, tends on the whole to value bases less than ships, but bases related to ships are more valuable to the Navy than bases that are not. The Army values forts with division headquarters and armor or infantry divisions more than it values training bases, particularly chemical-weapons training bases. So it placed Alabama's Fort McClellan on its closure list four times. But three of those four times BRAC struck Fort McClellan from the Army base-closure list.

Bureaucratic Politics and Base Closure

How did the services behave in the face of the base-closure process? Did they act to protect their share of the base-resource pie, as the Bureaucratic Politics Model would predict? Did they agree to shut down excess base structure so they could expand other more desirable programs that base expenditures had drained away? Or did they rise above parochial interests in recognition that the Cold War was over and all had to make sacrifices in the name of the national interest?

The BRAC processes of 1991, 1993, and 1995 saw the Air Force lose fewer bases than the other three services. That brought complaints of unfairness from the Army and the Navy, though the Air Force had one defense—it had lost more bases *prior* to BRAC, and so, Air Force officials could argue, they should lose fewer under BRAC. There is some support for that argument when comparing Air Force base structure before BRAC and after BRAC, noting which bases were closed before BRAC and which were shut down by the three BRACs examined in this book. Consider the states of Texas and Florida, two favorite sites for Air Force Bases. In 1958 both states were dotted with bases, but, by 1995, the landscape of both had changed considerably (see Table 6.1).

In Texas, Bergstrom, Carswell, and Reese AFBs were closed by BRACs—the Air Force closed the other bases. In Florida, the Air Force closed all but Homestead AFB. The reasons involve the cycle of Air Force buildup and downturn in response to changing Cold War requirements. Such changes drove Air Force base closure much more than did politics. In the 1950s, the Air Force built up its bomber bases in response to the "massive retaliation" doctrine, and it built up its fighter-interceptor bases to counter the potential for a Soviet response to "massive retaliation." As missiles replaced bombers, and the feared Soviet bomber threat never really materialized, the service found itself with considerable base infrastructure on hand. It also needed less aircraft-maintenance capacity, so it recommended closing the large aircraft depots at Brookley AFB in Alabama and Olmstead AFB in Pennsylvania. As noted earlier in the book, President Johnson allegedly closed Brookley for political reasons, but there was scarcely a whimper from the Air Force when the expensive base closed. It was designed largely to maintain the huge B-36 bomber, which the Air Force had dropped from its aircraft inventory in 1959.

Table 6.1: Active Air Force Bases, Texas and Florida

TEXAS		*FLORIDA*	
1958	*1995*	*1958*	*1995*
Amarillo AFB	Brooks AFB	Eglin AFB	Eglin AFB
Bergstrom AFB	Dyess AFB	Homestead AFB	Hurlburt Field
Biggs AFB	Goodfellow AFB	MacDill AFB	MacDill AFB
Brooks AFB	Kelly AFB	McCoy AFB	Patrick AFB
Bryan AFB	Lackland AFB	Orlando AFB	Tyndall AFB
Carswell AFB	Laughlin AFB	Palm Beach AFB	
Dyess AFB	Randolph AFB	Patrick AFB	
Ellington AFB	Sheppard AFB	Tyndall AFB	
Foster AFB			
Goodfellow AFB			
Gray AFB			
Harlington AFB			
James Connolly AFB			
Kelly AFB			
Lackland AFB			
Laredo AFB			
Laughlin AFB			
Perrin AFB			
Randolph AFB			
Reese AFB			
Sheppard AFB			
Webb AFB			

SOURCE: "Hearings to Authorize Certain Construction at Military Installations for Fiscal Year 1958," Committee on Armed Services, House of Representatives, 85th Cong., 2nd Sess.; "Hearings to Authorize Certain Construction at Military Installations for Fiscal Year 1995," Committee on Armed Services, House of Representatives, 104th Cong., 1st Sess.

These closures met several objectives. The services carried them out to reduce overhead. Civilian authority did not impose them. And as long as the services themselves shut their own bases down, the issue of interservice rivalry was muted. The services expected at least that the base-closing impact would neither favor nor punish a single service relative to others. That would not happen within each of the BRAC base-closing years. In each, year one service received larger cuts than the other. But, at the same time, BRAC made an effort to apportion those cuts more fairly across years (see Table 6.2).

Table 6.2: BRAC Closures, by Service Branch

	1991	*1993*	*1995*	TOTAL
Air Force	14	3	6	23
Army	8	1	10	19
Navy	12	17	8	47

The Air Force got the biggest cuts in 1991, the Navy in 1993, and the Army in 1995. Overall, BRAC reduced the Navy by almost twice the other services. The services, though, fought any closure pattern that placed an unequal burden on any particular service. Service subcomponents also fought unequal base-closure decisions.

An odd wrinkle appeared after the 1995 process indicating that base competition between services continues. The Navy really has two kinds of bases, shore bases and aircraft carriers. While the 1991-1995 BRACs reduced naval shore bases more than land bases of the other two services, the Navy carrier numbers remained constant at 12. The Air Force, though, saw a considerable loss of operating bases, potentially placing it as a weaker rival to the Navy. One Air Force answer is the "airpower expeditionary forces"—small mobile bases of 34 aircraft and 1,100 personnel that can be quickly deployed to a trouble spot. The Navy's defense of carriers lies in their capability for rapid deployment to a trouble spot, so the Air Force's "airpower expeditionary forces" emerge as a direct carrier competitor, except that they can actually put more aircraft on targets because the Navy uses a significant portion of carrier-based aviation to defend the carrier fleet.[6]

Another service priority over equity revealed itself in the 1995 closure round. The Air Force divides itself up in many ways, one being between operators and maintainers. The operators fly aircraft, and the maintainers fix and modernize them at depots. After the 1991 and 1993 BRAC rounds, many operating bases, but not a single depot, closed. Thus, the operators put pressure on the Air Staff to close at least two depots. They lost in the first Air Force submission to BRAC as depots recommended for closure by staffers were pulled by Air Force leadership at the last minute, reportedly after considerable political pressure from the White House. But BRAC added four of the five depots to its initial 1995 closure list and voted to close two in the final considerations. So while the operators did not "win" at the Air Force level, they at least got to see two depots on the final closure list.

Another indicator of organizational process-oriented behavior on the part of the services was their inability to combine functions in the face of base closure. One way to reduce unwanted base infrastructure would be to join up functions from two bases doing more or less the same thing. The Air Force and the Navy, for example, might combine undergraduate pilot training, which involves largely the same basic-skill development. Yet, both services maintained their own separate bases to perform this service. In a similar fashion, all of the services ran laboratories that sometimes tested for the same things, yet there was resistance to combining laboratories across services—creating, for example, a single service laboratory to test for materials strength or human stress performance. Only for the 1995 BRAC round did the Defense Department create the Joint Cross-Service Groups (JCSG) to consider such things, when, in fact, service jointness in such areas was called for by the Goldwater-Nichols Act passed in 1986.

While there is evidence of bureaucratic-politics behavior from the services on base closure, there is also counterevidence that the services were able to view closure as in the national interest and did little to thwart the process. Their input to the total closure process was valuable and important, but also smaller than that of the BRAC members and their staffs. In the end, in the 1991, 1993, and 1995 rounds examined here, the central authority was the BRAC, and service politics played second fiddle to BRAC commissioners when base-closure decisions were made.

LEARNING OVER TIME AS AN EXPLANATION

Some of the more notable successes in base closure came from the 1995 round of closures, while some of the more frustrating experiences came from earlier closures. Lesson drawing clearly took place; the questions are, how and when? At the BRAC level, lessons were sometimes limited by the fact that previous rounds remained incomplete. Hearing testimony during the 1995 decision process revealed that less than one-half of the closures mandated by previous rounds were complete.[7] Only by mid-1996 were all facilities ordered closed by the 1988 BRAC finally closed. Still, there were lessons.

Lesson One: Resist Closure or Convert?

The first issue was the choice to either resist base closure or prepare for closure and redevelopment of base property. Base supporters tried during earlier rounds to resist closure and invested comparatively little time and research in base alternatives, should resistance fail. By 1995, they realized however, that the BRAC process had improved and that a listed base would likely mean a closed base. At Myrtle Beach AFB in South Carolina, which made the 1991 BRAC list, little effort was put into alternatives, so, when the base closed in 1993, a few half-hearted efforts at commercial development fell through, and the only conversion is the base's golf course, which reverted to the city of Myrtle Beach. The city still must pay $2.1 million per year for base-caretaking fees for providing fire and police protection to the nearly empty site.[8] But in the case of the 1995 closure of the Fleet and Industrial Supply Center Oakland (FISCO), a reuse plan was in place by the time closure was announced. Base political figures, particularly Representative Dellums, had learned from previous base closures in the San Francisco Bay Area that resistance was likely to be futile. Thus, the 1995 closure saw Dellums shift his tactics from denouncing the closure decision to working with local officials, including the mayor of Oakland and the Port of Oakland, to proceed rapidly with economic redevelopment of the site and rapid remediation of its environmental problems.

Not all base-closure efforts generate useful lessons about advance preparations for closure, though. To put it another way, not all involved in base closure learn lessons from previous efforts. The case of Fort McClellan is instructive. By 1995, the base faced its fourth effort to close the facility, yet the tactics chosen by base supporters remained focused on resistance. Reuse plans, fairly common at other base-closure sites by 1995, were absent in the Fort McClellan case. One explanation appears to be that successive fights against closure had brought victory, and perhaps overconfidence set in among base supporters. They somehow refused to believe that they might lose in the final round and paid a high price for such refusal. Officials in the San Francisco area had been much less fortunate in that most of their closures were upheld, so by 1995 they were forced to adjust.

Another case of learning refusal appears at the Air Force depot level. The depots had been mentioned as candidates for closure in rounds previous to 1995 but had always escaped. Apparently, their supporters remained convinced that their high civilian employment levels and, in most cases, powerful political patrons could save them again in 1995. Interviews at Warner Robbins ALC in Georgia in early 1995 revealed a lackadaisical view of the closure prospects, including a statement of confidence from the base's newly elected U.S. representative, Republican Saxby Chambliss. In the end, Warner Robbins remained open, but only after BRAC listed it, along with three other depots, for closure. Sacramento ALC in California and San Antonio ALC in Texas were not so fortunate, though. Their lesson seemed to be learned more at the White House level than at the local level, when President Clinton drew from an Air Force study to propose privatization as a means of protecting their employment base.

Finally, lesson drawing differed across states as they prepared for the possibility of further base closure in 1999 and 2001. The State of Georgia, for example, survived BRAC without a major closure, but still created a Military Affairs Coordinating Committee to protect against future base closure.[9] Arizona also drew up plans to spend money to protect bases, but Colorado focused on future efforts to convert future base closures instead to attempting to prevent them.[10] However, neither Florida or Washington, still rich in base infrastructure, were planning any efforts to respond to future base-closure efforts.[11]

Lesson Two: Repackage and Streamline the Closure Process

One of the more adroit political learners was President Clinton himself. Clinton is the only president to preside over two rounds of base closure, and the combined weight of base closings in such key states as Texas, Florida, and California might have jeopardized his 1996 reelection chances. Clinton had experienced base closure himself as the governor of Arkansas and reflected bitterly upon the experience: "And nothing made it more clear to me than an experience I had as governor of my own state dealing with a base closing—when a base closed in a part of my state that already had double-digit unemployment before it closed. And they told me that I could have some of this land for a public park but not to put people back to work. They told me that we'd have to come up with all kinds of money if we wanted to convert the base. . . ."[12] Clinton's experience in his own state (which suffered the closure of Fort Chaffee, Blytheville AFB, and Eaker AFB) apparently helped him understand that the federal government needed to take both a dynamic and a symbolic role in base conversion. So during the 1996 presidential campaign, Clinton presided over the opening of California State University at Monterey Bay (the site of Fort Ord) and appeared at both Sacramento and San Antonio ALC to explain the benefits of the then-untested concept of base privatization.[13] Clinton performed in similar fashion at the Philadelphia Naval Shipyard, closed by the 1991 BRAC. While that action was taken before Clinton's presidency, he would inherit the damage done to Philadelphia's economy. So, in 1995 he touted his efforts to channel federal funds into base-conversion efforts: ". . . we have . . . committed over $100 million to this project. That's not counting the approximately $170 million in loan guarantees. . . ."[14]

The Defense Department appeared to recognize that the process could be packaged in ways to make it less politically costly. It paid political dividends, the department found out, to be prepared to eliminate or reduce impediments to efficient base closure. Thus, Assistant Secretary of Defense for Economic Security Joshua Gotbaum testified in glowing terms before the 1995 BRAC members as to his department's base-closure process. He outlined base closure as a part of the Clinton administration's "Reinventing Government" program—eliminating excessive regulation and streamlining the entire process.[15] He emphasized how new procedures would encourage economic development, speed environmental cleanup, and improve state-federal coordination.[16] He also offered his interpretation of DOD experience in previous base closures: "You will get plenty of pressure from local communities and sometimes from local commanders to modify a closure recommendation. . . . *Please don't.*"[17] Gotbaum apparently reflected thinking in the Clinton administration that, if packaged correctly, base closure could be made politically palatable.

Repackaging also meant accelerating the closure process. Nothing signified failure as much as a weed-strewn base with broken windows and empty parking lots. Rules regarding closure (including environmental rules,) could be streamlined to hasten the closure process. Local participation was also essential and would avoid problems incurred in previous closure decisions.[18] Previous commissions also learned lessons. The 1991 BRAC used the streamlined processes passed by Congress to reduce closure time to three years from the five years to close the 1988 BRAC bases.[19] Another study indicating the cumulative impact of learning was a Congressional Budget Office (CBO) report showing that, while the Defense Department closed only 22 percent of targeted bases four years after BRAC 1991, it shuttered 73 percent in the four years after BRAC 1993.[20]

Lesson Three: Closure and Reelection

The 1991-1995 base-closure years reflected another lesson from previous base closure-there is no evidence that base closure was responsible for even a single congressional or senatorial defeat in the election years following each round. While it is almost impossible to demonstrate direct links between electoral outcomes and political actions such as base closures, it is significant that no defeated member blamed his or her defeat solely on a closure decision in any of the three BRAC rounds considered in this book. The lesson learned from this is more complicated, though. In 1995, for example, the stated outrage of the California and Texas delegations over closures at Sacramento and San Antonio were just as tumultuous as were those of the Maine delegation over Loring's closing in 1991. There was as much maneuvering to save Long Beach Naval Shipyard in 1995 as there was to save Carswell AFB in 1991. Of course, neither action was successful, and, in the end, most such efforts failed to save a base from closure. But that may not be the point. A spirited effort by a representative against an apparently cold-hearted commission may have been the ingredient to successful reelection, regardless of the political outcome.

Lesson Four: Avoid Letting the Environmental Condition of a Base Delay Its Closure

The 1991 BRAC round sensitized those involved in base closure to the degree of contamination at most bases. The first lesson was that environmental rules had become much stricter in the last several decades, and their enforcement could well delay base closure or even prevent it altogether. The response to that lesson was to publicize toxins at bases in the hope that such information would prevent their closure due to the costs and delays imposed by cleanup requirements. But that tactic failed. In 1995, Commissioner Alton Cornella asked a DOD witness if she was aware of "any site that was not recommended for closure because of cleanup costs," and the answer was "no."[21] That view gets support from the number of polluted bases that did make the closure list, including shipyards, ammunition plants, and repair depots. The only possible exception was the Tooele Army Depot in Utah, stricken from the closure list because of the extent of contamination there. So those involved in base closures realized that the only avenue to speed closure and conversion was to comply with the stringent cleanup requirements. While that compliance might be satisfactory to those with an interest in conversion and the monetary opportunity it creates, it was of concern to community members who feared that the cleanup might never happen or happen incompletely, at best, leaving hazards behind.

Since this was a local problem, the answer was to involve members of localities by including them as members of Restoration Advisory Boards. A member of such a board at Watertown Arsenal in New York reflected the changed perception: "I used to say, 'It's us against the U.S. Army. . . ,' but now I talk of working with the installation's officials and the Army, to insure proper cleanup of the Arsenal. . . ."[22] By the end of fiscal 1995, 250 RABs had formed at both closing and operational bases. Community involvement in both closure and cleanup processes helped alleviate suspicions and gain political support for the entire process.

Lesson Five: Keep Policy Data Accurate

Another lesson learned appears to be the importance of accurate and objective data submission. In earlier BRAC rounds, the Defense Department in particular had been severely criticized by BRAC commissioners and staff members and by the General Accounting Office (GAO) for submitting faulty data. By 1995, DOD had come to learn that knowingly submitting bad data was fatal and could easily be used to overturn its decisions on base closure. It had also learned that errors in data made the DOD process seem inept, and decisions made on those data subject to reversal, and that those above the DOD review process suspected that the data had been manipulated to favor service and organizational positions because those who generated it were subject to personnel review by superiors with a stake in particular positions. To ease fears of reprisals for data not favorable to their superiors, by 1995 staff workers for base-closure issues were assured that their performance reports could not be written by direct superiors.

Lesson Six: Shifting Priorities, Power

Finally, a lesson about shifting priorities and decisional authority from federal to local levels appears to have materialized by the time the 1995 round occurred. In 1991, the Defense Department had responded to base-closure needs by creating a host of subagencies at the DOD level, and other federal agencies, including the Environmental Protection Agency and the General Accounting Office, had expanded their capabilities to handle base-closure investigation and implementation requirements. By 1995, though, in a shift that would mirror broader Clinton administration priorities in 1996, the emphasis shifted to local jurisdictions. Two acts of Congress, the Pryor Amendment to the National Defense Authorization Act for Fiscal Year 1995 and the Base Closure Community Redevelopment Act and Homeless Assistance Act of 1994, shifted responsibility away from federal rulemakers to local officials for final decisions on closure replacements. Local redevelopment agencies, along with Restoration Advisory Boards for waste cleanup, managed to speed the process of base redevelopment in a number of cases, though local agencies were not always able to mobilize sufficient resources to accomplish necessary tasks.

Did BRAC Depoliticize the Base-Closure Process?

BRAC produced base closure, something seemingly impossible in 1990 after Congress unceremoniously dumped Secretary of Defense Dick Cheney's base-closure list. It is difficult to imagine how Congress could have allowed such a dramatic reduction in bases without BRAC. Nor could presidents have inflicted as much political pain on politically important states without BRAC. So, in that sense, BRAC was successful in breaking through a political logjam that otherwise would have made base disposal much more difficult. The 1995 round was probably the most successful of all, in that the president and Congress approved all of the bases appearing on the BRAC list.

In another sense, though, BRAC failed to accomplish its assigned mission. There were 79 bases in all in just the 1995 round, but that was far fewer than originally predicted, and far less than the original legislation required. The total BRAC process did not close one-third of the nation's military installations, as required by the 1988 law. That may be seen as a failure if the standard is strict compliance with the law. Or it may be seen as the triumph of politics over process. Secretary of Defense William Perry stated early in 1995 that he believed that the national economic conditions of the time would not allow for "the mother of all base closings," as described in early press reports. Still, as in 1991, when BRAC recommended 31 bases for closure, and in 1993, when 28 bases were targeted, the process allowed for something that had been impossible for the preceding decade—base closures.

That did not happen, though, without considerable political interference. It came from the services, from the Defense Department, from local officials, from key members of Congress, and from presidents. In many cases, that interference was largely vocal, with politicians ranging from mayors to President Clinton denouncing the Base Realignment and Closure Commission as patently unfair, while realizing all along that the process had to go forward in the post–Cold War environment. Someone had to suffer. There were sincere efforts on the part of all involved in the process to try to ensure fairness. If the pain was spread equitably, there would perhaps be less opposition, both to the direct results and to the politicians who ultimately signed off on them. So, for example, shipyards on both coasts were shuttered (Hunter's Point Naval Annex and Long Beach in California, Charleston in South Carolina, and Philadelphia in Pennsylvania). The process also appeared designed to spread closures across the three services. If the Army lost more bases in one particular year, the Navy would lose more in the following round, and then the Air Force.

Congressional action was mixed. Representatives made clear efforts to use the powers of appointment to get key base supporters on the commission. There were also efforts behind the scenes to get targeted bases removed from the list. In some cases that amounted to a feeble protest, such as the one staged in 1990 by Senator Dale Bumpers (D-AR). He complained that the closure of Eaker AFB in his home state would lead to a 30 percent unemployment in the area,[23] but, beyond that, he did little to prevent it. Others were much more active in trying to keep a base in their state or district open. The entire Maine delegation fought the closing of Loring AFB from start to finish. They initially fought the closing itself, then worked feverishly to save employment in the area after closing became inevitable. But no representative probably found more unique ways to try to save an ultimately doomed base than Representative Glen Browder (D-AL). Browder raised the chemical-weapons issue to its most fearsome detail, noting the number of horrid weapons stored at Anniston Army Arsenal—a facility that nearby Fort McClellan, on the closure list, was required to assist in case of chemical emergency. Browder even used the Army's minuscule request for new museum money to defend his existing three Army museums at Fort McClellan. That he failed is not indicative of the creativity of his efforts. Browder was relatively junior, but the outcome of his efforts is comparable to that of Representative "Sonny" Montgomery (D-MS), who had 30 years of seniority and served on the House Armed Services Committee. Montgomery got Meridian NAS struck from the final BRAC base-closure list twice.

Browder, who wound up on the faculty of the faculty of the Naval Postgraduate School in Monterey, California, after a failed bid at the Democratic nomination to the United States Senate in 1996, succeeded three times but lost in the fourth round.[24] Who did better at rescuing a base? In the end, Montgomery prevailed as Meridian remains open, while the local community around Fort McClellan in 1996 struggled to find alternatives to the large base, scheduled to shut down in 1999. So, for that matter, did Representative C.W. "Bill" Young (R-FL), who worked with the commanders of the two major commands at MacDill AFB in Florida to ultimately keep the base open, even though the Air Force wanted to close it. Young's senior position on the House Defense Appropriations Subcommittee of the House Appropriations Committee probably did not hurt, but perhaps as important was his seniority and experience that helped him gain that committee assignment in the first place.

Senators with a vulnerable base in their state found another method to protect their facility. They nominated members to the Commission who were a sure bet to protect that base. Did BRAC keep partisan politics out of the base-closure process? Not if Senator Tom Dashle's (D-SD) nominee to the 1995 commission had close ties to Ellsworth AFB in South Dakota, or Senator Bob Dole's nominee had been previously involved in efforts to save Kansas's Fort Riley. Dole was the Senate majority leader; Dashle, the ranking Senate Democrat. Neither of their states lost a base in 1995. California, by way of contrast, lost a large number of bases in 1995, perhaps partly because California's two senators, Dianne Feinstein and Barbara Boxer, were both junior; each had not served even one full term. But the area that suffered the most from base closure in 1995 was Guam losing bases responsible for approximately 10 percent of the island's total work force. Guam has no senators, and only a single representative. The conclusion is that political clout and seniority make a difference in protecting states and districts from base closure, though, as in most political findings, there are exceptions. One was Senator Strom Thurmond, the venerable Republican from South Carolina. Thurmond reportedly left the Senate Judiciary Committee and transferred to the Senate Armed Services Committee to protect South Carolina's base structure. He failed to prevent the closing of Myrtle Beach AFB and, more important to the state's economy, the Charleston Naval Shipyard. Some argued that Thurmond was too old to have much clout in the Senate. Still, he was reelected to the Senate in 1996—proof that even a significant base closure was not sufficient to deny his reelection, even though he was also hampered with the charge that, at age 94, he was to old to serve.

Did BRAC prevent political punishment through base closings? Just ask California Representative Dellums, the liberal critic of many defense programs, who found virtually every base in his Northern California district closed in various BRAC rounds. While no conclusive proof exists, both Dellums and a large number of people living in the east San Francisco Bay Area believe that politics was the root cause of the base closures that literally moved the military out of the district. Representative George Brown, Jr. (D-CA), a long-term opponent of defense budgets and defense programs, lost two Air Force bases (George and Norton) either in or adjacent to his southern California district. Was this retaliation for attacking Air Force programs? It is almost impossible to tell for sure. Others argue that Senators Boxer and Feinstein were also punished for their antimilitary stances. Such may have been the case in Colorado, where liberal Democrat and frequent defense critic Representative Patricia Schroeder had Lowry AFB, Fitzsimmons Army Medical Center, and the Rocky Mountain Arsenal closed in her Denver district. There were even rumors that Republican Governor Pete Wilson of California was a target of California base closures to reduce his chances of obtaining the Republican presidential nomination in 1996.

Alternative explanations exist, though. Base-rich California was targeted for just that reason; it had an abundance of bases. Moderate Representative Stephen Horn (R-CA) of Long Beach lost his shipyard. San Diego's conservative and pro-military Representative Randy Cunningham, himself a Vietnam War fighter ace, lost the Naval Training Center in that city, along with several smaller facilities. Outside California, other pro-military Republican legislators also saw closures; Senator John McCain (R-AZ) of Arizona, also a Vietnam-era pilot and former prisoner of war, saw Williams AFB shut down. Virginia's Fort Pickett received a closure notice in 1995, along with some naval facilities in the home state of Senator John Warner (R-VA), a staunch friend of the military and former Secretary of the Navy. The pattern of closure, in other words, included a number of defense defenders as well as critics, militating against the argument that closure was a warning against military criticism.

Possibly the most strident criticism of closure politicization came from members of Congress, who accused President Clinton of violating the BRAC rules by removing the two Air Force depots at San Antonio and Sacramento and placing them under "privatization." Some saw the decision as a political ploy to gather votes in Texas and California, while others claimed that privatization would inject efficiency into depot operations and preserve wartime maintenance capacity should it be needed.

WILL "PRIVATIZATION" REPLACE PUBLIC BASES?

The Air Force originally proposed privatizing some of its functions long before President Clinton proposed it as a solution to the political fallout accompanying the closure of Sacramento and San Antonio ALCs. But, as of the 1995 closure round, it remained largely untested at the military base level. When the president said that Newark AFB was a pilot project for his decision to privatize the two large depots, the privatization of Newark had not begun and would not begin for more than a year. According to the cochair of the congressional depot caucus, Representative Browder of Alabama, a 1994 GAO study reported that the projected 1997 costs after privatization would be 107 percent higher than the projected costs under continued Air Force operation.[25] Was there evidence from other policy sources that the concept might work for other installations? The answer depends in part on what the purposes and objectives of privatization are. In some contexts, privatization means a complete replacement of a government function with a private function—a state-owned airline, for example, being sold to private investors. In the United States, though, the term more commonly refers to a change in the way goods and services are delivered, with funding still coming from state sources.[26] Privatization of defense processes does not necessarily mean greater efficiency, since the same facilities will be used, and the nature of competition is hardly clear. Congress did mandate the 60-40 rule that some 60 percent of depot work be sent to government depots, and that provision may still protect the privatized depots. There is, in other words, no assurance that privatization is nothing more than a way for President Clinton to avoid political damage in Texas and California. Says John D. Donahue, "There is a large element of nonsense in the privatization debate."[27] The credibility of privatization in Texas was shown in the plans of the Initial Base Adjustment Strategy Committee, a community group charged with planning San Antonio ALC's future. While the plans endorse privatization where it "makes sense," they also call for the creation of an additional 10,000 jobs in the area, diversification of the San Antonio economy, and the transfer of some base property for an industrial area.[28] A similar effort appeared in Sacramento as well, with the formation of the Mission McClellan Executive Advisory Committee. The group considered the range of responses to base closure, including studying other communities impacted by closure and forming an economic development corporation.[29] Such responses are politically understandable—privatization was an untried concept, and no large organization nor its supporting political leaders wanted to risk thousands of jobs and millions of dollars of income on it.

Privatization may be untried as a concept for military bases, but the Clinton Administration appears to be committed to it. Privatization of base housing was the next step, approved for trial facilities in 1996. Much base housing has deteriorated to the point that in 1996, 60 percent of the available units needed refurbishing at a projected cost of $20 billion and a 30- 40-year schedule for completion.[30] The alternative was to offer private contractors a series of incentives to provide private housing through renovation of existing units and the construction of new housing.

WHAT WAS SAVED (AND LOST) BY BRAC?

At the end of the 1995 BRAC process, BRAC closures and realignments promised $6 billion per year in savings. However, this figure would begin accruing mostly after 2001, in part because of the slow process involved in cleaning up and closing a base after decades of operation. One of the guiding principles of the 1995 process was the cost of closure, and the time required to complete the process.[31] Secretary of Defense Perry estimated that the 70 bases on the 1995 closure list would cost an initial $15 billion to close and that ". . . every year after that we will save about $4 billion a year in our defense budget."[32] Another source projected the savings over 20 years at $19.3 billion, though a starting time for the savings to begin accruing was not given.[33] Even as early as 1996, though, one year after the final BRAC round, savings began to appear in military-construction costs, which had declined more than 10 percent over the previous year. The military-construction budget for fiscal year 1997 projected another drop of 18 percent.[34] Not all of the reductions are attributable to the reduced base structure, though, and $2.5 billion in the fiscal 1997 budget request reflected additional base-closure cost.[35]

The $15 billion closing costs that Perry estimated included transferring service personnel and workers and their families fortunate enough to get relocationed. It also included the cost of early retirement for eligible workers at closed bases. In addition, there would be substantial environmental cleanup costs, security for bases while under the closure process, and a host of other smaller but additive expenses.

The accuracy of promised savings data has always been problematic at best. Base-closure supporters generally overestimated projected savings, only to revise those estimates later. For example, the first BRAC in 1988 was to generate considerable savings, but several years later those savings got a sharp readjustment, from $995 million to $23 million.[36] The following 1994 exchange between Senator Arlen Specter (R-PA), representing the Philadelphia Naval Shipyard, and then-Defense Secretary Les Aspin provides an even better sense of how much the estimates varied:

Q: According to the Navy's most recent cost estimate for closure of the Philadelphia Naval Complex, the closure costs have increased by over 350 percent, from an original estimate used during the 1991 base closure round of $126 million dollars to the current estimate of over $575 million. This cost excludes any environmental remediation activity. I am concerned that the estimates being presented during the base closure process are not adequately analyzed and that the return on investment and payback period can not be justified. Can you tell the committee how the Department is addressing the apparent lack of a cost analysis for past approved closures and how you intend to assure the Committee that the future defense budgets will be affected by base closure implementation costs that may be two three [sic] times larger than anticipated?

A: The costs, savings, and return on investment for the Philadelphia Naval complex were calculated using the Cost of Base Realignment Actions (COBRA) model. The total COBRA estimate for closing the Philadelphia Naval Complex was $183,274,000. The FY 1993 budget estimate (less environmental costs) submitted to Congress was $84,765,000. The FY 1994 budget estimate submitted to Congress was $140,091,000.[37]

The answer does not challenge Specter's 1991 estimate but does deflate his "current" cost estimate by more than half. Aspin also substitutes 1993 figures for Specter's 1991 figure. Who is correct? The quoted figures are quite spongy and subject to different interpretations. This has lead to fairly widespread doubt about the accuracy of cost figures, a concern noted by House International Security Committee Chair Floyd Spence (D-SC) in 1995: "A number of Members, including myself, have been skeptical when it comes to the rosy projections that have been made in previous base-closure rounds concerning the savings that will accrue to the military services."[38] That same year Representative Sam Farr (D-CA) stated that while the Army had costed the move of facilities at Fort Hunter Liggett at $6.7 million, he was in possession of internal Army documents showing the move costing three times that much.[39] A more recent GAO finding indicated that "existing financial data did not reliably portray actual costs associated with base closure and realignment."[40]

Whether the annual savings after the year 2000 is $4 billion or $6 billion (and the actual figure will probably be neither amount, given the difficulty of making such an estimate) how much does it matter? At the highest level, $6 billion is about 3 percent of an estimated $240 billion defense budget for 2000, not insignificant in itself, but not large considering the overall size of the budget. Even that may be deceiving, though. However, if the purpose is to save money from the DOD budget to free it up for something else, then DOD may ultimately benefit. However, if the purpose is also to cut overall federal governmental expenses, though, then the cost of closures becomes more significant. Some workers will lose their jobs altogether, forgoing tax payment in the process. Others will get new jobs at reduced pay, and pay less in taxes as a consequence. Yet others will get new jobs only after receiving federal assistance to find new jobs, which amounted to $559 million as of August 1996.[41] On the other hand, some base property that did not generate tax revenue under government ownership will do so if transferred to private ownership. But some of that revenue will be in the form of property taxes that will go to local, as opposed to federal, revenue coffers. Granted, some of that local-tax-base increase will perhaps offset federal payments to the local areas, though it is hard to predict how much. The bottom line for 1995 was that an estimated 43,742 jobs disappeared as a result of closure or realignment, and another 49,823 indirect jobs were lost in communities where the closed bases were located.[42]

WILL MILITARY EFFICIENCY IMPROVE WITH BASE CLOSURE?

The military's chief complaint against the congressionally mandated limits on base closure was that the services had to pay for a bloated and unnecessary base infrastructure that cost them billions of dollars each year to maintain. The BRAC process was supposed to alleviate that problem by helping the military rid itself of obsolete and excessive base stock to allow more money for such things as operations and maintenance, procurement, personnel, and other such wants. The process was well intended, but it has not worked, at least not in terms of reducing base numbers proportionate to service reductions. Since the end of the Cold War, service reductions have averaged 25 percent, but fewer than 10 percent of bases had closed as of mid-1995.

While another 10 percent of the bases were scheduled to close, service drawdowns continue apace as well, so there will probably be at least a 10 percent gap between service cuts and base cuts that could last until the end of the century. Also, there may be bases like Carswell AFB in Texas that "closed" only in name. Moreover, to privatize bases like the aviation depots at San Antonio and Sacramento means that tax dollars will still flow into them even though the Defense Department would no longer fund their infrastructure costs. The privatization of depots required the suspension of the old 60-40 rule mandating that the Air Force send at least 60 percent of its work to its own depots. Efforts in 1996 to repeal the rule met with stiff resistance, though, and the Clinton Administration's efforts along such lines met with a limited compromise. The House rejected the suspension of the rule entirely, and the Senate agreed only to reduce the 60 percent to 50 percent, with details to be worked out in conference.[43] The conferees, though, ultimately rejected the measure after the Defense Department released projections that the Army depot workload would fall to 56 percent, the Navy's to 51 percent, and the Air Force's to 46 percent.[44] While Deputy Secretary of Defense John White lobbied hard for the elimination of the rule, the depot caucus carried the day. The power of the depot labor unions was also present; John N. Sturdivant, national president of the American Federation of Government Employees, said: "Elimination of assurances that 60 percent of critical military hardware maintenance is performed in secure, stable government installations would have allowed the wholesale privatization of our defense depots."[45] That, of course, was the point of privatization, but the vote derailed administration efforts and left the fate of the "closed" depots in doubt. And while politics again prevailed over process in base closure, the "rational" solution of privatization still left questions about what the fate of the depots would have been under the concept. They might have become smaller in size (which could wind up making them less efficient), but they will remain nevertheless. The *question* remains: If the Air Force did not need them in 1995, what makes them necessary after their conversion to a private owner? The capacity, it would seem, is still surplus. In this case, "politics" appears to have won the day.

The existing basing structure also hampers the forward progress of service jointness. While the Goldwater-Nichols bill of 1986 tried to make the military more joint in many ways, bases are configured along service lines and designed for service-specific functions. Some of that structure is obviously necessary to service functions—naval vessels need shipyards, and aircraft need runways, for example. But bases also duplicate functions, with each service running its own training facilities, from recruit training to advanced officer training. Each service does almost all of its own maintenance on its weapons, despite some similarities in some of those weapons. That flew in the face of the 1990s emphasis on joint doctrine, joint weapons acquisition, joint training, and, ultimately, joint military operations. Of course, simply closing bases will not end the service-specific functions that remain. But the services may choose to move toward more consolidation of functions with the reduction of base infrastructure. For example, the Air Force formed "composite wings" in the early 1990s to make that service more compatible with the needs of the other services. One of the most efficient is the 23rd Composite Wing at Pope AFB in North Carolina, which was specifically tasked to support the 82nd Airborne at nearby Fort Bragg. The 23rd Composite Wing includes airlift to get the 82nd to its destination and A-10 ground-attack aircraft to provide them with close air support when they arrive. There may also be efficiencies in combining training and testing facilities. Both the Air Force and the Navy use the range at Columbus AFB with no noticeable problems, and the closure of ranges may simply lead to more consolidation. With fewer flying hours in both services, and fewer aircraft, crowding would not appear to be a problem. Testing could also be combined. The Army, Navy, and Air Force all maintain personnel laboratories in which things such as survival equipment are tested. Yet, a single joint laboratory could probably cut the costs by one-third and maintain almost all of the capacity needed for such testing. What little specialized testing that remains might be contracted out to private laboratories.

Military efficiency may also be hampered by political interference in military operations and funding due to efforts to mitigate negative base-closure impacts. For example, Section 8090 of the Defense Appropriations Act for Fiscal Year 1997 directs the Army to use the runway at George AFB in California (closed in 1988 but not successfully converted to alternative use) as an airhead for the National Training Center at Fort Irwin and prohibited the use of Edwards AFB for that purpose.[46] There is no other interpretation of this legislation except to keep a closed Air Force base minimally functional to keep a minimum number of jobs in the district. The same bill appropriated $7 million for California State University Monterey Bay at the site of closed Fort Ord.[47] While $7 million may be a drop in the Defense Department bucket of money, it represents no military worth to that department, which finds itself funding a state-supported university for apparent political reasons. That this was done in an election year may only be coincidental. But it does illustrate the hidden costs of base closure, draining defense money by requiring the military to spend money on bases from which it gets no further value.

THE COMMISSION PROCESS: HOW WELL DID IT WORK?

During televised hearings, the members of the 1995 BRAC were highly visible to fans of C-SPAN, and most likely to hundreds of thousands of viewers from communities located near a listed base. The hearings revealed a highly structured process in which witnesses testified on behalf of, or against, a particular base on the list. Deliberations were courteous and well informed, peppered with the arcane language of military things. After each base on the list received its hearing, the commission voted, with each commissioner's vote recorded for all to see. It had some of the appearance of the old New England town-hall meeting that has become enshrined in democratic myth. Everything was open and above board. Or so it seemed. In fact, traditional democratic practice had, to a degree, been short-circuited by the BRAC process.

First, the commission's open sessions were only the last part of the process. The initial deliberations were not always open. Nor was there any way to monitor the less formal, yet important, interaction among the BRAC members, nor the staff work that generated the rankings of bases, among other things. This, of course, does not make BRAC different from any other governmental commission; and the openness of *any* governmental process is relative. There will probably always be some commission business that will be conducted privately, and the openness of the final hearings should not blind anyone to that fact. But maybe the openness of the BRAC process (including the open regional hearings and the visits to selected bases) did at least create the impression that the pain that followed a base closure was meted out fairly. Given the growing public cynicism about American politics that dates back to Vietnam, Watergate, and the like, it is probably preferable that the victims of base closure believe that the process was open and that they had a chance to participate in it.

The process also raises questions of accountability. Granted that the president and Congress created the rules of BRAC, appointed the commission members, and signed off on the final decisions, the decisions themselves were made by a temporary body that disbanded after its final vote. Its members cannot now be held accountable for the decisions BRAC made, which will have an impact for many years to come around the nation as selected bases undergo the long process of closing or realigning. So while the president and Congress may bear final responsibility, both were able to pass off responsibility for hard decisions to a commission that no longer exists. In an era in which political accountability (and political courage) is more questioned than perhaps ever before, the BRAC process seemed to fit in well.

A TALE OF TWO CITIES: BASES AFTER CLOSURE

The Army's Presidio of San Francisco was the nation's oldest military base when it was first ordered to close in 1988.[48] In the summer of 1996, though, the large hilly tract of land it occupied near San Francisco Marina remained unconverted. Hundreds of buildings sat empty, slowly deteriorating from the salty air. Pershing Hall, a graceful three-story nineteenth-century brick building last used as a visiting-officer's quarters, sat curtainless with paint slowly peeling off exterior woodwork. Old red brick officers' houses meandered up the hills from the main base, all of them empty. The cannons remained outside the headquarters building, as did the World War II–era tank on the old parade ground. The new Letterman Army Hospital sat vacant, since the University of California reneged on its agreement to take over the facility, finding that the cost of upgrading the buildings to seismic standards was too expensive. The lawns were unmowed, the streets unswept, and the old base had simply become a ghost fort except for the occasional National Park Service employee.

The former base had environmental problems left over from its long operation, including underground storage tanks, landfills, a leaking fuel-distribution system, and PCB-contaminated electrical transformers. Pollutants included heavy metals, solvents, and pesticides. Yet between 1988 and 1996, only $50 million had been spent on cleanup, and negotiations remained "underway" among the National Park Service, the Army, and the state of California about where responsibility for what lay.[49] A site visit in the summer of 1996 revealed small colored flags placed along old pipelines, small exploration holes dug and unfilled, but no actual work underway to remove the offending pollutants—that, despite a 1994 survey that certified only 36 percent of the base's 1,487 acres as environmentally clean.[50] The only real evidence of cleanup effort were small paper signs taped to doors and windows of almost every building with faded lettering stating "ASBESTOS HAZARD" on them.

In the summer of 1996, legislation to free up more National Park Service money lay bottled up in a congressional committee, eight years after the Presidio was first ordered closed. In 1996, the Army agreed to pay "one-time costs" of $92.8 million for facility upgrades, to include water treatment, utility upgrades, road resurfacing, and other improvements. The problem was that this all represented "deferred maintenance" since 1991, and much of the money would pay to repair deterioration from previous neglect.[51] Moreover, the Army would get nothing back for its money, since it had lost the Presidio.

The opportunity is there at the Presidio for a major conversion. The base lies in downtown San Francisco, with a growing economy and a need for land. The old brick houses could be fixed up and sold on the commercial market, and the headquarters buildings used for shops. But, while under National Park Service jurisdiction, the base languished, unused and unwanted. This is why the Presidio Trust idea has gained support as an option, though years of implementation remain ahead.

Across the Bay Bridge lies the Fleet and Industrial Supply Center Oakland (FISCO), whose conversion to commercial use has proceeded ahead of schedule. The base's old buildings are to be bulldozed flat, and an innovative new multi-dimensional transportation facility linking the U.S. Pacific Coast with the growing Asian international market place will be in place after the turn of the century. The FISCO site remains somewhat dismal looking, with its weathered buildings, weed-infested roadways, and piles of phone poles, metal pipes, and other detritus accumulated over decades of use. But, in contrast to the still-graceful Presidio in San Francisco, FISCO in Oakland has a future—to generate income and jobs—and a connection to the dynamic Pacific region. Perhaps Oakland has played second fiddle to San Francisco in many ways, but not in base closure.

What are the political lessons from these contrasting outcomes? In Oakland, an aggressive partnership between private enterprise (the transportation industry) and the city government provided the Port of Oakland the power and the resources to actively involve itself in FISCO base closure. In San Francisco, the Army turned the Presidio over to a federal agency, the National Park Service, that was, and is, short on both funds and political clout. So in this case, Oakland, which often languishes in the shadow of its better-known neighbor across the bay, provides a success story in the politics of base closure while San Francisco lost the opportunity to land a prime piece of real estate within its borders.

THE POLICY LESSONS FROM BASE CLOSURE

What are the public policy lessons that flow from this study? What were the successes and disappointments from the base-closure rounds considered in this book? How well did the process work? How successful have base-closure conversions been?

Congress Surrenders Collective Power

BRAC reinforces a lesson about Congress, which is that Congress can and will give up decision making power when the collective interests of the institution and the nation are threatened by the individual interests of members. While the evidence of pork-related objectives was mixed at best, both at the overall defense-spending and military-base-spending levels, the charge of pork and the paralysis that resulted from ten years of no base closures provoked a change. Congress has since granted more budgetary power to the president when it passed the line-item veto in 1996. That decision should reduce the amount of pork-barrel spending, since the president can veto such expenditures.[52] Of course, a final test remains, and presidents may simply channel pork to favorite representatives or to politically important districts. The point is, though, that the executive branch has much more control of political spending relative to Congress, and this happened voluntarily. The 1996 congressional decision to give the president a line-item veto was yet another case in which Congress surrendered the power of budget making, since again the collective national interest in deficit reduction outweighed the congressional right to create and fund programs for constituency benefit.

Commission Politics Worked, If Imperfectly

Policy stalemate is likely to increase levels of commission policy making. Where political priorities produce policy paralysis, a commission is a way out. Elected officials can blame commissions for producing unpopular but necessary results. Commissions can delay decisions until after critical events like elections take place. Commissioners are not directly accountable to the electorate, and, often by the time the decisions are rendered, nobody remembers who appointed them. The commissioners then return to their normal positions and are themselves rarely remembered unless they headed the commission and lent it their name.

The commission charter allowed the pain and potential political cost of base closure to be spread out over four interations. As Richard Rose states, big changes are normally more difficult to implement than incremental changes.[53] By stretching the base-closure process over seven years, with small reductions each time, the shock was much less severe on both the president and members of Congress.

Other policy lessons emerge from the commission process chosen to decide the final fate of bases targeted by their services for closure. The commission method of decision making again prevailed in an area of policy paralysis. There are many other cases of policy paralysis in which lessons from base closure may fit. The National Park Service, for example, manages about 500 parks, but only about 100 are economically viable in that they generate return revenue from tourism or other commercial activities. From an economic point of view, it would make sense for the Park Service to eliminate those parcels that do not offset the cost of maintaining and policing them. But from a preservation perspective, the land-preservation efforts that date back to President Theodore Roosevelt would be lost. Both perspectives have strong constituencies, and, thus, policy paralysis is likely to occur if Congress makes a real effort to decide the issue. So the National Park Service may well recommend that an independent commission be created to take the politics out of the national-park issue, with hopefully as much success as the base-closure process.

NASA is another agency whose activities might be pared back by a commission. The subject of a booming growth pattern during the space race, NASA remains today a bloated bureaucracy in an era when space exploration is diminishing as a national objective. The Veterans Administration and its far-flung network of hospitals is another organization that remains intact even as the number of military veterans requiring health care at its facilities diminishes. A recent move to convert parts of some VA hospitals for public health care was defeated as a result of efforts of the powerful veterans lobby, indicating the clout that veterans have in preserving a care system in excess of the need. Amtrak, the publicly funded passenger rail network in the United States, also looms as a candidate for commission pruning. Amtrak has lost $750 million annually since 1988; yet, pressure by members of Congress continues to keep it running because it provides rail service to their states and districts.

BRAC Lessons for Other Policy Areas

There well may be efforts as well to expand the concepts behind BRAC to the larger issue of defense cutbacks in general. Jacques S. Gansler has proposed such an expansion of BRAC, suggesting that ". . . its objective would be privatizing the defense industrial base in all areas except for those functions that are inherently governmental. It would periodically submit an all-or-nothing list of balanced cutbacks for administration and congressional approval, as the Base Closure Commission now does."[54] Gansler's point is that, while much of the defense-industrial base has always been in private hands, an extension of that base is owned by the government. This infrastructure includes laboratories (including the large nuclear laboratories such as Lawrence Livermore in California, Los Alamos and Sandia in New Mexico, and Oak Ridge in Tennessee), depots, and arsenals. BRAC has closed some of the depots and arsenals, but the large laboratories have largely been untouched. Department of Energy (DOE) laboratories escaped closure since the BRAC mandate does not extend beyond the Department of Defense. There are 17 DOE laboratories that do a variety of work, much of it in the nuclear weapons or energy areas. It has been proposed that, in the post–Cold War era, some if not most of the these laboratories could be transferred to some other agency or privatized in order to diversify their products. A recent study by the Office of Technology Assessment recommended that a commission be created to study such a possibility.[55] So far, those laboratories have been labeled as clearly excessive of needs now that the United States is significantly reducing its nuclear arsenal. But they, just like many military bases, are located in states with political clout—California, Washington, Tennessee, and New Mexico. A commission may be just as necessary to reduce these laboratories as it was for military bases.

Commissions may provide solutions in other policy areas. President Clinton announced in October 1995 that he was forming another commission on crime, which he might have hoped would have more far-reaching impact than the Kerner Crime Commission of the 1970s. The acerbic debate in 1995 over Medicaid and Medicare reveals how divisive those issues are. Medicare, in particular, has a large recipient group whose members tend to be more politically active, given both their interest in the issue and their available time for participation. They also have a support group consisting of the next age cohort whose members know that, should Medicare be cut, they may have to contribute to the medical support of their parents. There are also a large number of beneficiaries of Medicare, including physicians, nursing homes, pharmaceutical companies, wheelchair manufacturers, and a host of others. But there are also millions of balanced-budget advocates who wonder whether caps should not be placed on Medicare benefits to upper-income claimants. Concern about excessive or fraudulent payments to Medicare providers also contributes to support for reducing the program. So Medicare appears to be a ready-made case for a commission. With the angst over the issue in the 1995 budget fights, the politically smart thing might be for both Republicans and Democrats to agree to submit the issue to a commission.

Potential Dangers from the Commission Process

There are potential dangers, though, in using the commission process as a substitute for politics. Political commentators often lament the difficulty of finding solutions to problems in the context of American politics, in which political power is balanced in ways that frustrate easy political answers. Local interests may combine, for example, to thwart what may otherwise be a collective national interest. That has clearly been the case for base closures. A commission is a way around what may be a perfectly legitimate and necessary expression of those local interests. Commissions are, after all, often charged with resolving *national* problems. Their members are selected from a national pool, and their charge from both Congress and the president is usually to get around the dilemmas posed by the divisions of power. Commissions are often a way of strengthening central power at the expense of local power. BRAC commissioners were not accountable to electors because they were unelected. They returned to whatever they did before their commission service. Members of Congress, on the other hand, were left lamenting the commission's work. Recall, for example, Representative Montgomery of Mississippi simply stating "I'm deeply disappointed" when learning of Meridian NAS's closure, or Senator Bumpers of Arkansas warning of a 30 percent unemployment rate around Eaker AFB should it close. Members of Congress, in this case, usually wound up fighting a symbolic battle that left few winners. But the will of the writers of the Constitution was probably not to have representatives overpowered by a national unelected commission.[56] The American political system was designed to respond to local interests, not to stymie them. And even though Senator Arlen Specter of Pennsylvania would ultimate lose his effort to have the commission's work overturned by the Federal court system, there may be merit in his argument.. By October 1995, the BRAC staffers were busy packing up their office and preparing documents for archive storage. By the end of 1995, there was no one to call about BRAC, as the office shut down and both commissioners and staff members scattered back across the country to other positions. Long-term accountability for decisions was not a burden for BRAC.

There are political implications here. Both the 1993 and 1995 BRAC decisions sometimes redressed grievances from previous closure and realignment decisions. Base supporters were sometimes able to argue that data originally presented and accepted as accurate later turned out to be in error, or that changed conditions were sufficient to warrant changes in the original decisions for that base. Carswell AFB in Texas, for example, was a beneficiary of the 1993 BRAC, which shifted units to that base in order to keep it open. The 1995 commission directed the Air Force to retain the airfield portion of MacDill AFB in Florida, closed by the 1993 BRAC. However, there was no BRAC scheduled after 1995. Decisions made earlier cannot easily be appealed even if a good reason exists for such an action. Members of Congress cannot reverse a BRAC decision, nor can the president. And after the Supreme Court's negative ruling on Senator Specter's challenge to BRAC's decision to close the Philadelphia Naval Shipyard, legal remedies are also not likely. So the long-term implications of decision by commission need to be considered within the broad context of the American political system and its values. To create a process that skips the sometimes-bruising political decision making processes in order to achieve a definitive purpose may appeal to the American preference for action over words and symbols, but it may also contradict other American values for political accountability and balance of power.

On a political-outcome level, though, BRAC clearly accomplished something that was, from a practical standpoint, necessary. The military clearly did not need the excessive base structure that remained from the Cold War. The taxpayers clearly did not need to pay excess billions of dollars each year to keep the bloated base infrastructure open so that the work force who benefited from it could remain employed. There was no reason that the flow of money to states and districts that had enjoyed a disproportionate share of defense spending for decades should continue on indefinitely. Between 1977 and 1988, not a single military base closed. Between 1988 and 1996, more than 130 bases closed. BRAC overcame a substantial political opposition that had prevented even a single base closure in ten years and, after three rounds, closed scores of bases. The factional nature of American politics that so often makes "optimal" political outcomes impossible to achieve had been overridden by BRAC. From a political standpoint, BRAC took power from the states and localities and centralized it. There were, though, enough compromises along the way to legitimate the process. BRAC procedures were fine-tuned each year in an effort to eliminate features that called the process into question. That process was made as open as possible, with an understanding that there is less likely to be public skepticism about a political process if the public can observe it. It was rational in that it relied heavily on objective information, a multi-tiered decision making process, and objective criteria. But, again, taking the politics out of the process, particularly at the local level, may run counter to some deeply held American political values. The push by the Republican Congress after 1995 to decentralize resources and authority back to states and localities, mirrors that. Suspicion of Washington at local levels includes suspicion of federal commissions that, though they may organize traveling road shows for the people at regional levels, return to Washington to make their decisions.

Conversion Works (Sometimes)

While the final outcome of the BRAC years considered here is pending in many cases, there are some identifiable results and lessons. First, successful conversion occurs when a significant portion of those faced with economic loss benefit by the replacement activities at closed bases. One of the more successful cases is FISCO, in which a large semiprivate agency, the Port of Oakland, moved rapidly to utilize FISCO facilities, using them in the short term and planning to demolish them over a longer time period and to build something new. Port of Oakland activities seem likely to absorb almost all of the lost jobs, and, in the end, to create far more jobs than existed before base closure. It would appear that a large commercial operator managing the entire base is the most successful way to convert. Loring AFB in Maine, on the other hand, is now the home of a group of unrelated activities that may bloom someday to fill the lost economic benefits of the base. The Loring Redevelopment Agency enabled some base transformation, but on nowhere near the scale of FISCO.

Some bases converted to other governmental activities, such as locating an office of the Defense Finance and Accounting Service or a branch of a state university. Such activities are more compatible with existing base structure than is commercial industry, since they primarily need office space and, in the case of a university, dormitory buildings that can be converted barracks or officer's quarters. The opportunity cost of such activities may be slower economic growth and fewer employment opportunities, though. Universities cannot hire shipyard workers and make them into faculty members, and the relatively low-paying and low-skill jobs at universities are far less than existed in a shipyard. Government bureaucracies often offer far fewer jobs than existed for a civilian workforce at a base. That is probably best illustrated by the conversion of the Presidio of San Francisco into a national park operated by the National Park Service. With the 1996 creation of a trust fund to support the operation of the park, there may still be an opportunity to keep it open and in the black financially. But it is unlikely that the activities there can match the employment offered by the Army during the Presidio's long history as a base.

Still, in the end, conversion managed to generate more employment and economic growth than did base operations. But that conclusion must be tempered with the finding that some conversions were remarkably successful economically, while others simply failed to create a real replacement economy in the impacted communities. Moreover, a number of conversion activities appeared to be driven more by the need to create post base employment than by viable economic choice. Conversions happened in these cases more because of free land and other government-provided inducements. That is hardly restricted to military base closures—governments often provide incentives for both private and public activities to locate within their jurisdictions. But the cost to the government to provide such incentives in base-closure cases must be weighted against the potential savings generated by closing the bases.

MORE BASE CLOSURES AHEAD?

Congress authorized four odd-year rounds of base closures in 1988; they have all now been completed. When the process began in 1988, the goal was to eliminate one-third of the nation's bases, but by 1995 the four rounds had closed only 21 percent. Will there be more base closings ahead?

Sound reasons exist to press ahead with at least one more round of base closings. Defense cutback continued into 1996, with defense taking a larger cut than all other cabinet-level agencies in both budget and personnel, as noted in Table 6.3:

TABLE 6.3: Proposed Personnel and Budget Changes, FY95-FY97

Agency	Fiscal FTE 1997 (in thousands of $)	% Change from FY95	FY97 budget authority (in billions of $)	% Change from FY95
Agriculture	104.6	.8	15.3	-1
Commerce	35.3	.5	4.3	5
Defense	767.4	-7.0	257.4	-14
Education	4.6	-4.0	25.6	4
Energy	18.5	-6.0	16.3	-5
EPA	18.0	3.0	7.0	17
HHS	58.9	-0.2	35.0	5
HUD	11.4	-6.0	21.7	8
Interior	72.2	-0.3	7.2	0
Justice	112.5	15.0	16.4	33
Labor	17.1	2.0	10.4	11
NASA	21.2	-5.0	13.8	-0.7
OPM	3.6	-14.3	0.1	0
State	23.5	-2.0	5.0	2
SSA	64.0	0.6	6.6	18.7
Transportation	63.9	1.0	12.5	12
Treasury	156.8	-0.4	11.5	7
VA	217.3	-2.5	18.9	4

SOURCE: *Government Executive*, May 1996, p. 12.

The numbers in Table 6.3 indicate the significant drop in defense spending over just two fiscal years. Defense clearly takes the largest cut in its budget and the second-largest reduction in personnel. The numbers may show something else as well. The Clinton Administration established its priorities in these numbers, and they were a guide for the second Clinton term. Funding rose for education, environmental protection, the aged, veterans, and crime prevention, while funding fell for defense and bureaucracy (OPM). While Clinton was hesitant to cut defense spending too far in his first term to avoid alienating constituencies in key electoral states, cuts early in his second term would cause less political damage and thus were more likely.

The Quadrennial Defense Review

A mechanism to pare defense spending emerged in the Quadrennial Defense Review (QDR), initiated in 1996 and scheduled to be repeated every four years. The QDR is actually two reviews, one by the services and one by an independent panel of nine non-military persons. Prior to its publication in May 1997, the QDR became the source of interesting speculation. Early predictions on the 1996 QDR were that the Army would take the largest cuts, since its 495,000 troops would be excessive should QDR replace the "two major regional conflicts" scenario of the early Clinton administration with a "one and a half major regional conflict" planning document.[57] According to one source, the Army would lose one or two divisions, while the Air Force was expected to take the smallest cuts.[58] The Army vice chief of staff produced a more drastic scenario under QDR, with the Army losing 56,000 troops, the equivalent of at least three heavy divisions.[59] Under the first scenario, the Army risked losing at least one major base, and probably some supporting bases, while the Air Force's basing structure would be more secure. Under the second, the Army would lose three major bases. Air Force and Navy cuts were more likely to occur in reductions in future fighter programs.[60] Those two services might hold on to older aircraft longer and thus might have fewer base closures. Of course, more Navy and Air Force base closures could free up more money for newer aircraft, something that both services could well push for.

The QDR service reviews attempted to minimize troop cuts and instead propose reduction in civilian support—accountants, logistics bureaucrats, secretaries, and so on. "That's where the bucks are," one source stated.[61] Assistant Secretary of Defense Edward Warner reinforced this view in March 1997 when he noted: "There has generally been a perception that the defense infrastructure has not come down as much as the forces have. . . . Many believe it is appropriate to go further."[62] He also said: "We need to get every dollar we can by reducing our infrastructure—to include committing ourselves to two BRAC rounds and the necessary changes in law to permit further outsourcing."[63] Defense Secretary Cohen thus opened the door to a political fight that would bring back echoes of the 1995 BRAC round. Anger in both the House and Senate over the President's alleged politicization of that process returned in a 66-33 vote on a measure in the Senate in July 1997 prohibiting further base closure until the costs and saving of previous closings were studied.[64] The House passed a similar measure in June. In response, President Clinton repeated his call for more base-closure rounds in 1999 and 2001 and then, anticipating congressional opposition, moved the next rounds to 2001 and 2005. For Clinton, the proposal was politically safe, since, by the start of the 2001 round, if there is one, he would be out of office.

Should the civilian QDR prevail, though, it could mean not only less military, but also less military in uniform. Civilianization of military functions, noted earlier in this book, continues at a fairly rapid pace. One indication of that is the growing number of civilian Defense Department employees deploying overseas with military operations. In the Desert Storm operation in 1990 and 1991, one in fifty Americans deployed in the theater were civilians; in the Bosnia peace support operation, one in ten were civilians.[65] Defense Department civilian employees have rarely been deployed to military theaters of operation, but as their ranks grow and they take over formerly uniformed military jobs, they are more likely to go to war or to keep peace. Civilians operate bases, maintain weapons and equipment, provide security, cook meals, and do thousands of jobs once done exclusively by military personnel.[66] The experience at Altus AFB in Oklahoma is reflective of this trend. Between 1994 and 1996, the civilian work force employed for aircraft maintenance increased from 40 to 750 while the overall number of maintenance workers was cut in half. Other bases experienced similar trends. In 1997, the GAO recommended more such conversions. Its study showed that 45 percent of uniformed personnel are assigned to support activities, which civilian workers could do for an average cost reduction of $15,000.[67]

What does this trend mean for the future of military bases? Civilianization is about saving money as much as anything. Civilians live at home and do not require the huge infrastructure that the uniformed military does. They shop in malls and supermarkets, use civilian hospitals, civilian golf courses, and so on. They are, moreover, *civilians,* the very kind of people that bases shielded from the military. So base requirements will shrink as civilians replace military personnel, allowing for base consolidation and thus fewer bases overall.

The Costs of Modernization

Another factor that may drive more base closings by the military is the future cost of weapons modernization. Much of the military hardware bought during the Reagan defense buildup will be retired at, or shortly after, the turn of the century. The cost of the replacements will be high—the Joint Chiefs of Staff want to spend $60 billion per year on it[68] According to Paul Kaminski, former undersecretary of defense for acquisition, the only way to find such money in the Pentagon's future budgets is to cut what is called the military's "last third" of the budget—real estate, depots, support equipment, and such.[69]

That would mean suspending the limits on work sent to private industry, and a new round of base closures.[70] So the military may well support another base-closure period simply to defend modernization. Secretary of Defense Cohen said as much at the time of his 1997 confirmation hearings, noting that force modernization might be funded partially with money saved from further base closures.[71] Having politically survived a painful base closure himself, Cohen argued that other legislators would also survive such closures and also benefit, in some cases, from the contracts for weapons modernization that might flow into their districts. He made this threat explicit in a letter to legislators in August 1997 where he noted that without further base closures, weapons modernization would be "extremely difficult."[72] After months of speculation, Cohen did indeed call for not one but two more rounds of base closure, one in 1999 and one in 2001.[73]

The costs of modernization are difficult to predict but likely to grow beyond the early predictions of the mid-1990s. The most painful may be the cost of new fighter aircraft desired by three of the four services. The combined cost of the F-22 (Air Force), the F/A-18E/F (Navy and Marine Corps) and the Joint Strike Fighter (Air Force, Navy, and Marine Corps) rose some $50 billion in early 1997 over previous estimates pegging the cost of the program at $300.[74] To cut even one of these programs would mean millions of dollars lost to a shrinking U.S. defense aerospace industry, and considerable job loss. Closing bases may well be easier, since the lessons of early closures suggest the potential of more job creation than offered by closed defense industry plant.

While there has been no outcry from the Defense Department about the continuing surplus of bases, there is still a sense that additional millions per year could be saved if more bases close.[75] As noted previously, the end of the 1995 BRAC saw a total reduction of 21 percent of bases, with the Army having eliminated 45 percent of its divisions, the Navy 37 percent of its ships, and the Air Force 44 percent of its tactical fighter wings.[76] Further, even substantial, reductions loom ahead. Clinton's then-Defense Secretary William Perry noted in 1993 during testimony before the Senate Appropriations Committee "I do want to report to you . . . that those closures and realignments were based on the so-called base force of the Bush program, and we see that force being reduced substantially in the years to come."[77] The Navy supported that view when it suggested that it would like to close some 16 bases in the two rounds proposed by the QDR, hoping to save some $500 million annually after an initial closing cost estimated at $2.4 billion.[78]

In his first appearance as Clinton's secretary of defense before the House National Security Committee, Cohen made it clear that base closure must continue. "Everything has to be on the table, including infrastructure," he stated.[79] Chairman of the Joint Chiefs of Staff Gen. John Shalikashvili echoed Cohen, noting that personnel were cut more than infrastructure, and, thus, ". . . the result is that we perhaps have more excess infrastructure today than we did when the base-closure process started...In the short run we need to close more facilities, as painful and expensive as that is.[80]

More hints of base closure came from the 1995 BRAC Chair, former Democratic Senator Alan J. Dixon of Illinois, who stated in June 1996 that more base closings were likely in coming years and that Scott AFB near St. Louis was a likely closure target.[81] In anticipation, both Illinois senators openly lobbied to Secretary of Defense Cohen to keep Scott open, partly because they argued that Illinois had suffered enough from previous base closures. Said Senator Carol Moseley-Braun (D-IL), "You can say I will fight to the death to keep Scott Air Force Base open."[82] Apparently, political leaders in Arizona came to the same conclusion, and mobilized to form plans to save Arizona bases from further closures.[83] Even senior members of Congress seemed ready to engage in battles to preserve bases. In 1997, Representative Ike Skelton of Missouri wrote to Air Force Chief of Staff Gen. Ronald Fogelman urging him to defend the B-2 bomber. Specifically, Skelton wrote: "In view of the current congressionally mandated Quadrennial Defense Review, a full evaluation is necessary to explore the unique effectiveness of long range conventional strike systems. . . . To this end I would like to propose and recommend further demonstrations of long range airpower's precision attack capacity. . . . This, in essence, would be a face-off between the B-2 GATS/GAM system and the cruise missile system launched from naval platforms."[84] The message was fairly clear: The B-2 would be safer under QDR scrutiny if it successfully competed with the Navy for the precision strike mission. For Skelton, the B-2's only base, Whiteman AFB in his Missouri district, would also be safer from closing if the B-2 proved its worth against the Navy, which had been increasingly critical of both its performance and its cost.

Alternatives to BRAC

While base closure seems likely in the next few years, Congress does not now appear eager to authorize additional rounds of base closures by re-creating BRAC. So what is most likely to happen? There may be a return to the kind of "nickel-and-dime" approach to base closure that shuttered a number of bases long before BRAC. It is useful to remember that in 1958 the Air Force maintained 163 major bases, but after 1996 only 67 remain in the continental United States. A significant majority of those bases closed *before* BRAC. But a large number of bases remain. Most of the Army's combat-related bases remain open. The Navy still has a large number of seaports—among them San Diego, California; Norfolk, Virginia; Mayport, Florida; and Pearl Harbor, Hawaii. The Air Force still maintains a number of "northern tier" bomber bases even in the wake of the Cold War—Fairchild AFB in Washington, Minot AFB in North Dakota, Ellsworth AFB in South Dakota, Malmstrom AFB in Montana, Francis E. Warren AFB in Wyoming, Offutt AFB in Nebraska, and other relics of the old Strategic Air Command days. Some of these now serve as Intercontinental Ballistic Missile (ICBM) bases, even though the value of the ICBM decreased after the end of the Cold War. The Air Force also has a number of large testing bases—Wright-Patterson AFB in Ohio, Eglin AFB in Florida, and Edwards AFB in California—but, with sharply declining orders for both new aircraft and new ordnance for them, this structure could probably be reduced and consolidated with testing facilities of other services (such as the Navy at China Lake in California) with little or no loss of capacity. In short, unless there is a fairly dramatic change in the world political climate, the services still have too many bases to maintain. Of course, there would be political ramifications in closing some of these facilities—Eglin AFB and Wright-Patterson AFB are huge facilities with considerable economic impact. In the late 1980s, Wright-Patterson was the fifth-largest employer in Ohio, with 30,000 people employed there.[85]

One approach would be to study the economic impact of closure and base conversion, to find what kinds of conversions work best, and under what circumstances. The Defense Department might arrive at a profile of the "best" conversions, looking at such things as the type of base, location, available infrastructure, and activity that might make the most efficient conversion. Then base closure could be accomplished on a case-by-case basis, beginning with negotiations concerning potential replacement activities and ending with a decision on closure only when there is a new tenant ready to move onto base property. Such a policy would have advantages in that the long delays and uncertainties that accompanied the BRAC closings would not have to happen again, with their accompanying drop of property values and forced migrations. But it also could hamper the capability of the military to close what it considers surplus bases. It might well be that there is not much of a match between the kinds of bases the military would like to close and the kinds that are the best candidates for conversion.

Another approach to excess basing might be to downsize bases while keeping essential parts of them open. That happened at the Norfolk Naval Station, where unused buildings were demolished and land offered to developers. Moreover the base struck an agreement with the Virginia Port Authority to allow the latter to build warehouses on surplus Navy property in exchange for cargo loading services.[86] Many other bases have surplus property which could be transformed or transferred in a similar way. Maxwell AFB in Alabama, for example, was once the site of a large pilot training activity, but now most of the base activity is related to professional military education, which takes up only a small fraction of the base's total acres. At least some of the base property could be sold off to private interests, or even other government activities, which would reduce the cost of maintaining the base while, at the same time, preserve the essential parts of it.

The experience from BRAC suggests that the process may simply be too traumatic to repeat. To ask base communities to hold their collective breath for six years was difficult to do. Moreover, there may not be enough bases left for closure to justify the creation of a new BRAC. And, given that some conversions were successful, members of Congress may not fight closure as adamantly as they once did. But that raises another problem that could also limit the flexibility of the Defense Department to choose what bases to close. If base closure returns to an ad hoc process, where two or three bases are closed at a time, the choice of bases may again be determined by the old political factors that existed before BRAC. Another president may threaten to close a base in an unsupportive representative or senator's district or state, or a senior member of Congress may offer up a base for closure in an uncooperative member's district.

The 1995 BRAC might have been mindful of this when it recommended that another round of base closings be held in 2001. The commissioners noted that all of the bases targeted for shutdown in 1995 would be closed by 2001 and that at that point further decisions on base capacity could be made.[87] It may be that by 2001 the political pain of the previous base-closure rounds will be sufficiently forgotten to allow another round. That may have been on Secretary Perry's mind when in 1995 he endorsed the call for another round of base closings "in three or four years."[88] At that time, a clearer sense of the military force structure for the next decade may allow for a clearer need statement for bases.

Opposition to further base closure centered on job loss in communities surrounding military facilities. But a RAND Corporation study found that some closures actually generated jobs. For example, the closure of Fort Ord in California in 1988 was expected to cause a 15 percent drop in the population of the surrounding communities, but the real drop was less than 3 percent.[89] Unemployment there was expected to jump by 7 percent, but it actually increased by 1 percent, and retail sales increased by 2 percent instead of sliding by an expected 25 percent.[90]

FINAL THOUGHTS

The purpose of this study has been to illuminate and explain the politics of military base closure. Those politics express themselves in a somewhat chaotic way, with unique circumstances surrounding most base closures. No two base closures are exactly alike, nor do politicians react in similar ways when they fought to protect their bases. Some seemed fixated on avoiding short-term losses, while others endeavored to remedy the problems that accompanied a closed base. Most politicians, though, stayed on the political high road; this study uncovered no examples of illegal actions. That is not to say there were none, nor was it the purpose of this study to find such cases. What it did find is that political figures fought hard, denounced loudly, compromised against principles, and did whatever they could to either prevent base closure or make the conversion to civilian activity as robust as possible. Their tactics were often unusual and interesting, but, by and large, they did the jobs they were elected to do.

The military wanted base closure, and in the end it got it. It was not always done evenhandedly, and sometimes military officers had to compromise with civilian public officials. Over the three BRAC rounds covered in depth in this research (1991, 1993, and 1995), the services were treated more or less equitably, both at the service and the sub-service level. The wake of the Cold War left the military with a host of problems, dealing with significant downsizing and a growth in nontraditional roles and missions such as peacekeeping and civil duties. Base closure was a real challenge for military officials, and they were not always happy with what they had to do to make base closure work smoothly (such as transfer of land and free equipment), but, like civilian politicians, the military adapted and tried hard to make base closure work.

This study has considered the base-closure process in the larger context of American politics. It has been a success story, but at the same time the outcome was less that what "optimal analysis" might have produced. Politics ultimately interfered with the rational process that the Base Realignment and Closure Commission epitomized. Fewer bases were closed than the services had recommended, and some that "closed" had a phoenixlike ability to survive when they were "rescued" by subsequent BRACs.

The writer Shelby Foote once claimed on the notable PPS series on the Civil War that the war happened because of the failure to do what Americans do best — to compromise. In a very real sense, the base-closure process succeeded to the extent that it did because in this case compromise was the key to the whole effort. Given the stakes—billions of dollars, hundreds of thousands of jobs, the lifeblood of entire communities, military preparedness, the stake of Congress in protecting assets in states and districts, and the need to respond to the real changes produced by the end of the Cold War, the compromises that made up the base-closure process from 1991 to 1995 were a genuine statement of the success of American democracy.

At the same time, BRAC did not take politics out of the process, but that is also a tribute to the nature of the American political system. Politics had stymied the base-closure process for decades before both Congress and the president realized that an alternative was necessary. BRAC allowed base closure to continue, while political interplay continued as well. In some cases political actors found more ingenious ways to protect their military installations, while in other cases "politics" consisted of rhetoric against the heartless and wrong-headed BRAC commissioners who were handy scapegoats for the impact of base closure. But politics is a part of the American experience, and while the name may have a negative connotation among a majority of American citizens, it is not easy to replace political input, bargaining, and, in some cases, under-handedness with the cold calculations of the commission process. In that sense, the fact that BRAC allowed politics to intervene in the base-closure process is, in the end, perhaps a fitting testimony to the success of the BRAC process.

Appendix I:
Gains and Losses by State, BRAC 1993

State	Loss/Gain	Sen 1	Sen 2	House
AL	-2,250	D	D	D
AR	-6,777	D	D	D
AZ	-146	D	R	R
CA	-26,869	D	D	4D, 3R
CO	-5,245	D	R	D
CT	-911	D	D	
FL	-18,850	D	R	R
GA	-3,811	D	D	D
HI	+1,247	D	D	D
ID	-1,200	R	R	
IL	+14,109	D	D	
IN	-8,024	R	R	2D, 1R
KY	+813	D	R	
LA	-5,563	D	D	R
MA	-3,776	D	D	D
MD	-781	D	D	
ME	-3,741	R	D	R
MI	-1,455	D	D	R
MO	+4,749	R	R	2D
MS	+818	R	R	
MT	+181	D	R	
NC	+703	R	D	
NE	+240	D	D	
NJ	-1,258	D	D	2R
NM	+1,755	R	D	
NY	+1116	D	R	
OH	-566	D	D	R
PA	-12,943	R	(e)	2D
RI	+873	D	R	
SC	+336	R	D	D
TX	+4,103	D	R	3D
VA	+2,290	R	D	
WA	+2,013	D	R	1R, 1D

NOTE: Sen 1 is the senior senator's party; party(ies) of congress indicated only where there is a base closure; some states gained jobs even though they also had base closures. (e) stands for "empty," in this case the seat was held by Republican Senator John Heintz until his death in a plane crash.
SOURCE: Congressional Quarterly, March 13, 1993, p. 617.

Appendix II:
Bases Closed by State, 1995

State	Facility	Service
AK	Adak NAS	Navy
AL	Fort McClellan	Army
CA	Long Beach NSY	Navy
CO	Fitzsimmons Hosp	Army
GM	Ship Repair Fac.	Navy
IN	NAWC	Navy
KY	NSWC	Navy
MA	S. Weymouth NAS	Navy
MD	Fort Richie	Army
	NSWC	Navy
MI	Selfridge Army Gar.	Army
MS	Meridian NAS	Navy
NJ	Bayonne Military Ocean Ter.	Navy
	Lakehurst NAWC	Navy
PA	Fort Indiantown Gap	Army
TN	Memphis NAS	Navy
TX	Brooks AFB	Air Force
	Red River Depot	Army
	Reese AFB	Air Force

NOTE: GM=Guam

SOURCE: Defense Base Closure and Realignment Commission, *Report to the President, 1995,* Ch.1; Congressional Directory, 1993.

Appendix III:
Gains and Losses by State, BRAC 1995

State	Loss/Gain	State	Loss/Gain
AK	-1,448	MN	-81
AL	-6,186	MO	-5,103
AR	-409	MS	+171
AZ	-438	MT	-963
CA	-42,208	NE	+506
CO	-4,071	NV	+35
CT	-5,441	NY	-320
DC	-212	NC	-3,562
FL	+4,328	ND	-1,085
GA	+341	OH	-1,107
GM	-5,296	OK	+7,472
HI	+2,956	PA	-6,829
ID	+163	PR	-257
IL	-1,992	RI	+1,064
IN	-2,724	SC	+5,008
KS	-22	TN	-2,661
KY	-2,096	TX	-32,857
LA	-248	UT	+12,406
MA	-185	VA	+3,436
MD	-3,284	WA	+1,131
ME	+306	WI	+8
MI	+217		

NOTE: GM=Guam; PR=Puerto Rico

SOURCE: Congressional Quarterly, March 4, 1995, p. 695.

Notes

INTRODUCTION

1. Kenneth R. Mayer and Anne M. Khademian, "Bringing Politics Back In: Defense Policy and the Theoretical Study of Institutions and Processes," *Public Administration Review,* Vol. 56 (March/April 1996), p. 181.

2. Richard Rose, *Lesson-Drawing in Public Policy: A Guide to Learning Across Time and Space.* Chatham, NJ: Chatham House, 1993.

CHAPTER ONE

1. Kenneth R. Mayer, "Closing Military Bases (Finally): Solving Collective Dilemmas Through Delegation," *Legislative Studies Quarterly,* Vol. 20 (August 1995), p. 396.

2. Gen. John Herres, quoted in Ann Markusen and Joel Yudken, *Dismantling the Cold War Economy.* New York: Basic Books, 1992, p. 195.

3. The various branches of the services have not been able to agree on what to call bases. Only the Air Force officially calls its bases "bases," the Army calls its bases "forts," and the Navy uses a variety of terms depending on the use of the base. Naval bases were once called "naval yards," but now that term refers to specialized facilities used for building, repairing, and modernizing naval vessels. Bases where ships are simply tied to piers are now called "stations," as are bases from which the Navy operates aircraft ("air stations"). The Navy calls its aircraft-maintenance bases "air rework facilities," while the Air Force calls its aircraft-maintenance bases "air logistics centers," though, unofficially, they are called "depots." Pronunciation is important here—the Air Force pronounces "depot" as "deppo" as opposed to "deepo." "Planes are fixed at deppos, trains go to deepos," goes the saying.

4. One interesting example of civilian co-location was land-based missile silos, which were often located in grain fields. Farmers would farm around them, becoming almost oblivious to the fact

that their fields were very high-priority on Soviet target lists during the Cold War.

5. Samuel P. Huntington, *The Soldier and the State: The Theory and Politics of Civil-Military Relations*. Cambridge, MA: Belknap Press of Harvard University, 1957, pp. 464-465.

6. Jerold E. Brown, *Where Eagles Land: Planning and Development of U.S. Army Air Fields, 1910–1941*. Westport, CT: Greenwood, 1990, pp. 98-101.

7. Before and during WWII, Air Corps bases were called "fields," often because that is exactly what they were: grass-covered pastures whose only requirement was that they were flat. When the Army Air Corps became the U.S. Air Force after WWII, the fields were renamed "Air Force Base."

8. Ibid., pp. 109-111.

9. Wesley Frank Craven and James Lea Cate (eds.), *The Army Air Forces in World War II*. Vol., 6, *Men and Planes*. Chicago: University of Chicago Press, 1955, p. 142.

10. *Annual Report to the President and the Congress,* William J. Perry, Secretary of Defense, February 1995, p. 53.

11. The precise economic impact of a base on its neighboring community is difficult to measure, given the impact of the so-called "multiplier effect" and the other sources of spending that come into any community. It is often difficult to determine just who is employed at a particular base, since the base does not always maintain records by employee town of residence. See Larry Lee Barron, "The Economic Impact of Tinker Air Force Base on Norman, Oklahoma". Unpublished Master's Thesis, University of Oklahoma, 1969. See also William Caldwell Griffin, "The United States Air Force in New York: An Example of the Impact of the Military Establishment on Regional and Local Economies." Unpublished Master's Thesis, Syracuse University, 1968.

12. United States Congress, *Base Closure,* Hearings Before the House. Committee on Armed Services, Subcommittee on Military Installations and Facilities, on H.R. 1583, 100th Cong., 2nd Sess. Washington, D.C.: GPO, June 1988, p.11.

13. Brian Friel, "Supermarkets," *Government Executive,* Vol. 29 (February 1997), p. 37.

14. Ibid., p. 38.

15. Those companies included Douglas, Northrop, Consolidated, North American, and Lockheed in California and Boeing in Washington.

16. See Ann Markusen, Scott Campbell, Peter Hall, and Sabina Deitrick, *The Rise of the Gunbelt: The Military Remapping of Industrial America.* New York: Oxford University Press, 1991, p. 237. See also Roger W. Lotchin, *Fortress California, 1910–1961: From Warfare to Welfare.* New York: Oxford University Press, 1992, esp. Ch. 4.

17. The "New Look" was President Eisenhower's response to a large buildup of Soviet military force after WWII. Eisenhower, though, believed that the U.S. response should be kept within tight fiscal limits and thus favored a buildup in strategic nuclear weapons, which were less expensive than a conventional-force alternative. See Samuel P. Huntington, *The Common Defense.* New York: Columbia University Press, 1961.

18. Such bases did not preclude other activity on them. The silos were dispersed among grain fields and pastureland, so, while technically the bases did cover thousands of acres, the actual military reservations were much smaller.

19. John E. Lynch, *Local Economic Development After Military Base Closures.* New York: Praeger, 1970. The Air Force cutbacks were a predictor of things to come, as Kennedy's secretary of defense, Robert McNamara, decided to reduce the number of Strategic Air Command bombers and replace them with ballistic missiles. See David S. Sorenson, *The Politics of Strategic Aircraft Modernization.* Westport, CT: Praeger, 1995, Ch. 1.

20. The figures come from Katherine McIntire Peters, "The Drawdown Drags On," *Government Executive,* Vol. 28 (March 1996), p. 20.

21. Ibid.

22. According to David Silverberg, the first reference to "pork" as a political payoff was made in 1862 by D.W. Mitchell, who declared that "to put myself in a position in which every wretch entitled to a vote would feel himself privileged to hold me under special obligations would be giving rather too much pork for a shilling." David Silverberg, "Days of Pork and Power," *Armed Forces Journal International,* Vol. 133 (June 1996), pp. 98-100.

23. Kenneth A. Shepsle and Barry R. Wingast, "Political Preferences for the Pork Barrel: A Generalization," *American Journal of Political Science,* Vol. 25 (February 1981), p. 107.

24. John A. Hird, "The Political Economy of Pork: Project Selection at the U.S. Army Corps of Engineers," *American Political Science Review,* Vol. 85 (June 1991), p. 432.

25. John Ferejohn, *Pork Barrel Politics: Rivers and Harbors Legislation, 1947–1968.* Stanford, CA: Stanford University Press, 1974.

26. Hird, "Political Economy of Pork," p. 449.

27. Morris P. Fiorina, *Congress: Keystone of the Washington Establishment.* New Haven, CT: Yale University Press, 1989, p. 43.

28. Randall Fitzgerald and Gerald Lipson, *Pork Barrel: The Unexpurgated Grace Commission Story of Congressional Profligacy.* Washington, D.C.: CATO Institute, 1984.

29. Robert M. Stein and Kenneth N. Bickers, "Congressional Elections and the Pork Barrel," *Journal of Politics,* Vol. 56 (May 1994), p. 390.

30. Ibid., p. 394.

31. David B. Magleby and Candice J. Nelson, *The Money Chase: Congressional Campaign Finance Reform.* Washington, D.C.: Brookings Institution, 1990, p. 28.

32. Senate Resolution 65, 105th Cong., 1st Sess., March 18, 1997, p. 1.

33. Barry M. Blechman, *The Politics of National Security: Congress and U.S. Defense Policy.* New York: Oxford University Press, 1990, p. 56.

34. Bruce M. Russett, *What Price Vigilance? The Burdens of National Defense.* New Haven, CT: Yale University Press, 1970, p. 179.

35. Representative Thomas Downey, quoted in Richard Stubbing, *The Defense Game.* New York: Harper and Row, 1986, p. 91.

36. Katherine McIntire Peters, "Tradeoffs Loom in Modern Force," *Government Executive,* Vol. 29 (May 1997), p. 60.

37. Senators Daniel Coats (R-IN) and Robert Byrd (D-WV). But Senator Byrd managed to direct military spending toward his state, as noted later in this book.

38. *Washington Post* (National Weekly edition), December 16-22, 1996, p. 33.

39. Roman Schweizer, "Maine Delegation Warns Navy not to Meddle with DDG-51 Construction," *Inside the Navy,* February 17, 1997, p. 1.

40. "Prodded by Office of Mississippi's Lott, Navy May Shift Work to His Home State," *Wall Street Journal*, February 24, 1997, pp. 1, 16.

41. "Navy Panel Rejects Bid for More Ships by Litton Yard," *Wall Street Journal*, April 11, 1997, p. A7A.

42. "Admiral Likes Shipyard's Plan," *Norfolk Virginian-Pilot*, April 23, 1997, p. D1.

43. Kenneth R. Mayer, "Congressional-DOD Relations After the Cold War: The Politics of Uncertainty," in Ethan B. Kapstein (ed.), *Downsizing Defense*. Washington, D.C.: Congressional Quarterly Press, 1993, p. 52.

44. *Washington Post* (Weekly edition), July 7, 1997, pp. 11-12.

45. Eric Schmitt, "Contrary to Senate, House Approves Adding Stealth Bombers," *New York Times*, September 8, 1995, p. 21.

46. "Hawaii Still Leaves Its Mark on Military Funding Measure, *Washington Post*, September 1, 1995, p. 21. One of Inouye's more creative expenditures was $1 million to combat the brown tree snake, infesting the island of Guam. Since, according to Inouye, the Hawaiian population feared the tree snake and its potential damage to Hawaii's exotic birds, and since the snake would most likely travel from Guam to Hawaii by military carrier (again according to Inouye), the defense budget was the best place to "set up a program to make certain that these snakes do not travel from Guam to Hawaii." By 1996, six brown tree snakes had been found on Hawaii, all associated with aircraft from Guam.

47. Rick Maze, "McCain Cites $2.6 Billion in 'Pork,'" *Navy Times*, August 4, 1997, p. 4.

48. *Wall Street Journal*, April 14, 1997, p. 1/16.

49. Ibid. Another representative who reportedly benefited from the C-130 project was Representative G.V. "Sonny" Montgomery (D-MS), who helped get orders through for a hurricane patrol in his state. Part of the plane's fuselage is built in his former district.

50. "Army: Florida Lawmaker Pushed Unwanted Project," *Philadelphia Inquirer*, June 24, 1988, p. 12.

51. Ibid.

52. "Firm Freed Rep. Chappell of Business Debt," *Washington Post*, July 1, 1988, p. 1.

53. "Rep. Biaggi, 4 Others Convicted in Wedtech Racketeering Case," *Washington Post*, August 5, 1988, p. 1.

54. "Defense Budget 'Add-Ons' (or Pork and Pet Projects) Manage to Survive," *New York Times*, July 19, 1996, p. 31. The article identified those gaining particular benefits as Senator Sam Nunn and House Speaker Newt Gingrich, both from Georgia, because of ". . . the F-16, which is assembled at the Lockheed-Martin plant in Marietta, Ga. . . . ." The Marietta plant, though, produces C-130 and P-3 aircraft, while the F-16 is assembled at the Lockheed-Martin plant in Fort Worth, Texas.

55. Defense-industry PACs rate high on the lists of both fund-raising and contributions. Tenneco (which has some defense business) rated Number One in corporate PAC fund-raising in 1980-1981, while the Fluor Corporation was seventh and General Dynamics and Grumman, both major defense contractors, came in at ninth and tenth. Fluor (which does construction for the Defense Department) was Number Five in contributions over the same time period, while United Technologies (parent of Sikorsky helicopters and Pratt & Whitney aircraft engines) was seventh and Grumman ninth. See Larry J. Sabato, *PAC Power: Inside the World of Political Action Committees*. New York: W.W. Norton, 1985, pp. 19-20.

56. See Nick Kotz, *Wild Blue Yonder: Money, Politics, and the B-1 Bomber*. Princeton, NJ: Princeton University Press, 1988, Ch. 15.

57. "In Test of Strength, Stealth Survives," *Washington Post*, September 24, 1995, p. 1.

58. *Defense Daily*, May 9, 1997, p. 238.

59. Craig Liske and Barry Rundquist, *The Politics of Weapons Procurement: The Role of Congress*. Monograph Series in World Affairs, Vol. 12, Monograph No. 1. Denver, CO: University of Colorado, 1974, pp. 62-63.

60. Markusen and Yudken, *Dismantling*, p. 196. Markusen and Yudken state specifically that the contract ". . . might be landed in Oakland's navy yard"; a strange statement since Oakland has never had a navy yard.

61. Kenneth R. Mayer, *The Political Economy of Defense Contracting*. New Haven, CT: Yale University Press, 1991, p. 217.

62. Ibid., Chs. 5, 8.

63. Paul Stockton, "Beyond Micromanagement: Congressional Budgeting for a Post–Cold War Military," *Political Science Quarterly,* Vol. 110, No. 2 (Summer 1995), p. 248.

64. West Virginia has a small naval radio station located at Sugar Grove, which is technically not a real base but does draw a small amount of money each year into its district.

65. Jonathan P. Decker, "US Lawmakers Salt Pentagon Budget with Job-Based Pork," *Christian Science Monitor,* August 2, 1996, p. 4.

66. Ibid.

67. Ibid. Representative Hunter misnamed his committee; it had changed to the National Security Committee in 1993.

68. Elias Huzar, *The Purse and the Sword: Control of the Army by Congress Through Military Appropriations, 1933–1950.* Ithaca, NY: Cornell University Press, 1950, pp. 46-52.

69. It should also not be surprising that the Navy has named an aircraft carrier each for Stennis and Vinson, a highly unusual honor but presumably in gratitude for the many favors both men did for the Navy when they were in office.

70. Charles W. Grindstaff, *War Baby of the South, 1940–1945.* Office of History, Warner Robins ALC, 1988, Ch. 1.

71. Jerome A. Ennels, *The Way We Were: A Pictorial History of Early Maxwell Air Force Base, 1918–1931.* Maxwell AFB, AL: 1990, p. 72.

72. Frank E. Moore, *The Saga of Norton Air Force Base.* Redlands, CA: A.K. Smedley Public Library, 1992, pp. 13-18.

73. Lotchin, *Fortress California,* pp. 27-28.

74. Frank Faulkner, *Westover: Man, Base, and Mission.* Springfield, MA: Hungry Hill, 1990, p. 11.

75. J. Ronald Fox, *The Defense Management Challenge.* Boston: Harvard Business School Press, 1988, p. 90.

76. Ibid.

77. "Dorgan Takes Democratic Seat on Senate Defense Appropriations," *Defense Daily,* January 30, 1997, p. 146.

78. The process is described in Gregory L. Vistica, *Fall from Glory: The Men Who Sank the U.S. Navy.* New York: Simon and Schuster, 1995, pp. 184, 288.

79. Ibid., p. 174.

80. R. Douglas Arnold, *Congress and the Bureaucracy: A Theory of Influence.* New Haven, CT: Yale University Press, 1979, p. 101.

81. Fitzgerald and Lipson, *Grace Commission,* pp. 15-16. President Johnson vetoed the measure.

82. Ibid., pp. 17-18.

83. Fred Thompson, "Why America's Military Base Structure Cannot Be Reduced," *Public Administration Review,* Vol. 48 (January/February 1988), p. 558.

84. Ibid.

85. Charles L. Wilson and James L. Weingartner, *Blame-Proof Policymaking: Congress and Base Closures.* Monterey, CA: Naval Postgraduate School, December 1993.

86. Senator John Glenn, quoted in James M. Lindsay, *Congress and Nuclear Weapons.* Baltimore: Johns Hopkins University Press, 1991, p. 142.

87. Thompson, "Why America's," p. 17.

88. Michael Barone, Grant Ujifusa, and Douglas Matthews, *The Almanac of American Politics.* Boston: Gambit, 1972, p. 506.

89. William J. Weida and Frank L. Gertchner, *The Political Economy of National Defense.* Boulder, CO: Westview, 1987, pp. 22-23.

90. Ibid.. p. 23. K.I. Sawyer was indeed closed, but not for another 12 years.

91. Douglas P. Gorgoni, *Expert Opinion on the Department of Defense Base Closure/Realignment Policy and Process: An Assessment of the Four Military Value Criteria.* Wright-Patterson Air Force Base, Ohio: Air Force Institute of Technology, September, 1991, p. 27.

92. See Alain C. Enthoven and K. Wayne Smith, *How Much Is Enough? Shaping the Defense Program, 1961-1969..* New York: Harper & Row, 1971, Ch. 3.

93. Hugh R. Leonard, Jr., *Handling the Hot Potato: Evolution and Analysis of the Base Closing Decision Process.* Washington, D.C.: Industrial College of the Armed Forces, 1992, p. 2.

94. The law would later come back to haunt Senator Cohen when it made the disposal of Loring AFB more difficult because the base did not comply with environmental standards.

95. Leonard, Jr., *Handling the Hot Potato,* pp. 3-4.

96. *The Plan for Joint Use of Military Airfields.* The Secretary of Defense and the Secretary of Transportation to the United States Congress, Washington, D.C.: GPO, 1984.

97. Ibid., p. iv.

98. L.R. Jones, "Management of Budgetary Decline in the Department of Defense in Response to the End of the Cold War," *Armed Forces and Society,* Vol. 19 (Summer 1993), p. 502.

99. Graham T. Allison, "Conceptual Models and the Cuban Missile Crisis," *American Political Science Review,* Vol. 63 (September 1969),. pp. 689-718.

100. Morton H. Halperin and Arnold Kanter, "The Bureaucratic Perspective: A Preliminary Framework," in Morton H. Halperin and Arnold Kanter (eds.), *Readings in American Foreign Policy: A Bureaucratic Perspective.* Boston: Little, Brown, 1973, pp. 8-9.

101. Ibid.

102. See James H. Lebovic, "Riding Waves or Making Waves? The Services and U.S. Defense Budgets, 1981–1993," *American Political Science Review,* Vol. 88 (December 1994), p. 840; Fen Osler Hampson, *Unguided Missiles: How America Buys Its Weapons.* New York: W.W. Norton, 1989.

103. Michael H. Armacost argues that the competition between the Army and the Air Force for an intermediate-range ballistic missile actually improved both services' product. See Michael H. Armacost, *The Politics of Weapons Innovation: The Thor-Jupiter Controversy.* New York: Columbia University Press, 1969, Ch. 8.

104. Stephen D. Krasner, "Are Bureaucracies Important? (or Allison Wonderland)," *Foreign Policy,* No. 7 (1972), pp. 159-179.

105. David A. Welch, "The Organizational Process and Bureaucratic Politics Paradigms: Retrospect and Prospect," *International Security,* Vol. 17 (Fall 1992), p. 136.

106. Edward Rhodes, "Do Bureaucratic Politics Matter? Some Disconfirming Findings from the Case of the U.S. Navy," *World Politics,* Vol. 47 (October 1994), pp. 1-41.

107. It is not exactly this clear, since all three branches have an air arm, and the Marine Corps performs in all mission areas.

108. Geoffrey Till, "Adopting the Aircraft Carrier: The British, American, and Japanese Case Studies," in Williamson Murray and Alan R. Millett (eds.), *Military Innovation in the Interwar Period*. Cambridge: Cambridge University Press, 1996, pp. 209-210. "Gen'l Mitchell" was Gen. William Mitchell, the ambitious head of the Army Air Service, who was at that point engaged in a campaign for a separate Army Air Corps, and who would try to demonstrate the value of Army air power by sinking a captured German battleship in Chesapeake Bay the next year.

109. Armacost, *Politics of Weapons Innovation*.

110. Raymond H. Dawson, "Congressional Innovation and Intervention in Defense Policy: Legislative Authorization of Weapons Systems," *American Political Science Review*, Vol. 61 (March 1962), pp. 48-50.

111. Wrote Enthoven and Smith: "The Services should not be expected to produce balanced and objective viewpoints on issues for which they are competing for funds or prestige." See Alain C. Enthoven and K. Wayne Smith, *How Much is Enough?* p. 92.

112. This is not the place to elaborate on the differences between the services and DOD; suffice it to say that each service has a service secretary who is senior in Pentagon pecking order to the senior officer of that service. Thus final decisions on bases at the DOD level are made by civilian officials. But those officials are or can be influenced by military officers, though some more easily than others. In the Reagan administration, for example, Navy Secretary John Lehman was known for his independence from the admirals, while Air Force Secretary Verne Orr was known for his deference to Air Force generals.

113. Mark Perry, *Four Stars*. New York: Houghton Mifflin, 1989.

114. A former official in the Reagan Administration relates how, in the early Reagan period, he went to get Secretary Orr's support against the Joint Chiefs, on a budget issue only to find him in his office with a group of Air Force generals, who had brought him a flak jacket and fighter pilot's helmet (which he was wearing) while they entertained him with war stories. Said the official: "It was too late; they had him bought off." Personal communication.

115. Morton K. Halperin, *Bureaucratic Politics and Foreign Policy*. Washington, D.C.: The Brookings Institution, 1974.

116. Carl H. Builder, *Masks of War: American Military Styles in Strategy and Analysis*. A RAND Corporation Research Study. Baltimore: Johns Hopkins University Press, 1989, Ch. 12.

117. I. M. Destler, *Presidents, Bureaucrats, and Foreign Policy: The Politics of Organizational Reform*. Princeton, NJ: Princeton University Press, 1972, p. 57.

118. Arnold Kanter, *Defense Politics: A Budgetary Perspective*. Chicago: The University of Chicago Press, 1979, Ch. 1.

119. Useful discussions of interservice rivalry can be found in Armacost, *Politics of Weapons Innovation;* Edmund Beard, *Developing the ICBM: A Study in Bureaucratic Politics*. New York: Columbia University Press, 1976; Asa a. Clark, "Interservice Rivalry and Military Reform," in Asa A. Clark IV, Peter W. Chiarelli, Jeffrey S. McKitrick, and James W. Reed, *The Defense Reform Debate: Issues and Analysis*. Baltimore: Johns Hopkins University Press, 1984, pp. 309-326; and Huntington, *Common Defense,* esp. Part VI.

120. There are clearly exceptions to such a general statement, but it tends to hold true for most American military officers. It depends on what is regarded as a "military" issue versus a "strategic" issue. Most professional soldiers, though, reject the interpretations of Gens. LeMay and Douglas MacArthur interpretation that strategy is too important to be left alone to the politicians and demand instead autonomy on things closer to their professional training, including operations, training, and maintenance.

121. See Peter Douglas Feaver, *Guarding the Guardians: Civilian Control of Nuclear Weapons in the United States*. Ithaca, NY: Cornell University Press, 1992, pp. 228-229; Paul Bracken, *The Command and Control of Nuclear Forces*. New Haven, CT: Yale University Press, 1982, pp. 93-94.

122. Richard Rose, *Lesson-Drawing in Public Policy: A Guide to Learning Across Time and Space*. Chatham, NJ: Chatham House, 1993, p. 1.

123. Jeffrey L. Pressman and Aaron Wildavsky, *Implementation*. Berkeley, CA: University of California Press, 1984, p. 125.

124. James H. Lebovic, *Foregone Conclusions: U.S. Weapons Acquisitions in the Post–Cold War Transition*. Boulder, CO: Westview, 1996, p. 79.

125. Arnold Kanter, *Defense Politics: A Budgetary Perspective*. Chicago: University of Chicago, 1979, Ch. 1.

126. Useful discussions of interservice rivalry can be found in Michael H. Armacost, *The Politics of Weapons Innovation: The Thor-Jupiter Controversy.* New York: Columbia University Press, 1969; Edmund Beard, *Developing the ICBM: A Study in Bureaucratic Politics.* New York: Columbia University Press, 1976; Asa A. Clark, "Interservice Rivalry and Military Reform," in Asa A. Clark IV, Peter W. Chiarelli, Jeffrey S. McKitrick, and James W. Reed, *The Defense Reform Debate: Issues and Analysis.* Baltimore: The Johns Hopkins University Press, 1984, pp. 309-326; and Samuel P. Huntington, *The Common Defense: Strategic Programs in National Politics.* New York: Columbia University Press, 1961, esp. Part VI.

127. Lebovic, *Foregone Conclusions.*

128. Thomas R. Wolanin, *Presidential Advisory Commissions: Truman to Nixon.* Madison, WI: University of Wisconsin, 1975, Ch. 2.

129. Ibid.

130. In mid-1995 White was elevated to the post of deputy secretary of defense.

131. *Defense Daily,* August 28, 1995, p. 288.

CHAPTER TWO

1. See William J. Bishop and David S. Sorenson, "Superpower Defense Expenditures and Foreign Policy," In Charles W. Kegley, Jr., and Pat McGowan (eds.), *Foreign Policy: USA/USSR.* Sage International Yearbook of Foreign Policy Studies, Vol. 7. Beverly Hills, CA: Sage, 1982, pp. 163-183.

2. "Military Sends Reagan 'Hit List' of Bases That Could Be Closed," *Washington Post,* May 12, 1981, p. 1.

3. Ibid.

4. *Defense Base Closure and Realignment Act of 1990,* Public Law 101-510, Section 2903, p. 5.

5. Ibid.

6. United States Congress, *Base Closure*, Hearings Before the House Committee on Armed Services, Subcommittee on Military Installation and Facilities, 100th Cong., 2nd Sess. Washington, D.C.: GPO, 1988, p. 97.

7. R. Douglas Arnold, *The Logic of Congressional Action*. New Haven, CT: Yale University Press, 1990, p. 139.

8. Kenneth R. Mayer, "Closing Military Bases (Finally): Solving Collective Dilemmas Through Delegation," *Legislative Studies Quarterly*, Vol. 20 (August 1995), p. 401.

9. This argument was made by Andrew D. Glassberg, "Military Base Closure: How the Process Has Changed," *Business & The Contemporary World*, Vol. 7, No. 1, (1995), p. 98.

10. United States Congress, *Base Closures*. Hearing before the Military Installations and Facilities Subcommittee, Committee on Armed Services, House of Representatives, 101st Cong., 2nd Sess. Washington, D.C.: GPO, 1991, p. 1.

11. Ibid., p. 2. Schroeder was referring to the B-2 Spirit bomber, which the Bush administration supported despite its controversial price tag.

12. *Report of Audit*, Management of the Air Force 1993 Base Closure and Realignment Evaluation Process, Phase 1. Air Force Audit Agency, July 29, 1992, p. 5.

13. "United States Air Force: DSS Provides Base Closure Analysis," Vienna, VA: MicroStrategy, 1995, pp. 1-2.

14. Douglas P. Gorgoni,., *Expert Opinion on the Department of Defense Base Closure/Realignment Policy and Process: An Assessment of the Four Military Value Criteria*. Wright-Patterson Air Force Base, OH: Air Force Institute of Technology, 1991, pp. 83-89. It is not known whether the Gorgoni recommendations were incorporated in future BRAC processes, but there is no direct evidence that they were.

15. Joshua Gotbaum, "Closing Excess Bases Makes Good Sense," *Defense 95*, No. 2, (1995), p. 23.

16. "Panel Questions Decision to Close Long Beach Yard," *Los Angeles Times*, March 7, 1995, p. 1.

17. "Long Beach Yard, 32 Other Bases Targeted to Close," *Los Angeles Times* (Washington edition), March 1, 1995, p. B1.

18. "Georgia Bases May Escape the Ax, Defense Chief Suggests During Visit," *Atlanta Constitution*, February 16, 1995, p. E4.

19. "Byrd Picks Navy Plum for W. Virginia," *Norfolk Virginian Pilot*, January 25, 1992, p. 1. Byrd had solicited money from the CIA, the FBI, the Treasury Department, the IRS, the Bureau of Alcohol, Tobacco, and Firearms, the Coast Guard, and the Navy Fleet Logistics Support Squadron 48. He gained more than $500 million by 1991. Senator Byrd did swear on a Holy Bible that he had not used his seniority to unduly influence decisions about federal money for West Virginia.

20. Ibid.

21. "Region's Military May Grow, Commanders Say," *Seattle Post-Intelligencer*, January 23, 1992, p. 1

22. *Congressional Record*, (House), September 8, 1995, p. H8687.

23. *New York Times*, December 27, 1994, p. 8.

24. *Los Angeles Times* (Washington edition), February 8, 1995, p. B6.

25. Supporters of Tinker were particularly adroit at creative ways to save the base. In May 1993, the Chamber of Commerce organized a human ring of support, in which around 50,000 citizens joined hands to form a symbolic community "embrace" of the base. Tinker also gained a more concrete means of saving itself when it garnered the Navy TACAMO aircraft mission, including its maintenance. Thus, the Navy became another supporter for Tinker. A joint Navy-Air Force communications unit was also moved from San Diego to Tinker, and Tinker tied itself in to the local phone network, ostensibly to provide service to the base. An additional cost to close Tinker would be to disrupt the regional phone network.

26. "Visiting Air Force Official Hears Pitch to Save Hamscom," *Boston Globe*, February 7, 1995, p. C2.

27. United States Congress, *Military Construction Appropriations for Fiscal 1992*, Hearings Before a Subcommittee of the House Committee on Appropriations, 102nd Cong., 1st Sess. Washington, D.C.: GPO, 1991, pp. 240-241.

28. Ibid., p. 176.

29. Karl D. Hoover, *Base Closure: Politics or National Defense Issue? Goodfellow Air Force Base, Texas, 1978–1981*. Randolph AFB, TX: His-

tory and Research Office, Headquarters Air Training Command, 1989. Hoover notes that, while a number of factors helped move Goodfellow from a threatened closure, ". . . It is . . . difficult to imagine . . . that Tower did not play an important role on behalf of Goodfellow" (p. 55).

30. The F-117 program was developed under extreme security measures that included efforts to disguise the mission of the aircraft by giving it an "F" designation for "fighter" when the plane actually carries no guns, and the "117" number, which would have indicated that it was the 117th fighter design accepted by the Air Force. It was not. When one crashed in California in the 1980s, the Air Force went so far as to scatter pieces of wreckage from an old F-101 at the F-117 crash site in order to hide the true nature of the F-117's revolutionary construction materials.

31. Holloman's history is told in George F. Meeter, *The Holloman Story.* Albuquerque: University of New Mexico Press, 1967.

32. In 1996, a wing of German Luftwaffe Tornado fighter-bombers was moved to Holloman in another re-missioning maneuver. The wing is the first element of a foreign air force to be housed at a U.S. base.

33. "New Mexico Hit Hardest in Cutbacks Proposed by Air Force," *Washington Post,* August 15, 1995, p. 4.

34. *Congressional Quarterly Weekly Report,* February 18, 1995, p. 539.

35. *Congressional Quarterly Weekly Report,* February 11, 1995, p. 467.

36. "Politicians Cheer Hanscom, Vow S. Weymouth Fight," *Boston Globe,* March 1, 1995, p. 6.

37. Peter J. Shelly and Mike Feeley, "Specter Vows Fight to Keep Depot Open," *Harrisburg Patriot,* January 25, 1992, p. 1. The reference "come up short" apparently referred to the Army's low ranking of the depot.

38. "California Emboldened to Fight for More Bases," *New York Times,* March 14, 1993, p. 30.

39. Ibid.

40. In reality, the base was vulnerable to closure when plans to move the Army Information Systems Command to Fort Devins from Fort Huachuca in Arizona were dropped after Senator Dennis

DeConcini (D-AZ) protested them. "Optimism Expressed on Fort Devens Future," *Boston Globe,* April 11, 1991, p. 19.

41. *Baltimore Sun,* June 13, 1995, p. B2. She did not indicate a requirement for keeping the facility.

42. *New York Times,* June 15, 1995, p. B6.

43. *Military Construction Appropriations for 1992.* Hearings Before a Subcommittee of the House Committee on Appropriations, 102nd Cong., 1st Sess. Washington, D.C.: GPO, 1991, p. 361.

44. "Air Force to Waste $16 million by Closing Base in '94, Group Says," *Kansas City Star,* January 15, 1992, p. 12.

45. "The Navy's Decision to Close Phila. Shipyard was Rigged, Lawmakers Say," *Philadelphia Inquirer,* January 29, 1992, p. B1.

46. *Chicago Tribune,* March 1, 1995, p. II2.

47. *Defense Base Closure and Realignment Commission, 1995.* Report To The President, (Washington, D.C.: The Commission, 1995), p. 80.

48. "Memorandum of Understanding Between the City of Chicago and the United States Air Force, signed by David R. Mosena, Commissioner, Department of Aviation, and Jimmy G. Dishner, Deputy Assistant Secretary of the Air Force (Installations), December 15, 1995, p. 4. See also "Closure Task Force II, 928 Airlift Wing, O'Hare IAP ARS," HQ Air Force Reserve, Robins AFB, GA, 29 April–3 May 1996.

49. Clifford J. Levy, "Bright Side to Base Loss?," *New York Times,* March 21, 1995, p. B1.

50. United States Congress, *Department of Defense Appropriations for Fiscal 1995,* Hearings Before a Subcommittee of the House Committee on Appropriations, 103rd Cong., 2nd Sess. Washington, D.C.: GPO, 1995, p. 508.

51. "George Air Force Base," via Internet, http://www.cedar.ca.gov/military/current_reuse_george.htm., pp. 1-2.

52. DOD News Briefing, December 1, 1993, Robert E. Bayer, DASD, Economic Reinvestment and Base Realignment and Closure, Mark F. Wagner, Special Assistant to the ASD for Economic Security, and Kathleen M. deLasky, ATSD, (PA), p. 9.

53. Ibid.

54. Ibid.

55. "Molinaris Tried to Save Blunder," *New York Daily News,* June 2, 1997, p. 1, 6.

56. "Hunter's Point Naval Annex," via Internet, http://www.cedar.ca.gov/military/current_reuse/ hunterpt.htm, p. 2.

57. *San Francisco Chronicle,* March 8, 1997, p. A1.

58. *Montgomery Advertiser,* August 13, 1995, p. 6C.

59. Andrew D. Glassberg, "Intergovernmental Relations and Base Closing," *Publius: The Journal of Federalism,* Vol. 25, No. 3, (Summer 1995), pp. 95-96.

60. *Congressional Record (House),* June 26, 1996, p. H6854.

61. One proposal to turn the base into a brothel in order to tighten down on prostitution in the rest of San Francisco was defeated by the City Council.

62. "California Military Base Closures: Current Status of Reuse Efforts." Sacramento, CA: Governor's Office of Planning and Research, November 1, 1996, p. 5.

63. *Transition Talk,* DOD Base Closure and Transition Office, December 1996, p. 3.

64. "Sacramento Army Depot" via Internet, http//www.cedar.ca.gov.military/current_reuse/sacdepot.htm, pp. 2-3.

65. *"Base Closure and Reuse Rules Changed to Speed Economic Recovery and Job Creation".* news release, Office of Assistant Secretary of Defense (Public Affairs), No. 618-94, November 2, 1994, p. 1.

66. *National Defense Authorization Act for Fiscal Year 1994,* Public Law 103-160, Section 2903 Title XXIX, Defense Base Closure and Realignment, Section 2903..

67. *California Base Closure News,* No. 7 (October 1995), p. 8.

68. *Frontline: An Alameda Neighborhood Newsletter,* Vol. 1 (July 22, 1995), p. 2.

69. Ibid.

70. *Montgomery Advertiser,* February 13, 1996, p. 2.

71. Richard L. Brandt, "The Town Uncle Sam Left Behind," *Business Week,* July 23, 1984, p. 24.

72. Why this happened is not exactly clear, but it might have had something to do with the fact that Leon Panetta, President Clinton's chief of staff, used to represent the district in Congress. California was clearly important to the president, who showed up in person for the dedication of Cal State Monterey Bay on Labor Day 1995. During his first term in office, Clinton visited California 28 times, more than President Reagan, who owned a house and a ranch there.

73. *San Francisco Examiner,* July 22, 1997, p. 1.

74. *California Base Closure News,* No. 11 (June 1996), pp. 12-13.

75. *National Defense Authorization Act for Fiscal Year 1994,* Public Law 103-160, Title XXIX, Defense Base Closure and Realignment, Section 2903.

76. See Murray Weidenbaum, *Small Wars, Big Defense: Paying for the Military After the Cold War.* New York: Oxford University Press, pp. 61-66.

77. By 1996 the facility had much more success, serving as a site for Honda, Borden, K-Mart, Wal-Mart, and ten airlines. "Rickenbacker International Airport," via Internet, http://atlas.lmi. org/cgi-bin-parcels/ refine_query.pl.

78. *California Base Closure News,* No. 10 (April 1996), p. 2.

79. Tracy Seipel,. "Air Freight Complex Proposed-Moffett Would Host 18 Daily Flights, *San Jose Mercury News,* December 14, 1995, p. 1; Tracy Seipel, "Sunnyvale Threatens To Sue S.J. Over Moffett Plan, *San Jose Mercury News,* January 11, 1996, p. 2;. *Sunnyvale Monitors Future of NASA,* 1995 Annual Report, City of Sunnyvale, n.d. Tini Tran, "Coalition Fights NASA's Plan for Moffett Field, *San Jose Mercury News,* April 6, 1996p. 1.

80. One of the more interesting cases of transfer to private interests was the sale of an Atlas ICBM silo in Kansas to a family who converted it to a home. They paid $40,000 for the silo, which had cost the Air Force about $3.5 million in 1961. With a 47-ton front door, the "house" was relatively safe from tornadoes or burglars. "Home on the (Missile) Range is 'Civilized Living' for Couple, " *Montgomery Advertiser,* November 12, 1995, p. 3A.

81. The nearby town of Roswell suffered initially from Walker's closure, but in recent years it has benefited from the alleged crash of a UFO, which brings in an estimated $5 million annually from

tourists interested in visiting the alleged crash site and a UFO Museum and Research Center located there.

82. "England Industrial Airpark and Community," via Internet, http://atlas.lmi.org/ cgibin/parcels/ refine_query.pl.

83. "Sacramento Army Depot," via Internet, http://www.cedar.ca. gov.military/current_reuse/sacdepot.htm, pp. 1-2.

84. *Christian Science Monitor,* March 2, 1995, p. 1.

85. *Air Force News Service,* via Internet, http://www.af.mil.news.

86. "Treasure Island Luxury Resort," *San Francisco Chronicle,* March 28, 1997, pp. A1, 3.

87. "Cutting Costs is Military Mission, and N.H. Air Base is First to Go," *Philadelphia Inquirer,* March 31, 1991, p. 9.

88. *California Base Closure News,* No. 11 (June 1996), p. 7.

89. "The ARMS Program: An Alternative to Base Closure," via Internet, http://www.openterprise.com/armsdesc.htm, n.d., p. 1.

90. Ibid.

91. *California Base Closure News,* No. 11 (June 1996), p. 3.

92. Ibid.

93. "Fauquier to Turn Secret Base Into Public Space," *Washington Post,* August 17, 1995, p. B3.

94. Steve Piacente, "Twice-Hit Charleston on the Mend," *Government Executive,* Vol. 26 (September 1994), p. 37.

95. *Review,* California State University, Long Beach, Vol. 23, Vol. 1 (Fall 1996), p. 5.

96. Ibid.

97. Ibid.

98. *New York Times,* June 18, 1997, p. A10.

99. *California Base Closure News,* No. 8 (December 1995), p. 8.

100. Reserve forces are directly attached to the Defense Department but comprise part-time personnel. National Guard forces are assigned to the state governor's office on a regular basis, although they can be mobilized by the president as federal forces in times of emergency. So while Reserve forces can use a regular federally owned military base, Guard forces use bases owned by the state.

Should a federal base revert to Guard forces, it must be transferred to state ownership.

101. *Montgomery Advertiser,* August 13, 1995, p. 6C.

102. John D. Donahue, *The Privatization Decision: Public Ends, Private Means.* New York: Basic Books, 1989, Chs. 1-2.

103. President's Private Sector Survey on Cost Control, *Report on Privatization.* Washington, D.C.: GPO, 1983, p. 2.

104. Ibid., p. 122.

105. BRAC specified that McClellan's electronic-communications work be transferred to the Tobyhanna Army Depot in Pennsylvania. "Clinton Plan Said to Save Only 800 Jobs," *New York Times,* July 7, 1995, p. 1, 14.

106. *Hilltop Times,* November 2, 1995, p. 1.

107. Ibid., p. 5.

108. "Tiny Base May Give Clues to Saving Jobs," *New York Times,* August 3, 1995, p. 16.

109. Ibid.

110. A few Air Force personnel remain to perform some highly specialized tasks after the Air Force decided that not all functions at Newark could be privatized.

111. James Kitfield, "Depots for Sale," *Government Executive,* Vol. 27 (December 1995), p. 44.

112. John Pulley, "U.S. Air Force, Inc.," *Federal Times,* July 8, 1996, p. 1.

113. "Newark AFB Workers Want to Transfer AFGE Representation to Private Sector, *San Antonio Express-News,* June 18, 1996, p. 2.

114. Privatization was not expected to reduce the work-force size much, though it was possible that some of the work could be relocated to other areas.

115. Interview with Col. Joseph Renaud, USAF, September 19, 1995.

116. "One City Hopes to Keep its Navy Base Afloat by Privatizing it." *Christian Science Monitor,* August 15, 1996, p. 3.

117. *Chicago Tribune,* December 20, 1994, p. IV.

118. Ibid.

119. *25 Years of Civilian Reuse: Summary of Completed Military Base Economic Adjustment Projects.* Washington, D.C.: Pentagon, April–May 1986, p. 1. One of the authors of the study was the Office of Economic Adjustment, created by Secretary of Defense McNamara in 1961 to ease the impact of base closure.

120. Ibid.

121. Ibid. for all of the above figures.

122. Richard D. Suttie and Arthur J. Ohanian, *The Political Economy of Military Base Closure.* Monterey, CA: Naval Postgraduate School, 1990, pp. 67-68.

123. Ibid., pp. 72-75.

124. The Inland Valley Development Agency signed a 1995 contract with Cal Tai Associates to build a $400 million Worldpointe International Trade Center at nearby Norton AFB that reportedly would create 5,000 jobs by September 1997. The facility was not completed, though, by early 1998. *California Base Closure News,* No. 7 (October 1995), p. 9.

125. Nearby Norton AFB, which closed two years later, was somewhat more practical, converting its runway to a drag strip. The demand was likely to be good, since southern California, once the heartland of drag racing, had seen more than ten drag strips close over the past two decades due to noise complaints and land values. With an increase in street racing, Norton's runways could provide both a public service and a few dollars of revenue to the area. Unfortunately, the drag strip did not last long.

126. "Military Base Closures: The Impact on California Communities," RAND Research Brief. Santa Monica: RAND Corporation, February 1996, p. 2.

127. Ibid., p. 4.

128. John E. Lynch, *Local Economic Development After Military Base Closures.* New York: Praeger, 1970.

129. Ibid., Ch. 4.

130. Ibid., Ch. 5.

131. Ibid., Chs. 7, 10, 11.

132. Henry A. Zimon, *The Effects of U.S. Military Base Closures on Regional and Local Economies: 1950–1980*. Maxwell AFB, AL: Air Command and Staff College, March 1983, p. 9.

133. Lewis J. Coyle, *The Economic Impact of Military Installations on Regional Economies*. Monterey, CA: Naval Postgraduate School, September 1992.

134. *California Base Closure News*, No. 7 (October 1995), p. 11.

135. *Christian Science Monitor,* March 25, 1996, p. 1.

136. Darwin W. Daicoff, "The Community Impact of Military Installations," in Bernard Udis (ed.), *The Economic Consequences of Reduced Military Spending*. Lexington, MA: Lexington Books, 1973, pp. 157-158.

137. Nora C. Buckley, *An Overview of Studies of the Impact of Military Installations and Their Closings on Nearby Communities*. The George Washington University School of Engineering and Applied Science, July 20, 1976, p. 29.

138. Edward R. Tufte, *Political Control of the Economy.* Princeton, NJ: Princeton University Press, 1978, esp. Ch. 2.

139. *Defense Base Closure and Realignment Act of 1990,* Public Law 101-510, Section 2905.

140. *California Base Closure News,* No. 8 (December 1995), p. 1.

141. "Hunter's Point Naval Annex, via Internet, http://www.cedar. ca.gov/military/current /_reuse_hunterpt.htm., p. 2.

142. Ibid.

143. *Atlanta Journal-Constitution,* March 23, 1991, p. B1.

144. The NPL is a list of areas that score above 28.5 on the Hazard Ranking System, devised by the EPA to measure the toxicity and mobility of contaminants and the dangers they may pose to health. See *Cleaning Up Defense Installations: Issues and Options.* Washington, D.C.: CBO, January 1995, p. 5.

145. Ibid., pp. 9-10.

146. In 1944, a leaking canister of German mustard gas was buried at what was then Columbus Field in Mississippi. The base is required by law to find the canister and dispose of it, but no one can remember where it was buried. Workers who buried it have been called back to try to find it, but the topography of the base

has changed so much that they cannot locate the place where the gas may lie. The search continues to this day, and the base (now Columbus AFB) cannot be closed until the canister is finally located and destroyed.

147. United States Congress, *Department of Defense Appropriations for Fiscal Year 1993*, Hearings Before a Subcommittee of the House Committee on Appropriations, 102nd Cong., 2nd Sess. Washington, D.C.: GPO, 1992, pp. 536-537.

148. *High Mach*, Vol. 42 (October 5, 1995), p. 12.

149. Restoration Advisory Board Meeting Minutes, August 8, 1996, pp. 1-12.

150. "Base Closure and Reuse: 24 Case Studies. Business Executives for National Security, via Internet, http://netsite.esa.doc.gov., p. 24.

151. Ibid., p. 22.

152. By most accounts, the military makes every effort to remain in compliance with environmental laws. There are more than moral incentives to do so; base commanders can be imprisoned for environmental-law violations. As one small example of this, the Naval Public Works Center on Guam detected unacceptable levels of PCBs in pretreatment water in September 1996, and discharge was immediately stopped. A series of costly actions was taken and a full report was made to both the Guam Environmental Protection Agency and the U.S. Environmental Protection Agency in San Francisco. Letter from Commander, Pacific Division, Naval Facilities Engineering Command, January 4, 1996, pp. 1-2.

153. *Congressional Quarterly Weekly Report*, March 27, 1993, p. 771.

154. *Improving the Department of Defense's Hazardous Waste Cleanup Program*. RAND Research Brief, February 1996, p. 1.

155. Boxer was later elected U.S. Senator from California.

156. United States Congress, *Report on the Defense Secretary's Commission on Base Realignment and Closure*. Hearings Before the House Committee on Armed Services, Military Installations and Facilities Subcommittee, 101st Cong., 1st Sess. Washington, D.C.: GPO, 1989, p. 263. Boxer's effort ultimately failed, and the base was closed.

157. "3,000 Military Base Sites Added to Toxic Cleanup List," *Washington Post,* March 29, 1991, p. 4.

158. Ibid.

159. "Report Cites the High Price of Cleaning Up," *Air Force Times,* October 30, 1995, p. 17.

160. *Cleaning Up Defense Installations,* p. 25.

161. Ibid.

162. United States Congress, *Department of Defense Appropriations for 1993,* Hearings Before a Subcommittee of the House Committee on Appropriations, Cong., 2nd Sess. Washington, D.C.: GPO, 1992, p. 386.

163. Ibid. Otis Air National Guard Base had previously been Otis AFB and had operated as a SAC bomber base.

164. "Air Force Wants to Hand Over Base Before a Cleanup," *St. Petersburg Times,* January 19, 1992, p. B3.

165. Ibid., p. 423.

166. *Cleaning up Defense Installations,* p. 12.

167. Ibid., p. 10. One of the first actions to halt live ammunition training fire came when the New England office of the EPA ordered the practice to be suspended at the Massachusetts Military Reservation, stimulating a search for nontoxic ammunition. "In a Peacetime Shift, Guns Give Way to Clean Water," *New York Times,* August 24, 1997, p. 1/18.

168. *Closing Military Bases: An Interim Assessment.* Washington, D.C.: CBO, December 1996, p. 35. Much of this land will transfer to the Interior Department Fish and Wildlife Service for use as wildlife preserves, while about 13 percent will be retained by the Defense Department.

169. *Congressional Quarterly Weekly Report,* March 27, 1993, p. 772. This problem was in addition to the other 68 toxic waste sites on its 10,000 acres.

170. *California Base Closure News,* No. 7 (October 1995), p. 13.

171. Ibid.

172. *California Base Closure News,* No. 10 (April 1996), p. 9.

173. These procedures are for conventional ordnance. Chemical shells or nuclear weapons pose their own special problems, though there is little evidence that such ammunition might be found on bases slated for closure. Of course, one can never be sure, and rumors persist of lost nuclear weapons, some of which might be in the remains of crashed aircraft, like the B-36 that still lies in the lake at the end of the runway at Carswell AFB in Texas, though those rumors have been strongly denied.

174. "U.S. Military Called Top Environmental Foe," *Chicago Tribune,* March 13, 1991, p. 8. Future base closures may be complicated by the more modern technology of ordnance. For example, pilots have used the range at Eglin AFB in Florida for years, some firing rounds made of depleted uranium. While these rounds are not highly radioactive, their levels exceed EPA acceptable levels, and the spent shells will have to be recovered if Eglin closes. Due to their mass (which is the reason for using depleted uranium) and the muzzle velocity of the 20-mm cannons that fire them (at rates of 1,000 rounds per minute), they can penetrate into soft earth to depths of hundreds of feet. Calculations of soil removal are staggering, particularly since the Eglin range covers 725 square miles, one-third of which has been used repeatedly for live-round tests.

175. *Closing Bases Right: A Commander's Handbook.* Washington, D.C.: Office of the Assistant Secretary of Defense for Economic Security, August 1995, p. 41.

176. Ibid.

177. Briefing by Rick Newsom, DASA (ESOH), 1995 Base Closure Commander's Conference, Arlington, VA, September 6-7, 1995.

178. *Transition Talk,* DOD Base Closure and Transition Office, August 1996, p. 4.

179. "Improving the Department of Defense's Hazardous Waste Cleanup Program," p. 1.

180. *California Base Closure News,* No. 9 (February 1996) ,p. 11.

181. United States Congress, Testimony of Hon. Robert B. Pirie, Jr., Assistant Secretary of the Navy (Installations and Environment), Before the Senate Appropriations Subcommittee on Defense, July 11, 1995, p. 17.

182. *Department of Defense Authorization for Appropriations for Fiscal Year 1994 and the Future Years Defense Program,* Hearings Before the

Senate Committee on Armed Services, 103rd Cong., 1st Sess. Washington, D.C.: GPO, 1993, pp. 814-815.

183. *Congressional Quarterly Weekly Report,* March 27, 1993, p. 770.

184. Ibid.

185. Thomas P. Azar, "Base Closure: Its Impact on Military Members," *Torch,* Vol. 2 (November 1995), p. 14. (*Torch* is the official safety magazine of the Air Education and Training Command.)

186. The 379th had an illustrious history as a WW II B-17 bomb wing, which participated in the bloody Schweinfurt raids in October 1943. The tail emblem was a "K" inside a triangle. Wurtsmith's B-52s reproduced the triangle K in honor of those earlier airmen and their B-17s.

187. See Richard Szafranski, *Closing Your Base.* Maxwell AFB, AL: Air War College, 1993. Szafranski was commander of the Seventh Bomb Wing at Carswell and was responsible for its closure as an Air Force base (though it actually remained open after Szafranski left).

188. Eric Yoder, "Military Links," *Government Executive,* Vol. 29 (May 1997), p. p. 54-55.

189. According to Kitfield, 65.4 percent of active-duty soldiers were married as of 1996. See James Kitfield, "A Watchful Eye," *Government Executive,* Vol. 28 (December 1996), p. 40. Of course, being married is no guarantee against unruly behavior. But married individuals are more likely to go home at night instead of wandering to the off-base bars, and, if they do the latter, their low pay rates and family financial obligations tend to leave less beer money in their pockets than is the case for singles.

190. Kitfield, "A Watchful Eye."

191. *California Base Closure News,* No. 9 (February 1996), p. 10.

192. Paul Barth, "Historic Preservation and Military Base Closures," 1996, via Internet, http://www.cedar.ca.gov/military/histpres.html, 1996, p. 1.

193. *California Base Closure News,* No. 9 (February 1996), pp. 8-9.

194. Barth, "Historic Preservation," p. 2.

195. "Midway Gaining New Identity," *Boston Globe,* October 6, 1996, p. A2.

196. Barth, "Historic Preservation," p. 4.

197. *California Base Closure News,* No. 11 (June 1996), pp. 9-10.

198. Ibid., p. 11.

199. *Los Angeles Times,* August 15, 1996.

200. United States Senate *Department of Defense Appropriations for Fiscal Year 1993.* Hearings before a subcommittee of the Senate Committee on Appropriations, 102nd Cong., 2nd Sess. Washington, D.C.: GPO, 1992, p. 881.

201. Fact Sheet, Naval Weapons Station Seal Beach, n.d.

202. As the United States Fish and Game Service was investigating how to protect the habitat, the Army conducted the Dragon Fire training exercise, destroying much of the area. Since then, the Army has adopted a number of policies to aid in preserving woodpecker habitat. David Rubenson, Jerry Aroesty, and Charles Thomsen, *Two Shades of Green: Environmental Protection and Combat Training.* Santa Monica, CA: The RAND Corporation, 1995, p. R-4220.

203. United States Congress, Testimony of Hon. Robert B. Pirie, Jr., Assistant Secretary of the Navy (Installations and Environment), Before the United States Congress, Senate Appropriations Subcommittee for Defense, July 11, 1995, p. 14.

204. Brenda Biondo, "In Defense of the Longleaf Pine," *Nature Conservancy,* Vol. 47 (September/October 1997, p. 14.

205. *Frontline: An Alameda Neighborhood Newsletter,* Vol. 1, No. 2 (August 5, 1995, p. 1.

206. *Washington Post National Weekly Edition,* April 21, 1997, p. 8.

207. Ibid.

208. As researchers marked its homes with little colored flags, they were dismayed to find that base closure was not its greatest threat; that came from the hundreds of feral cats living in the same area and described as "considerably overweight."

209. *New York Times,* June 17, 1997, p. A10.

CHAPTER THREE

1. United States Congress, *Department of Defense Appropriation for Fiscal Year 1991*, Hearings Before the Senate Committee on Appropriations, 101st Cong., 2nd Sess. Washington, D.C.: GPO, 1990, p. 21.

2. Ibid., p. 315.

3. "House Votes Bill That Could Bring Shutdown of 20 U.S. Bases in '89," *New York Times*, July 13, 1988, p. 1.

4. "House Panels Differ Over Base-Closing Bill," *Congressional Quarterly Weekly Report*, June 11, 1988, p. 16.

5. *New York Times, July 13, 1988, p. 1.*

6. "Panel Proposes Closing 86 Bases," *Los Angeles Times*, December 30, 1988, p. 1.

7. "Base Closings Would Cost 12,796 Jobs," *Los Angeles Times*, December 30, 1988, p.

3. Fort Dix would ultimately survive in reduced form.

8. This discussion draws heavily from Steven G. Koven, "Base Closings and the Politics-Administration Dichotomy Revisited," *Public Administration Review*, Vol. 52 (September/October 1992), pp. 526-531.

9. Hugh R. Leonard, Jr., Handling the Hot Potato: Evolution and Analysis of the Base Closing Decision Process. Washington, D.C.: Industrial College of the Armed Forces (1992) pp. 9-10.

10. The difference between "training bases" and "major training areas" is that training bases provide facilities and equipment for training individuals (like recruit training), whereas "major training areas" are firing ranges and areas where simulated battles are conducted.

11. Koven, "Politics-Administration Dichotomy," p. 528.

12. Ibid.

13. Ibid.

14. Defense Base Closure and Realignment Commission, *Report to the President, 1991,* (Washington, D.C.: The Commission), p. 2-2.

15. "Feud May Have Put Whidbey on the Hit List," *Seattle Post-Intelligencer,* April 13, 1991, p. 3.

16. Ibid.

17. Elizabeth A. Palmer, "Commission Comes to Life, Vowing a 'Fresh Look,'" *Congressional Quarterly Weekly Report,* April 20, 1991, p. 994.

18. *Orlando Sentinel,* April 17, 1991, p. 5.

19. Palmer, "Commission Comes to Life," "Plan to Close Bases is Met With Protests From Affected States," *New York Times,* April 13, 1991, p. 1.

20. Ibid.

21. "Base Closings Pit Some Republicans Against Bush," *New York Times,* April 15, 1991, p. 10.

22. United States Congress, *Department of Defense Appropriations for Fiscal Year 1991,* Hearings Before the Senate Committee on Appropriations, 101st Cong., 2nd Sess. Washington, D.C.: GPO, 1990, pp. 47-48.

23. Ibid., p. 76.

24. Ibid.

25. "Anxiety is High as Lawmakers Await Plan to Close Military Bases," *New York Times,* April 12, 1991, p. 12.

26. See Edward F. Gordon, *Base Closure and Realignment.* Washington, D.C.: Industrial College of the Armed Forces, April 1992.

27. Ibid., pp. 28-34.

28. United States Congress, *Base Closures,* Hearing Before the House Committee on Armed Services, Military Installations and Facilities Subcommittee, 102nd Cong., 1st Sess. Washington, D.C.: 1991, p. 161.

29. Ibid.

30. Defense Base Closure and Realignment Commission, *Report to the President, 1991,* pp. 5-9.

31. Spatz later changed the spelling of his name to "Spaatz" in an effort to stop its frequent mispronunciation.

32. One aircraft had the word "crack" chalked on almost all of its engine mounts, but most of the "crack" words were almost obliterated

by smoke from the engines, indicating that they had been there for a long time.

33. Defense Base Closure and Realignment Commission, *Message from the President of the United States Transmitting the Report of the Defense Base Closure and Realignment Commission, July 10, 1991.* Washington, D.C.: GPO, 1991, pp. 5-45.

34. "Local Base Stays Open," *Detroit News*, April 13, 1991, p. A3.

35. *Defense Base Closure and Realignment Commission, 1991*, pp. 5-45.

36. Ibid.

37. Levin was more fortunate in 1991—BRAC closed the Detroit Arsenal Tank Plant in 1995.

38. *Detroit News*, March 11, 1991, p. 1.

39. Ibid.

40. *Transition Talk*, DOD Base Closure and Transition Office, August 1996, p. 8.

41. *Congressional Quarterly Almanac*, 1993, p. 438.

42. Ibid.

43. *Dissolution of Wurtsmith Base Conversion Authority*, Executive Order No. 1994-12, May 1994, p. 1.

44. United States Congress, Statement of Joshua Gotbaum, Assistant Secretary of Defense (Economic Security) House, Before the House Committee on National Security, Military Installations and Facilities Subcommittee, February 23, 1995, p. 6.

45. *Transition Talk*, DOD Base Closure and Transition Office, December 1996, p. 2.

46. Ibid.

47. Much of the information on Air Force bases is drawn from *Air Force Bases*, Vol. 1, *Active Air Force Bases Within the United States of America on 17 September 1982*. Washington, D.C.: Office of Air Force History, USAF, 1989.

48. Defense Base Closure and Realignment Commission, *Report to the President, 1991*, p. 5-32.

49. Ibid.

50. "Possible Closure Clouds Future for Carswell Base," *Fort Worth Star-Telegram,* March 12, 1991, p. 1. The commentary had a ring of truth; Fairchild was indeed, spared. But two other large naval bases, the Puget Sound Naval Station and NAS, Whidbey Island, were put on the 1991 list.

51. "Carswell's Future," *Fort Worth Star-Telegram,* March 27, 1991, p. B6.

52. Letter to Mr. Bob Meyer, signed Pete Geren, Member of Congress, dated May 2, 1991. *Military Bases: Letters and Requests Received on Proposed Closures and Realignments.* Washington, D.C.: GAO, May 1991, pp. 60-61.

53. "Carswell Review Criticized," *Fort Worth Star-Telegram,* April 30, 1991, p. 1.

54. *Fort Worth Star-Telegram,* April 10, 1991, p. 1.

55. "Base Closure and Reuse: 24 Case Studies". Business Executives for National Security, April 1993, via Internet, http://www.netsite.esa.doc.gov., p. 19.

56. Ibid.

57. Ibid.

58. Ibid., p. 20.

59. Ibid.

60. "Environmental Report on Carswell Air Force Base", n.d., p. 2.

61. Ibid.

62. Defense Base Closure and Realignment Commission, *Report to the President, 1991,* p. 5-32.

63. Base Closure and Realignment Commission, *Report to the President,1993, (Washington D.C.: The Commission),* p. 1-26.

64. Interview, 1995.

65. Base Realignment and Closure Commission, *Report to the President, 1993,* p. 1-26.

66. *Air Force News Service,* via Internet , http://www.af.mil.news.

67. Carswell is not the only Air Force base to survive a closure decision. The Marine Corps recruiting offices, once sprinkled through the Kansas City area in leased properties, moved to the closed Richards-Gebaur AFB in Missouri. The move produced

considerable effort to clear up asbestos-laden buildings and other make improvements. Since the base is officially closed, the Marines must call it a "campus," sometimes producing confusion with a Bible college also located at the former base.

68.   "Loring AFB in Maine Also Slated for Closure," *Boston Globe,* April 13, 1991, p. 7. Brunswick pumped $141 million into the local economy, far more than did Loring.

69.   Gen. Cassidy's comment did not endear him to the citizens of the area, who produced a T-shirt with a picture of a horse's head on the front, and its rear on the back, with the general's name over the hindquarters.

70.   Some of this sentiment was noted in an article in *Down East* (Summer 1991), p. 10.

71.   Letter to the Honorable Sam Nunn, signed William S. Cohen, U.S. Senator, and George J. Mitchell, U.S. Senator, dated July 22, 1991, p. 1.

72.   Cohen speculated that the Air Force (and SAC, in particular) had included "quality of life" in its discussions with the BRAC commissioners but that the communications had been private. Cohen offered no evidence to support his suspicions, but presumably he believed that General Cassidy's previous position as Commander in Chief of SAC in the mid-1970s gave him a private conduit of information from SAC.

73.   Briefing by the Office of Economic Adjustment and the Department of the Air Force, Loring Officers Open Mess, September 6, 1991, p. 3.

74.   Letter to the Honorable Charles A. Bowsher, Comptroller of the United States, signed William Cohen, U.S. Senator, George J. Mitchell, U.S. Senator, Thomas H. Andrews, Member of Congress, and Olympia J. Snowe, Member of Congress, dated April 29, 1991. *Military Bases: Letters,* pp. 54-55.

75.   Ibid., p. 54.

76.   *The Stars and Stripes,* March 17. 1992, p. 3

77.   Letter to the Honorable Daniel Goldin, Administrator, National Aeronautics and Space Administration, signed by William S. Cohen and George J. Mitchell, dated October 26, 1992.

78. Letter to the Honorable Edward Madigan, Secretary of Agriculture, signed by William S. Cohen and George J. Mitchell, dated October 26, 1992, pp. 1-2.

79. *Congressional Record,* (Senate), September 8, 1992, p. S13064.

80. Ibid.

81. Letter to the Honorable William K. Reilly, Administrator, Environmental Protection Agency, signed by William S. Cohen and George J. Mitchell, dated October 26, 1992, pp. 1-2.

82. Letter to Admiral James D. Watkins, Secretary, Department of Energy, signed by William S. Cohen and George J. Mitchell, dated October 26, 1992, p. 1.

83. Letter to Senator George J. Mitchell, signed by Henry Cooper, Director, dated March 30, 1992. A similar letter dated February 24, 1992, was also sent to Representative Olympia Snowe, who had made a similar inquiry of Defense Secretary Dick Cheney.

84. Ibid.

85. Letter to Colonel David Cannan, Air Force Base Disposal Agency, signed by Hamid Butt, President, A & P Aviation, dated November 4, 1992.

86. Letter to Mr. Hamid Butt, President, A & P Aviation, signed by Colonel David M. Cannan, Director Headquarters Air Force Base Disposal Agency, dated November 12, 1992, p. 1.

87. Ibid.

88. Ibid.

89. Letter to Charles Connel, Loring Readjustment Committee, signed by Hamid Butt, A & P Aviation, dated October 29, 1992, p. 2 and undated statement from Charles Connell, p. 1.

90. Pilots never "dumped fuel," instead they "readjusted the gross weight of the aircraft."

91. In one of the more creative efforts to diffuse a situation, Loring's wing commander held a press conference to announce that he had peeked into the small hole in the building and had found no sources of radioactivity inside. The assembled reporters did not know that he had painted fluorescent dye around his eye. As he made his announcement, an aide illuminated his face with an ultraviolet lamp, which made his eye glow a lurid radioactive green.

The press reaction was not recorded, but there were no more stories of the "radioactive" building.

92. *Boston Globe,* January 12, p. 21; January 27, p. 16.

93. Letter to Sawyer Environmental, signed by Sean F. Crean, Procurement Center Representative, U.S. Small Business Administration, dated September 4, 1992.

94. Ibid.

95. *Bangor Daily News,* October 6, 1992.

96. Loring Commerce Centre, website, via Internet, www.loring. maine.com, August 1996.

97. Ibid.

98. News release, Office of Senator George J. Mitchell, June 10, 1992, p. 3.

99. Ibid.

100. Defense Base Closure and Realignment Commission, *Report to the President, 1991,* p. 5-37.

101. The 1991 BRAC rejected the Navy's recommendation to close Orlando because of prohibitive costs, but it did appear again on the 1993 Navy list, and in that year it did close.

102. As noted in Chapter Two, both New York senators delayed voting on the composition of the 1995 BRAC membership because of their anger over the fact that New York suffered more base closures than did New Jersey, a fact they attributed to the influence of former New Jersey Representative James Courter, who chaired the 1993 and 1995 BRACs.

CHAPTER FOUR

1. "Defense Chief Lists 31 Big Bases for Closing, and Outcry is Swift," *New York Times,* March 13, 1993, p. 1.

2. "Aspin Passes Along Unpopular Task as Panel Begins Base Hearings," *Congressional Quarterly Weekly Report,* March 20, 1993, p. 680.

3. The governor would get his wish two years later, when the Naval Station and most other Navy facilities made the 1995 BRAC list.

On a per capita basis, Guam lost more military jobs than any of the 50 states.

4. "Area Losses May Affect Thousands," *Washington Post,* March 13, 1993, p. 1.

5. "Appeals are not Expected to Save Bases," *Philadelphia Inquirer,* March 13, 1993, p. 1.

6. Ibid. Two facilities, the Navy's Aviation Supply Office, and the Naval Air Technical Services Facility, both made the initial 1993 closure list.

7. General Johnson actually headed two commands—the U.S. Transportation Command, a joint command incorporating both Air Force and Navy mobility assets; and the Air Mobility Command, in which the Air Force's transport aircraft were located.

8. United States Congress, *Department of Defense Appropriations, for Fiscal Year 1994.* Hearings Before the Senate Committee on Appropriations, 103rd Cong., 1st Sess. Washington, D.C.: GPO, 1994, p. 661.

9. DOD Briefing by Robert E. Bayer, DASD, Economic Reinvestment and Base Closure, Mark F. Wagner, Special Assistant to the ASD for Economic Security, Kathleen M. deLasky, ATSD (PA), December 1, 1993, p. 7.

10. Fort Monmouth would finally be realigned instead of closed completely.

11. *Congressional Quarterly Weekly Report,* March 13, 1993, p. 616.

12. "Fighting on the Home Front, Charleston Defends Itself," *Congressional Quarterly Weekly Report,* May 8, 1993, p. 1174-1175.

13. Ibid., p. 1175.

14. The following information was gathered in a series of interviews at Meridian NAS in July 1993.

15. Internal memorandum, Whiting NAS, dated February 12, 1993.

16. "Navy Meridian Team Major Points," internal memorandum, June 21, 1993.

17. Ibid.

18. Ibid. It was not clear whether the governor of Mississippi had approved the money, or, for that matter, whether state money could be spent on federal facilities for federal purposes.

19. Ibid. Apparently, putting "hurricane" in capital letters made it more prominent in the memo.

20. Ibid.

21. United States Congress, *Base Closures,* Hearings Before the Military Installations and Facilities Subcommittee of the House Committee on Armed Services, 101st Cong., 2nd Sess. Washington, D.C.: GPO, 1991, p. 205.

22. Ibid., p. 209.

23. Ibid.

24. *Congressional Quarterly Weekly Report,* June 11, 1988, p. 16.

25. *Philadelphia Inquirer,* March 13, 1995, p. 1.

26. Defense Base Closure and Realignment Commission, *Report to the President, 1993,* (Washington, D.C.: The Commission, 1993) p. 1-24.

27. Ibid., pp. 1-12.

28. Unfortunately, the Park Service needed more than half of its entire fiscal 1995 budget just to upgrade housing at the Presidio, and the University of California backed out of leasing the hospital complex, leaving the fate of the historical property highly uncertain. "Peacetime Vision for the Presidio in Jeopardy," *New York Times,* February 21, 1995, p. 1.

29. "Supplementary Summary of Responses to the Call for Interest, #1", via internet, http://gopher.well.sf.ca.us:70/0/Community/presidio/proposals/Supplemental-Feb-25-93.

30. "Presidio's Fate Nears Resolution–Park Bill in Cross Fire of Senate Political Battle," *San Francisco Chronicle,* March 4, 1996, p. A1.

31. "The Presidio as Ghost Post," *San Francisco Chronicle,* March 10, 1996, p. B10.

32. Ibid.

33. Ibid.

34. "Presidio Bill Hits a Snag in Senate," *San Francisco Chronicle,* March 21, 1996, p. A1.

35. Ibid.

36. "Presidio Trapped in Senate Politics," *San Francisco Chronicle,* March 26, 1996, p. A3.

37. Ibid.

38. "Presidio Bills Sinks in Senate," *San Francisco Chronicle*, March 28, 1996, p. A1.

39. Ibid.

40. "Senate Deal Clears Way for Presidio," *San Francisco Chronicle*, May 1, 1996, p. A1.

41. Ibid.

42. "Presidio Financing Approved by Senate," *San Francisco Chronicle*, May 2, 1996, p. A1.

43. "Only 200 Protest Clinton's S.F. Visit," *San Francisco Chronicle*, June 10, 1996, p. A1.

44. "Presidential Veto Threat," *San Francisco Chronicle*, September 26, 1996, p A1.

45. Ibid.

46. Ibid.

47. Ibid.

48. Ibid.

49. Ibid.

50. "GOP Rushing to Avert Veto on Parks Bill," *San Francisco Chronicle*, September 27, 1996, p. A3.

51. "Congressional Bickering Stalls Presidio Parks Measure," *San Francisco Chronicle*, September 28, 1996, p. A1.

52. Ibid.

53. Ibid.

54. "Presidio Bill Approved at Last Minute," *San Francisco Chronicle*, October 4, 1996, p. A1.

55. *San Francisco Chronicle*, October 26, 1996, p. A4. Republicans claimed that the delay was due to the difficulty of getting signatures from Republican Representatives anxious to leave Washington and hit the campaign trail.

56. "Presidio Trust Legislation," via internet, http://www.site2c.com/trust/trust.htm., n.d.

57. Ibid.

58. "Presidio Bill Approved at Last Minute," *San Francisco Chronicle*, October 4, 1996, p. A1.

59. A spirited fight broke out over the Presidio golf course, which the Army wanted to remain open for use by remaining military personnel. In a compromise, the Interior Department finally agreed to let the Army run the course pending its finding another way to keep it open. See Eric Yoder, "Military Links," *Government Executive*, Vol. 29 (May 1997, p. 54.

60. "Exhibit Hall Announced for Presidio," *San Francisco Chronicle*, April 27, 1996, p. A16.

61. "Waterfront Park Envisioned at S.F.'s Crissy Field," *San Francisco Chronicle*, June 19, 1996, p. A13.

62. "Mountain Lake's Real Menace," *San Francisco Chronicle*, August 27, 1996, p. A13.

63. "MacDill has Pentagon Point Man," *Tampa Tribune*, December 4, 1988, p. 17.

64. Edward F. Gordon, *Base Closure and Realignment*, Washington, D.C.: Industrial College of the Armed Forces, April 1992, p. 20.

65. *St. Petersburg Times*, June 23, 1995, p. 1

66. Ibid.

67. Ibid.

68. *Air Force News Service*, March 1995.

Chapter Five

1. Secretary of Defense Les Aspin, addressing a question from Senator Ted Stevens (R-AK) about the actual number of bases closed under previous BRACs. United States Congress, *Department of Defense Appropriations, Fiscal Year 1994*. Senate Hearings Before the Committee on Appropriations, 103rd Cong., 1st Sess. Washington, D.C.: GPO, 1994, p. 857.

2. *Congressional Record (House)*, September 8, 1995, p. H8692

3. James Kitfield, "A Tale of Two Cities," *Government Executive*, Vol. 26 (September 1994), pp. 30-31.

4. "Senate Floor Action," *Congressional Quarterly Almanac,* 1993, p. 438.

5. "Dole, White House Agree on Nominee to Panel," *Congressional Quarterly Weekly Report,* February 18, 1995, p. 539.

6. "Battle Lines Already Drawn as Clinton Names Panel," *Congressional Quarterly Weekly Report,* February 11, 1995, p. 468.

7. *Congressional Quarterly Weekly Report,* February 18, 1995, p. 539.

8. Ibid.

9. *Air Force Depot Maintenance: Privatization-in-Place Plans Are Costly While Excess Capacity Exists.* GAO/NSIAD-97-13. Washington, D.C.: GAO, December 31, 1996, p. 4.

10. Ironically, Odgen was the only one of the five depots that did not make the 1995 BRAC closure list. Ultimately, two depots were closed, but Hill never even came close.

11. The term "operational command" in Air Force parlance refers to those commands that operate aircraft (the Air Combat Command, the Air Mobility Command, the Special Operations Command, etc., whereas the "support commands" support the operators, includes the Air Force Logistics Command (which owns the depots).

12. Prior to the reorganization under Air Force Chief of Staff Gen. Merrill McPeak, the Air Force Material Command had been the Air Force Logistics Command.

13. *New York Times,* July 11, 1995, pp.1, 18.

14. Confusion can arise over the way Air Force depots (and sometimes laboratories) are named. Normally, the depot is located on the site of an Air Force base, in which is (named after the town or city in which it is located (i.e., Myrtle Beach AFB at Myrtle Beach, South Carolina) or after a deceased military aviator, while the depots are named after the town or city in which the host base is located. So San Antonio Air Logistics Center is located at Kelly AFB near San Antonio, Texas.

15. See John E. Lynch, *Local Impact Development After Military Base Closures.* New York: Praeger, 1970, Chs. 10 and 11.

16. *New York Times,* July 10, 1995

17. Barbara Boxer, "Base Essential to Security," *USA Today,* July 7, 1995, p. 10.

18. Ibid.

19. *Congressional Record (House),* September 8, 1995, p. H8700.

20. *San Antonio Express-News,* June 234, 1995, p. 1.

21. Ibid.

22. Ibid. Commissioners Cox and Montoya, both from California, voted against closing Sacramento.

23. Ibid.

24. Ibid. There was also unhappiness over the change in cost estimates to move the C-5 cargo aircraft repair to Oklahoma City— San Antonio leaders calculated the figure at $229 million, while BRAC analysts put the cost at $78 million.

25. *Congressional Record (House),* September 8, 1995, p. H8688.

26. *New York Times,* July 11, 1995, pp. 1, 18.

27. *Los Angeles Times,* (Washington edition), July 14, 1995, p. 3.

28. *Los Angeles Times* (Washington edition), July 7, 1995, p. B1.

29. *Defense Transition.,* Texas Defense Economic Adjustment Advisory Council Triennial Report, Texas Department of Commerce, December 4, 1995, p. 7.

30. Ibid.

31. Ibid., p. 8.

32. James Kitfield, "Depots for Sale," *Government Executive,* Vol. 27 (December 1995), p. 43.

33. *Washington Post,* April 1, 1996, p. 7.

34. Ibid.

35. *Congressional Record (House),* September 8, 1995, p. H8688.

36. Ibid., p. 44.

37. Ross Day, "C-5 First to Privatize," *Kelly Observer,* August 22, 1996, p. 2.

38. *Air Force Depot Maintenance: Privatization-in-Place Plans are Costly While Excess Capacity Exists.* GAO/NSIAD-97-13. Washington, D.C., General Accounting Office, December 31, 1996, p. 6.

39. Ibid., p. 11.

40. Ibid., p. 15.

41. "Angry Clinton Accepts Lists of Base Cutbacks," *Washington Post*, July 14, 1995, p. 1.

42. "Administration Seeks to Minimize Pain of Closures," *Air Force News Service*, August 1995., p. 2.

43. Ibid.

44. "Status of Site and Areas of Concern Identification", San Antonio Air Logistics Center, n.d., p. 1.

45. John E. White, "Playing Politics? The Charge is Baseless," *Washington Post*, July 27, 1995, p. 19.

46. Ibid.

47. Ibid.

48. Ibid.

49. Alan J. Dixon, "Military Bases: Painful but Prudent Closure," *Washington Post*, August 4, 1995, p. 22.

50. Ibid.

51. Ibid.

52. Ibid.

53. "House Action Assures Closing of 79 Bases," *New York Times*, September 9, 1995, p. 46.

54. *Congressional Quarterly Weekly Report*, March 4, 1995, p. 696.

55. Ibid.

56. Ibid.

57. "Ohio Gains Jobs from Base Closure," *Dayton Daily News*, March 3, 1995, p. 1.

58. United States Congress, *Base Closures*. Hearing Before the Military Installations and Facilities Subcommittee of the Committee on Armed Services, House of Representatives, 101st. Cong., 2nd Sess. Washington, D.C.: GPO, 1991, p. 228.

59. *Congressional Record (House)*, September 8, 1995, p. H8698.

60. Ibid.

61. Ibid.

62. United States Congress, *Department of Defense Appropriations for Fiscal Year 1994.* Hearings before a subcommittee of the Committee on Appropriations, House of Representatives, 103rd Cong., 1st Sess. Washington, D.C.: GPO, 1993, p. 576-577.

63. Ibid., p. 629.

64. Representative Glenn Browder, 3rd District of Alabama, Press Release, December 13, 1995, p. 1.

65. Ibid..

66. Ibid.

67. Studies continued, though. The National Research Council found some five different technologies to destroy chemical agents in place, including one that mixed the chemicals with sludge from a sewer treatment plant. "Neutralization of Mustard Agent Urged," *Baltimore Sun,* September 25, 1996, p. 2B.

68. *Congressional Record (House),* March 7, 1995, p. H2784.

69. *Congressional Record (House),* March 21, 1995, p. H3333.

70. *Congressional Record (House),* June 27, 1995, p. H6317.

71. *Congressional Record (House),* March 16, 1995, p. H3279; June 16, 1995, p. H6053.

72. United States Congress, *Military Construction Appropriations for 1997.* Hearings before a Subcommittee of the House Committee on Appropriations, 104th Cong., 2nd Sess. Washington, D.C.: GPO, 1996, p. 94.

73. Sgt. Alan Moore, *Redeveloping Fort McClellan,* via Internet.

74. Ibid.

75. *Montgomery Advertiser,* December 13, 1996, p. 3B.

76. Ibid.

77. "43 Employees to Lose Jobs at Oakland Naval Supply Center," *Oakland Post,* March 1, 1995, p. 6.

78. Roger W. Lotchin, *Fortress California, 1910–1961: From Warfare to Welfare.* New York: Oxford University Press, 1992, p. 62.

79. The Military Sea Transportation Service (later renamed the Military Sealift Command) is the Navy's transportation arm. Its responsibility, though, is limited to chartering civilian cargo and

research vessels, since the regular Navy retains control of fleet cargo and personnel transports.

80. Port of Oakland homepage, via Internet, http://www.portofoakland.com/ facts.html.

81. "Congressman Ronald Dellums: A Biography." Office of Representative Ronald V. Dellums, n.d., p. 1.

82. Letter to Hon. Charles A. Bowsher, Comptroller General of the United States, signed Pete Stark, Member of Congress and Ron Dellums, Member of Congress, March 7, 1991, *Military Bases: Letters and Requests Received on Proposed Closures and Realignments.* Washington, D.C.: GAO, May, 1991, pp. 7-8.

83. As the Vietnam conflict escalated in the mid-1960s, the Navy took a number of transports out of mothballs, and refurbished them to carry troops to Southeast Asia. Because the vessels were so old and were operated by civilian crews, the cost of running this operation quickly became prohibitive, and some ships sailed for less than a year before being retired and ultimately sent to the scrap yard.

84. Jeffrey L. Pressman and Aaron Wildavsky, *Implementation: How Great Expectations in Washington are Dashed in Oakland* Berkeley, CA: University of California Press, 1984, p. 16.

85. Ibid., p. 5.

86. Defense Base Closure and Realignment Commission, *Report to the President, 1993,* (Washington, D.C.: The Commission, 1993), p. 1-57.

87. Ibid., p. 1-56.

88. *San Francisco Chronicle,* August 14, 1993, p. 5.

89. Ibid.

90. "Oakland Port to Expand Under Base Conversion," *San Francisco Chronicle,* June 3, 1994, p. A19.

91. "Port Officials Hail Clinton Deal," *San Francisco Chronicle,* August 14, 1994, p. 4.

92. Ibid.

93. "Oakland Army Base Escapes Closure List," *San Francisco Chronicle,* February 28, 1995, p. A1.

94. "Oakland Base Spared—Muted Reaction," *San Francisco Chronicle,* March 1, 1995, p. A5.

95. Ibid.

96. "Oakland Base Again in Jeopardy," *San Francisco Chronicle,* May 11, 1995, p. A1.

97. Ibid.

98. Defense Base Closure and Realignment Commission, *Report to the President, 1995,* (Washington , D.C.: The Commission), 1995, p. 1-7.

99. Ibid.

100. Criteria 5 is "return on investment," and criteria 6 is "economic impact on communities," See ibid., p. H-1 for a full description of the 1995 closure criteria.

101. Defense Base Closure and Realignment Commission, *Report to the President, 1995,* p. 1-40.

102. Pressman and Wildavsky, *Implementation.*

103. *Congressional Record (House),* September 8, 1995, p. H8696.

104. Pressman and Wildavsky, *Implementation.*

105. *California Base Closure News,* No. 11 (June 1996), p. 13.

106. "Point Molate Naval Fuel Depot," via Internet, http://www.cedar. ca.gov/military/current_reuse/pt_molat.htm, p. 1.

107. *California Base Closure News,* No. 9 (February 1996), pp. 7-8.

108. "Save the Bay Programs," *Newsletter of the Save San Francisco Bay Association,* n.d., p. 6.

109. Ibid.

110. *San Francisco Chronicle,* August 28, 1991, p. 13.

111. Lotchin, *Fortress California,* pp. 175-176.

112. Ibid., p. 176.

113. "Private Shipyards Want Navy Competitors Closed," *Journal of Commerce,* December 1, 1988, p. B1.

114. Ibid.

115. "Shipyard in Long Beach Seen Choice for Closure," *Los Angeles Times,* December 2, 1988, p. 1.

116. Ibid.

117. Defense Base Closure and Realignment Commission, *Report to the President, 1995,* p. 45.

118. "Oakland Army Base to Close, Long Beach Also Added to Panel's List," *San Francisco Chronicle,* June 24, 1995, p. A1.

119. "Community, City Leaders Rally To Save Shipyard," *Forty-Niner Online,* March 20, 1996, p. 1.

120. Ibid.

121. "Boxer Continues To Call on President To Reject Base Closure List," newsletter Senator Barbara Boxer, July 6, 1995, p. 1.

122. Mario C. Aguilera, "San Diego Covets 2,500 More Jobs from Base Closure Plan," *Source Breaking News,* via Internet, http://www.sddt.com.

123. City of Long Beach News, via Internet, http://city.net/countries/united_states/ california/long_beach, p. 3.

124. *Journal of Commerce,* March 2, 1995, p. 1B.

125. *Congressional Record (House),* September 8, 1995, p. H8689.

126. Ibid.

127. Defense Base Closure and Realignment Commission, *Report to the President, 1995,* p. 1-45.

128. Ibid., p. 1-46.

129. The shipyard found itself unable to dispose of some surplus 16-inch gun barrels designed for battleships. The barrels, worth $9 million apiece in 1996 dollars, were sold to a scrap dealer, but environmental, health, and technical problems stymied efforts to cut them up. A plea was made to save them by moving them to another military base: "Remember that for a very long time to come, only battleships will be able [to] provide our troops with truly effective, all-weather fire support in another war." True or not, the barrels would have done little good without battleships to mount them on, and there was little support in the Navy to bring the battleships out from mothballs. See William L. Stearman, "Ink—and Vision—Can Save 16-Inch Tubes," *Proceedings,* Vol. 122 (September 1996), p. 82.

130. "Report Details Toxic Waste Produced at Naval Shipyard," *Los Angeles Times,* July 4, 1996, p. A5.

131. Long Beach Naval Complex Restoration Advisory Board, Minutes of Meeting, August 20, 1996, p. 4.

132. *Long Beach Press-Telegram,* March 30, 1996, p. 1.

133. Ibid.

134. Ibid. The report did not break down jobs by type (active military or civilian), but the official Navy figures for the base were more than 5,000 military and 4,200 civilian employees.

135. City of Long Beach News, Via Internet, p. 4. Http://www.ci.long beach.ca.us/press

136. Aguilera, "San Diego Covets."

137. "Council Decides on Port Plan for Long Beach Shipyard," *Los Angeles Times,* August 30, 1996, p. C6.

138. Ibid.

139. "Need to Keep Base, Navy Argues," *Los Angeles Times,* May 30, 1995, p. A10.

140. Ibid.

141. "Scenario," CR95-018, NAWCWD, Point Mugu, n.d., pp. 1-2, 1-3.

142. Ibid., p. 1-3.

143. This was not universally true; aircraft could fly directly to the range from carriers or fly up the coast over water from San Diego. But the specter of aircraft flying over land with live munitions was another political lever to help save the base.

144. "Scenario", p. 1-3.

145. Ibid., p. 1-4.

146. *Los Angeles Times,* May 30, 1995, p. A10.

147. "Statement of U.S. Senator Barbara Boxer to the Ventura County Board of Supervisors on the Base Realignment and Closure Commission Decision To Retain Point Mugu Naval Air Weapons Station Ventura, California," July 5, 1995, Office of Senator Barbara Boxer.

148. Restoration Advisory Board, Oxnard Plain Minutes of Meetings, July 11, 1996, May 2, 1996.

149. *The Plan for Joint Use of Military Airfields.* The Secretary of Defense and the Secretary of Transportation to the United States Congress. Washington, D.C.: GPO, 1984, p. 4.

150. Pat McKenna, "McClellan Inc.," *Airman,* (December 1995), p. 29.

151. Ibid., p. 30.

152. "Recovery Tools Available To Assist Base Closure Communities," Department of Defense newsletter, August 3, 1995.

CHAPTER SIX

1. *Congressional Record (House),* September 8, 1995, p. H8688.

2. United States Congress, Statement of Joshua Gotbaum, assistant secretary of defense economic Security, before the House Committee on National Security, Military Installations and Facilities Subcommittee, February 23, 1995, Washington, D.C.: GPO, 1995, p. 1.

3. The Charleston Navy Base had been so thoroughly closed by its official expiration date that the base had to borrow a destroyer from the Norfolk Naval Station to have a symbolic "last sailing" on the base's final day. *Atlanta Journal-Constitution,* September 17, 1995, p. F8.

4. See Michael O'Hanlon, *Defense Planning for the Late 1990s.* Washington, D.C.: Brookings Institution, 1995, p. 9.

5. "Senator Boxer Holds Hearings on Military Base Closures," press release, Office of Senator Barbara Boxer, December 10, 1993, p. 1.

6. "Air Chief Pushes for Balance of Power," *Newport News Daily Press,* July 31, 1996, p. C1.

7. Base Realignment and Closure Commission Hearings, March 16, 1995.

8. *California Base Closure News,* No. 8 (December 1995), p. 12.

9. CRB Note, Vol. 4 (May 7, 1997), p. 4. California Research Bureau, California State Library, Sacramento, CA. Georgians apparently realized their vulnerability to base closure after Senator Nunn's retirement from the Senate.

10. Ibid., p. 3.

11. Ibid., p. 48.

12. Remarks by the President, Military Personnel, Business Leaders and Citizens of the San Bernardino, California Area, San

Bernardino International Airport, San Bernardino, California, May 20, 1994. Washington, D.C.: White House, Office of the Press Secretary, May 20, 1994, p. 2.

13. It is not clear that Clinton indicated where some of the funding for the university came from—the Department of Defense budget, which contained a line item for $15 million to build a university owned and operated by the state of California.

14. Remarks by the President in Meeting with Community Leaders About the Philadelphia Naval Shipyard, Wyndham Franklin Plaza Hotel, Philadelphia, Pennsylvania, September 18, 1995. Washington, D.C.: White House, Office of the Press Secretary, September 18, 1995, p. 1.

15. "After Closure: Base Reuse and Job Creation," Statement of Joshua Gotbaum, Assistant Secretary of Defense (Economic Security), Before the Base Closure and Realignment Commission, March 16, 1995, pp. 1-3.

16. Ibid.

17. Ibid., p. 7. Italics in original.

18. Ibid.

19. Base Realignment and Closure Commission Hearings, February 23, 1995.

20. *Closing Military Bases: An Interim Assessment.* Washington, D.C.: CBO, December 1996, p. xiii.

21. Ibid.

22. Restoration Advisory Board, *Report to Congress for Fiscal Year 1995,* p. 2.

23. United States Congress, *Department of Defense Appropriations for Fiscal Year 1991,* Hearings Before the Senate Committee on Appropriations, 101st Cong., 2nd Sess. Washington, D.C.: GPO, 1990, p. 204. It is interesting that Senator Bumpers was the only member of the Senate Appropriations Subcommittee on Defense to question the service on the reasons to close a base.

24. Browder, a former political science professor at Jacksonville State University in Alabama, was defeated in the 1996 Democratic Party primary election for United States senator to replace retiring Senator Howell Heflin.

25. "Ending the Depot Dilemma: It's Time to Sensibly Think Through A Privatization Policy," Office of Representative Glen Browder, n.d., p. 2.

26. John D. Donahue, *The Privatization Decision: Public Ends, Private Means,* New York: Basic Books, 1989, p.222.

27. Ibid., p. 215.

28. "Presentation on Strategic Plan for the Development of Kelly Air Force Base, November 1, 1995," Initial Base Adjustment Strategy Committee, pp. 1-5.

29. Mission McClellan Executive Advisory Committee, Minutes of Meeting, September 25, 1995, p. 4.

30. "Military Housing Privatization Initiative," Statement of Robert E. Bayer, Deputy Assistant Secretary of Defense (Installations) Before the House National Security Committee, Military Installations and Facilities Subcommittee, March 7, 1996, Washington, D.C.: GPO, 1996, p. 2.

31. *New York Times,* March 1, 1995, p. B6.

32. William J. Perry, ""National Security Depends on Nontraditional Programs," *Defense 95,* No. 2, p. 10. Perry commented before the 1995 list was finalized at 79 closed and realigned bases.

33. "Base Closures Seen Despite Delay by Clinton," *Los Angeles Times,* (Washington edition), July 13, 1995, p. 4.

34. *Congressional Record (House),* May 30, 1996, p. H5660.

35. Ibid.

36. *Department of Defense Appropriations for Fiscal Year 1995.* Hearings Before a Subcommittee of the Committee on Appropriations, United States Senate, 103rd Cong., 1st Sess. Washington, D.C.: GPO, 1994, p. 872.

37. *Department of Defense Appropriations for Fiscal 1994,* p. 602.

38. *Congressional Record (House),* September 8, 1995, p. H8685.

39. *Congressional Record (House),* September 8, 1995, p. 8697.

40. Katherine McIntire Peters, "Money Woes," *Government Executive,* Vol. 29 (June 1997), p. 26.

41. *Interim Assessment,* p. 9.

42. *Washington Post,* July 13, 1995, p. 23.

43. *California Base Closure News,* No. 11 (June 1996), p. 15.

44. *Government Executive,* Vol. 28 (September 1996), p. 10.

45. Ibid.

46. United States Congress, *Defense Appropriations Act for Fiscal Year 1997.* via Internet, http://www.emissary.acq.BTOCONG.NSF.

47. Ibid.

48. The claim is a bit misleading. The Presidio of San Francisco was not the United States' oldest base when it closed; it had been a Spanish base before California became a part of the United States.

49. Presidio of San Francisco, via internet http://www.dtic.mil.environdod/derpreport/presidio.html.

50. Ibid.

51. *California Base Closure News,* No. 11 (June 1996), p. 5.

52. The legislation limited the veto, though, to items certified by the Joint Committee on Taxation as benefiting fewer than 100 persons or firms in one year.

53. Richard Rose, *Lesson-Drawing in Public Policy: A Guide to Learning Across Time and Space.* Chatham, NJ: Chatham House, 1993, p. 155.

54. Jacques S. Gansler, *Defense Conversion: Transforming the Arsenal of Democracy.* Cambridge, MA: The MIT Press, 1995, p. 231.

55. United States Congress, Office of Technology Assessment, *Defense Conversion: Redirecting R&D.* OTA-ITE-552. Washington, D.C.: G PO, May 1993, p. 31.

56. The writers themselves were a sort of commission, though.

57. "The Next Big Military Maneuver: Protecting the Budgets," *Washington Post,* December 3, 1996, p. C1.

58. Ibid.

59. *Defense Week,* April 14, 1997, p. 1

60. *New York Times,* April 29, 1996, p. 1.

61. "The Next Big Military Maneuver: Protecting the Budgets," *Washington Post,* December 3, 1996, p. C1..

62. *Aviation Week & Space Technology,* March 17, 1997, p. 35.

63. *Report of the Quadrennial Defense Review,* May, 1997, pp. 66-67.

64. *The New York Times,* July 9, 1997, p. 1.

65. Katherine McIntire Peters, "Civilians at War," *Government Executive,* Vol. 28 (July 1996), p. 24.

66. Ibid., pp. 24-27.

67. "Shift Military Support Jobs to Civilians, Close Inefficient Facilities, GAO Urges," *Baltimore Sun,* April 5, 1997, p. 4.

68. George C. Wilson, "A Kinder, Gentler Way to Balance the Budget," *Air Force Times,* January 20, 1997, p. 54.

69. Ibid.

70. Ibid.

71. "Cohen Wants Larger Pentagon Procurement Budget," *Defense Daily,* January 23, 1997, p. 105.

72. *Defense Daily,* August 8, 1997, p. 235.

73. *Washington Post,* May 7, 1997, p. 1.

74. "New Fighters to Cost More, Congress Told," *Baltimore Sun,* February 14, 1997, p. 1, C1.

75. The GAO report cited above noted that even after the four rounds of base closure, the military had a 35 percent excess capacity in research and development laboratories. *Baltimore Sun,* April 7, 1997, p. 4.

76. Defense Base Closure and Realignment Commission, *Report to the President,* 1995, p. 3-1.

77. *Department of Defense Appropriations, Fiscal Year 1994.* Senate Hearings Before the Committee on Appropriations, 103rd Cong., 1st Sess, Part 3. Washington, D.C.: GPO, 1994, p. 653. At the time of the hearings, Perry was Deputy Secretary of Defense.

78. *Inside the Navy,* June 30, 1997, p. 1.

79. "More Base Closures Urged," *European Stars and Stripes,* February 13, 1997, p. 1.

80. Ibid.

81. "Scott Air Base Beware, Dixon Warns," *St. Louis Post-Dispatch,* June 19, 1996, B-1,2.

82. *Chicago Tribune,* May 8, 1997, p. 3.

83. "State Works to Save Its Military Bases," *Arizona Republic,* October 27, 1996, p. B7.

84. Letter to General Ronald R. Fogleman, signed Ike Skelton, Member of Congress, dated January 11, 1997.

85. Lois E. Walker and Shelby E. Wickham, *From Huffman Prairie to the Moon: The History of Wright-Patterson Air Force Base.* Air Force Logistics Command (n.d.), p. 340.

86. Katherine McIntire Peters, "Funding the Fleet," *Government Executive,* Vol. 29 (January 1997), p. 43.

87. Defense Base Closure and Realignment Commission, *Report to the President, 1995,* p. 3-2.

88. "Secretary Perry Recommends Closing, Realigning 146 Bases," *DOD News* (BRAC), February 28, 1995, p. 1.

89. *Military Base Closures: The Impact on California Communities.* Santa Monica, CA: The RAND Corporation, February 1996., p. 3.

90. Ibid.

Bibliography

Air Force Bases. Vol. 1, *Active Air Force Bases Within the United States of America on 17 September 1982*. Washington, D.C.: Office of Air Force History, USAF, 1989.

Air Force Bases. Harrisburg, PA: Military Service Publishing, 1958.

Allison, Graham T., "Conceptual Models and the Cuban Missile Crisis," *American Political Science Review,* Vol. 63 (September 1969), pp. 689-718.

Annual Report to the President and the Congress. William J. Perry, Secretary of Defense, February 1993.

Armacost, Michael H., *The Politics of Weapons Innovation: The Thor-Jupiter Controversy*. New York: Columbia University Press, 1969.

Arnold, R. Douglas, *Congress and the Bureaucracy: A Theory of Influence*. New Haven, CT: Yale University Press, 1979.

————, *The Logic of Congressional Action*. New Haven, CT: Yale University Press, 1990.

Art, Robert F., *The TFX Decision: McNamara and the Military*. Boston: Little, Brown, 1968.

Azai, Thomas P., "Base Closure: Its Impact on Military Members," *Torch*, Vol. 2 (November, 1995), pp. 12-15.

Barone, Michael, Grant Ujifusa, and Douglas Matthews, *The Almanac of American Politics*. Boston: Gambit, 1972.

Barron, Larry Lee, "The Economic Impact of Tinker Air Force Base on Norman, Oklahoma." Unpublished Master's Thesis, University of Oklahoma, 1969.

Beard, Edmund, *Developing the ICBM: A Study in Bureaucratic Politics*. New York: Columbia University Press, 1976.

Biondo, Brenda, "In Defense of the Longleaf Pine," *Nature Conservancy*, Vol. 42 (September/October 1997, pp. 10-17.

Bishop, William J., and David S. Sorenson, "Superpower Defense Expenditures and Foreign Policy," in Charles W. Kegley, Jr., and Pat McGowan (eds.), *Foreign Policy: USA/USSR*. Sage International Yearbook of Foreign Policy Studies, Vol. 7. Beverly Hills, CA: Sage Publications, 1982, pp. 163-183.

Blechman, Barry M., *The Politics of National Security: Congress and U.S. Defense Policy*. New York: Oxford University Press, 1990.

Bracken, Paul, *The Command and Control of Nuclear Forces*. New Haven, CT: Yale University Press, 1982.

Brown, Jerold E., *Where Eagles Land: Planning and Development of U.S. Army Air Fields, 1910-1941*. Westport, CT: Greenwood, 1990.

Buckley, Nora C., *An Overview of Studies of the Impact of Military Installations and Their Closings on Nearby Communities*. Unpublished paper. George Washington University School of Engineering and Applied Science, July 20, 1976.

Builder, Carl H., *The Masks of War: American Military Styles in Strategy and Analysis*. A RAND Corporation Research Study. Baltimore: Johns Hopkins University Press, 1989.

Clark, Asa A., IV, "Interservice Rivalry and Military Reform," in Asa A. Clark IV, Peter W. Chiarelli, Jeffrey S. McKitrick, and James W. Reed (eds.), *The Defense Reform Debate: Issues and Analysis*. Baltimore: Johns Hopkins University Press, 1984, pp. 250-271.

Cleaning Up Defense Installations: Issues and Options. Washington, D.C.: CBO, January 1995.

Coulam, Robert F., *Illusions of Choice: The F-111 and the Problem of Weapons Acquisition Reform*. Princeton, NJ: Princeton University Press, 1977.

Coyle, Lewis J., *The Economic Impact of Military Installations on Regional Economies*. Monterey, CA: Naval Postgraduate School, September 1992.

Craven, Wesley Frank, and James Lea Cate (eds.), *The Army Air Forces in World War II.* Vol. 6, *Men and Planes.* Chicago: University of Chicago Press, 1955.

Daicoff, Darwin W., "The Community Impact of Military Installations," in Bernard Udis (ed.), *The Economic Consequences of Reduced Military Spending.* Lexington, MA: Lexington Books, 1973, pp. 149-166.

Dawson, Raymond H., "Congressional Innovation and Intervention in Defense Policy: Legislative Authorization of Weapons Systems," *American Political Science Review,* Vol. 61 (March 1962), pp. 42-57.

Defense Base Closure and Realignment Commission, *Report to the President, 1995.* Washington, D.C.: The Commission, 1995.

Defense Base Closure and Realignment Commission, *Report to the President, 1993.* Washington, D.C.: The Commission, 1993.

Defense Base Closure and Realignment Commission, *Report to the President, 1991.* Washington, D.C.: The Commission, 1991.

Destler, I. M., *Presidents, Bureaucrats, and Foreign Policy: The Politics of Organizational Reform.* Princeton, NJ: Princeton University Press, 1972.

Ennels, Jerome A., *The Way We Were: A Pictorial History of Early Maxwell Air Force Base, 1918-1931.* Maxwell AFB, AL: 1980.

Enthoven, Alain C., and K. Wayne Smith, *How Much Is Enough? Shaping the Defense Program, 1961-1969.* New York: Harper & Row, 1971.

Faulkner, Frank, *Westover: Man, Base, Mission.* Springfield, MA: Hungry Hill, 1990.

Feaver, Peter Douglas, *Guarding the Guardians: Civilian Control of Nuclear Weapons in the United States.* Ithaca, NY: Cornell University Press, 1992.

Ferejohn, John, *Pork Barrel Politics: Rivers and Harbors Legislation, 1947-1968.* Stanford, CA: Stanford University Press, 1974.

Fiorina, Morris P., *Congress: Keystone of the Washington Establishment.* New Haven, CT: Yale University Press, 1989.

Fitzgerald, Randall, and Gerald Lipson, *Pork Barrel: The Unexpurgated Grace Commission Story of Congressional Profligacy.* Washington, D.C.: CATO Institute, 1984.

Fox, J. Ronald, *The Defense Management Challenge.* Boston: Harvard Business School Press, 1988.

Gansler, Jacques S., *Defense Conversion: Transforming the Arsenal of Democracy.* Cambridge, MA: MIT Press, 1995.

Glassberg, Andrew D., "Military Base Closing: How the Process Has Changed," *Business & Contemporary Society,* Vol. 7, No. 1 (1995), pp. 96-106.

———— "Intergovernmental Relations and Base Closing," *Publius: The Journal of Federalism,* Vol. 25, No. 3 (Summer 1995) pp. 87-98.

Gordon, Edward F., *Base Closure and Realignment.* Washington, D.C.: Industrial College of the Armed Forces, April 1992.

Gorgoni, Douglas P., *Expert Opinion on the Department of Defense Base Closure/Realignment Policy and Process: An Assessment of the Four Military Value Criteria.* Wright-Patterson AFB, OH: Air Force Institute of Technology, 1991.

Griffin, William Caldwell, "The United States Air Force in New York: An Example of the Impact of the Military Establishment on Regional and Local Economies." Unpublished Master's Thesis, Syracuse University, 1968.

Grindstaff, Charles W., *War Baby of the South, 1940-1945.* Office of History, Warner Robins ALC, 1988.

Halperin, Morton H., *Bureaucratic Politics and Foreign Policy.* Washington, D.C.: The Brookings Institution, 1974

Halperin, Morton H., and Arnold Kanter, "The Bureaucratic Perspective: A Preliminary Framework," in Morton H. Halperin and Arnold Kanter (eds.), *Readings in American Foreign Policy: A Bureaucratic Perspective.* Boston: Little, Brown, 1973, pp. 1-42.

Hampson, Fen Osler, *Unguided Missiles: How America Buys Its Weapons.* New York: W.W. Norton, 1989.

Hird, John A., "The Political Economy of Pork: Project Selection at the U.S. Army Corps of Engineers," *American Political Science Review,* Vol. 85 (June 1991), pp. 429-456.

Hoover, Karl D., *Base Closure: Politics or National Defense Issue? Goodfellow Air Force Base, Texas, 1978-1981.* Randolph AFB, TX: History and Research Office, Headquarters Air Training Command, 1989.

Huntington, Samuel P., *The Soldier and the State: The Theory and Politics of Civil-Military Relations.* Cambridge, MA: Belknap Press of Harvard University, 1957.

———, *The Common Defense.* New York: Columbia University Press, 1961.

Huzar, Elias, *The Purse and the Sword: Control of the Army by Congress Through Military Appropriations, 1933-1950.* Ithaca, NY: Cornell University Press, 1950.

Jones, L.R., "Management of Budgetary Decline in the Department of Defense in Response to the End of the Cold War," *Armed Forces & Society,* Vol. 19 (Summer 1993), pp. 479-510.

Kitfield, James, "A Tale of Two Cities," *Government Executive,* Vol. 26 (September 1994), pp. 30-31.

———, "Depots for Sale," *Government Executive,* Vol. 27 (December 1995), pp. 41-44, 62.

Kotz, Nick, *Wild Blue Yonder: Money, Politics, and the B-1 Bomber.* Princeton, NJ: Princeton University Press, 1988.

Koven, Steven G., "Base Closings and the Politics-Administration Dichotomy Revisited," *Public Administration Review,* Vol. 52 (September/October 1992), pp. 526-531.

Krasner, Stephen D., "Are Bureaucracies Important? (Or Allison Wonderland)," *Foreign Policy,* No. 7 (1972), pp. 159-179.

Lebovic, James H., "Riding Waves or Making Waves? The Services and the U.S. Defense Budget, 1981-1993," *American Political Science Review,* Vol. 88 (December 1994), pp. 839-852.

——— *Foregone Conclusions: U.S. Weapons Acquisition in the Post–Cold War Transition.* Boulder, CO: Westview Press, 1996.

Leonard, Hugh R., Jr., *Handling the Hot Potato: Evolution and Analysis of the Base Closing Decision Process.* Washington, D.C.: Industrial College of the Armed Forces, 1992.

Lindsay, James M., *Congress and Nuclear Weapons.* Baltimore: Johns Hopkins University Press, 1991.

Liske, Craig, and Barry Rundquist, *The Politics of Weapons Procurement: The Role of Congress.* Monograph Series in World Affairs, Vol. 12, Monograph No. 1. Denver, CO: University of Colorado, 1974.

Lotchin, Roger W., *Fortress California, 1910-1961: From Warfare to Welfare.* New York: Oxford University Press, 1992.

Lynch, John E., *Local Economic Development After Military Base Closures.* New York: Praeger, 1970.

Magleby, David B., and Candice J. Nelson, *The Money Chase: Congressional Campaign Finance Reform.* Washington, D.C.: Brookings Institution, 1990.

Markusen, Ann, and Joel Yudken, *Dismantling the Cold War Economy.* New York: Basic Books, 1992.

Markusen, Ann, Scott Campbell, Peter Hall, and Sabina Deitrick, *The Rise of the Gunbelt: The Military Remapping of Industrial America.* New York: Oxford University Press, 1991.

Mayer, Kenneth R., *The Political Economy of Defense Contracting*. New Haven, CT: Yale University Press, 1991.

———, "Congressional-DOD Relations After the Cold War: The Politics of Uncertainty," in Ethan B. Kapstein (ed.), *Downsizing Defense*. Washington, D.C.: Congressional Quarterly Press, 1993, pp. 39-60.

———, "Closing Military Bases (Finally): Solving Collective Dilemmas Through Delegation, *Legislative Studies Quarterly*, Vol. 20 (August 1995), pp. 393-414.

Mayer, Kenneth R., and Anne M. Khademian, "Bringing Politics Back In: Defense Policy and the Theoretical Study of Institutions and Processes," *Public Administration Review*, Vol. 56 (March/April 1996), pp. 180-190.

McKenna, Pat, "McClellan Inc.," *Airman*, (December 1995), pp. 28-32.

Meeter, George F., *The Holloman Story*. Albuquerque, NM: University of New Mexico Press, 1967.

Military Bases: Letters and Requests Received on Proposed Closures and Realignments. Washington, D.C.: GAO, May 1991.

Moore, Frank, *The Saga of Norton Air Force Base*. Redlands, CA: A.K. Smiley Public Library, 1992.

O'Hanlon, Michael, *Defense Planning for the Late 1990s*. Washington, D.C.: Brookings Institution, 1995.

Peters, Katherine McIntire, "The Drawdown Drags On," *Government Executive*, Vol. 28 (March 1996), pp. 20-25.

———, "Funding the Fleet," *Government Executive*, Vol. 29 (January 1997), pp. 42-45.

———, "Trade-offs Loom in Modern Force," *Government Executive*, Vol. 29 (May 1997), p. 60.

———, "Money Woes," *Government Executive*, Vol. 29 (June 1997), pp. 24-29.

Piacente, Steve, "Twice-Hit Charleston on the Mend," *Government Executive*, Vol. 26 (September 1994), pp. 32-37.

The Plan for Joint Use of Military Airfields. The Secretary of Defense and the Secretary of Transportation to the United States Congress. Washington, D.C.: GPO, 1984.

President's Private Sector Survey on Cost Control, *Report on Privatization*. Washington, D.C.: GPO, 1983.

Pressman, Jeffrey L., and Aaron Wildavsky, *Implementation: How Great Expectations in Washington Are Dashed in Oakland*. Berkeley, CA: University of California Press, 1984.

Rhodes, Edward, "Do Bureaucratic Politics Matter? Some Disconfirming Findings from the Case of the U.S. Navy," *World Politics*, Vol. 47 (October 1994), pp. 1-41.

Rose, Richard, *Lesson-Drawing in Public Policy: A Guide to Learning Across Time and Space*. Chatham, NJ: Chatham House, 1993.

Rubenson, David, Jerry Aroesty, and Charles Thomsen, *Two Shades of Green: Environmental Protection and Combat Training*. Santa Monica, CA: RAND Corporation, R-4220, 1995.

Russett, Bruce M., *What Price Vigilance? The Burdens of National Defense*. New Haven, CT: Yale University Press, 1970.

Sabato, Larry J., *PAC Power: Inside the World of Political Action Committees*. New York: W. W. Norton, 1985.

Shepsle, Kenneth A., and Barry R. Weingast, "Political Preferences for the Pork Barrel: A Generalization," *American Journal of Political Science*, Vol. 25 (February 1981), pp. 96-111.

Sladkus, John, "The Transition of Mare Island Civilian Workers Before Base Closure." Unpublished paper, Institute of Industrial Relations, University of California at Berkeley, 1995.

Sorenson, David S., *The Politics of Strategic Aircraft Modernization*. Westport, CT: Praeger, 1995.

Stein, Robert M., and Kenneth N. Bickers, "Congressional Elections and the Pork Barrel," *Journal of Politics*, Vol. 56 (May 1994), pp. 377-399.

Stockton, Paul, "Beyond Micromanagement: Congressional Budgeting for a Post–Cold War Military," *Political Science Quarterly*, Vol. 110, No. 2 (Summer 1995), pp. 233-259.

Stubbing, Richard, *The Defense Game*. New York: Harper & Row, 1986.

Suttie, Richard D., and Arthur J. Ohanian, *The Political Economy of Military Base Closure*. Monterey, CA: Naval Postgraduate School, 1990.

Szafranski, Richard, *Closing Your Base*. Maxwell AFB, AL: Air War College, 1993.

Thompson, Fred, "Why America's Military Base Structure Cannot Be Reduced," *Public Administration Review*, Vol. 48 (January/February 1988).

Till, Geoffrey, "Adopting the Aircraft Carrier: The British, American, and Japanese Case Studies," in Williamson Murray and Allan R. Millett (eds.), *Military Innovation in the Interwar Period*. Cambridge: Cambridge University Press, 1996, pp. 191-226.

Tufte, Edward R., *Political Control of the Economy*. Princeton, NJ: Princeton University Press, 1978.

United States Congress, *Defense Department Appropriations for Fiscal Year 1991*, Committee on Appropriations, 101st Cong., 2nd Sess. Washington, D.C.: GPO, 1990.

United States Congress, *Land Withdrawals from the Public Domain for Military Purposes*, Hearings before the Senate Committee on Energy and Natural Resources, Subcommittee on Public Lands, Reserved Water, and Resource Conservation, 99th Cong., 2nd Sess. Washington, D.C.: GPO, 1987.

United States Congress, Office of Technology Assessment, *Defense Conversion: Redirecting R&D*. OTA-ITE-552. Washington, D.C.: GPO, May 1993.

Vistica, Gregory L., *Fall from Glory: The Men Who Sank the U.S. Navy*. New York: Simon and Schuster, 1995.

Walker, Lois E., and Shelby E. Wickham, *From Huffman Prairie to the Moon: The History of Wright-Patterson Air Force Base*. Wright-Patterson AFB, OH: Air Force Logistics Command, [n.d.].

Weida, William J., and Frank L. Gertcher, *The Political Economy of National Defense*. Boulder, CO: Westview, 1987.

Weidenbaum, Murray, *Small Wars, Big Defense: Paying for the Military After the Cold War*. New York: Oxford University Press, 1992.

Welch, David A., "The Organizational Process and Bureaucratic Politics Paradigms: Retrospect and Prospect," *International Security*, Vol. 17 (Fall 1992), pp. 112-146.

Wilson, Charles L., and James L. Weingartner, *Blame-Proof Policymaking: Congress and Base Closures*. Monterey, CA: Naval Postgraduate School, December 1993.

Wolanin, Thomas R., *Presidential Advisory Commissions: Truman to Nixon*. Madison, WI: University of Wisconsin Press, 1975.

Yoder. Eric, "Military Links," *Government Executive*, Vol. 29 (May 1997), pp. 53-56.

Zimon, Henry A., *The Effects of U.S. Military Base Closures on Regional and Local Economies: 1950-1980*. Maxwell AFB, AL: Air Command and Staff College, March 1983.

Index